Leveraging Consumer Behavior and Psychology in the Digital Economy

Norazah Mohd Suki
Universiti Utara Malaysia, Malaysia

Norbayah Mohd Suki
Universiti Utara Malaysia, Malaysia

A volume in the Advances in Marketing, Customer Relationship Management, and E-Services (AMCRMES) Book Series

IGI Global
DISSEMINATOR OF KNOWLEDGE

Published in the United States of America by
IGI Global
Business Science Reference (an imprint of IGI Global)
701 E. Chocolate Avenue
Hershey PA, USA 17033
Tel: 717-533-8845
Fax: 717-533-8661
E-mail: cust@igi-global.com
Web site: http://www.igi-global.com

Library of Congress Cataloging-in-Publication Data

Names: Mohd Suki, Norazah, 1977- editor. | Mohd Suki, Norbayah, 1976- editor.
Title: Leveraging consumer behavior and psychology in the digital economy / Norazah Mohd Suki and Norbayah Mohd Suki, editors.
Description: Hershey : Business Science Reference, 2020. | Includes bibliographical references and index. | Summary: "This book provides current research on topics relevant to consumer behavior, consumer psychology, consumer value, customer satisfaction, and loyalty. It also examines how to best utilize this research on consumer behavior and psychology in the digital economy"-- Provided by publisher.
Identifiers: LCCN 2019047075 (print) | LCCN 2019047076 (ebook) | ISBN 9781799830429 (h/c) | ISBN 9781799852711 (s/c) | ISBN 9781799830436 (ebook)
Subjects: LCSH: Consumer behavior--Psychological aspects. | Technological innovations--Psychological aspects.
Classification: LCC HF5415.32 .L473 2020 (print) | LCC HF5415.32 (ebook) | DDC 658.8/342--dc23
LC record available at https://lccn.loc.gov/2019047075
LC ebook record available at https://lccn.loc.gov/2019047076

This book is published in the IGI Global book series Advances in Marketing, Customer Relationship Management, and E-Services (AMCRMES) (ISSN: 2327-5502; eISSN: 2327-5529)

British Cataloguing in Publication Data
A Cataloguing in Publication record for this book is available from the British Library.

For electronic access to this publication, please contact: eresources@igi-global.com.

Advances in Marketing, Customer Relationship Management, and E-Services (AMCRMES) Book Series

Eldon Y. Li
National Chengchi University, Taiwan & California Polytechnic State University, USA

ISSN:2327-5502
EISSN:2327-5529

Mission

Business processes, services, and communications are important factors in the management of good customer relationship, which is the foundation of any well organized business. Technology continues to play a vital role in the organization and automation of business processes for marketing, sales, and customer service. These features aid in the attraction of new clients and maintaining existing relationships.

The Advances in Marketing, Customer Relationship Management, and E-Services (AMCRMES) Book Series addresses success factors for customer relationship management, marketing, and electronic services and its performance outcomes. This collection of reference source covers aspects of consumer behavior and marketing business strategies aiming towards researchers, scholars, and practitioners in the fields of marketing management.

Coverage

- Cases on CRM Implementation
- Relationship Marketing
- Text Mining and Marketing
- Electronic Services
- CRM and customer trust
- Ethical Considerations in E-Marketing
- B2B marketing
- CRM strategies
- Customer Relationship Management
- Data mining and marketing

IGI Global is currently accepting manuscripts for publication within this series. To submit a proposal for a volume in this series, please contact our Acquisition Editors at Acquisitions@igi-global.com or visit: http://www.igi-global.com/publish/.

The Advances in Marketing, Customer Relationship Management, and E-Services (AMCRMES) Book Series (ISSN 2327-5502) is published by IGI Global, 701 E. Chocolate Avenue, Hershey, PA 17033-1240, USA, www.igi-global.com. This series is composed of titles available for purchase individually; each title is edited to be contextually exclusive from any other title within the series. For pricing and ordering information please visit http://www.igi-global.com/book-series/advances-marketing-customer-relationship-management/37150. Postmaster: Send all address changes to above address.

Titles in this Series

For a list of additional titles in this series, please visit:
https://www.igi-global.com/book-series/advances-marketing-customer-relationship-management/37150

Millennial Consumer Trends and Their Impact on the Global Economy
Abhijit Pandit (Amity University, India) and Jayjit Chakraborty (University of Calcutta, India)
Business Science Reference • © 2020 • 300pp • H/C (ISBN: 9781799844297) • S $215.00

Anthropological Approaches to Understanding Consumption Patterns and Consumer Behavior
Valentina Chkoniya (University of Aveiro, Portugal) Ana Oliveira Madsen (CEGE, Católica Porto Business School, Portugal & Universidade Católica Portuguesa, Porto, Portugal) and Paata Bukhrashvili (Ilia State University, Georgia)
Business Science Reference • © 2020 • 546pp • H/C (ISBN: 9781799831150) • US $215.00

International Approaches to Marketing, Communication Media, and Management of Government Policies
Oscar Odiboh (Covenant University, Nigeria) Eno Akpabio (University of Namibia, Namibia) and Piet Kommers (University of Twente, The Netherlands)
Business Science Reference • © 2020 • 280pp • H/C (ISBN: 9781799830726) • US $225.00

Emotional, Sensory, and Social Dimensions of Consumer Buying Behavior
Ana Maria Soares (School of Economics and Management, University of Minho, Portugal) and Maher Georges Elmashhara (School of Economics and Management, University of Minho, Portugal)
Business Science Reference • © 2020 • 424pp • H/C (ISBN: 9781799822202) • US $215.00

Examining Cultural Perspectives in a Globalized World
Richard Brunet-Thornton (University of Economics, Prague, Czech Republic)
Business Science Reference • © 2020 • 350pp • H/C (ISBN: 9781799802143) • US $215.00

Managing Social Media Practices in the Digital Economy
Shirin Alavi (Jaypee Institute of Information Technology, India) and Vandana Ahuja (Amity Business School, Amity University, Noida, India)
Business Science Reference • © 2020 • 312pp • H/C (ISBN: 9781799821854) • US $215.00

Handbook of Research on Decision-Making Techniques in Financial Marketing
Hasan Dinçer (Istanbul Medipol University, Turkey) and Serhat Yüksel (İstanbul Medipol University, Turkey)
Business Science Reference • © 2020 • 646pp • H/C (ISBN: 9781799825593) • US $395.00

IGI Global
DISSEMINATOR OF KNOWLEDGE

701 East Chocolate Avenue, Hershey, PA 17033, USA
Tel: 717-533-8845 x100 • Fax: 717-533-8661
E-Mail: cust@igi-global.com • www.igi-global.com

Table of Contents

Detailed Table of Contents

The digital economy shows a challenging environment, and three main players have entered the arena (digital platforms, online communities, new technologies). The aim of this chapter is to provide a new multidimensional framework for exploring multiple signals. The study leverages the signaling theory, since signals help companies and sellers to mitigate information asymmetries. In the virtual context of the digital economy, credible and observable information improve the decision-making process of consumers. The work opted for a multidimensional framework and proposes that four types of signals (social network, social capital, certification, social identity) influence consumer behavior. Furthermore, the study suggests that also the interactions/combinations between these signals could affect consumer behavior. This contribution offers a conceptual framework without testing empirically the propositions; thus, it offers the opportunity of further research. This work has interesting implications for several actors of the digital ecosystem (firms, entrepreneurs, platform managers, consumers, etc.).

This chapter looks at the phenomenon of social media and its consequences on marketing and consumer behavior. To express an opinion, the authors first define the notion of "social media," review their different types as well as the decisive moments that marked their history. Then, they focus on the influence of these media on marketing practices by referring to the changes that have affected the marketing approach from the stage of the market study to the stage of control of marketing actions companies. Finally, they are very interested in the changes that have affected the traditional decision-making process and are announcing useful recommendations to respond to this set of changes.

This chapter explores participation and co-production in affective media experiences in Johnny & Associates' online fan communities. Johnny & Associates is a Japanese all-male talent management company established in the 1960s. As a pioneer in the idol industry, Johnny & Associates and artists under its management have been highly influential in the contemporary Japanese entertainment industry. These artists are collectively known as Johnny's idols or Janīzu. Much of the data are collected through participant-experiencer and interviews. The originality of this case study stems mainly from the empirical data for Johnny & Associates, Janīzu, and the global fan base during Johnny & Associates' transition to a social media platform. This chapter analyses marketing strategy, audience awareness, and behaviour in relation to a mass media phenomenon. The complex interaction among Johnny & Associates, Janīzu, and fans generates tensions and contradictions that mirror the modern mediated life.

The advent of internet-based technologies and social media has drastically affected how people communicate and share information. Electronic word-of-mouth (E-WOM) communication is one of those communication methods, and it has attracted the attention of scholars because of its effects on the consumer's decision-making process. However, there is a fragmentation of the E-WOM communication literature because of the broad range of platforms and different E-WOM formats. Therefore, the purpose of this chapter is to provide a comprehensive understanding of the antecedents, motivations, and consequences of E-WOM communication for consumers in the digital economy.

This study aimed to investigate mobile game addiction through perceived game value. According to this aim, the relationship between mobile game addiction and consumption values was tested. From 500 e-survey forms, 386 forms were accepted for analysis. To measure perceived value, Sheth, Newman, and Gross's consumption values model was adapted. Lemmens, Valkenburg, and Peter's game addiction model were used in this study to measure mobile game addiction. With the help of canonical correlation analysis, it was tested whether there was a significant relationship between perceived value and mobile game addiction. Consequently, it was found that perceived values were significantly related to mobile game addiction. Especially, functional, emotional, and conditional values had a strong correlation with mobile game addiction. This study provides some evidence that perceived game value can influence game addiction.

discussed at the end of this paper.

This paper details about the qualitative study of proactive and responsive export market orientation. An interview series was conducted to assess whether the issue of proactive and responsive export market orientation exist among exporters, identification of the exporters' characteristics (antecedents) and understand the behaviors effect on performance consequences. Findings from the interview were recorded in a qualitative codebook. Discussions and conclusion made on the qualitative findings revealed that the issue of proactive and responsive export market orientation is present, different characteristics lead to different behaviors, and the behaviors affect the exporters' performance consequences differently.

This study emphasizes the overview of technology innovation that comprises the definition and the technological innovation categories distinction; the overview of consumer attitude towards product innovation focused on the consumer demand on innovative products, the stimulus purchasing factor, and the consumer satisfactory factors over product innovation; overview of sustainability innovation; innovation management as part of the strategic management; and challenges on innovative strategy formulation and implementation. Innovation strategy formulation requires detailed assessments on potential technological advancement, consumers' attitudes on innovative products, and sustainability impact on innovative initiatives. Innovation strategy is perceived as part of the strategic management, and the implementation depends on intra-organizational factors. The employee innovation adoptions as the connection between technological innovation, consumer behavior towards product innovation, and innovative sustainability for innovation strategy formulation can be further studied.

In the past, the economy was solely dependent on natural resources, but it moved to manufacturing and is now focusing on service delivery. Government roles in implementing policies are needed in order to ensure natural resources are transformed. The production of business delivery is getting more innovative; therefore, research and development are aligned with the goals for sustainability.

Flipped learning is basically a pedagogical model that reverses classroom activities. Materials or contents

Preface

With the increasing prevalence of information, communication, and technology including social media in the digital economy, leveraging consumer behavior and psychology have become a dominant ground for researchers and practitioners to inspect the trends, opportunities and challenges to SNS developers and online firms. These platforms have become the key channel for social interactions and networking among individuals, and online communities to leverage business activity in respect of products and services visibility and sustainability via the Internet.

Leveraging Consumer Behavior and Psychology in the Digital Economy provides current research on topics relevant to consumer behavior, consumer psychology, consumer value, customer satisfaction, and loyalty and how best to utilize this research consumer behavior and psychology in the digital economy. Emphasizing critical topics in the field of consumer behavior research, this publication is a wide-ranging resource for professionals, practitioners, marketers, retailers, business managers, academics, researchers, and graduate-level students interested in the latest material on consumer behavior and psychology in the digital economy. The research handbook would also be suitable for use as a teaching aid and suited for class discussions in a variety of courses in different disciplines both at undergraduate and postgraduate level around the globe.

The book is organized into 16 chapters. A brief description of each of the chapters as follows.

Chapter 1: Multiple Signals and Consumer Behaviors in the Digital Economy – Implementing a Multidimensional Framework

The digital economy shows a challenging environment and three main players have entered the arena (digital platforms, online communities, new technologies). The aim of this chapter is to provide a new multidimensional framework for exploring multiple signals. The study leverages signaling theory, since signals help companies and sellers to mitigate information asymmetries. In the virtual context of the digital economy, credible and observable information improve the decision-making process of consumers. The work opted for a multidimensional framework and proposes that four types of signals (social network, social capital, certification, social identity) influence consumer behavior. Furthermore, the study suggests that also the interactions/combinations between these signals could affect consumer behavior. This contribution offers a conceptual framework without testing empirically the propositions, thus it offers the opportunity of further research. This work has interesting implications for several actors of the digital ecosystem (firms, entrepreneurs, platform managers, consumers, etc.).

Chapter 2: Social Media, Marketing Practices, and Consumer Behavior

This chapter looks at the phenomenon of social media and its consequences on marketing and consumer behavior. To express an opinion, the authors first define the notion of "social media", review their different types as well as the decisive moments that marked their history. Then, they focus on the influence of these media on marketing practices by referring to the changes that have affected the marketing approach from the stage of the market study to the stage of control of marketing actions companies. Finally, they are very interested in the changes that have affected the traditional decision-making process and are announcing useful recommendations to respond to this set of changes.

Chapter 3: Challenges and Opportunities for News Media and Journalism in an Increasingly Digital, Mobile, and Social Media Environment

This paper reviews challenges and opportunities for news media and journalism in today's changing media environment. It documents that we are moving towards an increasingly digital, mobile, and social media environment with more intense competition for attention. More and more people get news via digital media, they increasingly access news via mobile devices (especially smartphones), and rely on social media and other intermediaries in terms of how they access and find news. In this environment, a limited number of large technology companies enable billions of users across the world to navigate and use digital media in easy and attractive ways through services like search, social networking, video sharing, and messaging. As a consequence, these companies play a more and more important role in terms of (a) the distribution of news and (b) digital advertising.

Chapter 4: Conspicuous Consumption via Social Media

Conspicuous consumption was explored since 19th century, focusing on its conceptual or mathematical modelling. It has gained widespread attention in the Western culture as compared to East. However, the increased performance of luxury market and strong demand for luxury goods in developing countries urged investigation on the spread of this consumption pattern. This chapter examines conspicuous consumption in Malaysia via social media usage. A research was carried out involving 387 respondents in Klang Valley, Malaysia. The results suggest Malaysian are moderately materialistic and propend to conspicuous consumption. Through the exposure to social media, consumers are being situated in comparison with other social media users and inclined to learn and pick up the consumption styles that are being exposed to. Thus, high level of social media usage can lead to high inclination in consuming conspicuously.

Chapter 5: The Behavior and Motivation Factor of Scammer and Victimization Consequences

This chapter presents the overview of how the online fraud began; and how in starting to spread around the world. Mastering the motivation factor fraudster to do scamming. Also the perspectives of victim attitude, social media; the emerging trends of community attitudes and IT among public community among youngster or even among elders; the concept of motivation factors, by fraudsters; the characteristics of victim by dividing to gender and age stages; sustainable online media; sustainable long hours of consuming internet; the importance of sustainable consumption, sustainability, and sustainable deterrence to avoid people being online scam victim. Mastering how this case working is essential for modern police organizations that seek to serve public and nation, reduce the loses are facing by victim in the future, strengthen strategy in combating online scam. It's also emphasized thoroughly the effect, and the consequences after victim got cheated by online. The chapter argues that mastering fraudster and victim attitude and knowledge to enhance the awareness and reduce online scam.

Chapter 6: The Affective Economy and Online Fan Communities – A Case Study of Johnny & Associates

This chapter explores participation and co-production in affective media experiences in Johnny & Associates' online fan communities. Johnny & Associates is a Japanese all-male talent management company established in the 1960s. As a pioneer in the idol industry, Johnny & Associates and artists under its management have been highly influential in the contemporary Japanese entertainment industry. These artists are collectively known as Johnny's idols or Janīzu. Much of the data are collected through participant-experiencer and interviews. The originality of this case study stems mainly from the empirical data for Johnny & Associates, Janīzu, and the global fan base during Johnny & Associates' transition to a social media platform. This chapter analyses marketing strategy, audience awareness and behavior in relation to a mass media phenomenon. The complex interaction among Johnny & Associates, Janīzu and fans generates tensions and contradictions that mirror the modern mediated life.

Chapter 7: Antecedents, Motivations, and Consequences of Electronic Word-of-Mouth Communication

The advent of internet-based technologies and social media has drastically affected how people communicate and share information. Electronic word-of-mouth (E-WOM) communication is one of those communication methods, and it has attracted the attention of scholars because of its effects on the consumer's decision-making process. However, there is a fragmentation of the E-WOM communication literature because of the broad range of platforms and different E-WOM formats. Therefore, the purpose of this chapter is to provide a comprehensive understanding of the antecedents, motivations, and consequences of E-WOM communication for consumers in the digital economy.

Chapter 8: Examining Perceived Value Influence Mobile Game Addiction – A Case of Turkish Young Adults

This study aimed to investigate mobile game addiction through perceived game value. According to this aim, the relationship between mobile game addiction and consumption values was tested. From 500 e-survey forms, 386 forms were accepted for analysis. To measure perceived value, Sheth, Newman and Gross's consumption values model was adapted. Lemmens, Valkenburg and Peter's game addiction model were used in this study to measure mobile game addiction. With the help of canonical correlation analysis, it was tested whether there was a significant relationship between perceived value and mobile game addiction. Consequently, it was found that perceived values were significantly related to mobile game addiction. Especially, functional, emotional and conditional values had a strong correlation with mobile game addiction. This study provides some evidences that perceived game value can influence game addiction.

Chapter 9: Antecedents of Global Brands Preference Among Generation Y in Malaysia

Consumers in Asia are known for preferring global brands as opposed to the locally manufactured ones. The emergence of global brands in the marketplace has brought many benefits as well as many obstacles, especially for local marketers. This study explored the antecedents of global brands preference among Gen-Y in Malaysia, notably country-of-origin, quality, design, and advertising. 300 students of higher learning institutions in Malaysia were selected to take part in the study. Multiple regression analysis were used to analyze the data. It was found that the country-of-origin, quality, and design positively influence global brands preference among Gen-Y. However, advertising was found to influence preferences negatively. The findings could help local marketers develop and execute their marketing plan better and global marketers to improve their strategies and be more competitive. Marketers should focus on the above aspects in their marketing plan to capture the markets of Gen-Y in Malaysia and thus addressing their needs and wants better.

Chapter 10: Understanding Cultural Hybridization and Globalization Through the Benefits and Risks on Economic Growth

The purpose of this study is to examine various issues and understanding the main talking point in globalization which is the impacts it brings to the economic growth and the benefits and risks associated with it. In a fast pace world where information and communication is power, globalization in a nutshell is a worldwide agenda that primarily targeted to bring the best out of each and every members of the economic cycle. Globalization in the world's business is undeniably known as a catalyst that paved the way for aspiring entrepreneurs and business entity to acquire new wealth elsewhere by venturing into a new territory. The development of an ascending trend of integrated and holistic global economy has made globalization a worldwide agenda that implies the open up of a border for foreign business to come in and vice versa. The act of it often focused on three major elements involved which is resoundingly crucial, such as the inception of a free trade, allowing a free flow of capital and the exploitation of cheaper foreign labor markets. Together with those objectives, corporations and business entities alike are keen to fully utilize the technological advancement at their disposal for expanding their respective businesses with the help of effective information and communication technology system that interconnected within the business cycle. These factors have brought the world closer and as world economy become closer and closer, the competition become higher.

Chapter 11: A Decent Work and Economic Growth – The Potential of Asnaf Entrepreneur in Achieving Sustainable Development Goals (SDGs)

Asnaf entrepreneur is a micro SME entrepreneur who plays a significant role in the contribution of the economic sectors. In 2018, Malaysia registered a total of 907,065 SMEs, with micro-enterprises accounting for 2.3% (20,612) of the total. The poor and needy entrepreneur is also part of the successful key to support Malaysian to achieve Sustainable Development Goals (SDGs). The objective of this study is to identify the potential of poor and needy entrepreneur in Kedah Zakat Board (LZNK) to achieve SDGs. This paper uses a conceptual study method and explore the literature as a guide for enhancing knowledge on this area. This paper suggests a potential sustainable development model with four variables of poor and needy entrepreneurs in achieving SDGs goals. The contributions and implications of the study are discussed at the end of this paper.

Chapter 12: Proactive and Responsive Export Market Orientation Behaviors, Antecedents, and Firm Performance – A Qualitative Study on Exporting SMEs

This paper details about the qualitative study of proactive and responsive export market orientation. An interview series was conducted to assess whether the issue of proactive and responsive export market orientation exist among exporters, identification of the exporters' characteristics (antecedents) and understand the behaviors effect on performance consequences. Findings from the interview were recorded in a qualitative codebook. Discussions and conclusion made on the qualitative findings revealed that the issue of proactive and responsive export market orientation is present, different characteristics lead to different behaviors, and the behaviors affect the exporters' performance consequences differently.

Chapter 13: Managing Innovation – Technology, Consumer, and Sustainability Perspective and the Challenges

This study emphasizes the overview of technology innovation which comprises the definition and the technological innovation categories distinction; the overview of consumer attitude towards product innovation focuses on the consumer demand on innovative products, the stimulus purchasing factor and the consumer satisfactory factors over product innovation; overview of sustainability innovation; innovation management as part of the strategic management and challenges on innovative strategy formulation and implementation. Innovation strategy formulation requires detail assessments on potential technological advancement, consumers' attitude on innovative products and sustainability impact on innovative initiatives. Innovation strategy is perceived as part of the strategic management and the implementation is very much depends on intra-organizational factor. The employee innovation adoptions as the connection between technological innovation, consumer behavior towards product innovation and innovative sustainability for innovation strategy formulation can be further studied.

Chapter 14: The Implication of Sustainability Innovation – Blue Ocean Strategy

The global economy has been shifting from one phase to another as they are trying to move the country's economy moving forwards as it evolves.in the past economy was solely dependent on natural resources, moving to manufacturing and now currently focusing on the services delivery. Government roles in implementing policies are needed in order to ensure natural resources to be transformed as it getting more sustain and positively contribute to social wellbeing of the people. The production of business delivery is getting more innovative; therefore, research and development are aligned with the goals for sustainability. Thus, it is significant for business to include sustainability innovation for Industrial Revolutions 4.0. Business unsustainability is putting such value and its significance towards the stakeholders, the environment and also the society. It is the ability or capability to maintain or sustain without endangering the potential of the next generation in carrying out businesses. The sustainability innovation should be applied all level of generations and aspect of our leathery should use the concept of sustainability and innovation to be embedded in the culture of the company for longer survival in the market and prosperity. The blue ocean strategy with sustainable innovation are the concept that help business to seek for solution that not only innovative the products but also the process; will be discussed thoroughly throughout this finding.

Chapter 15: Inverted Grammar Classroom – Detecting Grammar Errors in Students' Video Presentation

Flipped learning is basically a pedagogical model which reverses classroom activities. Materials or contents are provided online (in learning management system or other learning platforms) and students will study the material prior to the lesson. Therefore, classroom time can be used to engage in activities such as problem-solving, discussion and analysis. This study is an extended study of a previous research which explored the effects of the flipped learning approach in a grammar classroom. For this study, the focus is shifted to the grammatical errors made by students in their video presentation during the flipped learning session. The analysis of the findings showed that students' grammar errors are mainly on missed formation errors, addition error, omission error and lastly improper ordering The findings of this study give ESL practitioners a better insight into student errors and should lead to improved grammar usage in the classroom through blended learning.

Chapter 16: Green Consumer Behavior – Integration of Theory of Planned Behavior and Technology Acceptance Model

Environment preservation is a global concern. Textile industry disposes of chemicals which effects environment and human life (water borne diseases). United Nations develops 17 Sustainable Development Goals (UNSDG's) to protect environment. Five SDG's addressing textile industry namely good health and well-being, clean water and sanitation, responsible production and consumption, climate action and life below water. Role of textile industry to achieve SDG's is inevitable. Textile policy of Pakistan 2014-19 confirms that international buyer is concerned about the environment which evidently shows potential of green marketing in textile sector of Pakistan. Green marketing encourages environment friendly marketing practices (product, price, place, promotion). The objective of this study is to integrate the theory of planned behavior and technology acceptance model. Green consumer behavior of textile sector of Pakistan is conceptualized with this extended lens. This study enhances the body of knowledge by conceptualizing green consumer behavior of textile sector through extended model. Practically, this study remains beneficial for marketing professionals and researchers to understand green consumer behavior of textile sector. Success of green marketing is the success of society to curb environmental problems.

Norazah Mohd Suki
Universiti Utara Malaysia, Malaysia

Norbayah Mohd Suki
Universiti Utara Malaysia, Malaysia

REFERENCES

Lemmens, J. S., Valkenburg, P. M., & Peter, J. (2009). Development and Validation of a Game Addiction Scale for Adolescents. *Media Psychology*, *12*(1), 77–95. doi:10.1080/15213260802669458

Sheth, J. N., Newman, B. I., & Gross, B. L. (1991). *Consumption Values and Market Choices-Theory and Applications*. Cincinnati, OH: South-Western Publishing Co.

Acknowledgment

The editor would like to acknowledge each one of the authors for their contribution to this book. Without their support, this book would not have become materialized. The editor also wish to thank the valuable contributions of the reviewers to improve the quality, and content presentation of chapters.

Norazah Mohd Suki
Universiti Utara Malaysia, Malaysia

Norbayah Mohd Suki
Universiti Utara Malaysia, Malaysia

Chapter 1
Multiple Signals and Consumer Behavior in the Digital Economy:
Implementing a Multidimensional Framework

Ciro Troise
https://orcid.org/0000-0002-8899-8949
Department of Management, University of Campania Luigi Vanvitelli, Capua, Italy

ABSTRACT

The digital economy shows a challenging environment, and three main players have entered the arena (digital platforms, online communities, new technologies). The aim of this chapter is to provide a new multidimensional framework for exploring multiple signals. The study leverages the signaling theory, since signals help companies and sellers to mitigate information asymmetries. In the virtual context of the digital economy, credible and observable information improve the decision-making process of consumers. The work opted for a multidimensional framework and proposes that four types of signals (social network, social capital, certification, social identity) influence consumer behavior. Furthermore, the study suggests that also the interactions/combinations between these signals could affect consumer behavior. This contribution offers a conceptual framework without testing empirically the propositions; thus, it offers the opportunity of further research. This work has interesting implications for several actors of the digital ecosystem (firms, entrepreneurs, platform managers, consumers, etc.).

INTRODUCTION

The current era is characterized by the advent of the digital and the spread of new technologies. At the same time, the rise of the so-called "Industry 4.0" (Lasi, Fettke, Kemper, Feld, & Hoffmann, 2014) and the development of ICT (Information and Communications Technology) (Sassi & Goaied, 2013) had a

DOI: 10.4018/978-1-7998-3042-9.ch001

strong impact on the global economy. In this changing and evolving scenario, some new players have entered the arena. Among them, the most promising are digital platforms (Dou, He, & Xu, 2016; Parker, Alstyne, & Choudary, 2016), online communities (Kozinets, De Valck, Wojnicki, & Wilner, 2010; Sun, Rau, & Ma, 2014) and new technologies (also known as "Technologies 4.0") – which include a multitude of categories such as mobile apps, Fintech, IoT, and so on. These new players have emerged in the last few years and have radically changed people's lifestyles and companies' activities.

The digital revolution offers many challenges and opportunities for several stakeholders, in particular for SNS developers and online companies. However, inevitably, the digital revolution raises a number of questions on the outlook for the traditional systems. In this vein, the main research questions that attract both scholars and practitioners are related to the impact of these new players and to the improvement of the understanding of consumer behavior.

Thus, there is a significant call for more research that contributes to shed some lights in this field. Understanding the consumer behavior – and the related buying process – plays a key role for the strategies of many companies. Consumer marketing strategies mainly follow new trends, for example the large use of social media (Hughes, Rowe, Batey, & Lee., 2012) represents an essential factor for both demand and supply sides. Changing consumer behavior is being joined by new digital technologies to drive a new era of innovation in marketing services.

In this digital revolution era, both the social networks and the so-called "digital natives" affect the success and the growth of digital businesses. Over the last years, some companies such as AirBnb, Alibaba, BlaBlaCar, MyTaxi and Uber, had a relevant impact on the market. In particular, sharing economy platforms (Basili & Rossi, 2019) are a successful business model in the digital economy (Denning, 2014). The digital economy and online markets present a challenging environment for consumers to evaluate the real value of products/services and company offers. In this context characterized by high uncertainty, the signals that companies send to consumers can affect their decision-making process. Observable and credible signals can mitigate the problem of information asymmetries (Connelly, Certo, Ireland, & Reutzel, 2011; Spence, 1973).

In the digital economy scenario, many companies operate through virtual platforms. These platforms are characterized by the absence of personal interactions and by a virtual space in the exchange process. One of the most important challenges facing companies and platform managers is to communicate information about the business or product/service in order to involve consumers. Thus, the signals must be credible and attractive to actually capture the attention of consumers. These signals could play a key role in limiting uncertainty associated with online purchases and overcoming typical problems related to information asymmetries, such as adverse selection and moral hazard (Akerlof, 1970).

The decision-making process of consumers is affected by several factors, for example social networks, motivation, emotions, passion, cognitive or relational aspects, and so on. More research that delve into aspect of consumer behavior and psychology in the digital economy is deemed necessary (Ling Chang, Ling Tam, & Suki, 2016; Nathan, Fook Chiun, & Suki, 2016; Suki, 2016). Accordingly, the present study tries to shed some light on the nascent research field related to consumer behavior in the digital economy by leveraging the signaling theory (Spence, 1973). Precisely, this work proposes a multidimensional framework in order to examine multiple signals and their influence on consumer behavior.

Multidimensional framework is a recurrent method to investigate a new phenomenon and useful to support decisions-making process (Flood & Jackson, 1991; Keszei, Murphy, & Loeur, 2018; Mavlanova, Benbunan-Fich, & Koufaris, 2012; Xu & Ouenniche, 2011; Yablonsky, 2018; Yigitcanlar et al., 2018; Yang, Yang, & Plotnick, 2018). The study focuses on multiple signals (Cho & Sobel, 1990; Ramey,

1996; Worsham & Gatrell, 2005), a technique that allows the exploitation of different signals. The main signals considered in this work belong to four main pillars: social network, social capital, certification and social identity.

The proposed framework suggests that individual dimensions can influence consumer behavior and – furthermore – also combinations and interactions (or intersection) between these dimensions can also have a significant impact. The study provides several propositions that could be used in future developments of this research in order to test the influence of signals – and their related interactions – in affecting consumer behaviors. The discovery could enhance our understanding of signals and their interactions/combinations. Furthermore, the study could have future useful implications for a multitude of stakeholders, in particular online sellers and platform managers.The remainder of this chapter is structured as follows. First, the three main players of the digital economy – i.e. digital platforms, online communities and new technologies – are analyzed. Second, an overview of the signaling theory is provided, followed by the description of the multidimensional framework and the analyses of the multiple signals. Finally, the conclusion provides a summary of the work, addressing some limitations of the research and future research directions.

DIGITAL ECONOMY

As the International Monetary Fund (IMF) (2018) argued, "the lack of a generally agreed definition of the 'digital economy' or 'digital sector' and the lack of industry and product classification for Internet platforms and associated services are hurdles to measuring the digital economy". Many times, the term "digital economy" indicate the spread of digitalization (e.g., the use of Internet, ICT services, online platforms, etc.) across all sectors of the economy, from agriculture to warehousing. In recent years, the measurement of the digital economy has become a significant topic of several discussions. One of this topic is the inclusion (or exclusion) – within the digital economy – of digital platforms, digital products, new technologies (e.g. new forms of financial technologies, i.e. Fintech).

According to the latest classifications – such as the latest version of the United Nations' International Standard Industrial Classification (ISIC) and of Central Product Classification (CPC) – both ICT sector and content or media sector belong to the digital economy. However, IFM (2018) suggested that it is important to consider also the recent growth of digital activities and products, such as the spread of online platforms and platform-enabled services. These platforms include sharing economy portals, collaborative finance (e.g. P2P lenging) and crowdsourcing platforms (e.g., Freelancer, and Upwork). In this virtual scenario, online communities are increasingly widespread and numerous.

The digital economy is growing rapidly over the years and the numbers are significant worldwide (OECD, 2017, 2019). In fact, IMF (2018) reported some of the main indicators of several major countries and highlights that:

- China's digital economy amounted to 30% of GDP in 2016 (Tencent, 2017);
- Services of online platforms (including distribution margins of e-commerce platforms), were estimated to amount to 1.5% of U.S. GDP in 2015 (IMF, 2018);
- Open source (free) software production were estimated at 0.2% of U.S. GDP in 2015 (estimated in $35 billion) (Ahmad, Ribarsky, & Reinsdorf, 2017; Greenstein & Nagle, 2014);

Figure 1.

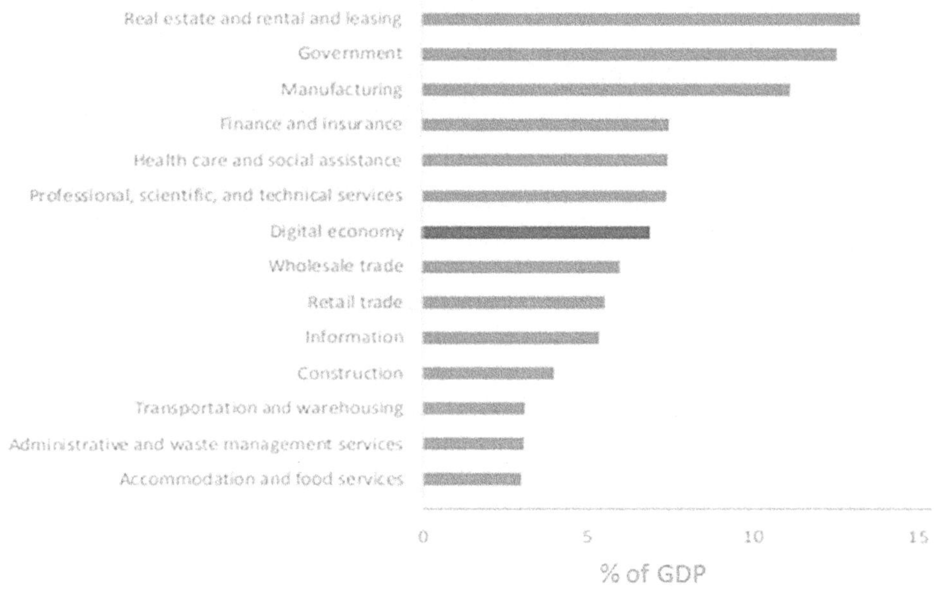

- Free media from online platforms (funded by advertising) were estimated at 0.1% of U.S. GDP in 2015 (Nakamura, Samuels, & Soloveichik, 2017);
- Fixed capital formation by platforms that make their own servers is overlooked in 2015 (Byrne et al., 2017);
- The digital portion of worldwide output of U.S. multinational enterprises (MNEs) were estimated at 0.4% of U.S. GDP in 2017 (Guvenen, Mataloni, Rassier, & Ruhl, 2017);
- Businesses with an online presence accounted for 87% of turnover and 86% of employment in the business sector in the Netherlands in 2015 (Oostrom et al., 2017);
- The total welfare from digital products (including consumer surplus) in U.S. GDP in 2016 will increase in the following years (by about 30%) (Brynjolfsson, Eggers, & Gannamaneni, 2017).

According to some recent statistics released by the Bureau of Economic Analysis (BEA) (2019), the digital economy accounted for 6.9% of the U.S. GDP, i.e. \$1.35 trillion, in 2017. In this new emerging field, BEA (2019) data shows two other significant parameters of the digital economy. Firstly, the digital economy supported 5.1 million jobs in 2017, i.e. 3.3% of total U.S. employment (of 152.1 million jobs). It is interesting to note that the digital economy's share of total employment is about same as the transportation and warehousing industry's share. Second, employees working in the digital economy earned \$132,223 in average annual compensation in 2017, compared to \$68,506 per worker for the total U.S. economy. Table 1 summarizes the main and significant numbers of the digital economy.

This study shares the main classifications of digital economy provided by IMF, ISIC, OECD, BEA and other main organizations. Thus, three main players (see Figure 2) that entered the digital economy arena are discussed: digital platforms, online communities and new technologies. The present study acknowledges the importance of these players and also the key role that signals play for them. Thus,

Table 1. The numbers of the digital economy

Country	Numbers of Digital Economy	Percetanges	Year
China	China's Digital economy	30% of GDP	2016
Netherlands	Turnover business online presence	87% (sector)	2015
Netherlands	Employment business online presence	86% (sector)	2015
U.S.	Services of online platforms	1.5% of GDP	2015
U.S.	Open source software production	0.2% of GDP	2015
U.S.	Free media from online platforms	0.1% of GDP	2015
U.S.	Digital worldwide output of MNEs	0.4% of GDP	2017
U.S.	U.S. - Digital economy	6.9% of GDP	2017
U.S.	Jobs supported in the digital economy	3.3% of U.S. Employement	2017
U.S.	Employees (average) earnings	193% higher (compared to average U.S. workers)	2017

Source: author's elaboration on IMF (2018) and BEA (2019) data

this work analyzes multiple signals that could affect consumer behavior and represent successful driver for the three players.

Digital Platforms

Digital platforms are certainly the main players in the digital economy. In fact, sometimes the digital economy is defined as the sum of online platforms and activities that owe their existence to such platforms (IMF, 2018). In order to describe the power and the impact of digital platforms, Parker et al. (2016) reported: "How can a major business segment be invaded and conquered in a matter of months by an upstart with none of the resources traditionally deemed essential for survival, let alone market dominance? And why is this happening today in one industry after another? The answer is the power of the platform – a new business model that uses technology to connect people, organizations, and resources in an interactive ecosystem in which amazing amounts of value can be created and exchanged".

Figure 2.

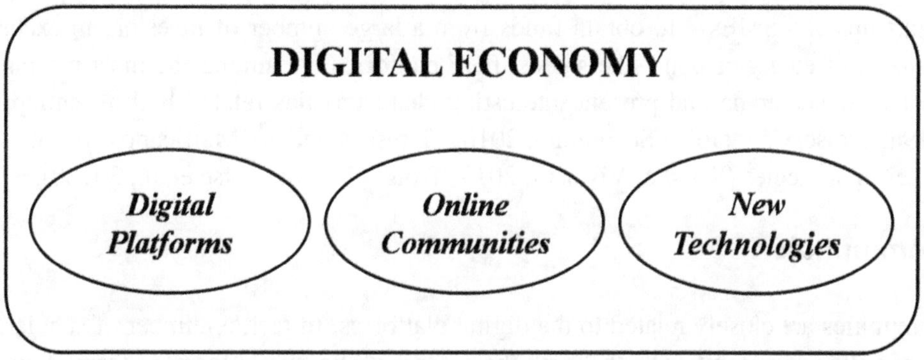

The digital economy is a vibrant field in which the digital platforms are an established feature and are main elements to foster the digital ecosystem and economic growth (Kenney & Zysman, 2016; Parker et al., 2016). Over the last years, a growing number of companies (e.g. AirBnb, Uber, etc.) focused their business on digital platforms and had a significant impact on both the market and the global economy. Those platform-based digital businesses are challenging established new companies that approach a market with different business models. The literature on digital platforms is rich in studies that specifically examined the two-sided platforms (Armstrong & Wright, 2008; Evans, 2003; Katz & Shapiro, 1985; Rochet & Tirole, 2006). As Armstrong & Wright (2008) suggested, many industries in the current global scenario "are organized as so-called two-sided markets in which platforms enable interactions between two groups of users, each of which cares about the size and attributes of the other group on the same platform".

Two sided-platforms are a well-known business configuration that "enable interactions between end-users, and try to get the two sides 'on board' by appropriately charging each side" (Rochet & Tirole, 2006, pp. 645). These platforms act as match-makers between two different groups of customers and mediate transactions between them (Eisenmann, Parker, & Van Alstyne, 2006; Hagiu & Wright, 2011). The interactions between consumers and sellers create surplus for both the groups. Representative examples in this field are: travelers and hosts (e.g. for Airbnb) or riders and drivers (e.g. for Uber or MyTaxi), creating the so-called indirect network effects (Katz & Shapiro, 1985). Digital platforms could create more surplus for the parties by offering value-added service (Dou et al., 2016; Kuo et al., 2009) and improving the quality and attractiveness of both the sides (Bakos & Katsamakas, 2008; Caillaud & Jullien, 2003; Evans, 2003).

Digital platforms are spreading all over the world and among the most important types are: sharing-economy platforms such as carsharing (e.g. Drivy or Turo) and ridesharing (e.g. BlaBlaCar or Lyftshare) (Basili & Rossi, 2019), hospitality platforms (e.g. Airbnb) (Guttentag, 2015), and taxi-hailing platforms (e.g. MyTaxi, GetTaxi or Uber) (Cramer & Krueger, 2016).

In the global scenario, other two emergent types of digital platforms are: open innovation platforms and crowdfunding platforms. Open innovation platforms (OIPs), are virtual places where innovation seekers (e.g. companies) launch an online open call in order to collect ideas from users and thus support their initiatives (Chesbrough, 2003; Troise, Matricano, & Sorrentino, 2019). OIPs provide useful services and favor the exchange of knowledge and cooperation between the participants (De Silva, Howells, & Meyer, 2018; Troise et al., 2019; West & Lakhani, 2008).

Since the main goal of crowdfunding is to collect money, crowdfunding platforms connect funding seekers to small investors, i.e. the crowd. There are four main categories of crowdfunding: reward, donation, equity and lending. Among them, equity crowdfunding (ECF) platforms help companies – in particular start ups and SMEs – to obtain funds from a large number of investors in exchange for a specified amount of equity or bond-like shares. ECF platforms are among the most promising in the entrepreneurial finance arena and present interesting characteristics related both to entrepreneurship (Troise, 2019a; Troise, Candelo, & Sorrentino, 2018a; Troise, Candelo, Matricano, Sorrentino, 2018b) and to services or strategies (Rossi & Vismara, 2018; Troise, 2019b; Troise et al., 2018b).

Online Communities

Online communities are closely related to the digital platforms. In fact, a number of scholars leverage the concept of online communities to deal with the success of digital platforms in term of open innovation projects (Parmentier & Gandia, 2013; Wang, Nickerson, & Sakamoto, 2018) and growth of sharing economy phenomenon (Richter, Kraus, Brem, Durst, & Giselbrecht, 2017). These communities are "online social networks in which people with common interests, goals, or practices interact to share information and knowledge, and engage in social interactions" (Chiu, Hsu, & Wang, 2006, pp. 1873). Many scholars worldwide embrace the idea that communities create new knowledge and share experience (Brown & Duguid, 1991; Hsu, Ju, Yen, & Chang, 2007; Kozinets, Hemetsberger, & Schau, 2008).

These online communities are virtual associations formed by groups of people who have several interests or values in common and shares some goals (Cohen, Prusak, & Prusak, 2001; Hsu et al., 2007; Inkpen & Tsang, 2005; Kozinets, 1999; West & Lakhani, 2008).

Belonging to a community promotes both the creation of a strong relational network and the sharing of knowledge among the members. This favors the process of collective invention and influences the outcome of communities (Chiu et al., 2006; Kosonen, 2009).

In this vein, some prior works argued that the transfer of knowledge could play a key role in this context by affecting the solutions for innovative challenges (i.e. the new problems that innovation solvers try to solve) (Jeppesen & Lakhani, 2010; Lovett & Anderson, 1996; Lüthje, Herstatt, & Von Hippel, 2005). In fact, the members of the community – especially with different expertise – can leverage the body of knowledge embedded in the community or spur new connections (Jeppesen & Lakhani, 2010; Novick, 1988). Several studies highlighted that the size of online communities (i.e. the number of community members) is a significant proxy in digital platforms contexts such as online P2P lending (Chen, Zhou, & Wan, 2016) and OIPs (Troise et al., 2019).

In these online communities, the so-called WoM (word of mouth) is a major part of online consumer interactions and represents one of the most important communications channels within this virtual environment (Brown, Broderick, & Lee, 2007; Kozinets et al., 2010). The main audience of online communities sare the so-called "Millennials" (Keszei et al., 2018; Taken Smith, 2012). A recent report by Goldman Sachs (2015, pp. 7) reported that "Millennials are the agent of change in shifting behaviors".

New Technologies

A more difficult task is to examine the wide range of new technologies. In the last few years a large number of new technologies have been developed in many fields. For example in the financial industry, the financial technologies, better known as "Fintech", represent significant novelties (BCBS, 2018; IOSCO, 2017). "The term 'Financial Technologies or Fintech' is used to describe a variety of innovative business models and emerging technologies that have the potential to transform the financial services industry" (IOSCO, 2017, pp. 2). As for innovative Fintech business models, they typically offer one or more specific financial products or services through the use of the internet. Well-known examples are ECF platforms (intermediate share placements) and P2P lending platforms (intermediate or sell loans). As for emerging technologies, typical examples are cognitive computing, machine learning, artificial intelligence, and distributed ledger technologies (DLT). These technologies support both Fintech new entrants and traditional incumbents. The Fintech landscape shows eight main categories (IOSCO, 2017): payments, insurance, planning, lending and crowdfunding, blockchain, trading and investments, data and analytics, and security.

Other typical examples of the new technologies in this field are initial coin offerings (ICOs), cryptocurrencies and blockchain (Adhami, Giudici, & Martinazzi, 2018; BCBS, 2018). Among them, ICOs are topical since this category adopts innovative technologies based on 'blockchains' and token mechanism (Adhami et al., 2018).

The current economy is characterized by the spread of the so-called "apps". The term app has recently entered the global lexicon and is short for the word "application". As OECD (2013, pp. 8) reported "an app is a standardised piece of software that runs on a computing platform". This new form of technology had a strong impact on the global economy (OECD, 2013; Troise & Ferrara, 2016; Vision Mobile, 2015). Many scholars in this research stream investigated app business models or consumer behaviors (Arora, Ter Hofstede, & Mahajan, 2017; Chen, Zhang, & Zhao, 2017; Dinsmore, Swani, & Dugan, 2017).

Finally, it is important to recall that the classification of new technologies include cloud computing (Sultan, 2010; Zhang, Cheng, & Boutaba, 2010) and IoT (Internet of Things) (Wortmann & Flüchter, 2015; Yang, Yang, & Plotnick, 2013). The development of new technologies offer significant opportunities for several markets. The spread of digital technologies is a crucial parameter to foster business growth and in particular big data represent an important resource (Trabucchi, Buganza, Dell'Era, & Pellizzoni, 2018).

SIGNALING THEORY

Signaling theory is one of the main research framework under which consumer behavior has been investigated. This well known theory originates from the seminal paper of Spence (1973). The scholar introduced the concept of signals, i.e. visible features of an object that a signaler send to an audience (specific or indifferent target). These features can be altered according to a signaler's preference, thus favoring potential moral hazard issues. The asymmetric information held by sellers and buyers can lead to inefficient exchanges and cause adverse selection problems (Akerlof, 1970).

In fact, sellers could convey hidden or limit quality information to another party, i.e. buyers, in order to influence consumer behavior (Zmud, Croes, Shaft, & Zheng, 2010) and facilitate a purchase or exchange (Wells, Valacich, & Hess, 2011). Precisely, signaling theory helps to explain the behavior of sellers and buyers when they have access to different information (Connelly et al., 2011). The main focus of the signaling theory lies in the intentional communication of information by sellers in order to provide observable characteristics useful to mitigate the problem of information asymmetry.

Signaling theory has been used to explain which types of information lead consumers to choose a specific product or service (Celani & Singh, 2011; Mavlanova et al., 2012; Benbunan-Fich, & Lang, 2016; Price & Dawar, 2002). However, not all the information are effective signal useful to overcome the problem of information asymmetry. Credible and observable signals (Connelly et al., 2011) that sellers disclose can convey positive information which enables buyers to identify good quality products. In this way, buyers can make more accurate assessments of quality, especially in presence of limited or scarce product information (Kirmani & Rao, 2000; Richardson et al., 1994). Also signals originated from third parties mitigate the asymmetries (Fischer & Reuber, 2007). Furthermore, some information can better be understood as "cheap talk".

The online environment increases the uncertainty for buyers. Information asymmetries between the two parties, i.e. sellers and buyers, emerge since a buyer possesses incomplete or imperfect information with respect to the seller. For example, e-commerce is a note example of virtual channels characterized for the absence of personal interactions, thus signals are fundamental for buyers to alleviate the problem of product evaluation (Mavlanova et al., 2016; Wells et al., 2011). In this context, online buyers face difficulties since the quality of products and information about sellers are uncertain (Dimoka, Hong, &

Pavlou, 2012; Ghose, 2009). Specific signals introduced by sellers disclose both the quality of products and the validity of sellers (Pavlou, Liang, & Xue, 2007). Sometimes this signals represent a cost for sellers (Donath, 2007), even if these costs are low in the online market.

The digital economy is a challenging environment to evaluate the quality of products/services. In the current literature, a recurrent research question (little investigated) is which information or strategies affect consumer behavior and are preferred by several typologies of buyers, in particular Millennials (Taken Smith, 2012). In this vein, signaling theory is the most suitable theory to provide new insights for research in the digital economy. The present study leverages this theory and provides a multidimensional framework that considers multiple signals. The work acknowledges the importance of multiple signals and their combinations/interactions, thus it focuses on signals deriving from four areas and their related theories: social network; social capital; certification; social identity.

MULTIDIMENSIONAL FRAMEWORK

The study opted for a multidimensional framework to examine multiple signals in the digital economy. This methodology is commonly used by several scholars in order to explain new emergent phenomenon or support decisions. A growing number of studies in fact leverage this method since it offers the possibility to explore multiple dimensions or parameters simultaneously. In this vein, Flood & Jackson (1991) argued that this method is useful to explore complex problems that comprise several components (e.g. social, behavioral or exploitative) and require their combinations to develop different orientations.

Over the years, there has been a growing interest in utilizing multidimensional framework and – in fact – several scholars adopt this method. Among them: Yigitcanlar et al. (2018) explored smart cities; Mavlanova et al. (2012) classified website signals in online commerce; Keszei et al. (2018) focused on American Millennials; Yablonsky, (2018) investigated digital platform innovation; Xu & Ouenniche (2011) focused on performance evaluation of forecasting models; Yang et al. (2018) analyzed political ties in China. The purpose of this study is to propose a multidimensional framework to shed light on multiple signals in the digital economy. The work suggests that these signals could influence consumer behavior.

MULTIPLE SIGNALS

The present work leverages the signaling theory and focuses on four types of signals. Multiple signals is a well-known technique that allows the exploitation of different signals (Cho & Sobel, 1990; Daley & Green, 2014; Mavlanova et al., 2016; Ramey, 1996; Worsham & Gatrell, 2005). The main signals considered in this work belong to the above cited four main pillars (social network, social capital, certifications and social identity).

Social Networks

Several scholars leverage social network theory in order to promote innovation (Leyden et al., 2014) or crowdfunding success (Vismara, 2016), but the vast majority of them tried to analyze consumer behavior (e.g. Campbell, Ferraro, & Sands, 2014; Coulter & Roggeveen, 2012; Dholakia, Bagozzi, & Pearo, 2004; Heinonen, 2011).

Figure 3.

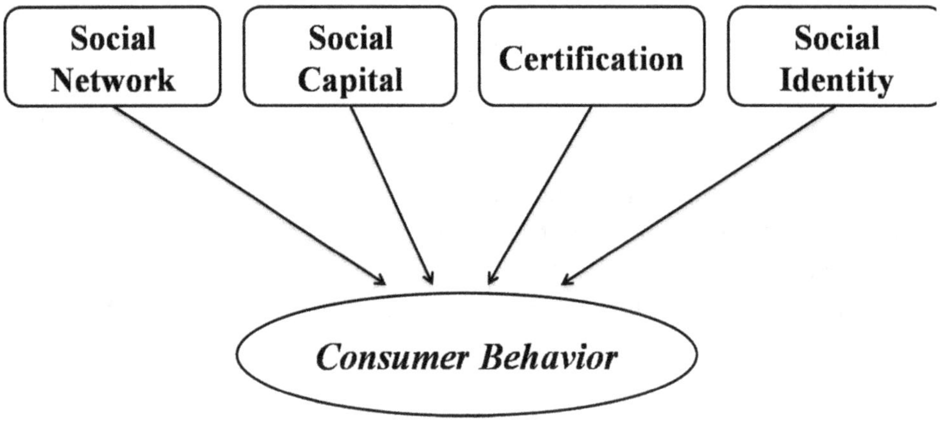

The strong diffusion of social networks (e.g. Facebook, LinkedIn, Twitter, YouTube) and the development of digital platforms have created new opportunities for the exchange process between buyers and sellers. In this scenario, social network connections represent important factors for the success of initiatives. Social networks (in particular Facebook) are becoming a significant source of information for both sellers and buyers (Hermida, Fletcher, Korell, & Logan, 2012). In fact, social networks help sellers to promote their products/services and help buyers to improve their understanding of products/services.

It is common that consumers are segmented on the basis of attitudes toward social networks (Campbell et al., 2014). The growing interest in social networks suggest that consumers actively contribute to marketing content (Heinonen, 2011). In the last few years, social networks know a great development (Boyd & Ellison, 2008; Shao, 2009) and many of them focused on characterizing content for consumers (Krishnamurthy & Dou, 2008). Social networks enable users to interact, socialize and share information (Kaplan & Haenlein, 2010; Park, Kee, & Valenzuela, 2009).

Figure 4.

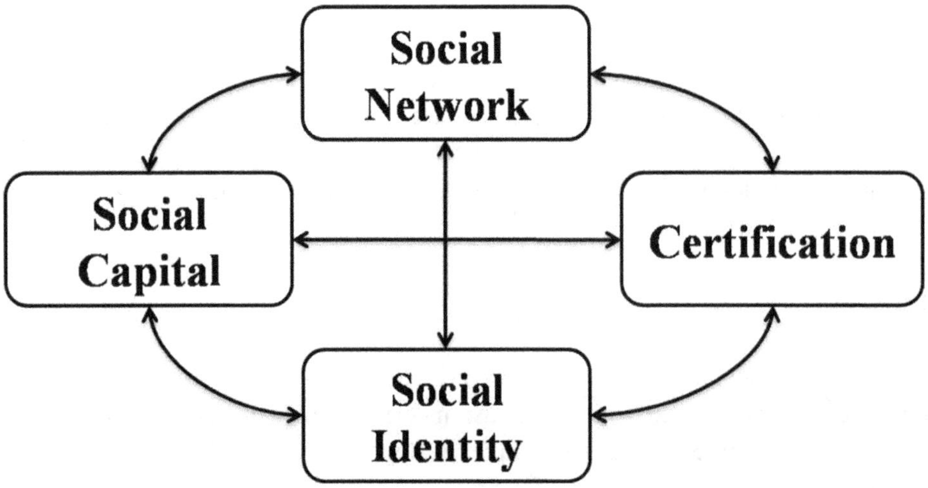

Other scholars focused on the key role played by social networks in this digital economy. Janssen & Jager (2006) showed the importance of social networks in explaining the dynamics of markets. Dholakia et al. (2004) investigated these networks focusing specifically on virtual communities. Other scholars explored social networks dynamics and communication. For example Coulter & Roggeveen (2012) examined how consumers respond to a WoM communication in an online social network (e.g. Facebook), while Smith, Coyle, Lightfoot, & Scott (2007) analyzed the nature, the characteristics and the influences of social networks.

Social networks facilitate WoM and create communities (Goldman Sachs, 2015). In the current era, there are several types of adopters, but Millennials are the main target (Goldman Sachs, 2015; Taken Smith, 2012). Social networks act as signals for buyers. Sellers leverage these signal in order to involve a large number of buyers. These social networks favor both interactions and the diffusion of information. Social network exploitation is very important in the digital era characterized by a growing number of online contexts. This work proposes the following proposition.

P1: Social networks influence consumer behavior.

Social Capital

The theory of social capital is one of the most important in management studies (Cohen et al., 2001; Inkpen & Tsang, 2005) and this type of capital – differently from other types of physical capital – lies in an individual's social structure (Coleman, 1988). Coleman (1998, pp. 98) argued that social capital (in terms of its functions) "is not a single entity, but a variety of different entities, with two elements in common: they all consist of some aspect of a social structure, and they facilitate certain actions – whether persons or corporate actors within the structure".

Social capital has been described as the combination of intangible resources that individuals and groups gain from their connections to one another (Bourdieu 1986; Paxton 1999).

Several scholars (e.g. Castaneda, Martinez, Marte, & Roxas, 2015; Mathwick, Wiertz, & de Ruyter, 2008) leveraged social capital theory and adopted a consumer behavior perspective in order to investigate the effects of social capital within a community on some consumer behaviors.

Many studies suggested that social capital is a multidimensional concept (Coleman, 1998; Hazleton & Kennan, 2000; Nahapiet & Ghoshal, 1998). It operates on multiple levels and affect the quality of the relationships within communities (Michaelson, 1996; Minkoff, 1997) and consumption interests (Holt, 1997; Kozinets, 2002).

In the management literature, one of the main classification of social capital is the repartition in three dimensions, i.e. structural (e.g. network ties and network configuration), relational (e.g. obligations, expectations, and trustworthiness) and cognitive (e.g. shared language, shared narratives and shared meanings) (Nahapiet & Ghoshal, 1998).

The significant role of social capital in relationships between consumers and sellers is widely recognized, however recent studies are showing its impact also in other contexts such as crowdfunding (Colombo, Franzoni, & Rossi-Lamastra, 2015). In this vein, Colombo et al. (2015) discussed the importance of founder's social capital – i.e. the internal social capital developed within the platform – in affecting campaign's success. Social capital plays a strategic signaling role for sellers to involve buyers. This work proposes the following proposition.

P2: Social capital influences consumer behavior.

Certifications

Certification theory suggests that a third-party can certify quality information (Booth & Smith, 1986). The third parties have access to inside information and act as certifiers of the quality of a product/service and of the company reputation. In the global market, certifying organizations play an active role. Credible and reputable certifiers provide endorsement and help alleviate the information gap between the parties (Megginson & Weiss, 1991). Several quality ratings or certifications – such as ISO (International Organization for Standardization) and FDA (Food and Drug Administration – are effective signals of the underlying quality of a product/service or a entity (King et al., 2005).

Certifications are quality cues that mitigate information asymmetries in several fields (Dimara & Skuras, 2003). For example, Mishra (2006) explored the role of certification signals in service relationships, while Lee & Turban (2014) investigated third-party certification in order to investigate consumer trust in Internet shopping (e-commerce). Instead, other scholar focused on certification applied to food safety or quality and to the environment (Caswell & Mojduszka, 1996; Tregear, Kuznesof, & Moxey, 1998).

In this research stream, several scholars focused on the effectiveness of certification logos on consumer behavior (Jiang, Jones, & Javie, 2008; Sparks, Perkins, & Buckley, 2013). Logos, awards, grants and IPRs are some well known examples of certifications that play a signaling role for consumers (Long, 2002; Sparks et al., 2013; Tregear et al., 1998). Jiang et al. (2008, pp. 839) suggested that "a key strategy to increase consumer trust in ordering has been participation in third-party certification programs". The scholars found that: Web site certification can reassure potential customers and increase the probability of purchase; perceptions of third-party logos are related to intensity of seal exposure, importance of trust factors in online shopping, and disposition toward third-party certification; perceptions and the level of consumer trust in online shopping are positively related to transfer of trust from certification to online e-marketers.

Certification transforms unobservable credence attributes into observable search attributes (Auriol & Schilizzi, 2003) and represents the main solution to the problem of signaling the quality of products/services. In fact, many times the quality of products and services is not observable (or only partially) to consumers. Auriol & Schilizzi (2003, pp. 3) defines certification as "a process whereby an unobservable quality level of some product is made known to the consumer through some labeling system, usually issued by a third independent party". The scholars discussed the importance of certification in affecting the consumer confidence, i.e. the credibility of the certification process.

Certifications are useful signal that sellers use in order to involve a large number of buyers. These certifications play a signaling role to the extent they show the quality of the product/service and of the company. Consumers rely on signals and compare quality disclosure with other parameters/signals to make their decisions. Certifications help to mitigate asymmetries between the parties. This work proposes the following proposition.

P3: Certifications influence consumer behavior.

Social Identity

Social identity is a topic that caught the attention of many scholars in different areas or domains such as psychology, marketing, economy and organization contexts (Bhattacharya & Sen, 2003; Brewer & Kramer, 1986; Forehand, Deshpande´, & Reed, 2002; Madrigal, 2001; Marin, Ruiz, & Rubio, 2009; Reed, 2004; Tajfel, 1988; Tajfel & Turner, 1986). Since its origin, social identity theory (Tajfel & Turner, 1979, 1986) represents a recurrent theme in management literature since it explains intergroup behavior (Tajfel & Turner, 1979). According to this well-known theory, people classify themselves into a multitude of social categories and demonstrate a sense of belonging (Abrams & Hogg, 1988; Tajfel, 1988). People manifest multiple identities associated to different social groups in which they play a specific role (Tajfel & Turner, 1986). McLeod, (2008) argued that individuals perceive others as part of "ingroups" with which they socially identify (or "outgroups" with which they do not). Norms and attitudes affect groups' interactions.

Social identity affects consumer attitudes, judgments, and behaviors (for example what they buy or why they do it) (Forehand et al., 2002; Reed, 2002). A particular social identity is relevant to evaluate a brand, a product/service and a company (Reed, 2004). People commit more resources and efforts to support initiatives and products/services that resonate with their social identity (Aaker & Akutsu, 2009). Arnett, German, & Hunt (2003) discussed the consumption decision making which involves social identity and suggested that a social identity is an activated conceptual structure in the consumer's working self-concept.

Marin et al. (2009, pp. 65) found that "activating identity salience of a particular consumer social identity (a company) will affect consumer reactions to product stimuli, increasing consumer loyalty". Social identity is also relevant to evaluate a company (Reed, 2004). Companies that disclose distinctive characteristics or configurations – such as a distinctive culture, strategy or structure – are the main target for consumers' identification (Bhattacharya & Sen, 2003; Tajfel & Turner, 1986).

Companies through specific marketing communications attempt to connect a product or brand to a social identity (Reed, 2004). In doing this, they should consider that social identity is valued by the target consumers and should focus on specific aspects that can be leveraged to increase perceptions of self-importance associated with that identity (Reed, 2004).

In the digital era characterized by developed communications channels, social identity plays a key role in affecting consumer behavior. Social identity is strategic for companies and product/service evaluation. Communication activity cues about how the company or product/service is related to the identity that is relevant to the consumer. This work proposes the following proposition.

P4: Social identity influences consumer behavior.

Signal Interactions and Combinations

This study proposes that the above discussed four dimensions – i.e. social networks, social capital, certifications and social identity – could interact and be combined. The interaction and combination of dimensions enhance and reinforce the impacts of the signals. Each dimension interacts with the other three dimensions considered. It is reasonable to assume that these intersections and combinations could influence consumer behavior. In fact, social networks, social capital, certifications and social identity could increase their signaling role by their combinations. Hence, it is posited that:

Figure 5.

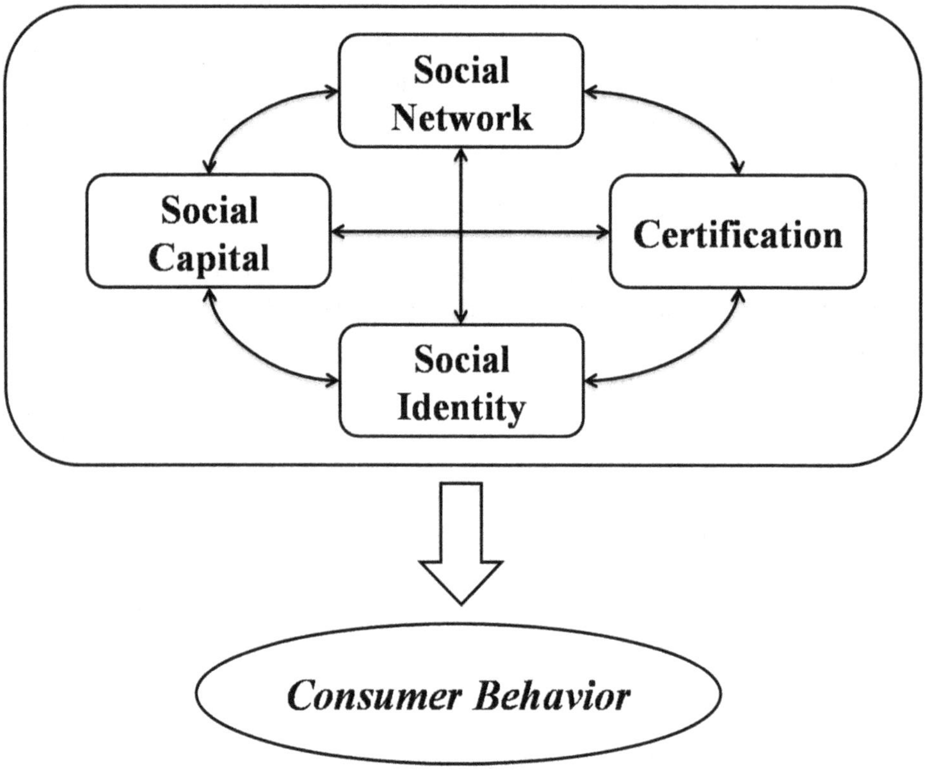

P5: The interactions between the dimensions (social networks, social capital, certification and social identity) and their combinations influence consumer behavior.

An Extension of the Final Multidimensional Framework

As additional step, this study proposes a possible extension (and expansion) of this framework. Following the contribution by Kim, Ferrin, & Rao, (2018), the framework includes three parameters, i.e. consumer trust, perceived benefit and perceived risk.

The present work acknowledges the importance of these three parameters, thus proposes that they could be influenced by multiple signals and (consequently) in turn affect consumer behavior. The logic of this final multidimensional framework is that consumers behaviors are affected by their perception of benefit, risk and trust toward the selling entity. In the digital market, most of the selling entities are Internet entity, thus the virtual environment is characterized by high uncertainty and asymmetries.

In this context, multiple signals are strategic drivers and can influence consumer trust (Bhattacherjee, 2002; Gefen, 2002; Rousseau, Sitkin, Burt, & Camerer, 1998) and their perception of benefits (Margherio, 1998; Peter & Tarpey, 1975) and risks (Bhatnagar, Misra, & Rao, 2000; Peter & Ryan, 1976). Trust, benefits and risks are key parameters to consider to the extent that they affect consumer behavior. In particular, consumers make their purchasing decisions based on their intentions.

CONCLUSION

The aim of this chapter is to provide a new multidimensional framework for exploring multiple signals able to influence consumer behavior. The digital economy presents a challenging environment for consumers to evaluate companies and their products/services. In this context characterized by high uncertainty and several virtual environments, sellers could leverage signals in order to influence consumer behavior and improve their knowledge on their decisions and actions. The signals that companies and sellers send to consumers influence their decision-making process. Observable and useful signals can mitigate the problem of information asymmetries.

In the digital economy scenario, a growing number of companies operate through virtual platforms. These platforms show virtual spaces for the exchange process. The interactions between the parties are based on virtual interactions, while personal interactions are absent. Since a significant challenge facing companies (and also many platform managers) is to communicate useful information about the product/service and the business, they try to involve consumers through credible signals. In fact, observable and credible information effectively attract consumers and influence their behaviour. This study firstly describes the three main players of the digital economy, i.e. digital platforms, online communities and new technologies – then introduces a multidimensional framework with the related multiple signals construct.

The work considers four types of signals and also their interactions/combinations. The four dimensions analyzed are: social network, social capital, certification and social identity. These types of signals could affect consumer behavior and represent successful driver in the digital economy and thus for its players (including the above cited: digital platforms, online communities and new technologies). This study suggests that also the interactions/combinations of these signals could play a key role in the context of digital economy by affecting consumer behavior. This multidimensional framework and the interactions/combinations between signals present new challenges and show new horizon of consumer behavior analysis and decision support system. The contribution proposes an original framework for the study of multiple signals, thus improving the understanding of the digital economy, a new emerging phenomenon and scenario. There is little knowledge about multiple signals in this digital context, thus the work could add new knowledge in this research field.

This chapter has interesting implications for many and different actors of the digital ecosystem: digital companies, entrepreneurs, companies, platform managers, consumers, public agencies, authorities and policy makers. Future researchers might consider the use of multidimensional signals and the use of multidimensional approaches, both in order to better measure sellers/companies actions and the main activities useful to affect consumer behavior. The framework can be expanded by adding new signals and leveraging other main theories. Similar to many qualitative studies, this contribution offers a conceptual framework with no empirical data to test the propositions. Thus, this work calls for future research to empirically explore these five propositions.

REFERENCES

Aaker, J., & Akutsu, S. (2009). Why do people give? The role of identity in giving. *Journal of Consumer Psychology*, *19*(3), 267–270. doi:10.1016/j.jcps.2009.05.010

Abrams, D., & Hogg, M. (1988). Comments on the motivational status of self-esteem in social identity and intergroup discrimination. *European Journal of Social Psychology*, *18*(4), 317–334. doi:10.1002/ejsp.2420180403

Adhami, S., Giudici, G., & Martinazzi, S. (2018). Why do businesses go crypto? An empirical analysis of initial coin offerings. *Journal of Economics and Business*, *100*, 64–75. doi:10.1016/j.jeconbus.2018.04.001

Ahmad, N., Ribarsky, J., & Reinsdorf, M. (2017). *Can Potential Mismeasurement of the Digital Economy explain the Post-Crisis Slowdown in GDP and Productivity Growth?* OECD Working Papers, 2017/09.

Akerlof, G. A. (1970). The market for 'lemons': Quality uncertainty and the market mechanism. *The Quarterly Journal of Economics*, *84*(3), 488–500. doi:10.2307/1879431

Armstrong, M., & Wright, J. (2008). Two-Sided Markets. The New Palgrave Dictionary of Economics. doi:10.1057/978-1-349-95121-5_2758-1

Arnett, D. B., German, S. D., & Hunt, S. D. (2003). The Identity Salience Model of Relationship Marketing Success: The Case of Nonprofit Marketing. *Journal of Marketing*, *67*(2), 89–105. doi:10.1509/jmkg.67.2.89.18614

Arora, S., Ter Hofstede, F., & Mahajan, V. (2017). The Implications of Offering Free Versions for the Performance of Paid Mobile Apps. *Journal of Marketing*, *81*(6), 62–78. doi:10.1509/jm.15.0205

Auriol, E., & Schilizzi, S. G. M. (2003). Quality Signaling through Certification. *Theory and an Application to Agricultural Seed Market*. IDEI Working Papers 165.

Bakos, Y., & Katsamakas, E. (2008). Design and Ownership of Two-Sided Networks: Implications for Internet Platforms. *Journal of Management Information Systems*, *25*(2), 171–202. doi:10.2753/MIS0742-1222250208

Basel Committee on Banking Supervision (BCBS) (2018). *Sound Practices: implications of fintech developments for banks and bank supervisors*. Author.

Basili, M., & Rossi, M. A. (2019). (in press). Platform-mediated reputation systems in the sharing economy and incentives to provide service quality: The case of ridesharing services. *Electronic Commerce Research and Applications*.

Bhatnagar, A., Misra, S., & Rao, H. R. (2000). On risk, convenience, and internet shopping behavior. *Communications of the ACM*, *43*(11), 98–114. doi:10.1145/353360.353371

Bhattacharya, C. B., & Sen, S. (2003). Consumer-Company Identification: A Framework for Understanding Consumers' Relationships with Companies. *Journal of Marketing*, *67*(2), 76–88. doi:10.1509/jmkg.67.2.76.18609

Bhattacherjee, A. (2002). Individual trust in online firms: Scale development and initial test. *Journal of Management Information Systems*, *19*(1), 211–242. doi:10.1080/07421222.2002.11045715

Booth, J. R., & Smith, R. L. II. (1986). Capital raising, underwriting and the certification hypothesis. *Journal of Financial Economics*, *15*(1), 261–281. doi:10.1016/0304-405X(86)90057-7

Bourdieu, P. (1986). The Forms of Capital. In J. Richardson (Ed.), *Handbook of Theory: Research for the Sociology of Education* (pp. 241–258). New York: Greenwood.

Boyd, D. M., & Ellison, N. B. (2008). Social Network Sites: Definition History, and Scholarship. *Journal of Computer-Mediated Communication, 13*(1), 210–230. doi:10.1111/j.1083-6101.2007.00393.x

Brewer, M. B., & Kramer, R. M. (1986). Choice behavior in social dilemmas: Effects of social identity, group size, and decision framing. *Journal of Personality and Social Psychology, 50*(3), 543–549. doi:10.1037/0022-3514.50.3.543

Brown, J., Broderick, A. J., & Lee, N. (2007). Word of mouth communication within online communities: Conceptualizing the online social network. *Journal of Interactive Marketing, 21*(3), 2–20. doi:10.1002/dir.20082

Brown, J. S., & Duguid, P. (1991). Organizational learning and communities-of-practice: Toward a unified view of working, learning, and innovation. *Organization Science, 2*(1), 40–57. doi:10.1287/orsc.2.1.40

Brynjolfsson, E., Eggers, F., & Gannamaneni, A. (2017). Using Massive Online Choice Experiments to Measure Changes in Wellbeing. *5th IMF Statistical Forum.*

Bureau of Economic Analysis (BEA). (2019). *Digital Economy Accounted for 6.9 Percent of GDP in 2017.* Author.

Byrne, D., Corrado, C., & Sichel, D. (2017). The Rise of Cloud Computing: Minding Your P's, Q's and K's. *5th IMF Statistical Forum.*

Caillaud, B., & Jullien, B. (2003). Chicken & egg: Competition among intermediation service providers. *The RAND Journal of Economics, 34*(2), 309–328. doi:10.2307/1593720

Campbell, C., Ferraro, C., & Sands, S. (2014). Segmenting consumer reactions to social network marketing. *European Journal of Marketing, 48*(3/4), 432–452. doi:10.1108/EJM-03-2012-0165

Castaneda, M., Martinez, C., Marte, R., & Roxas, B. (2015). Explaining the environmentally-sustainable consumer behavior: A social capital perspective. *Social Responsibility Journal, 11*(4), 658–676. doi:10.1108/SRJ-02-2014-0019

Caswell, J. A., & Mojduszka, E. M. (1996). Using informational labeling to influence the market for quality in food products. *American Journal of Agricultural Economics, 78*(5), 1248–1253. doi:10.2307/1243501

Celani, A., & Singh, P. (2011). Signaling theory and applicant attraction outcomes. *Personnel Review, 40*(2), 222–238. doi:10.1108/00483481111106093

Chang, L. D. M., Ling Tam, A. Y., & Suki, N. M. (2016). Moderating effect of races towards consumers' feeling of TCM usage. Handbook of Research on Leveraging Consumer Psychology for Effective Customer Engagement, 306-323.

Chen, Q., Zhang, M., & Zhao, X. (2017). Analysing customer behaviour in mobile app usage. *Industrial Management & Data Systems, 117*(2), 425–438. doi:10.1108/IMDS-04-2016-0141

Chen, X., Zhou, L., & Wan, D. (2016). Group social capital and lending outcomes in the financial credit market: An empirical study of online peer-to-peer lending. *Electronic Commerce Research and Applications*, *15*, 1–13. doi:10.1016/j.elerap.2015.11.003

Chesbrough, H. W. (2003). *Open innovation the new imperative for creating and profiting from technology*. Boston: Harvard Business School Press.

Chiu, C. M., Hsu, M. H., & Wang, E. T. (2006). Understanding knowledge sharing in virtual communities: An integration of social capital and social cognitive theories. *Decision Support Systems*, *42*(3), 1872–1888. doi:10.1016/j.dss.2006.04.001

Cohen, D., Prusak, L., & Prusak, L. (2001). *In good company: How social capital makes organizations work* (Vol. 15). Harvard Business School Press Boston.

Coleman, J. (1988). Social capital in the creation of human capital. *American Journal of Sociology*, *94*, 95–120. doi:10.1086/228943

Colombo, M. G., Franzoni, C., & Rossi-Lamastra, C. (2015). Internal social capital and the attraction of early contributions in crowdfunding. *Entrepreneurship Theory and Practice*, *39*(1), 75–100. doi:10.1111/etap.12118

Connelly, B. L., Certo, S. T., Ireland, R. D., & Reutzel, C. R. (2011). Signaling theory: A review and Assessment. *Journal of Management*, *37*(1), 39–67. doi:10.1177/0149206310388419

Coulter, K., & Roggeveen, A. (2012). Like it or not. *Management Research Review*, *35*(9), 878–899. doi:10.1108/01409171211256587

Cramer, J., & Krueger, A. B. (2016). Disruptive change in the taxi business: The case of Uber. *The American Economic Review*, *106*(5), 177–182. doi:10.1257/aer.p20161002

Daley, B., & Green, B. (2014). Market signaling with grades. *Journal of Economic Theory*, *151*, 114–145. doi:10.1016/j.jet.2013.10.009

De Silva, M., Howells, J., & Meyer, M. (2018). Innovation intermediaries and collaboration: Knowledge–based practices and internal value creation. *Research Policy*, *47*(1), 70–87. doi:10.1016/j.respol.2017.09.011

Denning, S. (2014). An economy of access is opening for business: Five strategies for success. *Strategy and Leadership*, *42*(4), 14–21. doi:10.1108/SL-05-2014-0037

Dholakia, U. M., Bagozzi, R. P., & Pearo, L. K. (2004). A social influence model of consumer participation in network- and small-group-based virtual communities. *International Journal of Research in Marketing*, *21*(3), 241–263. doi:10.1016/j.ijresmar.2003.12.004

Dimara, E., & Skuras, D. (2003). Consumer evaluations of product certification, geographic association and traceability in Greece. *European Journal of Marketing*, *37*(5/6), 690–705. doi:10.1108/03090560310465099

Dimoka, A., Hong, Y., & Pavlou, P. A. (2012). On product uncertainty in online markets: Theory and evidence. *Management Information Systems Quarterly*, *36*(2), 395–426. doi:10.2307/41703461

Dinsmore, J. B., Swani, K., & Dugan, R. G. (2017). To "Free" or Not to "Free": Trait Predictors of Mobile App Purchasing Tendencies. *Psychology and Marketing*, *34*(2), 227–244. doi:10.1002/mar.20985

Donath, J. (2007). Signals in social supernets. *Journal of Computer-Mediated Communication, 13*(1), 231–251. doi:10.1111/j.1083-6101.2007.00394.x

Dou, G., He, P., & Xu, X. (2016). One-side value-added service investment and pricing strategies for a two-sided platform. *International Journal of Production Research, 54*(13), 3808–3821. doi:10.1080/00207543.2016.1148275

Eisenmann, T., Parker, G., & Van Alstyne, M. W. (2006). Strategies for Two-Sided Markets. *Harvard Business Review, 84*(10), 92–102.

Evans, D. S. (2003). Some Empirical Aspects of Multi-Sided Platform Industries. *Review of Network Economics, 2*(3), 191–209. doi:10.2202/1446-9022.1026

Fischer, E., & Reuber, R. (2007). The good, the bad, and the unfamiliar: The challenges of reputation formation facing new firms. *Entrepreneurship Theory and Practice, 31*(1), 53–75. doi:10.1111/j.1540-6520.2007.00163.x

Flood, R., & Jackson, M. (1991). *Creative Problem Solving: Total Systems Intervention.* Wiley.

Forehand, M. R., Deshpande´, R., & Reed, A. (2002). Identity Salience and the Influence of Differential Activation of the Social Self-Schema on Advertising Response. *The Journal of Applied Psychology, 87*(6), 1086–1099. doi:10.1037/0021-9010.87.6.1086 PMID:12558216

Gefen, D. (2002). Reflections on the dimensions of trust and trustworthiness among online consumers. *ACM SIGMIS Database, 33*(3), 38–53. doi:10.1145/569905.569910

Ghose, A. (2009). Internet exchanges for used goods: An empirical analysis of trade patterns and adverse selection. *Management Information Systems Quarterly, 33*(2), 263–291. doi:10.2307/20650292

Greenstein, S., & Nagle, F. (2014). Digital Dark Matter and the Economic Contribution of Apache. *Research Policy, 43*(4), 623–631. doi:10.1016/j.respol.2014.01.003

Guttentag, D. (2015). Airbnb: Disruptive innovation and the rise of an informal tourism accommodation sector. *Journal Current Issues in Tourism, 18*(12), 1192–1217. doi:10.1080/13683500.2013.827159

Guvenen, F., Mataloni, R. J. J., Rassier, D. G., & Ruhl, K. J. (2017). *Offshore Profit Shifting and Domestic Productivity Measurement.* NBER Working Paper 23324.

Hagiu, A., & Wright, J. (2011). *Multi-Sided Platforms.* Harvard Business School.

Hazleton, V., & Kennan, W. (2000). Social capital: Reconceptualizing the bottom line. *Corporate Communications, 5*(2), 81–87. doi:10.1108/13563280010372513

Heinonen, K. (2011). Consumer activity in social media: Managerial approaches to consumers' social media behavior. *Journal of Consumer Behaviour, 10*(6), 356–364. doi:10.1002/cb.376

Hermida, A., Fletcher, F., Korell, D., & Logan, D. (2012). Share, like, recommend. Decoding the social media news consumer. *Journalism Studies, 13*(5-6), 815–824. doi:10.1080/1461670X.2012.664430

Holt, D. B. (1997). Poststructuralist Lifestyle Analysis: Conceptualizing the Social Patterning of Consumption in Postmodernity. *The Journal of Consumer Research, 23*(4), 326–350. doi:10.1086/209487

Hsu, M. H., Ju, T. L., Yen, C. H., & Chang, C. M. (2007). Knowledge sharing behavior in virtual communities: The relationship between trust, self-efficacy, and outcome expectations. *International Journal of Human-Computer Studies*, *65*(2), 153–169. doi:10.1016/j.ijhcs.2006.09.003

Hughes, D., Rowe, M., Batey, M., & Lee, A. (2012). A tale of two sites: Twitter vs. Facebook and the personality predictors of social media usage. *Computers in Human Behavior*, *28*(2), 561–569. doi:10.1016/j.chb.2011.11.001

Inkpen, A. C., & Tsang, E. W. (2005). Social capital, networks, and knowledge transfer. *Academy of Management Review*, *30*(1), 146–165. doi:10.5465/amr.2005.15281445

International Monetary Fund (IMF). (2018). *Measuring the Digital Economy.* IMF Policy Papers.

IOSCO (International Organization of Securities Commissions). (2017). *Research Report on Financial Technologies*. Fintech.

Janssen, M. A., & Jager, W. (2006). Simulating Market Dynamics: Interactions between Consumer Psychology and Social Networks. *The MIT Press Journals*, *9*(4), 343–356. PMID:14761255

Jeppesen, L. B., & Lakhani, K. R. (2010). Marginality and Problem-Solving Effectiveness in Broadcast Search. *Organization Science*, *21*(5), 955–1123. doi:10.1287/orsc.1090.0491

Jiang, P., Jones, D. B., & Javie, S. (2008). How third-party certification programs relate to consumer trust in online transactions: An exploratory study. *Psychology and Marketing*, *25*(9), 839–858. doi:10.1002/mar.20243

Kaplan, A. M., & Haenlein, M. (2010). Users of the world, unite! The challenges and opportunities of Social Media. *Business Horizons*, *53*(1), 59–68. doi:10.1016/j.bushor.2009.09.003

Katz, M. L., & Shapiro, C. (1985). Network Externalities, Competition, and Compatibility. *The American Economic Review*, *75*(3), 424–440.

Kenney, M., & Zysman, J. (2016). The rise of the platform economy. *Issues in Science and Technology*, *32*(3), 61–69.

Keszei, D., Murphy, K., & Loeur, N. (2018). An Evaluation of American Millennials Leading Global Teams: A Multidimensional Framework for Planning and Optimizing Success. *Journal of Management Policy and Practice*, *19*(1), 10–16.

Kim, D. J., Ferrin, D. L., & Rao, H. R. (2008). A trust-based consumer decision-making model in electronic commerce: The role of trust, perceived risk, and their antecedents. *Decision Support Systems*, *44*(2), 544–564. doi:10.1016/j.dss.2007.07.001

King, A. A., Lenox, M. J., & Terlaak, A. (2005). The strategic use of decentralized institutions: Exploring certification with the ISO 14001 management standard. *Academy of Management Journal*, *48*(6), 1091–1106. doi:10.5465/amj.2005.19573111

Kirmani, A., & Rao, A. R. (2000). No pain, no gain: A critical review of the literature on signaling unobservable product quality. *Journal of Marketing*, *64*(2), 66–79. doi:10.1509/jmkg.64.2.66.18000

Kosonen, M. (2006). Knowledge sharing in virtual communities-A review of the empirical research. *International Journal of Web Based Communities*, *5*(2), 144–163. doi:10.1504/IJWBC.2009.023962

Kozinets, R. V. (1999). E-Tribalized Marketing?: The Strategic Implications of Virtual Communities of Consumption. *European Management Journal*, *17*(3), 252–264. doi:10.1016/S0263-2373(99)00004-3

Kozinets, R. V. (2002). Can Consumers Escape the Market? Emancipatory Illuminations from the Burning Man. *The Journal of Consumer Research*, *29*(1), 20–38. doi:10.1086/339919

Kozinets, R. V., De Valck, K., Wojnicki, A. C., & Wilner, S. J. S. (2010). Networked Narratives: Understanding Word-of-Mouth Marketing in Online Communities. *Journal of Marketing*, *74*(2), 71–89. doi:10.1509/jm.74.2.71

Kozinets, R. V., Hemetsberger, A., & Schau, H. J. (2008). The wisdom of consumer crowds: Collective Innovation in the Age of Networked Marketing. *Journal of Macromarketing*, *28*(4), 339–354. doi:10.1177/0276146708325382

Krishnamurthy, S., & Dou, W. (2008). Advertising with User-Generated Content: A Framework and Research Agenda. *Journal of Interactive Advertising*, *8*(2), 1–7. doi:10.1080/15252019.2008.10722137

Kuo, Y. F., Wu, C. M., & Deng, W. J. (2009). The Relationships among Service Quality, Perceived Value, Customer Satisfaction, and Post-purchase Intention in Mobile Value-added Services. *Computers in Human Behavior*, *25*(4), 887–896. doi:10.1016/j.chb.2009.03.003

Lasi, H., Fettke, P., Kemper, H. G., Feld, T., & Hoffmann, M. (2014). Industry 4.0. *Business & Information Systems Engineering*, *6*(4), 261–264. doi:10.100712599-014-0334-4

Lee, M. K. O., & Turban, E. (2014). A Trust Model for Consumer Internet Shopping. *International Journal of Electronic Commerce*, *6*(1), 75–91. doi:10.1080/10864415.2001.11044227

Leyden, D. P., Link, A. N., & Siegel, D. S. (2014). A theoretical analysis of the role of social networks in entrepreneurship. *Research Policy*, *43*(7), 1157–1163. doi:10.1016/j.respol.2014.04.010

Long, C. (2002). Patent signals. *The University of Chicago Law Review. University of Chicago. Law School*, *69*(2), 625–679. doi:10.2307/1600501

Lüthje, C., Herstatt, C., & Von Hippel, E. (2005). User-innovators and "local" information: The case of mountain biking. *Research Policy*, *34*(6), 951–965. doi:10.1016/j.respol.2005.05.005

Madrigal, R. (2001). Social Identity Effects in a Belief-Attitude-Intentions Hierarchy: Implications for Corporate Sponsorship. *Psychology and Marketing*, *18*(2), 145–162. doi:10.1002/1520-6793(200102)18:2<145::AID-MAR1003>3.0.CO;2-T

Margherio, L. (1998). *The Emerging Digital Economy*. Washington, DC: U.S. Department of Commerce.

Marin, L., Ruiz, S., & Rubio, A. (2009). The Role of Identity Salience in the Effects of Corporate Social Responsibility on Consumer Behavior. *Journal of Business Ethics*, *84*(1), 65–78. doi:10.100710551-008-9673-8

Mathwick, C., Wiertz, C., & de Ruyter, K. (2008). Social Capital Production in a Virtual P3 Community. *The Journal of Consumer Research*, *34*(6), 832–849. doi:10.1086/523291

Mavlanova, T., Benbunan-Fich, R., & Koufaris, M. (2012). Signaling theory and information asymmetry in online commerce. *Information & Management*, *49*(5), 240–247. doi:10.1016/j.im.2012.05.004

Mavlanova, T., Benbunan-Fich, R., & Lang, G. (2016). The role of external and internal signals in E-commerce. *Decision Support Systems*, *87*, 59–68. doi:10.1016/j.dss.2016.04.009

McLeod, S. (2008). *Social identity theory*. Simply Psychology.

Megginson, W. L., & Weiss, K. A. (1991). Venture capitalist certification in initial public offerings. *The Journal of Finance*, *46*(3), 879–903. doi:10.1111/j.1540-6261.1991.tb03770.x

Michaelson, K. L. (1996). Information, Community and Access. *Social Science Computer Review*, *14*(1), 57–59. doi:10.1177/089443939601400118

Minkoff, D. C. (1997). Producing Social Capital. *The American Behavioral Scientist*, *40*(5), 606–619. doi:10.1177/0002764297040005007

Mishra, D. P. (2006). The role of certification in service relationships: Theory and empirical evidence. *Journal of Retailing and Consumer Services*, *13*(1), 81–96. doi:10.1016/j.jretconser.2005.08.005

Vision Mobile. (2015). *European App Economy 2015: creating jobs e driving economic growth in Europe*. Author.

Nahapiet, J., & Ghoshal, S. (1998). Social capital, intellectual capital, and the organizational advantage. *Academy of Management Review*, *23*(2), 242–266. doi:10.5465/amr.1998.533225

Nakamura, L., Samuels, J., & Soloveichik, R. (2017). Measuring the 'Free' Digital Economy within the GDP and Productivity Accounts. *5th IMF Statistical Forum*.

Nathan, R. J., Fook Chiun, D. C., & Suki, N. M. (2016). An online marketing strategies assessment for companies in airlines and entertainment industries in Malaysia. Handbook of Research on Leveraging Consumer Psychology for Effective Customer Engagement, 1-15.

Novick, L. R. (1988). Analogical transfer, problem similarity, and expertise. *Journal of Experimental Psychology. Learning, Memory, and Cognition*, *14*(3), 510–520. doi:10.1037/0278-7393.14.3.510 PMID:2969945

OECD. (2013). *The App Economy*. Digital Economy Papers, No. 230.

OECD. (2017). *Digital Economy Outlook 2017*. Paris: OECD Publishing.

OECD. (2019). *Measuring the Digital Transformation: A Roadmap for the Future*. Paris: OECD Publishing.

Oostrom, L., Walker, A., Staats, B., Slootbeek-Van Laar, M., Ortega Azurduy, S., & Rooijakkers, B. (2016). *Measuring the Internet Economy in The Netherlands: A Big Data Analysis*. CBS Discussion paper 2016-14.

Park, N., Kee, K. F., & Valenzuela, S. (2009). Being Immersed in Social Networking Environment: Facebook Groups, Uses and Gratifications, and Social Outcomes. *Cyberpsychology & Behavior*, *12*(6), 729–733. doi:10.1089/cpb.2009.0003 PMID:19619037

Parker, G. G., Alstyne, M. W., & Choudary, S. P. (2016). *Platform revolution: How networked markets are transforming the economy and how to make them work for you*. WW Norton.

Parmentier, G., & Gandia, R. (2013). Managing sustainable innovation with a user community toolkit: The case of the video game Trackmania. *Creativity and Innovation Management*, *22*(2), 195–208. doi:10.1111/caim.12021

Pavlou, P. A., Liang, H., & Xue, Y. (2007). Understanding and mitigating uncertainty in online exchange relationships: A principal-agent perspective. *Management Information Systems Quarterly*, *31*(1), 105–136. doi:10.2307/25148783

Paxton, P. (1999). Is Social Capital Declining in the United States? A Multiple Indicator Assessment. *American Journal of Sociology*, *105*(1), 88–127. doi:10.1086/210268

Peter, J. P., & Ryan, M. (1976). An investigation of perceived risk at the brand level. *JMR, Journal of Marketing Research*, *13*(2), 184–188. doi:10.1177/002224377601300210

Peter, P. J., & Tarpey, L. X. Sr. (1975). A comparative analysis of three consumer decision strategies. *The Journal of Consumer Research*, *2*(1), 29–37. doi:10.1086/208613

Price, L. J., & Dawar, N. (2002). The joint effects of brands and warranties in signaling new product quality. *Journal of Economic Psychology*, *23*(2), 165–190. doi:10.1016/S0167-4870(02)00062-4

Ramey, G. (1996). D1 Signaling Equilibria with Multiple Signals and a Continuum of Types. *Journal of Economic Theory*, *69*(2), 508–531. doi:10.1006/jeth.1996.0066

Reed, A. II. (2004). Activating the Self-Importance of Consumer Selves: Exploring Identity Salience Effects on Judgements. *The Journal of Consumer Research*, *31*(2), 286–295. doi:10.1086/422108

Richardson, P. S., Dick, A. S., & Jain, A. K. (1994). Extrinsic and intrinsic cue effects on perceptions of store brand quality. *Journal of Marketing*, *58*(4), 28–36. doi:10.1177/002224299405800403

Richter, C., Kraus, S., Brem, A., Durst, S., & Giselbrecht, C. (2017). Digital entrepreneurship: Innovative business models for the sharing economy. *Creativity and Innovation Management*, *26*(3), 300–310. doi:10.1111/caim.12227

Rochet, J. C., & Tirole, J. (2006). Two-Sided Markets: A Progress Report. *The RAND Journal of Economics*, *37*(3), 645–667. doi:10.1111/j.1756-2171.2006.tb00036.x

Rossi, A., & Vismara, S. (2018). What do crowdfunding platforms do? A comparison between investment-based platforms in Europe. *Eurasian Business Review*, *8*(1), 93–118. doi:10.100740821-017-0092-6

Rousseau, D. M., Sitkin, S. B., Burt, R. S., & Camerer, C. (1998). Not so different after all: A cross discipline view of trust. *Academy of Management Review*, *23*(3), 395–404. doi:10.5465/amr.1998.926617

Sachs, G. (2015). *The Future of Finance - The Socialization of Finance*. Equity Research.

Sassi, S., & Goaied, M. (2013). Financial development, ICT diffusion and economic growth: Lessons from MENA region. *Telecommunications Policy*, *37*(4-5), 252–261. doi:10.1016/j.telpol.2012.12.004

Shao, G. (2009). Understanding the Appeal of User-Generated Media: A Uses and Gratification Perspective. *Internet Research, 19*(1), 7–25. doi:10.1108/10662240910927795

Smith, T., Coyle, J. R., Lightfoot, E., & Scott, A. (2007). Reconsidering Models of Influence: The Relationship between Consumer Social Networks and Word-of-Mouth Effectiveness. *Journal of Advertising Research, 47*(4), 387–397. doi:10.2501/S0021849907070407

Sparks, B. A., Perkins, H. E., & Buckley, R. (2013). Online travel reviews as persuasive communication: The effects of content type, source, and certification logos on consumer behavior. *Tourism Management, 39*, 1–9. doi:10.1016/j.tourman.2013.03.007

Spence, M. (1973). Job Market Signaling. *The Quarterly Journal of Economics, 87*(3), 355–374. doi:10.2307/1882010

Suki, N. M. (2016). *Handbook of Research on Leveraging Consumer Psychology for Effective Customer Engagement*. https://www.igi-global.com/book/handbook-research-leveraging-consumer-psychology/149284

Sultan, N. (2010). Cloud computing for education: A new dawn? *International Journal of Information Management, 30*(2), 109–116. doi:10.1016/j.ijinfomgt.2009.09.004

Sun, N., Rau, P. P. L., & Ma, L. (2014). Understanding lurkers in online communities: A literature review. *Computers in Human Behavior, 38*, 110–117. doi:10.1016/j.chb.2014.05.022

Tajfel, H. (1988). *Social Identity and Intergroup Behavior*. Cambridge, University Press.

Tajfel, H., & Turner, J.C. (1979). An integrative theory of intergroup conflict. *The Social Psychology of Intergroup Relations, 33*(47), 74.

Tajfel, H., & Turner, J. C. (1986). The Social Identity Theory of Intergroup Behavior. In S. G. Worchel & W. G. Austin (Eds.), *Psychology of Intergroup Relation* (pp. 7–24). Chicago: Nelson-Hall Publishers.

Taken Smith, K. (2012). Longitudinal study of digital marketing strategies targeting Millennials. *Journal of Consumer Marketing, 29*(2), 86–92. doi:10.1108/07363761211206339

Tencent. (2017). China's Digital Transformation: An Analysis from a Socio-economic Perspective. *5th IMF Statistical Forum*.

Trabucchi, D., Buganza, T., Dell'Era, C., & Pellizzoni, E. (2018). Exploring the inbound and outbound strategies enabled by user generated big data: Evidence from leading smartphone applications. *Creativity and Innovation Management, 27*(1), 42–55. doi:10.1111/caim.12241

Tregear, A., Kuznesof, S., & Moxey, A. (1998). Policy initiatives for regional foods: Some insights from consumer research. *Food Policy, 23*(5), 383–394. doi:10.1016/S0306-9192(98)00044-X

Troise, C., Candelo, E., Matricano, D., & Sorrentino, M. (2018b). The role of Entrepreneurial Quality in Equity Crowdfunding success: An explorative analysis of Italian platforms. *ICSB Conference*.

Troise, C., Candelo, E., & Sorrentino, M. (2018a). Equity Crowdfunding: Investigating the Role of Entrepreneurial Quality in Affecting the Success of the Campaigns. *Sinergie Conference*, 315-319.

Troise, C., & Ferrara, E. (2016). App economy: impact and effects of the phenomenon. *MC - Diritto ed economia dei mezzi di comunicazione, 2*, 7-28.

Troise, C., Matricano, D., & Sorrentino, M. (2019). Open innovation platforms: exploring the importance of knowledge in supporting online initiatives. *Ifkad Conference*, 1646-1658.

Troise. (2019a). Entrepreneurship and Equity Crowdfunding: Does It Matter? *International Journal of Business and Management, 14*(10), 72-86.

Troise. (2019b). Marketing Strategies in Equity Crowdfunding: a Comparative Study of Italian Platforms. *International Journal of Marketing Studies, 11*(4), 16-29.

Vismara, S. (2016). Equity retention and social network theory in equity crowdfunding. *Small Business Economics*, *46*(4), 579–590. doi:10.100711187-016-9710-4

Wang, K., Nickerson, J., & Sakamoto, Y. (2018). Crowdsourced idea generation: The effect of exposure to an original idea. *Creativity and Innovation Management*, *27*(2), 196–208. doi:10.1111/caim.12264

Wells, J. D., Valacich, J. S., & Hess, T. J. (2011). What signal are you sending? How website quality influences perceptions of product quality and purchase intentions. *Management Information Systems Quarterly*, *35*(2), 373–396. doi:10.2307/23044048

West, J., & Lakhani, K. (2008). Getting clear about communities in open innovation. *Industry and Innovation*, *15*(2), 223–231. doi:10.1080/13662710802033734

Worsham, J., & Gatrell, J. (2005). Multiple Principals, Multiple Signals: A Signaling Approach to Principal-Agent Relations. *Policy Studies Journal: the Journal of the Policy Studies Organization*, *33*(3), 363–376. doi:10.1111/j.1541-0072.2005.00120.x

Wortmann, F., & Flüchter, K. (2015). Internet of Things: Technology and Value Added. *Business & Information Systems Engineering*, *57*(3), 221–224. doi:10.100712599-015-0383-3

Xu, B., & Ouenniche, J. (2011). A multidimensional framework for performance evaluation of forecasting models: Context-dependent DEA. *Applied Financial Economics*, *21*(24), 1873–1890. doi:10.1080/09603107.2011.597722

Yablonsky, S. (2018). A Multidimensional Framework for Digital Platform Innovation and Management: From Business to Technological Platforms. *Systems Research and Behavioral Science*, *35*(4), 485–501. doi:10.1002res.2544

Yang, J., Ma, J., Zhang, Y., & Hong, J. H. (2018). With whom should you have dinner? A multidimensional framework for understanding political ties in China. *Business Horizons*, *61*(6), 891–898. doi:10.1016/j.bushor.2018.07.010

Yang, L., Yang, S. H., & Plotnick, L. (2013). How the internet of things technology enhances emergency response operations. *Technological Forecasting and Social Change*, *80*(9), 1854–1867. doi:10.1016/j.techfore.2012.07.011

Yigitcanlar, T., Kamruzzamanf, M., Buys, L., Ioppolo, G., Sabatini-Marques, J., Moreira da Costa, E., & Yun, J. H. J. (2018). Understanding 'smart cities': Intertwining development drivers with desired outcomes in a multidimensional framework. *Cities (London, England), 81*, 145–160. doi:10.1016/j.cities.2018.04.003

Zhang, Q., Cheng, L., & Boutaba, R. J. (2010). Cloud computing: State-of-the-art and research challenges. *Journal of Internet Services and Applications*, *1*(1), 1–7. doi:10.100713174-010-0007-6

Zmud, R. W., Croes, H., Shaft, T., & Zheng, W. (2010). Systematic differences in firm's information technology signaling: Implications for research design. *Journal of the Association for Information Systems*, *11*(3), 149–181. doi:10.17705/1jais.00223

Chapter 2
Social Media, Marketing Practices, and Consumer Behavior

Nozha Erragcha
Tunis Business School, University of Tunis, Tunisia

Hanene Babay
University of Monastir, Tunisia

ABSTRACT

This chapter looks at the phenomenon of social media and its consequences on marketing and consumer behavior. To express an opinion, the authors first define the notion of "social media," review their different types as well as the decisive moments that marked their history. Then, they focus on the influence of these media on marketing practices by referring to the changes that have affected the marketing approach from the stage of the market study to the stage of control of marketing actions companies. Finally, they are very interested in the changes that have affected the traditional decision-making process and are announcing useful recommendations to respond to this set of changes.

INTRODUCTION

Since Tim Berners-Lee's shocking invention in 1989, the Web has transfigured the Internet to the point that it has become a synonym for some. Being simple to use, the web has been massively adopted by the general public and its success has generated the need to make it evolve since its first version 1.0 which dates from the 90s. This first version, also called traditional web, is static. It focuses on the distribution of information and does not solicit the intervention of users. Thus, according to this form of the web, the first e-commerce sites were product-oriented sites whose main purpose is to present the products to consumers by offering them online access to information about these products. But the individual consumer of this content could not interact with the website in question. It is compared in its non-interactive design to a television program.

DOI: 10.4018/978-1-7998-3042-9.ch002

Nevertheless, in the early 2000s, new applications appeared on the Web giving users the ability to interact and generate content themselves. As an indication, the YouTube app allows everyone to upload a video for free broadcast worldwide. Other media and applications also appeared as blogs, wikis, podcasts, social networks, social bookmarks, microblogging, etc. Through these applications, the web 2.0 has totally changed perspective and has become a social web that favors the sharing and exchange of information and content (text, video, images or other). Therefore, the intervention of consumers is tolerated or even desired and their opinions are now solicited permanently. They then enrolled in a virtual socialization that offers them a growing pleasure. Little by little, social media has become an integral part of the lives of consumers who now use them to connect with friends and family, keep up to date and even entertain themselves. That's why around 4 billion people around the world today use social media.

The interest and commitment shown by consumers to social media has not been without consequences for marketing. Companies have had to adapt their marketing strategies to exploit the potential offered by these media, particularly to inform, seduce, convince and retain their customers. At the same time, these media have had a very significant impact on consumer behavior, in particular their motivations and brakes with respect to buying online and the way in which their decision-making process works. This process seems to undergo a real metamorphosis that should be considered more closely and draw conclusions and useful recommendations.

More research that delve into aspect of consumer behavior and psychology in the digital economy is deemed necessary (Ling Chang, Ling Tam, & Suki, 2016; Nathan, Fook Chiun, & Suki, 2016; Suki, 2016). Accordingly, this study focus on the rise of social media and the consequences of this boom on marketing and consumer behavior. To do this, they first come back to the definition of social media and their classification in order to clarify the reader about what is called "social media".Then, they will focus on the influence of these media on marketing practices and on the various stages of the decision-making process.

SOCIAL MEDIA - DEFINITION, TYPOLOGY AND HISTORY

What is Social Media?

According to Kaplan and Haenlein (2010), social media is defined as "a group of Internet-based applications that build on the ideological foundations of Web 2.0, and that allow the creation and exchange of user generated content".

In other words, Social media refers to all sites and web platforms that offer so-called "social" features to users. These platforms are based on the collaborative creation of content as well as the exchange of information between individuals (forums, blogs open to comments, etc.). Social media is understood as the different forms of online communication used by people to create networks, communities and collectives to share information, ideas, messages and other content, such as videos.

From this definition, two important characteristics of social media are to highlight:

1. Social media includes online communication, which means that the story of social media can not begin before the invention and the widespread adoption of the Internet.

2. Social media depends on user-generated content. That's why classic websites and blogs are not part of the social media world. Only some people can post on these sites, and there are significant restrictions on the types of content that are downloaded.

These two features make it possible to distinguish social media from other applications on the web and emphasize concepts such as collaboration, interactivity and sharing that particularly characterize this type of media.

Moreover, it is clear that social media contain a wide range of elements. Indeed, social media applications include messaging applications like WhatsApp and Viber, platforms based on profiles like Facebook and LinkedIn, video portals like YouTube, and email clients such as GMail. These elements lend themselves to being categorized according to their own characteristics and the purposes to which they respond. Thus, the authors propose to draw up a typology which highlights the different types of elements constituting the social media in order to better understand this vast notion.

The Different Types of Social Media

Social media apps vary in scope and functionality. Thus, to better understand the potential of social media in the digital strategies of companies, it is essential to understand the specificities of each category or type of social media. Social media can focus on mass targeting or professional networking or sharing photos, videos and knowledge (Kietzmann et al., 2011). The classification depends on the user's use and the need he / she wants to meet and achieve (Kaplan & Haenlein, 2010, Hanna et al., 2011, Kaplan & Haenlein, 2012, Zolkepli and Kamarulzaman, 2011, Kaplan, 2012).

Social Networks

This includes platforms that allow their users to connect to other users with common interests. Usually, they rely on creating a profile to interact with other users. Members are linked bilaterally or through groups. The most popular today are Facebook and LinkedIn.

Platforms Of Social Bookmarking

They record, organize, and manage links to web resources that the user finds useful. Most of them allow to "mark" the links to make easier their reunion and sharing. The most famous are Pinterest and StumbleUpon.

Sharing Services

They allow uploading, sharing photos, videos or audio content on a website to make them accessible anywhere in the world. The majority of these services offer additional social characteristics such as the addition of a user profile or the possibility of commenting on the content. The most popular are YouTube or Flickr.

Micro-Blogging Sites

These are publishing, sharing and discussion services. Each individual member has a public profile where the latest messages are listed. This member can subscribe to other people's profiles and view their publications. These sites focus on short updates that are visible to anyone who has subscribed to receive. The most known sites are Twitter and Instagram.

Forums

This is a public chat room where messages are displayed in chronological order. A message posted by a user could be approved before by a moderator. The content posted by Internet users are categorized by themes, subjects. They are at least temporarily archived.

Blogs

This is a special form of website, with specific features. A blog is characterized by the more or less regular publication of articles, usually classified in reverse chronological order on the main page. Articles are dated and each has a unique URL with a comment box. There are many known and influential blogs. The blog also participates in SEO optimization of a company on a search engine.

Collaborative Media

Social and information sites that tend to relay content in a relatively neutral and factual way. Collaboration, mutual aid and exchange are embodied in this type of social media. These sites are particularly powerful collaborative spaces. The best known are Wikipedia and Commentçamarche.net.

History of Social Media

The history of social media has been marked by decisive moments, relative to the launch of certain sites and platforms whose footprint was particularly salient. These have contributed to the evolution of "social media" as well as the success gained by these media so far. In what follows, the authors will return to the key dates that characterize the history of social media since the advent of web 2.0.

In the year 2000, a site called Hot or Not was launched to invite users to post photos of themselves in order to be rated by other users based on their charm. This site would have fed the lack of confidence of millions of people, which made its success at the time and led to say that it even inspired the creators of Facebook.

In 2002, a dating site called Friendster was launched. This site allows users to meet friends of their friends. This is to create a profile, include "status updates" and indicate mood. The site had a messaging service that also allows sending messages to friends of friends. This site has had incredible success in just one year and has reached a peak of popularity to which the creative company was unprepared. So the servers were and so the users started to connect elsewhere.

In 2003, the "MySpace" site was created as a place for friends. Disappointed users of Friendster service have abandoned it for the benefit of the newborn baby who has become the favorite haunt for millions of trendy teens. This site has made it possible to create public profiles that are customizable and visible to everyone, unlike private Friendster profiles, which are reserved for registered users.

From 2003 to 2005, social media particularly gained ground. Indeed, Mark Zuckerberg has launched Facebook. At the same time, LinkedIn is making an appearance by targeting the business community. Photo sharing sites like Photobucket and Flickr or bookmarks like del.ici.ous or blogging like WordPress are born. YouTube also entered the scene in 2005 with the first video in which a man comments on his visit to the zoo in front of the elephant enclosure. This video has so far made 56 million views. In the same year, the Reddit Community Social News website was also launched.

In 2006, the Facebbok network took off and became a truly global network. Twitter has also taken off.

In 2007, YouTube launched a partnership program with its creators of popular content, which marked a turning point for the site. The microblogging also arrives thanks to Tumblr. This year was also marked by the advent of the hashtag, a symbol that mobilized, promoted and sensitized around critical (and not so critical) social issues.

In 2009, Twitter totally adopted the hashtag after realizing that this symbol is more than just a way to organize content, but a unique language to express ideas and emotions on the Internet. The hashtag energizes the platform and seduces new users.

The year 2009 was also marked by the new family hobby: FarmVille. This addictive social game has even featured in the list of the worst inventions in the world, published by TIME Magazine). Second, users were noticeably attracted by the foursquare geolocation application, which is one of the first applications that allows users to indicate where they are and publish check-ins, recommending certain neighborhoods or cities to their family and to their friends. Since then, this application has been a social phenomenon par excellence.

In 2010, the digital culture was jostled by the adoption of emoji by the Unicode standard. Since this adoption, emojis have become popular at lightning speed and have been legitimized as language. At the same year, Instagram enters the scene by giving birth to the phenomenon of publishing retouched photos with a Polaroid type filter.

In 2011, social networks played a fundamental role in the protest movements against the regime of Zine el-Abidine Ben Ali in Tunisia and later that of Hosni Mubarak in Egypt. The success of these protests sparked similar movements, collectively known as the "Arab Spring," which swept the countries of the Middle East and North Africa in the hope of overthrowing the powers that be and to bring to peoples positive changes. According to several reports, social networks have contributed significantly to the success of these events by allowing organizers to mobilize and shape opinion. The most popular Twitter hashtags (#Egypt, # Jan25, #Libya, #Bahrain and #protest) were tweeted millions of times in the first three months of 2011. Facebook usage has grown throughout the Arab region and doubled in some countries. The government manages to block all access to Facebook and Twitter briefly, but soon activists find other creative ways to organize themselves, inspiring viewers around the world. Since these facts, social networks have acquired an inescapable importance.

Also in 2011, the Snapchat application was launched and was an immediate success because it draws on the ephemeral nature of the moments of life. With this application, users publish content ("snaps") that disappear after 24 hours. This disappearance of snaps seduced teenagers, who were the first to use the application. For teens, Snapchat is the perfect alternative to find their friends - and to flee their family on Facebook.

In 2012, Facebook celebrated a billion users contacted through this network.

2014 was named the Year of the Selfie because of Ellen DeGeneres' selfie at the Oscars, which was retweeted over three million times, setting a new record on Twitter and winning the Twitter award " Golden tweet of the year.

In 2015, the streaming war begins. Meerkat is the first app to create the craze for live video. Shortly after, Twitter launches Periscope and wins the first war of streaming.

In 2016, Facebook launched Facebook LIVE to join the battle of live video. Instagram launched the Stories. With the help of filters, stickers, polls, hashtags and highlights, the Stories manage to make the Instagram application even more addictive, even though it seemed impossible.

The year 2016 was also marked by the crisis of fake news on social media related to the American elections. An information war was cleverly waged using "troll factories" on social media to spread false information (including false statements and conspiracy theories) during US presidential elections. Opinion leaders in mainstream media such as journalists, experts and politicians (up to Hillary Clinton and Donald Trump) are spreading content that is said to have been shared on social networks by bots. Since then, Facebook has revealed that 126 million Americans had been exposed to content published by Russian agents during the elections.

In 2018, representatives of Facebook, Twitter and Google appear before the US Congress to give their testimony in connection with investigations into Russian interference in the US presidential election. At the beginning of 2018, we learn that Facebook has authorized a researcher from Cambridge Analytica, who worked on Donald Trump's presidential campaign, to acquire the data of 50 million users of the social network without their consent. Following this, a campaign named #DeleteFacebook (#DeleteFacebook) spreads on the Internet to protest this scandal by massively suppressing their Facebook profiles. Yet the number of Facebook users seems to continue to climb. BUT, Zuckerberg had to participate in five days of hearings before the US Congress following strong pressure to respond to the problem of protection of personal data. That same year, Instagram launched the IGTV app to allow its users to publish long videos that can last an hour.

All these events, evolutions and revolutions attached to social media seem to have significant consequences for human life on more than one plan. Their fallout seems to be difficult to define definitively. Thus, it is inevitable to be interested in the impact of these social media on marketing and consumer behavior.

INFLUENCE OF SOCIAL MEDIA ON MARKETING

For years, the rate of companies using social media for marketing purposes has visibly increased and the budget allocated by these companies for the implementation of their marketing strategy on these networks continues to grow as well. Companies are increasingly investing in the potential of social media as they offer significant advantages over conventional channels of marketing:

First, social media gives businesses the space they need to reach their target. Indeed, given the surprising increase in the number of connected consumers (no less than 70% of the workforce is well anchored in social media) and the increased time spent by these consumers on these virtual spaces, it is important for any company to be present in order to ensure an omnipresence in the daily lives of its customers.

Secondly, by being present on these media, marketers can easily identify influencer groups that are likely to play the role of promising brand ambassadors and thus contribute to the success of the brand.

And thirdly, all this is done at almost no cost (compared to traditional customer outreach programs) because in most cases, social networking sites are free.

Social media is then associated with a very attractive potential that should never be overlooked. Thus, to ensure a presence that allows them to achieve their profitability, image and sustainability goals, companies are forced to implement a methodical process to properly address the digital space. They must then be aware of the influence of these media on the marketing approach and the opportunities that it is important to grasp to properly carry out each step of this process.

Conduct a Market Research on Social Media

Social media is a unique opportunity for companies that want to do a study of their market. These media provide invaluable information that is relatively inaccessible through conventional data collection methods. In fact, individuals do not behave in the same way when responding to an inquiry as when they are talking with friends or colleagues or when they are under anonymity on a forum. Thus, to access the words of these individuals in these different situations makes it possible to collect information with an essential wealth around the needs and opinions of the consumers. Consumer-to-consumer conversations are particularly relevant because they provide a closer view of reality and help to better understand the public's view.

Nevertheless, the use of social media to carry out a market study does not mean that traditional methods of market research are no longer effective. These media are particularly useful for complementing conventional methods or verifying the results that result from them in order to reach more generalized and realistic conclusions. In addition, thanks to these media, it is possible to carry out several market studies at the same time which would allow the company to improve its performance in several areas including customer service, product development, crisis management, e-reputation, etc. Thus, the use of social media to carry out a market study makes it possible to:

- Access information faster and cheaper

Conducting market research through social media provides very quick access to information that exists on millions of sites, forums, and networks around the world, but also divides, analyzes, and compares data collected as wish the company. On the basis of these data, it is also possible to create different reports, depending on the needs of different teams or departments of the company and as precisely or generally as necessary. This would be significantly more expensive with conventional methods of data collection.

- Validate the results obtained during a classical market study

If the results obtained through traditional methods are reflected on social media, then there is no doubt that these results are accurate.

- Develop a good competitive intelligence

The analysis of the competition is essential to study a market well. Competitive intelligence makes it possible precisely to follow the actions taken by the competitors, to know their marketing strategies, to observe their strengths and weaknesses, to know their products and the services as well as their innovations. As such, social media provide valuable assistance to companies that want to operate a competitive intelligence. Indeed, beyond conversations about the brand itself, the real benefit of conducting a market research with social media is the ability to access discussions about competitors and, above all, from consumer to consumer. This is where the most valuable information is. The collection of such information could inspire the company to react in time. Once the market study is completed, the company could save its requests to continue to observe its audience and access this information at any time.

- Know consumers better

Social media is a huge help in getting to know the intended audience. Indeed, the sample that the company can observe on these media is much larger relative to any panel used. The company could also access the spontaneous personal opinions expressed when consumers discuss with each other. Indeed, there are thousands of conversations on the web just waiting to be analyzed. This concerns both current discussions and those archived on different online discussion platforms. It is then possible to carry out retroactive searches in order to collect the information sought.

- Discover the trends of the sector

Social media monitoring also allows you to discover trends and key topics from conversations around a brand, as well as an entire industry. This allows the company to know and control its environment. In this respect, social media offers an effective tool for quickly accessing important insights for the company. The Brandwatch Signals function does just that by informing the business automatically as soon as a crisis or trend emerges.

Several examples can illustrate the importance of social media in conducting a market study. Two concrete examples are cited in this regard. The first example concerns the banking sector. In fact, one credit card company conducted a classic market survey and another on social media, in order to observe consumers' behavior towards their debts and their financial situation. It turned out that the results obtained were very different. Indeed, while the "physical" group described themselves as responsible with their money, consumers who voted on online discussion forums were much more open about their financial problems. This means that the informality and anonymity provided by these forums can reveal another face of consumers that they dare not show in other situations. It is therefore important to combine the two methods of market research in order to obtain a more realistic view of its market.

The second example is Sony. Indeed, by analyzing the keywords related to its field of activity, the marketing team of Sony realized that the word "mom" returned constantly. For example, Sony was a pioneer in targeting mothers as part of its marketing campaign while its competitors continued to address a young male audience at the time. This example shows how important it is to listen to and analyze discussions on the social web to discover opportunities to exploit. Standby tools enable the company to observe what its customers say beyond its brand or competitors and thereby broaden its knowledge of the market, its players and its audience.

It is also possible, through these media, to analyze the demographic Insights of an audience. Several features make it possible, like Brandwatch Analytics, which offers a very practical feature for market research and sociological studies: Demographics. This feature analyzes, for example, the demographics of twittos that discuss a brand or product in conversations with Brandwatch Analytics and provides access to numerous dashboards and charts to organize this data, as well as to many tools and filters to analyze, understand and derive actuable insights. This feature is not the only one to offer such services. There's also the built-in Snapchat Insights analytics tool that collects multiple types of data including user demographics: age, location, gender, and interests.

Then, in the case where the company wants to launch a given innovation, the social media also offer an essential space to perform product testing on a large sample. Thus, developing a market study seems to be easier but also more exciting and more interesting on these media.

Develop Marketing Strategy on Social MEDIA

Like market research, the development of the marketing strategy has been influenced by the advent of social media. The concepts segmentation, targeting and positioning are now boosted by these media. In fact, beyond the sociodemographic segmentation criteria frequently used in a classic segmentation (age, sex, income, occupation, etc.), segmentation via social media is more and more using psychographic criteria (tastes, hobbies, events, interests, etc.) and behavioral. The likes, comments and shares unveil the expectations and preferences of consumers connected to these media.

Segmentation is a very important step in defining the company's marketing strategy on social media. This segmentation process begins with an analysis of the points of view of the targets as well as their activities: place and condition of life, passions, interests, priorities,... And then the company must think about the way of consumption of its customers: motivations, rhythm, who are their influencers? Who pushes them to consume? ... Then she has to identify on which social networks her audience is most present: Facebook, Twitter, LinkedIn, Quora, Pinterest, Viadeo, Snapchat, Instagram,... Finally she must follow her audience on these social networks through the frequency and type of posts they post, the time they spend on these networks, etc.

The analysis of this information would allow the company to clearly identify the characteristics of its target (persona). It could also easily get in touch with customers interested in its products or services. Through the social media, the company can easily reach a niche clientele, not only locally but also globally thanks to the power of the internet.

Finally, having defined its position relative to the competitors, the company can use social media to communicate this positioning effectively and this, by prioritizing its presence on the social media most consistent with this positioning. In addition, the company is called upon to present content to this audience that attracts it to attract its attention and engage it in a conversation around its offer, thanks to the techniques and tools of content marketing. It can also check via these media if the positioning conveyed is correctly perceived by the target and this, detecting as and when its reactions.

What Influence of Social Media on the Marketing Mix?

Social media has significantly changed the 4P. First, around the product policy, social media have imposed the addition of certain features to the product marketed on these media. Indeed, it is no longer enough to offer consumers features to meet their essential needs. The products offered must be particularly meaningful. They must have additional value that can occur intrinsically and / or through an improved and much richer brand experience. These products are in fact aimed at consumers who use more and more tools such as Facebook, Twitter and comparison sites and reviews, which offer them early knowledge and significantly wider than many companies. They are therefore more demanding and very knowledgeable. Thus, products must be designed with sophisticated promises to meet the expectations and aspirations of this type of customers.

Regarding pricing policy, companies are more than ever asked to price their products and services in a fair and competitive manner across all distribution channels. Indeed, the extended digital connectivity today imposes price transparency. The most obvious example is travel, especially the sale of airline tickets. In this respect, studies have shown that price is one of the main reasons why consumers go to companies' social media sites. In addition, the Internet and the mobile Web allow customers to check prices. These will publicly claim the company concerned if they detect inconsistencies on it. This can be mobilized in the service of competitors who sell less expensive.

In terms of distribution, apart from retail stores, direct sales, print catalogs and / or the website, the company must be present on social media to ensure a strong presence within a wide range of competing offers. This includes all platforms and applications to reach the target of the company. On these platforms, it is also important to focus on conversations between consumers. Companies need to determine if their prospects, customers and the general public want to socialize around their products and / or brand. This virtual socialization is a real asset for the marketing of the company's products, whether to attract prospects or to retain current customers.

In terms of communication, social media has imposed a revolution in communication practices. In fact, classical marketing relied on its promotional activities to communicate the attributes of the offer to the public in a single direction from business to consumer. Social media, on the other hand, has imposed new rules according to which it is the consumers who make known the performance and the value of the products. Today, communication is not limited to the virtues of the offer but must focus on what makes the special brand, original, different to the point that consumers want to join. Social media marketing is conversation-based rather than product-driven and needs to be integrated at every stage of the buying process, even at the post-purchase stage. This requires constant content and support that helps engage consumers.

Can Social Media Gauge the Effectiveness of the Marketing Strategy?

The commercial strategy undertaken on social media certainly deserves to be evaluated. Indeed, measuring the effectiveness of marketing actions allows the company to adjust its choices and plan future actions. There are several indicators to gauge the effectiveness of these actions. In what follows, the authors will look at the most relevant indicators starting with key indicators, which do not depend on a particular sector of activity, such as community growth and user responses.

The Size Of The Audience

The success of the business strategy is reflected in the correct size of the community on the business page and the fact that the community is active. Nevertheless, checking these indicators on each social network separately is tedious. It also causes a waste of time. Tools such as SEMrush provide all the useful statistics on a single dashboard. These tools can also provide a detailed report on audience engagement for each social network.

Commitment

Companies are certainly interested in detecting customer engagement and seeking to measure that engagement through the reactions and behaviors they display on social media. The signs of commitment are relatively comparable from one social network to another. However, each platform admits its own specificities and the indicators can also have different names and meanings:

Likes

Like is the most standard way people use to respond to content. Being very used and widespread, this modality is present on all social networks. As an indication, Facebook has introduced a number of "reactions" in the form of symbols and emoji to allow users to express their feelings about a post or publication. By a simple click, the consumer individual reveals his attitude towards a given content.

Comments

Comments are the most direct and expressive means of expression of the audience. Through their comments, customers of a particular brand express their appreciations around the offer and express that they wish to interact with the company. In addition, if consumers write positive comments about a brand, it may mean that the brand's efforts are being made in the right direction. On the contrary, the negative comments, if they are numerous, call to diagnose the situation.

Shares

Shares, retweets, and re-releases prove that a particular strategy, offering, or theme has impacted the target audience. Sharing also reflects a level of trust in content and the company that published it. Indeed, when a person shares content, it means that they believe the information is valid and useful.

The Engagement Rate

The size of the community and the number of likes are two important indicators, but they are not representative of each other. One hundred Likes may reflect a high level of success for an account with 1,000 subscribers, but perhaps less for an account that counts 100,000. The Engagement Rate measures the involvement of a hearing, its reactivity to the content published by the company and further its fidelity. It is essential for the company to study this indicator if it wants its subscribers to change from fan to customer. SEMrush's Social Media Tracker tool allows enterprise publications to be ranked by engagement rate to determine the types of content that work best on each social network. This information helps to target audiences' interests in an efficient way.

Other Specific Indicators

Apart from the indicators already mentioned, the company is called upon to collect data related to its own objectives and competitors in order to ensure that it is progressing towards the achievement of these objectives. In this respect, some indicators seem interesting, including:

The Growth Dynamics Of Audiences

It is appropriate for a company to measure the visibility of its products or services to potential customers. Social networks are a good way to do this because they are free and therefore a good option for small businesses with limited budgets. The audience growth indicator is particularly important for young brands who want to see how fast their community is evolving and what type of activity contributes most to growing their audience.

Comparative Indicators

The company must also monitor its competitors especially when it works in a congested business niche. To do this, it is necessary to identify, in particular, the content that best suits them, their strengths and weaknesses, the audiences they neglected to target, the influencers they mention, and so on., to be able to develop a strategy that will allow it to be competitive.

Traffic on Social Networks

Most companies use social networks to generate leads. But, the likes do not make money to the company if they do not lead to a conversion. Thus, it is essential to measure the share of traffic on social networks that directly generates a conversion. Google Analytics is the best tool to see the traffic coming from company accounts on social networks, but SEMrush also allows to compare these results with those of the competitors and to see especially how much of the traffic goes, from the social networks, towards the competitors' websites rather than the company's website.

IMPACT OF SOCIAL MEDIA ON CONSUMER BEHAVIOR

Long before the advent of social media, the buying path was relatively basic. Indeed, consumers went to the store to acquire products that meet their needs, including following the advice of sellers. At that time, media such as television, the press and magazines exerted some influence on the purchasing but the bulk of the consumption was in store when the consumer went there to buy. Today, social media has upset this classic pattern of consumption. Indeed, a study conducted in January 2017 on 3648 women between 18 and 64 years old having bought at least one beauty product during the last three months in the United Kingdom, France, Germany or the United Arab Emirates (survey conducted by GFK for Facebook) showed that 72% of female consumers are influenced by their online experience.

E-commerce accounts for a large share of purchases, but in-store sales remain the most popular channel for consumers (69%). In this respect, it is clear that consumers who appropriate their purchases still in store now go there with a clear idea of what they want. If this is not the case, these consumers use their smartphones in store especially to compare prices directly or to search for information on similar products. These assertions show that the in-store journey and the use of social networks are not contradictory acts. However, the influence of social media on the purchase path is indisputable. This journey has undergone a real revolution, which arouses the interest to study closely the behavior of the connected consumer. The study online consumer behavior goes beyond the traditional field of marketing and in turn becomes a current of research in its own right. Indeed, the advent of web 2.0 has transformed the profile of the consumer and its use of the Internet in the context of buying and consuming.

In this chapter, the authors are particularly interested in the impact of social media on consumer behavior by returning to each step of its decision-making process. They propose to describe the peculiarities of online consumer behavior by going through the main stages of its decision-making process: information retrieval, evaluation of alternatives, purchase and post-purchase evaluation (Engel, Blackwell and Kollat, 1968).

The Online Information Search Phase

During this phase, the consumer will enter a process of research and information processing allowing him to choose the product that best meets his needs (Zaoui et al., 2008). In this respect, social media has upset the situation. Indeed, these media have become the first source of information consulted by consumers, even if these consumers will later choose to make their purchases elsewhere, especially through conventional channels. The primacy granted to these media comes from the fact that they offer an unavoidable convenience in the search for information. The consumer can find on the sites of these media information from several sources at once. They can learn from their knowledge, consult the opinions of other consumer members in interactive groups and visit the pages of companies created on these media. The latest figures and statistics reflecting consumer behavior during this phase are both meaningful and very meaningful. Indeed, according to a study conducted by GlobalWebIndex in 2018, about 54% of social media followers use them to search for products. Consumers are increasingly joining social networks to seek advice and recommendations. In addition, these media are increasingly perceived as sources of credible information and that is why they are relatively privileged compared to official sources such as brand sites. This is because consumers are more likely to trust the opinions of other consumers than the best creative.

Nevertheless, this trend should not deter companies from promoting their products and services via social networks. Indeed, the more the brand selects the content published delicately, the more it manages to capture the attention of its fans and generate interest in the prospects generally.

The Evaluation Phase of Alternatives Online

The search for information on the Internet will allow the consumer to form his evoked set, consisting of alternatives from which he will choose the product or service he will buy on the Internet or in stores (Alba et al., 1997; Howard, 1989; Meyer, 1982; Wu, 2003). The choice of the individual will then be made on the basis of a set of criteria which also served to constitute the evoked ensemble (Andrews and Srinivasan, 1995). The possibilities offered by social media to help the consumer to constitute his evoked whole and to evaluate the various alternatives are immense (Alba et al., 1997) which can cause an information overload and consequently the confusion, the abandonment of research (Biswas, 2004) or the adjournment of the decision (Dhar and Nowlis, 1999). The challenge is to seduce the target with attractive content and a distinctive offer. In addition, we must always seek to identify influencers to help the consumer to focus on the company's offer compared to competing offers. Studies have shown that 49% of consumers rely on influencer recommendations on social networks before making their purchases. (Fourcommunications, 2018). This means that if the consumer has confidence in the influencer, he will tend to buy the product. This statistic shows that brands have every interest in relying on the power of influencers as part of their social media marketing.

Among these influencers, there are consumers who have had a positive experience with the brand. According to a study by GlobalWebIndex (2018), 71% of these consumers tend to recommend the brand to their friends and family. Their testimony is of great credibility. These consumers could greatly influence prospects and guide them towards a definite choice. Thus, the company must make sure to take advantage of the influence that these consumers can have on social networks. In addition, there are opinion leaders who play an important role in these new procurement processes. They can exert a strong influence by distributing, in social networks, articles, photos, video tutorials on certain products, they guide consumers in their choices. Thus, companies could benefit from the influence of these thought leaders to guide the choice of consumers.

The role of influencers is not at all marginalized. Nearly 40% of consumers say they are more likely to buy a brand they see on Facebook or Instagram. This is due in particular to the quality of the visuals posted or the opinions and tests made by the influencers. The brand is then credited by all the voices that boast. Thus, it is no longer just a salesperson who advises the consumer, but it is consumers who redesign the buying process by interacting with each other.

The Phase of Passing the Order Online

In our opinion, the online transaction consists of two phases: the online ordering phase and the online payment phase. The authors chose to separate these two phases because they can be conducted separately on the Internet. Placing an order online is a decision that may depend on several factors that may encourage or slow down consumer behavior in this regard. On the social networks, companies have the opportunity to use purchase incentive techniques to push consumers to place their order. Among these techniques, there is live chat. Customers appreciate this form of interaction with the brand because they benefit from real-time support. The response time is a crucial element of this support by chat, it must be less than 30 seconds, and otherwise the customer could abandon the purchase. Studies have shown that 57% of customers say they will give up their shopping cart if they do not find an answer to their questions quickly. In addition the company must master the organization of these live video to make the customer feel that it is unique and is listening to it despite being solicited by other customers. In addition, this chat support does not automatically lead to boost sales. The customer must be pushed to the purchase of a clever and intelligent way and this, by applying the techniques of sale suitable. These include:

- Make flash sales: The flash sale is a very fashionable concept right now. This is to create a sale with a very limited duration and this, to create a state of emergency, while advancing a very convincing advantage: an interesting discount for example. Combining the limited time and the large reduction will prompt the client to make his decision quickly. In addition, offering gifts or additional benefits would cause the customer to buy from the company that grants him such benefits and not from competitors especially that it is constrained by the limited time of the offer.
- Announce a limited number of products available in stock: when the company displays a limited number of products available, it could prompt the customer to make a quick decision to take advantage of it before the stock runs out. The company can also limit the number of customers who will enjoy its exceptional offer during the live instead of limiting the number of products available.

Online Payment Phase

Buying on the Internet is a remote transaction, with high uncertainty due to the transfer of money and the disclosure of personal information through "open" technology to a virtual vendor "hiding" behind a screen (Hoffman et al., 1999). As such, buying online can be considered risky, and remains one of the most obvious barriers to the development of online shopping (Forsythe and Shi, 2003, Hoffman et al., 1999, Miyazaki and Fernandez 2001, Pavlou 2003, Tan 1999, Tan and Thoen 2001). Looking at the profile of online shoppers and non-shoppers shows that online shoppers are less concerned about the financial risks of buying online, while the majority of non-shoppers are concerned about financial risk and fear for their data financial and personal (Lee and Tan 2003, Swinyard and Smith, 2003). The presence of the consumer on social media means that the consumer already shares personal information with the community. Users of these social media also have the habit of sharing the most personal data in private messages, which reassures these users more. Regarding payment, note that companies and brands that use these media to sell tend to postpone payment upon receipt of the order. This modality is used in particular to provide a remedy for the financial risk perceived by the customers but could be at the origin of certain problems for the companies which send the orders to customers who prove not solvent or who renounce the purchase after have gone through all the previous steps to payment.

Product Delivery Phase

Except for digitized products, whose possession is immediate, there is a gap between the placing of the order and the possession of the product (Zaoui et al., 2008).

The "no immediate possession" of the product is another characteristic of online shopping that hinders some consumers (Zaoui et al., 2008). It has been established that there is a negative relationship between delivery times and the tendency to change from buying an offline circuit to an online circuit (Gupta et al., 2004). Several consumers were also faced with a problem of receiving a product damaged or not meeting the advertised criteria. As such, social networks have been used by companies to reassure customers and prospects in this regard. These companies constantly publish testimonials from their satisfied customers by the company's delivery performance, to provide proof of their professionalism. These testimonials are usually presented in terms of screenshots of private conversations between the company and its customers or in terms of spontaneous thank-you messages sent by customers to the company.

The Online Post-Purchase Phase

Contrary to what one might think, the post-purchase stage is of paramount importance for companies and brands. In fact, it is no longer sufficient to sell one's products and services. The most important thing would be to maintain a privileged and lasting relationship with the customers. That said, studying consumer behavior in the post-purchase phase is essential in order to establish, develop and maintain a lasting customer relationship. The importance of loyalty is well established today and there is a growing need to harness the potential of social media to achieve this goal. Social media can help the company maintain a favorable relationship with its customers through a set of measures such as:

- Create a dialogue with customers: social networks are a particularly interesting communication channel because it allows companies to conduct both a one-to-many communication when the brand speaks to all its subscribers and a one-to-one communication when the brand responds directly to the requests and comments of its consumers. Thanks to these media, the brand and its customers are in constant interaction, which is the basis of maintaining their exchange relationship.

- Generate a base of contacts to promote the brand: social media can bring together diverse and varied profiles of people interested in the brand and who can communicate with each other. For companies, this dynamic is to be maintained to be exploited in order to encourage the most passionate customers to play the role of promising ambassadors of their brands.
- Provide after-sales service: Facebook and Twitter are used by companies to manage after-sales service issues and turn complaints or requests into constructive communication, which could positively impact brand perception.

To do this, it is important to accompany consumers from the curious stage, visitors and try to keep consumers who reach the status of ambassadors. If this happens, dissatisfied customers can hurt the image of the company when they talk about it to others. Thus, the marketing strategy on social media must integrate the 4 steps presented in the visual above. We are talking here about Inbound Marketing. The fourth step of this approach is essential for the company since it allows to optimize the returns on investment and then facilitate the communication strategy on the Internet. Indeed, by increasing customer loyalty, encouraging them to promote it, the company certainly gains in efficiency.

In addition, to better manage consumer behavior in the post-purchase phase, it is important to pay particular attention to virtual communities. Social media has created thousands of virtual communities that have developed spontaneously by fans and continue to be managed by them. In addition, many communities are now managed by the companies themselves. These communities are commercially oriented but manage to create community spirit among members and generate strong brand loyalty (Mathwick, 2002). Virtual communities are generally important because they help businesses better understand the concerns of their consumers, leading to satisfaction and retention (Hagel, 1997). These concerns can be unveiled in many ways including negative comments. In this case, the brand should not see these comments as a danger but rather as an opportunity to propose an individual solution to the dissatisfied consumer. Claims processing is the key to creating a constructive and mutually beneficial relationship with clients.

In the end, it is clear that the process of buying online admits features making it more complex. This offers cyber-consumers more leeway to act and reverse the balance of power with companies. However, it is important for these companies to understand the ways in which they can benefit from them in order to achieve their objectives and to minimize the potential harm affecting their journey.

CONCLUSION

For years, social media has been growing exponentially. Their major asset is simplicity and speed. Indeed, for most users, these media are intuitive, do not require real expertise and have no difficulty in accessing information. It is enough for a user to discover a product, a service or a person that interests him, so that he immediately informs his entire community. The potential of these media is therefore enormous for companies that want to develop their customer base, their brand image and their turnover. Today, the use of these media is inevitable, they acquire a more strategic role.

Social media has also influenced consumer behavior. It is more and more demanding and better informed through the use of the internet and social media. And yet, social media has managed to influence its attitudes, product valuation, purchase intent and loyalty (Safi et al., 2018). The impact of these media is so great that it is illusory to think to have definitively identified.

REFERENCES

Alba, J., Lynch, J., Wietz, B., Janiszewski, C., Lutz, R., & Sawyer, A. (1997). Interactive home shopping: Consumer, retailer, and manufacturer incentives to participate in electronic marketplaces. *Journal of Marketing*, *63*(3), 38–53. doi:10.1177/002224299706100303

Andrews, R. L., & Srinivasan, T. C. (1995). Studying consideration effects in empirical choice models using scanner panel data. *JMR, Journal of Marketing Research*, *32*(1), 30–41. doi:10.1177/002224379503200105

Biswas, D. (2004). Economics of information in he web economy, towards a new theory? *Journal of Business Research*, *57*, 724–733. doi:10.1016/S0148-2963(02)00355-7

Chang, L. D. M., Ling Tam, A. Y., & Suki, N. M. (2016). Moderating effect of races towards consumers' feeling of TCM usage. Handbook of Research on Leveraging Consumer Psychology for Effective Customer Engagement, 306-323.

Dhar, R., & Nowlis, S. M. (1999). Consumer preference for the no-choice option. *The Journal of Consumer Research*, *24*(2), 215–231. doi:10.1086/209506

Engel, J. F., Kollat, D. T., & Blackwell, R. D. (1968). *Consumer Behavior*. New York: Holt, Rinehart &Winston.

Forsythe, S. M., & Shi, B. (2003). Consumer patronage and risk perception in internet shopping. *The Journal of Consumer Research*, *56*, 863–875.

Gupta, A., Su, B., & Walter, Z. (2004). An empirical study of consumer switching from traditional to electronic channels: A purchase-decision process perspective. *International Journal of Electronic Commerce*, *8*(3), 131–161. doi:10.1080/10864415.2004.11044302

Hagel, J. I. (1997). Net gain, expanding markets through virtual communities. *The McKinsey Quarterly*, *1*, 141–153.

Hanna, R., Rohm, A., & Crittenden, V. L. (2011). We're all connected: The power of the social media eco system. *Business Horizons*, *54*(3), 785–807. doi:10.1016/j.bushor.2011.01.007

Hoffman, D. L., Novak, T. P., & Peralta, M. (1999). Building consumer trust online, in (coord.). *Communications of the ACM*, *42*(4), 80–85. doi:10.1145/299157.299175

Howard, J. A. (1989). *Consumer behavior in marketing strategy*. Academic Press.

Kaplan, A. M. (2012). If you love something, let it go mobile: Mobile marketing and mobile social media 4x4. *Business Horizons*, *55*(2), 129–139. doi:10.1016/j.bushor.2011.10.009

Kaplan, A. M., & Haenlein, M. (2010). Users of the world, unite! The challenges and opportunities of Social Media. *Business Horizons*, *53*(1), 59–68. doi:10.1016/j.bushor.2009.09.003

Kaplan, A.M., and Haenlein, M. (2012). Social Media: Back to the Roots and Back to the Future. *Journal of Systems and Information Technology, 14*(2), 101-104.

Kietzmann, J. H., Hermkens, K., McCarthy, I. P., & Silvestre, B. S. (2011). Social media? Get serious! Understanding the functional building blocks of social media. *Business Horizons*, *54*(3), 241–251. doi:10.1016/j.bushor.2011.01.005

Lee, K. S., & Tan, S. J. (2003). E-retailing versus physical retailing, a theoretical model and empirical test of consumer choice. *Journal of Business Research*, *56*(11), 877–885. doi:10.1016/S0148-2963(01)00274-0

Mathwick, C. (2002). Understanding the online consumer: A typology of online relational norms and behavior. *Journal of Interactive Marketing*, *16*(1), 40–55. doi:10.1002/dir.10003

Meyer, R. J. (1982). A descriptive model of consumer information search behavior. *Marketing Science*, *1*, 1.

Miyazaki, A. D., & Fernandez, A. (2001). Consumer perceptions of privacy and security risks for online shopping. *The Journal of Consumer Affairs*, *35*(1), 27–44.

Nathan, R. J., Fook Chiun, D. C., & Suki, N. M. (2016). An online marketing strategies assessment for companies in airlines and entertainment industries in Malaysia. Handbook of Research on Leveraging Consumer Psychology for Effective Customer Engagement, 1-15.

Pavlou, P. A. (2003). Consumer acceptance of electronic commerce: Integrating trust and risk with the technology acceptance model. *International Journal of Electronic Commerce*, *7*(3), 101–134. doi:10.1080/10864415.2003.11044275

Safi, H., Azouri, M., & Azouri, A. (2018, May). L'influence des réseaux sociaux sur le comportement du consommateur: Le cas de l'industrie des biens luxueux. *La Revue Gestion et Organisation*, *10*(1), 29–35. doi:10.1016/j.rgo.2018.04.001

Suki, N. M. (2016). *Handbook of Research on Leveraging Consumer Psychology for Effective Customer Engagement*. https://www.igi-global.com/book/handbook-research-leveraging-consumer-psychology/149284

Swinyard, W. R., & Smith, S. M. (2003). Why people (dont) shop online: A lifestyle study of the internet consumer. *Psychology and Marketing*, *20*(7), 567–597. doi:10.1002/mar.10087

Tan, S. J. (1999). Strategies for reducing consumers' risk aversion in internet shopping. *Journal of Consumer Marketing, 16*(2), 163.

Tan, Y.-H., & Thoen, W. (2001). Toward a generic model of trust for electronic commerce. *International Journal of Electronic Commerce*, *5*(2), 61–74.

Wu, J., & Rangaswamy, A. (2003). A fuzzy set model of search and consideration with an application to an online market. *Marketing Science*, *22*(3), 411–434. doi:10.1287/mksc.22.3.411.17738

Zaoui, I., Ben Ammar Mamlouk, Z., & Trahand, J. (2008). Analyse du processus d'achat sur Internet: nouvelles influences, nouveaux comportements, nouveaux challenges. *Actes du congrès de l'AFM*.

Zolkepli, I. A., & Kamarulzaman, Y. (2011). Understanding social media adoption: The role of perceived media needs and technology characteristics. *World Journal of Social Sciences*, *1*(1), 188–199.

Chapter 3
Challenges and Opportunities for News Media and Journalism in an Increasingly Digital Mobile:
Challenges and Opportunities for Social Media.

Kheder Omar Lawa
Universiti Utara Malaysia, Malaysia

ABSTRACT

This paper reviews challenges and opportunities for news media and journalism in today's changing media environment. It documents that we are moving towards an increasingly digital, mobile, and social media environment with more intense competition for attention. More and more people get news via digital media, they increasingly access news via mobile devices (especially smartphones), and rely on social media and other intermediaries in terms of how they access and find news. In this environment, a limited number of large technology companies enable billions of users across the world to navigate and use digital media in easy and attractive ways through services like search, social networking, video sharing, and messaging. As a consequence, these companies play a more and more important role in terms of (a) the distribution of news and (b) digital advertising.

INTRODUCTION

A well–functioning democracy requires free and diverse news media capable of keeping people informed, holding powerful actors to account, and enabling public discussion of public affairs. Existing research suggests that quality journalism can increase levels of political knowledge, participation, and engagement and can furthermore help reduce corruption and encourage elected officials to represent their constituents

DOI: 10.4018/978-1-7998-3042-9.ch003

more effectively. The freedom, diversity, and ability of news media to enable democracy depend on the institutional structure of individual countries' media environment. Today, these media environments are changing in part as a result of technological and market developments largely associated with the rise of digital media. More research that delve into aspect of consumer behavior and psychology in the digital economy is deemed necessary (Ling Chang, Ling Tam, & Suki, 2016; Nathan, Fook Chiun, & Suki, 2016; Suki, 2016). Accordingly, the purpose of this study is to review evidence–based research on the opportunities and challenges these developments represent for news media and their role in democracy in different contexts. We will rely on research carried out at the Reuters Institute for the Study of Journalism, other up–to–date relevant academic work, as well as industry data and analysis. Our primary focus is on Europe with some additional consideration of developments in other high– to medium–income regions with relatively high levels of digital media use. The precise nature of change in the media environment varies in important ways from country to country, but there are some clear, high–level commonalities that represent both opportunities and challenges for journalism, media organizations, and public debate.

The three most important developments driven by technological and market forces today are:

1. The move to an increasingly digital, mobile, and social media environment with increasingly intense competition for attention where legacy media like broadcasters and especially newspapers, while remaining very important news producers are becoming relatively less important as distributors of news and are under growing pressure to develop new digital business models as their existing operations decline or stagnate.
2. The growing importance of a limited number of large technology companies that enable billions of users across the world to navigate and use digital media in easy and attractive ways through services like search, social networking, video sharing, messaging, etc. and who as a consequence play a more and more important role in terms of (a) the distribution of news and (b) digital advertising.
3. The development of a high–choice media environment where internet users have access to more and more information in convenient formats and often for free, across a range of increasingly sophisticated personal and mobile devices, and in ways that enable new forms of participation—an environment where those most interested in news embrace these new opportunities to get, 8 share, and comment on news, but a larger number of people opt for more casual and passive forms of use.

These three developments are broadly common across most high– and medium– income countries with wide access to digital media. They are enabled by technology and some of the most pressing accompanying challenges to journalism are associated with the market implications, but it is important to recognize that they are driven by media users. Technology is changing media and media markets, but primarily because audiences and advertisers have embraced them. Technologies enable change. People and organizations enact change.

TECHNOLOGICAL AND MARKET DEVELOPMENTS

A More and More Digital Media Environment

During the last two decades, the media environment has become increasingly digital with the development of ever more advanced and often cheaper digital devices, improved connectivity, and increased supply of digital media content, products, and services. Generally speaking, print readership is declining, television viewing has been broadly stable (but the audience is aging), and time spent with digital media has increased rapidly. In high income democracies with high levels of internet use, over half of all time spend with media is now spend with digital media, including both internet use via personal computers and the use of mobile devices like tablets and especially smartphones.2 Most medium income countries with a relatively developed technical infrastructure are rapidly developing in the same direction as more and more people get internet access at home and via mobile devices and as digital media account for a larger and larger share of overall media use. The implications for how people get news can be illustrated by the cases of France and the United Kingdom, two European countries with historically quite different media environments. As is clear from Figure 1, television

Figure 1. Sources of News in France and the UK (2013–2016)
Source: Data from the Reuters Institute Digital News Report 2015–2018.

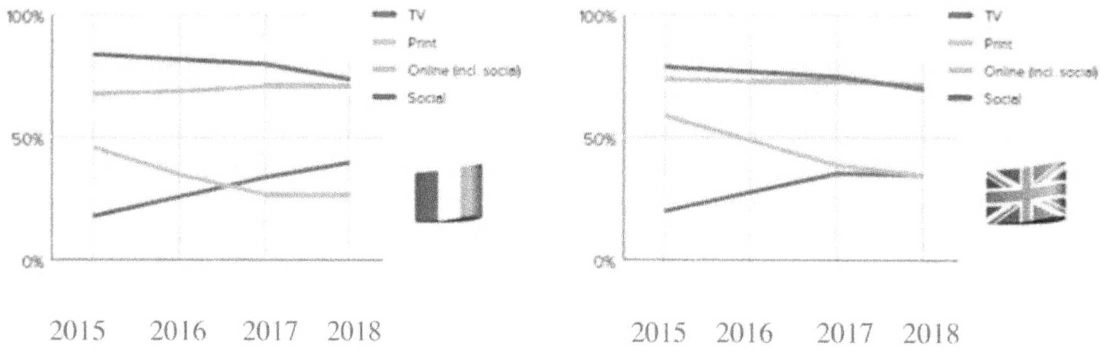

remains an important, but gradually eroding, source of news in both countries, print is far less widely used, and more and more people name online media, especially social media, a source of news—in the United Kingdom more than name television.

The importance of digital media as a part of people's overall media use, and the increasing number of people who rely on online sites for news has been a gradual development unfolding since the late 1990s with the rise of internet. In recent years, however, the gradual move towards digital media has accelerated and changed in potentially profound ways as the desktop and search–based internet of the 2000s is increasingly complemented by a mobile and social internet in the 2010s.

The move towards a mobile centered media environment:

Since the launch of the iPhone in 2007 and the first Android models in 2008, smartphone use has spread very rapidly across the world, and not only in high income countries. In 2010, mobile media use accounted for an estimated 8 percent of the time Americans spend using media, and internet access via personal computers 25 percent. By 2015, mobile media had grown to 25 percent and overtaken internet access via personal computers, which was down to 22 percent. As is clear from Figure 2, the number of people who say they rely on mobile media for news has grown rapidly in parallel and show no signs of slowing down. In a number of countries including several of the Nordic countries, the UK, and highly developed markets in the Asia–Pacific region, more people rely on smartphones than on personal computers for accessing digital news.

Figure 2. Smartphone Use for News in Selected Countries:
Source: Data from the Reuters Institute Digital News Report 2015–2018.

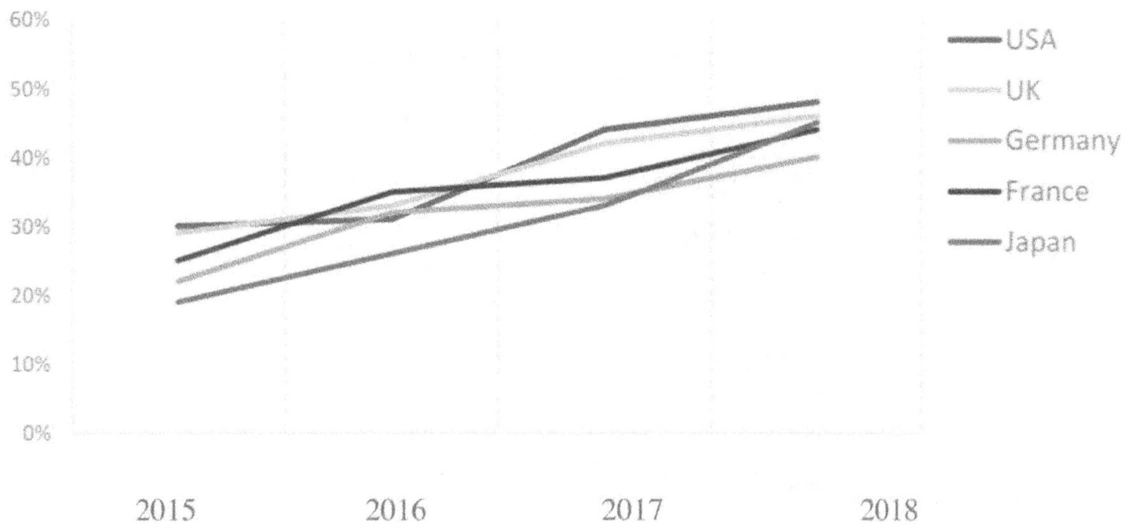

An Increasingly Social Media Environment

The move to mobile media has been accompanied by the rise of social media, most importantly Facebook but also increasingly video–sharing sites like YouTube and Vimeo, messaging services likes WhatsApp and Snapchat, photo sharing sites like Instagram and Pinterest, and microblogging tools like Twitter. Several of these services are offered by a small number of large technology companies that occupy a central position in the digital media environment Google owns YouTube, for example, and Facebook owns WhatsApp and Instagram. Social media are not only widely used to share experiences and stay in touch with friends and family. They also play an increasingly important role as sources of news as more and more people come across news on these platforms. Figure 3 presents first the percentage of all respondents across the 26 countries covered in the 2018 Reuters Institute Digital News Report that say they have used the platform in question for any purpose in the last week (in blue), and second, the percentage who say they have used it as a source of news (in red). With 44 percent reach across 26 countries and 1.7 billion active users globally, Facebook, a company founded in 2004, now reaches more people with news than any media organization in the world. The biggest platforms are increasingly important for the distribution of news, but invest little or nothing in news production.

Social media are an increasingly widely used way of accessing and finding news. How important varies significantly across countries, as can be seen in Figure 4. In countries characterized by historically strong news media who enjoy relatively high levels of trust and have aggressively invested in building attractive digital products and services like the Nordic countries and the United Kingdom social media are widely used for news, but rarely named as people's main source of news. In countries where news media have either historically been weaker, or have been harder hit by digital disruption in recent years, and where people tend to truest news media less like parts of Southern Europe and the United States social media is more frequently named a main source of news.

From direct contact to distributed media:

Figure 3. Top social networks for news (and for any purpose) in all countries
Source: Data from the Reuters Institute Digital News Report 2018.

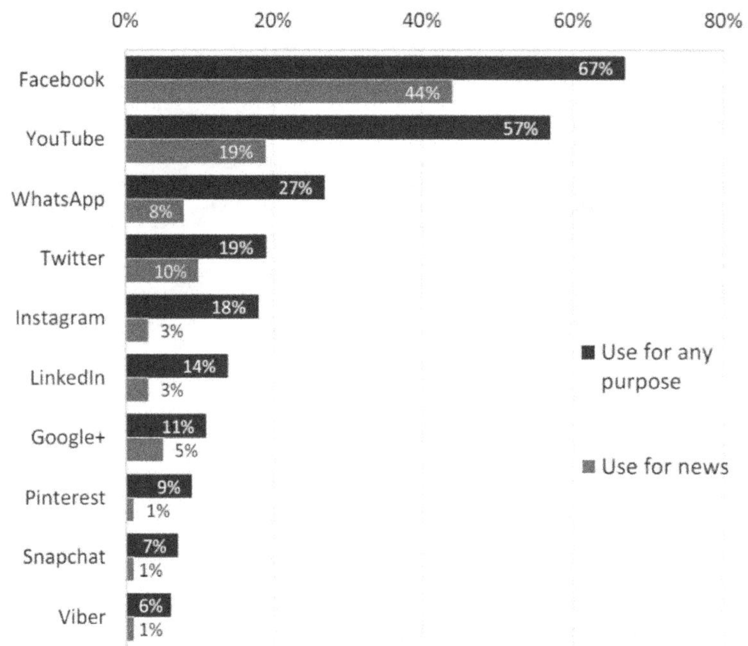

Figure 4. Growth in social media as main source of news between 2017 and 2018
Source: Data from the Reuters Institute Digital News Report 2017–2018.

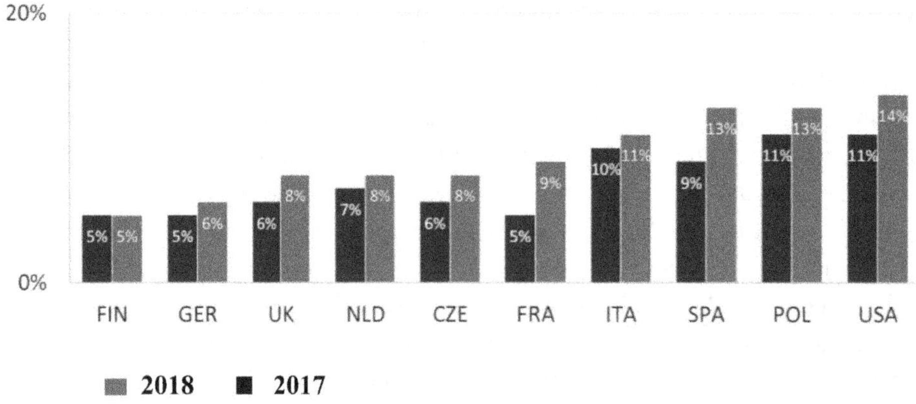

The move towards a more digital, more mobile, and more social media environment points towards a situation where news media are still very important for news production, but are relatively less important for news distribution than they were in the past. We are moving from an environment where audiences found news by going directly to the various channels offered by news media broadcast and print, websites and email newsletters, and today increasingly mobile apps and alerts to an environment characterized by "distributed discovery", where direct access is still important, but increasingly supplemented by people coming across news via search engines, social media, aggregators, and the like. As is clear from Figure 5,

Figure 5. Ways of coming across news online 2018
Source: Data from the Reuters Institute Digital News Report 2018.

	UK	GER	FRA	FIN	GRE	POL
Direct entry	47%	27%	27%	62%	44%	27%
Search	20%	37%	35%	15%	54%	62%
Social Media	25%	21%	26%	24%	55%	38%
Aggregator	6%	6%	5%	9%	6%	8%
Email	7%	15%	22%	6%	21%	14%
Mobile Alerts	9%	8%	14%	5%	8%	7%

the relative importance of each form of discovery varies significantly from country to country, but overall, distributed discovery via third party platforms like search engines and social media are clearly becoming more widespread and important.

The move towards distributed discovery has been going on for some time as first aggregators, then search engines, and later social media have become more and more important for how people find news online. The development is continuing with the rise of "distributed content", where news is not only found via, but consumed on, platforms controlled by third–parties that do not produce their own content. The most important examples of this are the launch of Snapchat Discover (2017), Facebook Instant Articles (2017), and Apple News (2017), all initially open only to a few partners but gradually opened up to and embraced by more and more media organizations. The rise of these "off–site" formats, where publishers can reach audiences without relying on their own websites or apps, and the way in which brands like BuzzFeed have built significant reach beyond their own channels, have led some to suggest the future of news will be entirely distributed with news organizations focusing on production and platform companies controlling distribution. Most news organization's still, however, insist on investing in channels for direct communication with their target audiences through legacy channels as well as digital channels including websites, mobile apps, alerts, notifications, and email letters. There is a keen awareness amongst both private sector and public service news media that what a platform gives, it can also take away sometimes suddenly and that technology companies are primarily focused on what they see as their users' and their own best interests.

A More Polarized Pattern of News Media Use

How people engage with the changing media environment depends in part on their access to digital media and news, in part on socio–economic factors like age, gender, education, and income, and in part on interest in news. A general tendency is towards a more and more polarized environment along lines of interest, which in turn is associated in part with education and income. The move from a low choice media environment towards a high choice media environment that started with the spread of cable and satellite television has accelerated with the rise of digital media, and increasingly, the gap between those most interested in news (who embrace many of the new opportunities available) and those least interested (who embrace digital media, but not necessarily for news) is likely to grow. Internet users have access to more and more information from more and more different sources, increasing the opportunities people have to use diverse sources and encounter different perspectives. An increasingly digital media environment offers more diverse opportunities than ever before in most respects (though, as we note below, the diversity of original professionally produced content in small markets, less lucrative niche issue areas, and at the local level is under pressure as media industry revenues and investment in news production decline). How much people avail themselves of these opportunities depend on access to digital media as well as on interest in news. Across the 26 countries, Casual Users outnumber News Lovers by more than 2 to 1—as shown by Figure 6. Clearly, an abundant supply of diverse information and ease of access does not in itself guarantee wide dissemination of news.

Figure 6. Segmentation by frequency of access and interest in news
Source: Data from the Reuters Institute Digital News Report 2018.

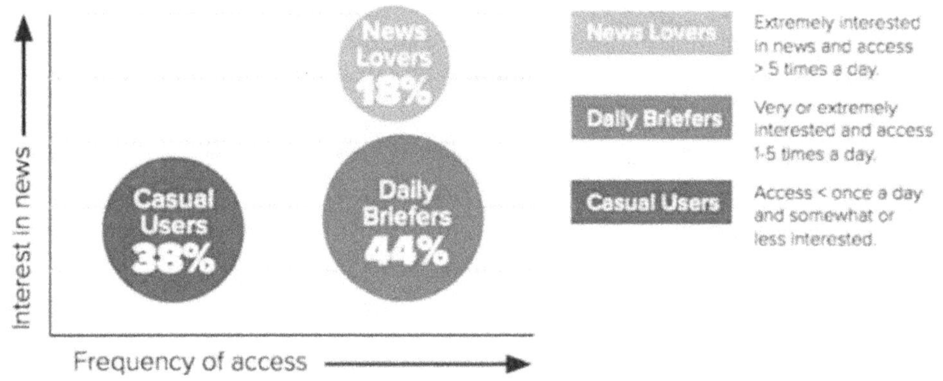

Generational differences in news and media use:

News and media use is highly habitual and people's media habits are generally shaped in their youth. Older people adopt new media and new forms of media use, but often as a supplement to rather than instead of their established routines. Today, the majority of the population has grown up in a pre-digital media environment, but many of those who are under 35 have grown up with digital media. The generational differences are very pronounced when we look for example at what people identify as their main source of news (see Figure 7).

As they grow older, people's media habits change as their circumstances evolve (professionally and personally), but they rarely age into previous generations' dominant forms of media use. People who came of age in the 1960s did not abandon television in favor of print and radio, and we should not expect people who come of age in the 2010s to abandon digital media in favor of linear scheduled television and newspapers.

Opportunities and Challenges for News Media

Many news media, including both newspapers and broadcasters, already have therefore invested substantial resources in digital media and have built significant audience reach online. Across the 26 countries covered in the 2018 Reuters Institute Digital News Report, the majority of internet users go to established news

Figure 7. Main source of news by age
Source: Data from the Reuters Institute Digital News Report 2018.

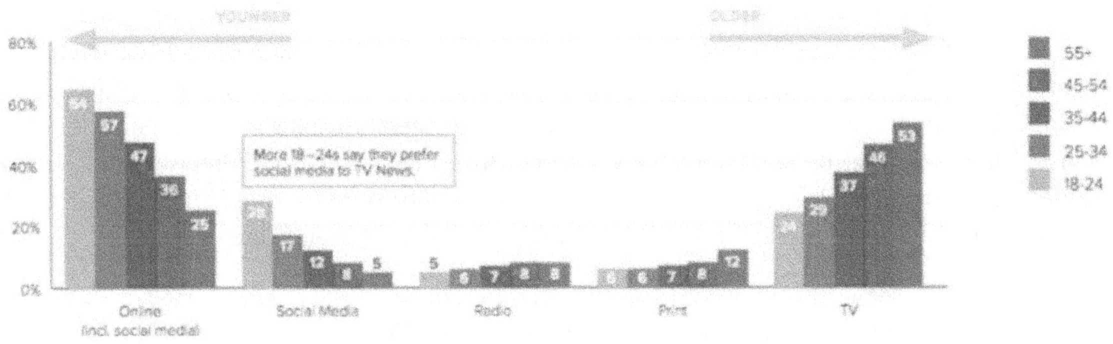

media organizations for online news, and more people go to newspaper brands and broadcaster brands than go to digital–born outlets like BuzzFeed, the Huffington Post, or various domestic online–only news sites. (See Figure 8.) The most successful media today have digital audiences far larger than what they have historically been able to attract to their legacy print or broadcast offerings. News organizations are clearly still not only key producers of news, but also important distributors of news, even as people also rely on aggregators, search engines, and social media.

Figure 8. Proportion that use each type of news brand online
Source: Data from the Reuters Institute Digital News Report 2018.

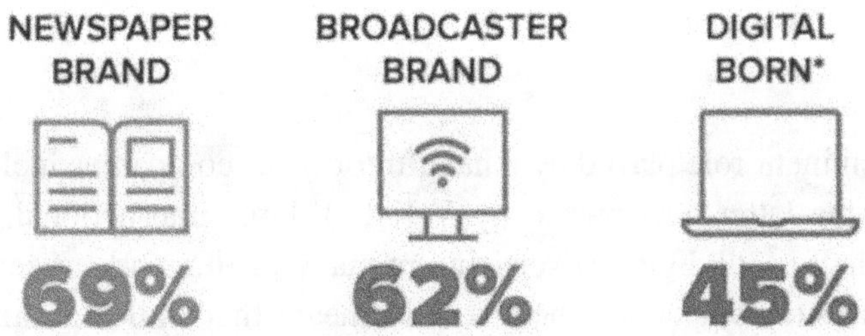

Audience reach, however, does not necessarily translate into a significant share of audience attention and by extension advertising and consumer sales. The developing digital media environment is in important ways dominated by a few large players who have developed very successful and popular products and services used frequently by large numbers of people. They in turn attract a large share of attention and advertising. The trend towards the concentration of audience attention around a few large players can be seen across both the internet and in the mobile/tablet app environment and can be illustrated with data from the United Kingdom.

Digital Advertising

In terms of advertising, news media face (1) fierce competition from large technology companies that provide high audience reach, data for highly targeted advertising, and low rates enabled by their economies of scale and capture the majority of digital advertising, as well as a very large number of other, less prominent websites where advertisers can advertise at very low prices enabled by advertising exchanges, (2) the move to a more mobile environment with less space for advertising and so far lower advertising rates and (3) the increasingly widespread use of ad–blockers. First, the central positions occupied by the most successful large technology companies is reflected not only in their large number of users, their increasingly important role in how people discover news, or their significant share of attention online. It is also reflected in their success when it comes to attracting digital advertising. Precise estimates vary, but some suggest that Google alone accounts for more than 30 percent of digital advertising globally, and Facebook more than 10 percent. Figure 9 provides an estimate of their share over time.

Figure 9. Estimated Global Digital Advertising Revenues 2008–2018
Sources: Ian Maude, Be Heard Group, data from Google, Facebook, and estimates from Enders Analysis.

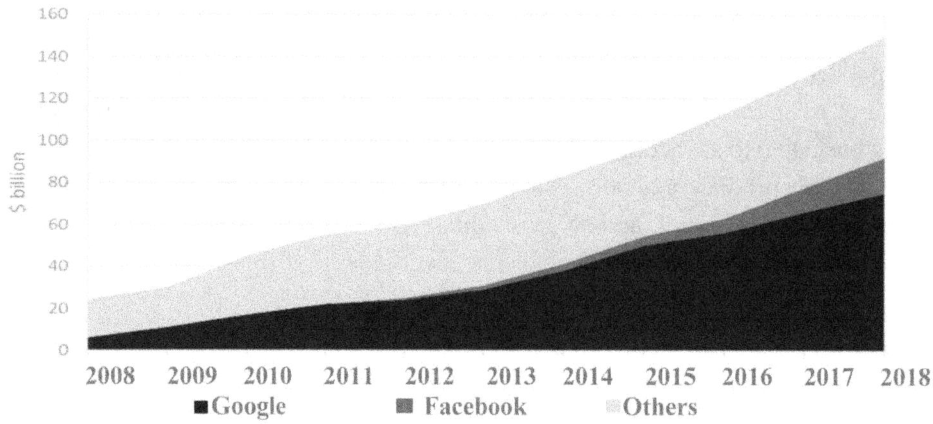

Considering the prominent role played by a handful of other companies including Amazon, Apple, Microsoft and Yahoo (the latter now owned by Verizon), large international technology companies account for more than half of all digital advertising in many media markets, leaving domestic content producers and other actors to compete for the rest. This means that while digital advertising is growing rapidly (as shown in Figure 3.3 above), much of it goes to a few very successful companies who do not invest in news production, even as they do enable news distribution (through distributed discovery) and increasingly news consumption (through distributed content). Second, the rapid move from a desktop internet to a mobile web is changing the business of digital news. Several media organizations already get a large majority of their traffic from mobile devices. But the mobile advertising market is particularly challenging because the space on the screen for ads is more limited, the rates are low, and technology companies are even more dominant than in desktop advertising. Audiences have also in many cases moved to mobile much faster than advertisers have, as illustrated by the variable advertising spend per mobile user observed across Europe seen in Figure 10. Mobile advertising will grow for years to come, but news organizations face tough competition for a share of these revenues.

Third, online news users frustrated by slow load times and intrusive advertising on many sites are increasingly installing and using ad–blocking software. Ad–blockers are popular across the world, but particularly so in some countries such as Poland and Greece (see Figure 11). Although it is a worry in

Figure 10. Mobile advertising expenditures per head, 2012–2016
Source: 2016 Ofcom International Communication Markets (figure in parenthesis last year on year growth).

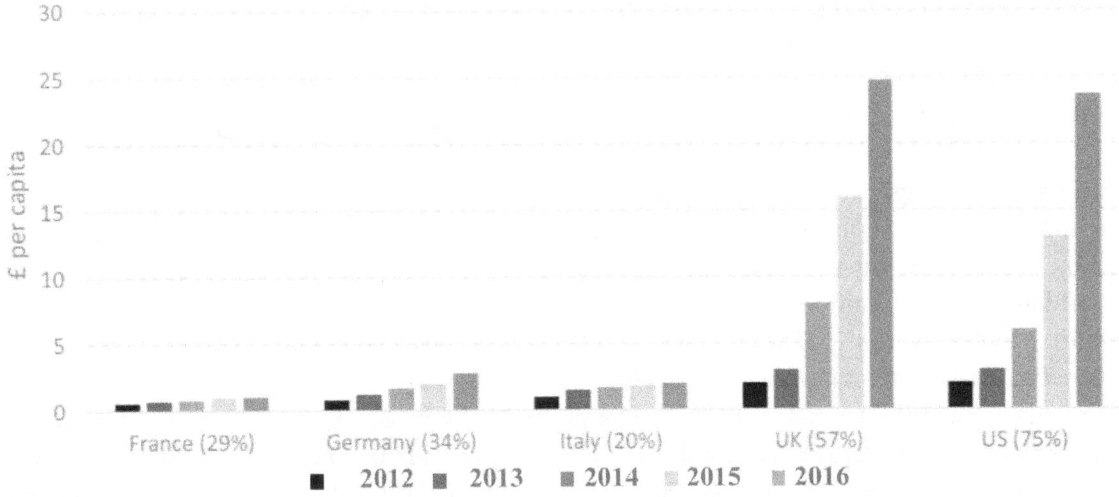

Figure 11. Use of Ad–blocking software across select markets
Source: Data from the Reuters Institute Digital News Report 2016.

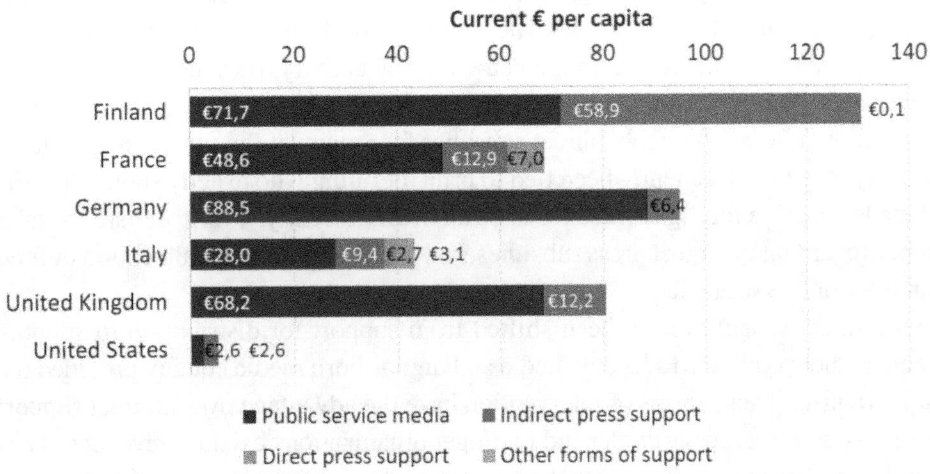

many news organizations, only a few have adopted concrete actions to combat it: The German tabloid Bild is one of the first European national bands to block all content on its website for users with an active ad–blocker.15 Fundamentally, ad–blocking is an industry built on audiences' response to a poor user experience resulting in large part from the advertising surrounding content that people otherwise value.

Despite the pressures on digital advertising, a significant number of news media still offer digital news free at the point of consumption, and base their business primarily on advertising. This is the strategy of a number of newspapers with very large online audiences (e.g. the British Mail Online, the Italian La Repubblica, and the Polish Fakt), most commercial broadcasters (Sky, RTL, Mediaset, etc.), as well as many digital– born news media (both international players like BuzzFeed and the Huffington Post and domestic players like Uusi Suomi in Finland and the Lad Bible in the UK). But it is clear that more and more publishers no longer believe that digital display advertising alone can support professional content production, and more and more, including both newspapers and digital–born news sites like MediaPart in France, are pursuing pay models instead.

Indirect and Direct Support for Private Sector Media

Indirect support for private sector media have historically primarily come in the form of VAT exemptions or other tax benefits normally targeted specifically at newspaper publishers, in some countries also other indirect forms of support including reduced rates for travel, postal and telephone services. Indirect support has provided significant support for private sector news media and researchers have suggested these arrangements have helped increase both news provision and news plurality. Indirect support through tax benefits today however faces a series of challenges. First, these benefits are normally tied to printed newspapers specifically and not available for digital media products. Changing this is difficult because it is easier to define who exactly are entitled to indirect support offline (newspapers with a defined proportion of general interest news that appear with a certain regularity) than who are entitled to indirect support if these schemes were moved online.

Second, the value of these benefits is directly tied to the revenues generated by the news organizations that benefit from them, and are thus cyclical rather than counter– cyclical forms of intervention—very valuable when revenues are high, less significant as revenues shrink. Finally, some countries have in addition provided direct subsidies to some or all newspapers to reduce distribution costs, increase circulation, and increase diversity. The exact arrangements vary by country, from general subsidies (available to all titles meeting certain minimum requirements) to targeted subsidies (available only to a minority of news organizations). As a policy tool, direct subsidies face many of the same issues as indirect subsidies—historically they have frequently been tied to print, defining who exactly should benefit if similar support was made available for digital media can be difficult. Recently, a vivid debate has taken place in Italy and France regarding the direct press subsidies, and there are calls for reallocation of funds towards media research for online strategies.

In Denmark, direct subsidies have been shifted from support for distribution to support for news production and are now available to legacy media and digital-born media equally provided they employ professional journalists. These forms of intervention have the advantage over indirect support that they unlike tax benefits do not necessarily depend on target organizations existing revenues. They have the disadvantage that direct support can create the perception or reality that news media organizations are dependent on public money and thus more vulnerable to government and political influence. No up-to-date estimates exist of the overall value of different forms of direct and indirect public support for media, but as policies in this area have generally change only incrementally, the 2008 figures reported in Figure 12 provides an indication of the relative composition in a range of different high income democracies, including both public funding for public service media, indirect support for private sector media, and direct support for private sector media.

Other possible forms of indirect or direct support for private sector include (1) legal changes to make it easier to operate non-profit news organizations and more attractive to support them and (2) public investments in incubators like Media Lab Bayern intended to enable innovation in digital journalism to benefit the wider media environment rather than individual existing companies.

Figure 12. Public support for media (2010)
Source: Nielsen and Linnebank (2011).

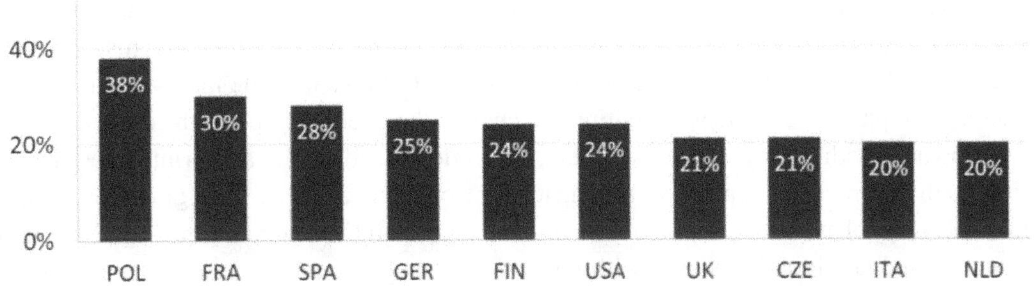

CONCLUSION

In this report, we have provided an overview of opportunities and challenges for news and media in an increasingly digital, mobile, and social media environment and reviewed responses from media and policymakers. Our overall analysis is that we are moving towards a media environment where most people have access to more and more news and information about many issues, in large part enabled by digital media and the products and services of large technology companies, but where many do not necessarily engage with this information (because they find other offers more relevant, interesting and valuable than news) and where the media industry that has historically produced most of this news is under significant pressure.

We have identified three underlying trends in how news and media in otherwise different high– and medium–income countries are evolving:

1. The move to an increasingly digital, mobile, and social media environment with increasingly intense competition for attention. This puts increasing pressure on legacy media like broadcasters and newspapers. These remain important news producers but are becoming relatively less important as distributors of news. As their existing operations decline or stagnate, the development of new, sustainable business models for digital news production become more urgent.
2. The growing importance of a limited number of large technology companies with billions of users across the world who play an increasingly important role in the distribution of news through services like search, social networking, video sharing, messaging and who capture a large share of attention and advertising by virtue of their attractive products.
3. The development of a high–choice media environment where internet users have access to more and more information, a range of increasingly sophisticated devices, and new forms of participation, and where people increasingly engage on the basis of interest—those most interested in news embrace these new opportunities to get, share, and comment on news, but a larger number of people opt for more casual and passive forms of use.

These developments mean that Internet users will have access to more and more information from more and more sources even as the media environment they navigate is increasingly dominated by a limited number of very large players and see consolidation and cost-cutting elsewhere in the media landscape which can over time reduce media pluralism by undermining the diversity of original, professional news production. All of these three developments are underway across otherwise different countries and all three of them are likely to continue for two reasons. First, digital 35 technologies continue to develop at a rapid pace, with industry observers predicting further disruptions of existing media industries if digital technologies like virtual reality, messaging apps empowered by artificial intelligence/machine learning, and new user interfaces across a more distributed internet–of–things become mainstream.

30 Second, the passing of time will continue to change the overall shape of the audience as people who have grown up with legacy media like linear, scheduled broadcasting and printed newspapers and use digital media more as a supplement than instead of older media forms are gradually replaced by new generations who have grown up native to a more digital and on–demand media environment accessed via personal and mobile devices with few reasons to seek out broadcast and print media. The implications for news production and distribution depend on the details of these general developments in media technology and media markets and how they vary from country to country, and in particular on how audiences and the business of media evolve. But they also depend on media policy makers and whether they identify and implement policies to enable the kind of free and diverse news media capable of keeping people informed, holding powerful actors to account, and enabling public discussion of public affairs that a well–functioning democracy depends on. This concerns basic issues like protecting professional journalists and individual citizens alike from censorship, intimidation, and legal harassment that are real issues in many countries but beyond the scope of this report. It also highlights the importance of revisiting twentieth century media policies to ensure they are fit for a twenty–first century media environment and strike the right balance between the interests of media organizations, technology companies, and media users.

REFERENCES

Benson, R., & Powers, M. (2011). *Public media and political independence. Lessons for the Future of Journalism from Around the World.* http://newstv.mediasapiens.ua/sites/mediaosvita.com.ua/files/mariastv/public– media–and–political–independence_4.pdf

Brüggemann, M., Humprecht, E., Nielsen, R. K., Karppinen, K., Cornia, A., & Esser, F. (2015). Framing the Newspaper Crisis. *Journalism Studies, 17*(5), 533–551. doi:10.1080/1461670X.2015.1006871

Bruno, N., & Nielsen, R. K. (2012). *Oxford: Reuters Institute for the Study of Journalism.* http://reutersinstitute.politics.ox.ac.uk/sites/default/files/Survival%20is%20Success%20Journalistic%20Online%20Start-Ups%20in%20Western%20Europe_0.pdf

Chang, L. D. M., Ling Tam, A. Y., & Suki, N. M. (2016). Moderating effect of races towards consumers' feeling of TCM usage. Handbook of Research on Leveraging Consumer Psychology for Effective Customer Engagement, 306-323.

Cornia, A., Sehl, A., & Nielsen, R. K. (2016). *Private Sector Media and Digital News.* http://reutersinstitute.politics.ox.ac.uk/sites/default/files/Cornia%20- %20Private%20Sector%20Media%20and%20Digital%20News%20FINAL.pdf

EAO. (2016). *Yearbook 2015: Television, VOD, Cinema and Video in 39 European States: Markets and Players, Services and Usage.* Strasbourg: European Audiovisual Observatory.

EAO. (2010-2014). Yearbook 2010-2014: Television, Cinema, Video and On-Demand Audiovisual Services – the Pan-European Picture. Strasbourg: European Audiovisual Observatory.

EBU (European Broadcasting Union). (2013). *Viewpoint: Media Freedom and Pluralism*. http://www3.ebu.ch/files/live/sites/ebu/files/Publications/ebuviewpoint-MediaFreedom_eN.pdf

Herzog, C., & Kari, K. (2014). Policy Streams and Public Service Media Funding Reforms in Germany and Finland. *European Journal of Communication*, *29*(4), 416–432. doi:10.1177/0267323114530581

Ibarra, A., Karen, E. N., & Kuhn, R. (Eds.). (2015). *Public Service Media in Europe: A Comparative Approach*. London: Routledge. doi:10.4324/9781315722290

Mediatique. (2012). *The provision of news in the UK*. Author.

Meeker, M. (2016). *Internet Trends 2016*. http://www.kpcb.com/internet–trends

Napoli, P. (2015). *Assessing the Health of Local Journalism Ecosystems: A Comparative Analysis of Three New Jersey Communities*. Prepared for the Democracy Fund, the Geraldine R. Dodge Foundation, and the John S. and James L. Knight Foundation. http://wp.comminfo.rutgers.edu/mpii-new/wpcontent/uploads/sites/129/2015/06/Assessing-Local-Journalism_Final-Draft6.23.15.pdf

Nathan, R. J., Fook Chiun, D. C., & Suki, N. M. (2016). An online marketing strategies assessment for companies in airlines and entertainment industries in Malaysia. Handbook of Research on Leveraging Consumer Psychology for Effective Customer Engagement, 1-15.

Newman, N. (2016). *Media, Journalism and Technology Predictions 2016*. Oxford: Reuters Institute for the Study of Journalism. http://digitalnewsreport.org/publications/2016/predictions-2016/

Suki, N. M. (2016). *Handbook of Research on Leveraging Consumer Psychology for Effective Customer Engagement*. https://www.igi-global.com/book/handbook-research-leveraging-consumer-psychology/149284

Chapter 4
Conspicuous Consumption via Social Media

Lee Kar Wai
Universiti Putra Malaysia, Malaysia

Syuhaily Osman
Universiti Putra Malaysia, Malaysia

ABSTRACT

Conspicuous consumption has been explored since 19th century, focusing on its conceptual or mathematical modelling. It has gained widespread attention in the Western culture as compared to East. However, the increased performance of luxury market and strong demand for luxury goods in developing countries urged investigation on the spread of this consumption pattern. This chapter examines conspicuous consumption in Malaysia via social media usage. A research was carried out involving 387 respondents in Klang Valley, Malaysia. The results suggest Malaysian are moderately materialistic and propend to conspicuous consumption. Through the exposure to social media, consumers are being situated in comparison with other social media users and inclined to learn and pick up the consumption styles that are being exposed to. Thus, high level of social media usage can lead to high inclination in consuming conspicuously.

INTRODUCTION

The worldwide luxury market has continued to shine in recent years. The Luxury Goods Worldwide Market Study, Fall–Winter 2018 conducted by Bain and Company found that the luxury market had shown positive performance across the industry and grew about 5%, an estimation of €1.2 trillion globally. As the emerging luxury market, 70% of consumers in China, Russia, and United Arab Emirates had reported an increase in their spending on luxury purchases (Deloitte, 2017). Consumers in developing countries such as Asian countries are now more exposed to prestige and luxury goods as well (Wan-Ismail, Zakaria, & Abdul-Talib, 2016). Indeed, Malaysians are increasingly brand conscious throughout the years (Bagheri, 2014). Luxury market has also shown increasing growth due to the important contribution

DOI: 10.4018/978-1-7998-3042-9.ch004

of the youth (Giovannini, Xu, & Thomas, 2015), particularly consumers from Generation Y has shown more interest in international brands (Tee, Gharleghi, & Chan, 2013).

There are analyses of globalism mentioned that consumer culture is spreading from the West to different parts of the world, where consumers from developing countries started to prefer luxury brands as similar to those Westerns (Ger & Belk, 1996). Social media can be a major contributor to this effect due its availability of variety data and information from the mass media, international tourism, and multinational marketing (Durvasula, Lysonski, & Watson, 2015; Zhou & Belk, 2004).

Moreover, according to statistic from Multimedia and Communications Ministry in 2017, Malaysia has a 117.3% of household broadband penetration and 98% out of the 24.5 million active internet are using social media. Assessing social media has become a daily routine for people where Malaysians spend up to three hours daily to access the internet on their mobile phones, and up to three and a half hours on social media. Through all the time spending on social media, users get to know and learn about new brands and luxury goods are not exceptional. According to The Star, 94% of Malaysians discover products and brands on Facebook and 62% of them make a purchase after the discovery (Lee, 2016). Supporting that, a study of Hajli (2014) had proved that social media can influence consumers purchase decisions; and high intensity of assessing to social media can also have direct influence on conspicuous consumption (Thoumrungjore, 2014).

Previous studies revealed the connection between consumers' attributes and conspicuous consumption, particularly social visibility, materialism, self-esteem, individualism, and desire for uniqueness (Chaudhuri et al., 2011). Among the values of luxury consumers, materialism is the crucial one (e.g., Fournier and Richins, 1991). According to Kasser (2003), it is characterized as the propensity to ascribe noteworthy significance to material belongings and eminence. Hence, individuals, who are highly materialistic, are bound to display high social status through the purchase of luxury goods (Fournier and Richins, 1991; Wang and Wallendorf, 2006). Specifically, materialism enhances interest in luxury brands (Gil, Kwon, Good, & Johnson, 2012) and a preference for luxury goods (Prendergast & Wong, 2003; Wong & Ahuvia, 1998). However, it was revealed that desires which driven by acquisition of money and possessions frequently prompt to problematic consequences as the association between endorsement of materialism and well-being very often were inverted (Dittmar, Bond, Hurst, & Kasser, 2014; Twenge et al., 2010).

Consumers in the Western countries seek brands that make them comfortable with; however, for consumers in Asian countries, the most elevated need in brands is with respect to status seeking. These attitude, value and practices encompassing conspicuous consumption are especially crucial to investigate because they are originally viewed as western ideals and have started to be a norm in East Asian due to the globalization (Podoshen, Li, & Zhang, 2011).

Conspicuous Consumption

Conspicuous consumption was originally coined by American economist Thorstein Veblen (1889) in his book, "The Theory of the Leisure Class", indicating wealthy people obtain products and services with the purpose to show monetary power as the motivations behind achieving or keeping up social status (Veblen, 1899). Likewise, Veblen goods are defined as luxury goods for which the quantity demanded increases as the price increases which against the law of demand. Initially, these concepts were heavily linked with the upper classes of society, whom are affordable to spend their disposable income on goods and services that are not based on the functionality; instead, on how luxury the product is in order to display wealth and gain higher social status.

The economics studies on conspicuous consumption remained consistent since the commence of Veblen's theory. Traditionally, this kind of demonstration-oriented consumption has connected with the display of status and wealth. Although the focus had been more on durables purchases, immaterial purchases are claimed to also demonstrate status (Chen, Yeh & Wang, 2008). For example, it can reveal different implications, including ethnicity, age, sexuality, hobbies, individual qualities, signalling of value, and other types of personality (Blumer, 1969; Davis, 1992).

Besides facilitating the understanding on the issue, these economic studies also recommended the policy makers to intervene conspicuous consumption with policy measures. For instance, the progressive consumption taxes, which penalize high levels of consumption, or the luxury taxes, which penalize specific status-conferring consumption such as purchases of high-end cars or boats (Becker, Murphy, and Werning 2005; Frank 1985b). Nonetheless, these measures have not been effective intervention due to three important points. Firstly, these measures were seek to increase equality in income and serve as part of the redistribution of wealth mechanism, yet there are limited evidence on the effectiveness of increasing equality in increase savings and reduce consumption (Ordabayeva & Chandon, 2010). Secondly, these measures neglected the conspicuous consumption among the lower classes, those who are most severely impact if they overspend (Trigg, 2001; Wan-Ismail, Zakaria, & Abdul-Talib, 2016). Thirdly, the economic studies tend to take a macro perspective and neglect individual consumers and their proclivity toward conspicuous consumptions.

In the context of Malaysia, the sector of luxurious goods in Malaysia has been developing alongside with countries around the world in the course of the years (Run, Butt & Nee, 2010), consumers are also more aware about the brands they are buying from, especially with the young generation. The young generation are more preferring luxury brands and products particularly undergraduates and young adults in the workforce (Kamaruddin & Mokhlis, 2003), limited attention has been devoted on the issue of conspicuous consumption. Mat et al. (2016) employed purposive sampling and mall-intercept survey at high-class shopping malls located in Kuala Lumpur, to investigate the luxury consumption of 400 luxury fashion consumers. The researchers define conspicuous consumption behaviour as luxury consumption behaviour; and reported that attitude, brand image, patron status, role model – celebrities, and quality found to be statistically significant in influencing conspicuous consumption behaviour. The findings showed that attitude is the most influential factor that predicts the assumption of luxury fashion products.

The phenomenon where a higher portion of expenditure was not spent on basic needs but on luxuries is seen in households with higher income levels. However, observations made in recent years over conspicuous consumption highlighted that in developing countries, lower class groups were also suggested in further studies to adapt with conspicuous consumption (Hamilton & Catterall, 2005; Trigg, 2001; Wan-Ismail et al., 2016). The overconsumption and preference towards luxury products had led to overspending and poorer financial management actions such as high level of personal debt and credit card debt, which describes a large group of Malaysian Consumers (Kapeller & Schütz, 2015; Sandhu & Paim, 2015). As indicated by the report from The Malaysian Reserved, thousands of Malaysians had been pulled into bankruptcy due to excessive personal loan and credit card usage (Hani, 2019). For many of those who are married, this situation is causing financial pressure to their families. As shown by the statistics from the Malaysian Department of Insolvency, the main reasons that lead to bankruptcy include personal loans (27.76%), hire purchase (24.73%), housing loans (14.09%), as well as credit cards debt (9.91%).

In the current age digital, social media has transform the ways users interacts and lives. It has become a platform where users share various elements of life including stories, experiences, activities and consumptions to friends and followers in social media (Yenicioglu & Christodoulides, 2014). While on the other hand, it also become a battlefield for corporations and brands to market products and engages consumers (Ashley & Tuten, 2015). These idealized personality and lifestyles advertised in social media can cause pressure on consumers to purchase conspicuous goods base on image and price instead of functionality (Escobar, 2016).The traditional conspicuous consumption theory has clearly changed along with the globalization and the advent of social media (Yenicioglu & Christodoulides, 2014). Nonetheless, there is a dearth of research on investigating social media usage in conjunction with conspicuous consumption. Further, Wilcox and Stephen (2012) had recommended future studies on the consumer to look into the effect of social media towards customers' choices to purchase luxuriously. These findings indubitably urge for further investigation on the issue.

Although past studies have attempted to examine the influence of social media to consumer behaviour such as decision making, purchase intention and buying behaviour (Goh, Heng, & Lin, 2013; Hajli, 2014; Wang, Yu, &Wei, 2012), a comprehensive model illustrates influence of social media usage to the conspicuous consumption is not prevalent. Due to the shifting of attitudes towards the display of wealth and the wide spreading of luxury products (and information about them) (Atsmon, Dixit, & Wu, 2011), this study adopted conspicuous consumption as the main discussion focus in order to gain more understanding upon linking social media usage and conspicuous consumption. Indeed, more research that delve into aspect of consumer behavior and psychology in the digital economy is deemed necessary (Ling Chang, Ling Tam, & Suki, 2016; Nathan, Fook Chiun, & Suki, 2016; Suki, 2016).

Materialism

Materialism is an aspect related to consumption that has gained widespread attention. In theory, the word "materialism" is alludes to the philosophical conceptualization that nothing exists aside from matter and its movement (Scott, 2009). According to Lange (1873-75), materialism is then noticed as a belief in "material, self-existent things." Today, in like manner use, materialism is related with an inclination to consider material belonging and physical solace as more essential than spiritual qualities. Materialism is a complex, multi-faceted marvel (Larsen, Sirgy, & Wright, 1999), broadly studied by researchers from different fields, for example advertising, anthropology, consumer behavior and marketing, economics, psychology, political science, and social sciences (Mannion & Caolan, 1995).

Two types of materialism that are most widely known are personality materialism and value materialism (Ahuvia & Wong, 2002; Srikant, 2013; Kasser et al., 2004). Belk (1984; 1985) has conceptualized materialism as a personality trait composed of possessiveness, non-generosity, envy, and preservation (Ger & Belk, 1996) which also known as personality materialism. These constructs are selected and defined as a general trait rather than an attitude towards only a particular target person and possession. In the Richins and Dawson's (1992) conception (value materialism), materialism refers to an instrumental or terminal value (Rokeach, 1973). Although both Richin and Dawson's measure (1992) and Belk's measure (1985) share some adapted items in common, Richins and Dawson's (1992) measure interprets materialism differently. According to them, materialism is an enduring belief in the desirability of acquiring and possessing things. Operationally, the Richins and Dawson's scale (1992) comprised three dimensions: acquisition centrality, the role of acquisition in happiness, and the role of possessions in defining success.

Materialism has been associated with various consumer behaviours including social consumption motivation (Fitzmaurice & Comegys, 2006), compulsive buying (Rindfleisch, Burroughs & Denton, 1997; Roberts, Manolis & Tanner, 2003), brand perception (Kamineni, 2005), attitude towards advertising

(Yoon, 1995), self-doubt and insecurity (Chang & Arkin, 2002), social influence conformity (Schroeder & Dugal, 1995), and self-esteem contingent on praise (Deci & Ryan, 1995). Although there are two different understanding of materialism as mentioned, they both implied a consistency in the popular belief that materialistic person likes to display luxury goods (Wong, 1997). Conspicuous consumption is one of the behaviour that is most frequently related to materialism, in which the satisfaction from using a product is not derived from the functionality of it; instead, the audience reaction. Richin (1994) stated that people who are materialistic prone to value things that can be shown in public more. In addition, they often feel more satisfaction in showing the products than actually using them. Based upon such indications, it is believed that individual high in materialism may incline to purchase conspicuously.

In addition, the influence of social media usage towards materialism was proven to be significant (Kamal, Chu, & Pedram, 2013). A more current study found that highly materialistic consumer tend to pay more attention to what is displayed as luxurious and branded (Audrin, Brosch, Sander & Chanal, 2018). In addition, it is worth to highlight that the more a materialistic consumer is exposed to luxuries and branded, the more it will lead to luxury purchases. Thus, being highly exposed to social media will not only provides consumers with more frequent exposure to luxuries, it will also affect the consumer intention to consumption conspicuously.

Social Media Usage

Social media is web-based service that allows users to interact, collaborate, and communicate through the creation, modification, and sharing of content (McCay-Peet & Quan-Haase, 2017). There are a variety of purpose for the usage of social media, such as entertainment, social interaction, personal identity, information, and empowerment (Muntinga, Moorman, & Smit 2011).

Prior study has proposed that consumers' traditional media consumption can affect their materialism level (Ger & Belk 1999; Goldberg & Gorn 1978) because the media caters consumers with values and norms which acted as factors towards consumption. Previously, researches that suggested the connection between media usage and materialism are generally domain in television consumption and print advertising (Churchill & Moschis 1979; Lens, Pandelaere, & Warlop 2010; Richins, 1987). Past studies revealed that television viewership can influence viewers' materialism in the East and in the West (Chu, Windels, & Kamal, 2016). The existence of this relationship is explained by Richins (1987) partly because of the advertisements found in TV. However, this relationship between TV consumption and materialism is significant only when the commercials are guesstimated as realistic and authentic by individuals. Due to the fact that materialistic person will compare more between their standards of living and others'; in which media consumption provides sources for that (Schiffman & Kanuk, 2004).

Although the consumption of television and printing media is decreasing throughout the years, materialism and conspicuous consumptions remain on the rise (Lim et al., 2014). This may due to the advancements in the usage of social media. Social media settings enable social interactions between consumers, as well as enable consumers to openly display their lifestyle. This platform appears to provide a setting that enhances social comparison behaviour (Vogel, Rose, Roberts, & Eckles, 2014) whereby social media support consumers by having an access data to friends.

In particular, Facebook is a setting that encourages social comparison behaviour with the accompanying reasons. First, when social media, one can freely see data about how others are doing. Rich data about others' livestyle can be a worthwhile resource for individuals who search out comparison targets for self-assessment. Second, given that most Facebook friends tend to have identical background,

comparison targets sought on Facebook will probably have similar characteristics than those sought in different settings (Hargittai, 2007). Besides, social media makes it simpler for user to interface with both weak and strong ties (strength of users' relationship closeness to their friends on the network), data stream inside any given social network usually relies on the strength of those ties (Frenzen & Nakamoto 1993). Thus, on the off chance that one frequently utilizes Facebook, she or he will probably to encounter comparison targets and has chances to do comparison with those targets. At that point, it is normal that, as one's usage intensity is high, she or he will probably involve in social comparison activities (Jang, Park & Song, 2016), regardless of the culture (Chu, Windels, & Kamal, 2016). According to Ozimek and Förster (2017), people who score high in materialism are using social media especially Facebook to satisfy their need to do comparison with others. Rest on that finding, higher Facebook use is said to be triggered by materialistic comparison condition than the non-materialistic comparison condition.

Moreover, increasingly more luxury brands have turned towards marketing communication in social media (Kim & Ko, 2012) such as Facebook, Twitter, YouTube, and Instagram (Schwedt, Chevalier, & Gutsatz, 2012). Prior researches stated that social media marketing is a promising promotional strategy in marketing luxury brands as well (Kim & Ko, 2012; Phan, Thomas, & Heine, 2011; Schwedt et al., 2012). Besides influence from marketers, individuals now can be influenced not only by their close family and friends, they can be influenced by public figure such as bloggers, influencer in social media, and celebrities. All of these are due to the available of access to view and intimate idealized personality and lifestyles of others in social media (Escobar, 2016). Hence, it was reasonable to suggest that these exposures in social media, the idealized media pictures of riches in social media will strengthen and fuel the drive to get a greater amount of the wanted products and leads to increasing motivation of acquisition of luxurious products to show status which is conspicuous consumption.

The Study

Due to the scenario discussed above and based on the previous research findings as well, the following section of this chapter will discuss about the research undertook to examine such issues in Malaysian context. Particularly, this research is conducted to have a clearer view about to what extent that the conspicuous consumption can be related to social media. The research involved 387 respondents who were selected from shopping malls in Klang Valley, Malaysia through systematic sampling method. The research data was collected through the use of self-administrated questionnaire which contained the items questioning about the respondents social media usage and also the perception towards their conspicuous consumption.

Background of Respondents

In the demographic profile section, gender, age, ethnic, marital status, monthly income, and education level were examined. The summary of respondents' demographic data is presented in percentage form as shown in Figure 1.

The gender distribution of the respondents consisted of 41.9% male and 58.1% female. For age distribution, the respondents were consisted of 39.1% aged less than 25, followed by 37.4% aged more than 30, and 23.5% aged between 26 and 30. In term of the ethnic distribution, slightly more than half of the respondents (51.9%) were Chinese, followed by Malay (38.3%), Indian (9.3%), and lastly other ethnicity (0.5%). The reported ethnic ration found to be different from the actual ethnic ration in Malaysia. This

Figure 1. Demographic background of the respondents

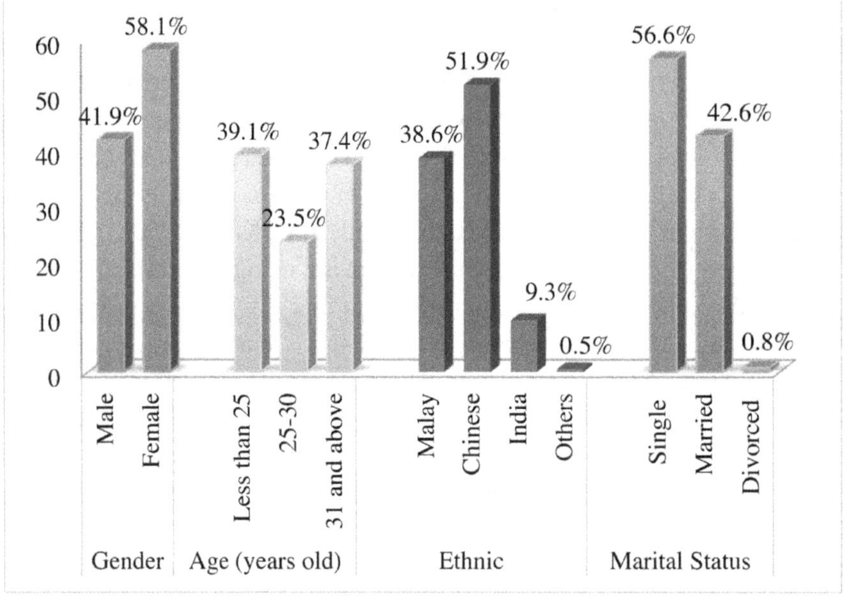

might due to the tendency of luxury products to be more well-liked by Chinese than other ethnics (Mat et al., 2016). Data on marital status of the respondents showed that the highest number respondents are married (42.6%), and the rest are single (56.6%) and divorced (0.8%).

With respect to socio economic background (Figures 2 and 3), only two variables were asked from respondents, i.e., monthly income and highest education level. The data for monthly income shows that

Figure 2. Respondents' monthly income

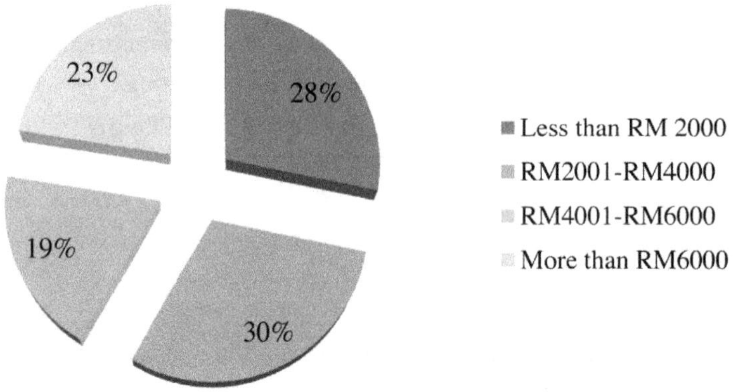

the largest income group comprised of income ranging from RM2001 to RM4000 (30.2%), followed by the group whom income less than RM2000 (28.2%). For those with income ranging from RM4001 to RM6000 and above RM6000 are accounted for 19.1% and 22.5% respectively.

Figure 3. Respondents' highest education level

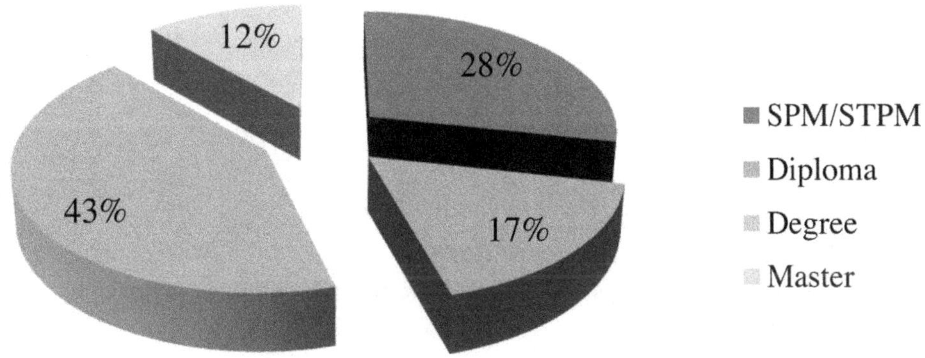

Meanwhile, in term of highest education level, largest proportion of respondent (41.3%) is degree holders, followed by SPM/STPM holders (27.6%). Others are diploma (16.8%) and master (11.4%) holders. PhD took the smallest proportion of respondent which occupied only 2.9% of total. This shows that most of the respondents had tertiary education level.

According to the Internet Users Survey 2017 done by Malaysian Communications and Multimedia Commission, more than half of the social media users in Malaysia are young adults aged below 35, who had at least secondary/post-secondary education or above with monthly above RM1000. Comparing to this statistics of the Internet user general demographic distribution in Malaysia, the social media users in this survey showed consistency where half of the social media users in current survey were consisted of young adults aged below 30 who most of them possess at least a tertiary certificate with monthly income ranged between RM2001 and RM4000.

Social Media Usage

The assessment of social media usage is consisted of two parts, usage pattern and absorption. Social media usage pattern includes self-reported assessments of social media behaviour, designed to measure the extent to which the respondents were actively engaged in social media activities, while absorption is referred to the extent of an individual's attention focuses in accessing social media.

Figure 4 shows that in terms of frequency, more than half of the respondents (59.4%) will access the social media as frequent as more than 5 times in a day. Only as little as 9.6% of the respondents access the social media less than 3 times a day. This shows that, social media site users are regular visitors where accessing the social media have become a daily routine. Aside from the daily usage frequency, in order to find out the exact amount of time consumers spent on social media, respondents were asked about how many hours they spent on using social media in a day. It was found that about 35.1% of the respondents spend less than 2 hours surfing on social media sites. Besides that, near to half of the respondents (47.0%) spend about 2 to 4 hours on using social media daily. Since half of the respondents are accessing the social media frequently, this pattern is considered sensible as according to Achariam (2015), Malaysians spend about 3 hours and 27 minutes on social media.

Furthermore, among the three social media sites listed (Facebook, Twitter, and Instagram), Facebook is the most used social media site, followed by Instagram. About 69.6% of the respondents primarily use

Figure 4. Social media usage pattern

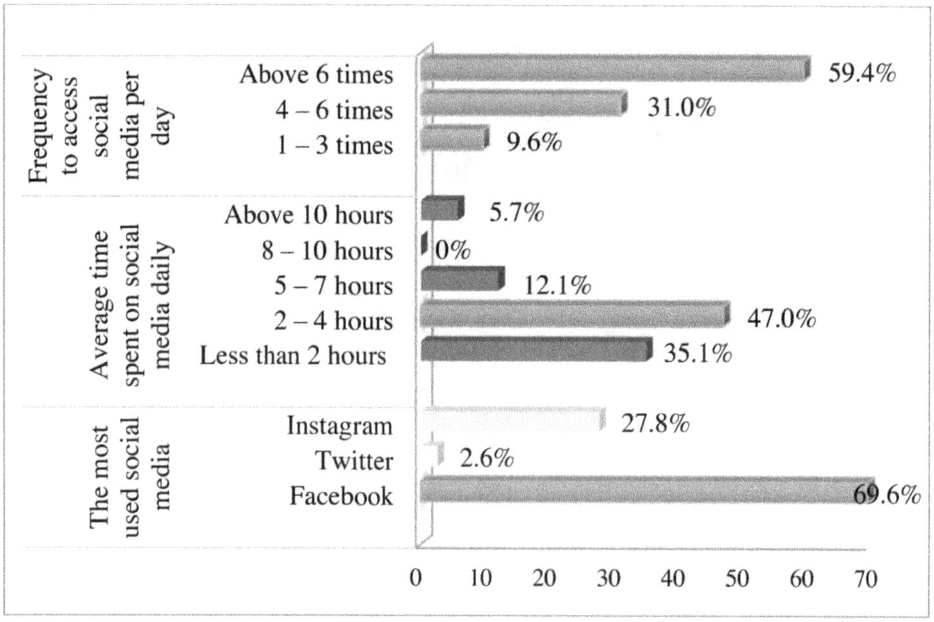

Facebook the most, and only as little as 1.6% of the respondents do not own a Facebook account. According to the report of Malaysia Internet Users Survey 2017 done by Malaysian Communications and Multimedia Commission, the highest percentage of Internet users owned a Facebook account (97.3%), followed by Instagram (56.1%) in year 2016. The result for current study which showed Facebook as the most used social media site, followed by Instagram is seen to show similarity as reported in the Internet Survey 2017.

In addition, with the purpose to find out the audience consumers own in the social media environment, respondents were asked about the amount to friends and followers they have for each social media site (Figure 5). More friends and followers in social media means more audiences are able to view the content a user delivered through the form of news feed. The result showed that more than half of the respondents (59.5%) own less than 1000 Facebook friends, followed by 1001 to 2000 Facebook friends (32.3%), and 6.2% of the respondents own more than 2000 Facebook friends. This indicates that Facebook provided the most opportunities not only for the users to view but also deliver contents in the news feed.

As for the second most used social media site, Instagram is reported as the second most used social media site (27.8%). Result shows that 17.6% of the respondents not owning an Instagram account and more than half of the respondents (65.6%) have less than 500 Instagram followers. Although Twitter is listed as one of the most used social networking site for Malaysian and the ownership of Twitter has saw an increased as reported in Internet Users Survey 2017, Twitter is reported as the least used social media site (2.6%), and more than three quarter of the respondents (77.5%) do not own a Twitter account.

Overall, most of respondents own more than one social media user account. Social media is highly accessed by consumers with frequency up to 5 times a day. Lastly, the result enclosed that, the respondents owned biggest audience group in the platform of Facebook site, which it is seem acceptable since most of respondents were primarily using Facebook as the main social media site.

Figure 5. Number of friends/followers

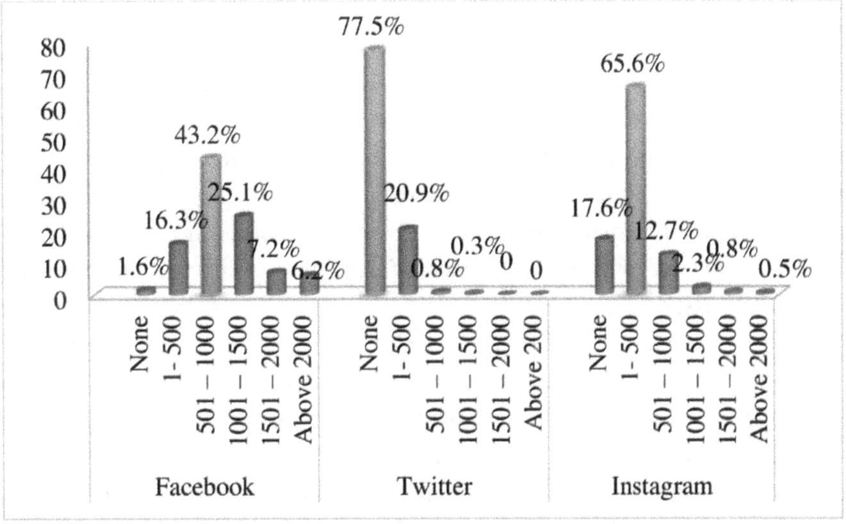

Based on the data shown in Table 1 about the absorption towards social media usage as perceived by the respondents, it was found that more than half of the social media users (67.5%) enjoy spending time on using social media. A total of 41.6% of them reported that social media can help to forget about daily problems. However, they will not get too involved in using social media until they forget about everything else outside the social media world (49.6%). Besides that, near to half of the users (49.4%) also remain neutral for the idea that they care a lot about using social media. Looking from these results, respondents were genuinely enjoying their time when using social media. However, as much as the respondents feel involved in using social media, they are not completely absorbed to the extent that they will forget everything else.

Table 1. Absorption towards social media usage

No.	Statement	Total Frequency/ (%)				
		1	2	3	4	5
1.	I genuinely enjoy the time spending on the social media.	4 (1.0)	10 (2.6)	112 (28.9)	188 (48.6)	73 (18.9)
2.	I feel that the social media helps me forget about daily problems.	25 (6.5)	57 (14.7)	144 (37.2)	119 (30.7)	42 (10.9)
3.	I feel totally absorbed while I am using the social media.	12 (3.1)	68 (17.6)	156 (40.3)	117 (30.2)	34 (8.8)
4.	I get so involved while using the social media that I forget everything else.	65 (16.8)	127 (32.8)	107 (27.6)	76 (19.6)	12 (3.1)
5.	I couldn't care less about using social media.	8 (2.1)	79 (20.4)	191 (49.4)	98 (25.3)	11 (2.8)

Materialism

In determining materialism of consumers, results showed more than half of the respondents (69.2%) tried to minimise possessions in order to keep their life simple. It was also enclosed that less than a quarter of respondents (22.7%) were likely to own many luxury possessions. This indicated that respondents are less prone to treat material possession as the central of living. However, only as low as 23.8% and 23.0% of respondents opposed the idea that they admired people with expensive belongings, and material possessions are important achievements in life respectively. Therefore, it is reasonable to say that there is still a considerable amount of respondents possessed neutral to positive opinion towards the idea that possession can show success.

Furthermore, the results also showed more that more than half of the respondents (65.2%) would be happier if they could own nicer things and afford to buy more things. In addition, only low amount of respondents (19.3%) felt okay for not being able to buy all the things that they like. This result also signified that respondents were treating possessions as the lead to happiness.

Figure 6 showed the percentage of respondents falling in different category of materialism, namely low, moderate and high. The border score for each category is 11-25 (low), 26-40 (moderate), 41-55 (high). Majority of the respondents are moderately materialistic (85.0%). Only as little as 8.3% and 6.7% of the respondents are high and low in materialism respectively. This result indicates that consumers showed moderate level of materialism. Comparing this result to the result of past studies done (Kamal, Chu, & Pedram, 2013; Podoshen, Li, & Zhang, 2011), it is found that consumers in recent years are consistent compared to previous year which was also moderate for both Asian and American sample. These indicate that the respondents now are not highly inclined to show materialism as according to the frequency distribution, although respondents believed success is judged by the things people own and acquiring more possessions can lead to happiness, they did not treat material belongings as central of living.

Figure 6. Category of materialism

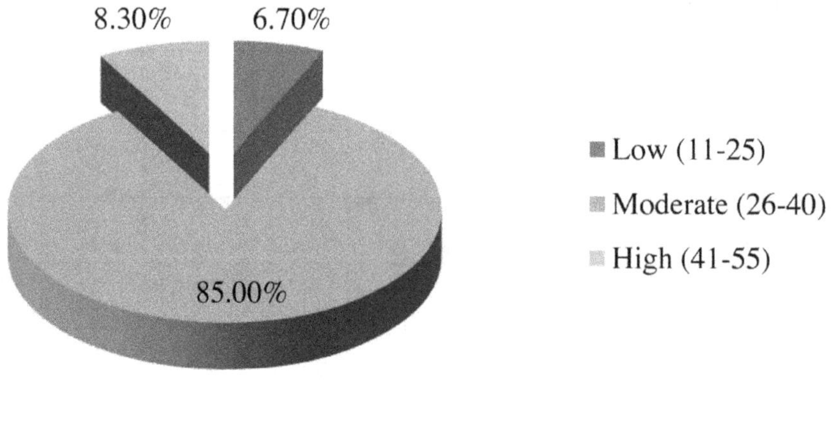

Table 2. Materialism

No.	Statement	Total Frequency/ (%)				
		1	2	3	4	5
	Acquisition of Centrality					
2.	I try to keep my life simple without having many material possessions.	3 (0.8)	27 (7.0)	89 (23.0)	199 (51.4)	69 (17.8)
5.	Buying things gives me a lot of pleasure.	20 (5.2)	75 (19.4)	145 (37.5)	122 (31.5)	25 (6.5)
6.	I like a lot of luxury in my life.	53 (13.7)	119 (30.7)	127 (32.8)	67 (17.3)	21 (5.4)
	Success					
8.	I admire people who own expensive cars, homes, and clothes.	29 (7.5)	63 (16.3)	124 (32.0)	128 (33.1)	43 (11.1)
9.	I think some of the more important achievements in life include buying material possessions.	24 (6.2)	65 (16.8)	149 (38.5)	127 (32.8)	22 (5.7)
11.	The things I own say a lot about how I am doing in life.	11 (2.8)	73 (18.9)	159 (41.1)	132 (34.1)	12 (3.1)
12.	I like to own things that impress people.	27 (7.0)	98 (25.3)	153 (39.5)	98 (25.3)	11 (2.8)
13.	I do not pay much attention to the material objects other people own.	11 (2.8)	57 (14.7)	162 (41.9)	130 (33.6)	27 (7.0)
	Happiness					
15.	My life could be better if I could buy certain things I do not currently own.	12 (3.1)	65 (16.8)	156 (40.3)	132 (34.1)	22 (5.7)
17.	I would be happier if I could afford to buy more things.	5 (1.3)	20 (5.2)	110 (28.4)	198 (51.2)	54 (14.0)
18.	It sometimes irritates me that I cannot afford to buy all the things I like.	11 (2.8)	64 (16.5)	162 (41.9)	130 (33.6)	20 (5.2)

Perception Towards Conspicuous Consumption

In the section designed to determine the consumer perception towards conspicuous consumption, all of the items showed more negative responses as compared to positive. Based on data shown in Table 2, near to three quarter of the respondents (73.9%) opposed that their purchases are for the purpose to show their wealth. Besides that, respondents opposed frequent purchases of top-of-the-line products (67.7%).

In addition, slightly more than half of the responses dissented about wanting to be different by choosing product with exotic design (58.9%), wanting to show sophistication (54.5%), and wanting to know what others think about brands of their choices (53.7%). However, there were still about more than a quarter of respondents do consider products that can make good impression (32.3%), and make purchases which they feel can create style that others admire (30.8%). This might because of products' brand image can help to indicate quality and status (Mat et al., 2016). Conspicuous consumption as demonstration-oriented consumption can provide satisfaction not only from the consumption itself; it also provides satisfaction from the admiration received from others (Ekşi & Candan, 2018).

From the frequency distribution shown in Table 2, the three categories of consumer perception towards conspicuous consumption namely low, moderate, and high was determined. It can be seen in Figure 7 that the border score for reach category are 12-27 (Low), 28-43 (Moderate), and 44-60 (High). Data showed slightly more than half of the respondents (54.5%) are moderately propended

Table 3. Conspicuous consumption

No.	Statement	Total Frequency/ (%)				
		1	2	3	4	5
1.	I buy some products because I want to show others that I am wealthy.	141 (36.4)	145 (37.5)	79 (20.4)	18 (4.7)	4 (1.0)
2.	It says something to people around me when I buy a high priced brand.	70 (18.1)	143 (37.0)	111 (28.7)	54 (14.0)	9 (2.3)
3.	I would be a member in a businessmen's posh club.	94 (24.3)	160 (41.3)	93 (24.0)	39 (10.1)	1 (0.3)
4.	I would buy an interesting and uncommon version of a product otherwise available with a plain design, to show others that I have an original taste.	61 (15.8)	124 (32.0)	128 (33.1)	70 (18.1)	4 (1.0)
5.	By choosing a product having an exotic look and design, I show my friends that I am different	83 (21.4)	145 (37.5)	102 (26.4)	54 (14.0)	3 (0.8)
6.	I choose products or brands to create my own style that everybody admires.	50 (12.9)	92 (23.8)	126 (32.6)	106 (27.4)	13 (3.4)
7.	I always buy top-of-the-line products.	115 (29.7)	147 (38.0)	89 (23.0)	32 (8.3)	4 (1.0)
8.	I show to others that I am sophisticated.	81 (20.9)	130 (33.6)	120 (31.0)	51 (13.2)	5 (1.3)
9.	Before purchasing a product, it is important to know what friends think of different brands or products I am considering.	86 (22.2)	122 (31.5)	99 (25.6)	68 (17.6)	12 (3.1)
10.	Before purchasing a product, it is important to know what kinds of people buy brands or products I am considering.	67 (17.3)	127 (32.8)	97 (25.1)	79 (20.4)	17 (4.4)
11.	Before purchasing a product, it is important to know what others think of people who use certain brands or products I am considering.	64 (16.5)	117 (30.2)	120 (31.0)	78 (20.2)	8 (2.1)
12.	Before purchasing a product, is important to know what brands or products to buy to make a good impression on others.	53 (13.7)	100 (25.8)	109 (28.2)	107 (27.6)	18 (4.7)

in conspicuous consumption. Near to half of the respondents (41.3%) have low perception towards conspicuous consumption, and only as little as 4.1% of consumers are highly conspicuous. This result indicated that consumers in Malaysia are somehow low to moderately propend in conspicuous consumption. There is difference with the result from Western cultured sample that reported higher involvement in conspicuous consumption (Segal & Podoshen, 2013). Overall, it can be concluded that the results show moderate inclination of Malaysian in conspicuous consumption. Although Malaysian are less involved in conspicuous consumption as compared to Westerns, the affection for luxury is exceptionally pervasive in Asia Pacific area (Sandhu & Paim, 2015). Schaefer, Hermans, and Parker (2004) mentioned that East Asians might also have pressure to engage in this kind of consumption due to the need to maintain stature in the community.

Figure 7. Category of perception towards conspicuous consumption

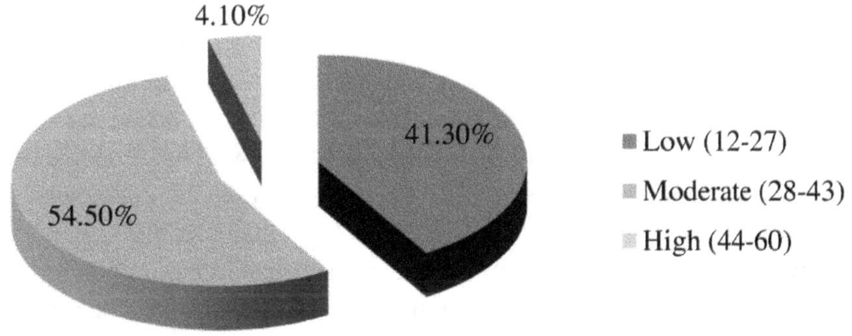

Effect of Social Media Usage on Materialism and Conspicuous Consumption

It was suggested that social media can influence materialism and conspicuous consumption. It is not hard to find that social media has become the key contribution to the success of luxury brands' marketing effort (Phan et al., 2011). More corporations and brands are turning to market products and engages consumers through social media (Ashley & Tuten, 2015). Aside from marketers, social media users will more likely to only present the best sides of themselves and their lives on social media platforms (Lin & Utz, 2015). These digital contents play some roles in brand expressions, triggering aspirations and provoking desires to be special and feel special, therefore influencing consumers on materialism as well as luxury consumption (Kamal, Chu, & Pedram, 2013; Escobar, 2016).

Although majority of respondents are moderately materialistic, only half of the respondents are moderately conspicuous in their consumption. Not to overlook, near to half of the respondents fell into the category of low involvement in conspicuous consumption. Despite these result, materialism was found to have direct influence on consumer perception towards conspicuous consumption (.Podoshen & Andrzejewski, 2012). Materialists believe that success and happiness can be visibly exhibited by the possession they own, which can be the reason for the demonstration-oriented consumption. This derivation is affirmed by empirical proof that discovered in contrasted with individual low in materialism, highly materialistic individuals are bound to value items that show monetary power (Richins, 1994a).

Looking at the effect of social media on link between materialism towards conspicuous consumption, it was discovered that under the influence of social media usage, there is a positive interaction effect of materialism on conspicuous consumption. It can be said deduced that social media usage showed positive moderation in the relationship of materialism and conspicuous consumption. When social media usage is high, high materialism becomes a strong predictor of conspicuous consumption. This result indicated that consumers who are highly materialistic are more inclined to do purchases conspicuously. By adding the influence of social media usage, idealized media pictures of riches in social media will strengthen and fuel the drive to consume getter amount of conspicuous products. According to Audrin et al. (2018), highly materialistic individuals tend to pay more visual attention on luxurious condition such as designer brands and products. In addition, the more highly materialistic individual exposed to visual images of luxurious products, the more they will select luxury products. This provides explanation on why intensive usage of social media can cause high materialism to be more intending to consume conspicuously.

CONLCUSION

Based on this study, Malaysia portrays a market where the use of social media and demand of luxury products has increased due to the growth of the nation's economy. Although the emphasize on overt display of consumption to demonstrate financial achievement had been rooted in Asian norm, this consumption pattern had not been widely spread as the results suggested only low to moderate consumer perception towards conspicuous consumption. However, with more common practice of luxury display in social media, there is possibility for more consumers to pick up such demonstration-orientated consumption pattern as social media usage was discovered to affect consumer purchasing behaviour. This effect of social media usage can be seen more critical on individuals who value material possessions. Materialists pay extra attention on material objects that are branded, expensive and visible. This information selection allows them to be only surrounded by luxuries and the comparison of luxuries, triggering them to involve more in conspicuous consumption.

This chapter provides more comprehensive understanding on the effect of social media usage towards materialism and conspicuous consumption. Besides that, the social media usage pattern and the extent of materialism and perception towards conspicuous consumption of consumer in Malaysia are disclosed. These results are relevant to two parties including market researchers and consumers. In exploring the effect of social media usage on materialism and conspicuous consumption, a new finding has given vital connotations to the theory, as well as to the practice. Current study implies to the literature by showing the effect of social media usage in the relationship between materialism and conspicuous consumption. Aside from the consistent result found between materialism and conspicuous consumption, this research reveals the effect of social media environment on the predictability of materialism towards conspicuous consumption. Intensive usage of social media can strengthen the drive to consume conspicuously, and it can be seen especially for those who are more materialistic.

The study identified the potential impacts of social media users' characteristics (materialism) able to exert an influence on conspicuous consumption. Consumers need to be aware that the dependence on the utilization of conspicuous goods to compensate for societal and situational underestimation or to adjust their status and self-esteem is inappropriate. The formal curriculum syllabus can advocate the young generations to abstained themselves from materialism and conspicuous consumptions; instead, focusing on developing social identity through knowledge, skills and abilities.

REFERENCES

Achariam, T. (2015). Malaysians use the internet an average of 12 hours a day. *The Sun Daily*. Retrieved from: https://www.thesundaily.my/news/1633825

Ahuvia, A. C., & Wong, N. Y. (2002). Personality and values based materialism: Their relationship and origins. *Journal of Consumer Psychology*, *12*(4), 389–402. doi:10.1207/S15327663JCP1204_10

Ashley, C., & Tuten, T. (2015). Creative strategies in social media marketing: An exploratory study of branded social content and consumer engagement. *Psychology and Marketing*, *32*(1), 15–27. doi:10.1002/mar.20761

Atsmon, Y., Dixit, V., & Wu, C. (2011). *Dimensions of brand personality.* Insights & Publications, McKinsey & Company. Retrieved from www.mckinsey.com/insights/marketing_sales/tapping_chinas_luxury-goods_market

Audrin, C., Brosch, T., Sander, D., & Chanal, J. (2018). More than meets the eye: The impact of materialism on information selection during luxury choices. *Frontiers in Behavioral Neuroscience, 12*, 12. doi:10.3389/fnbeh.2018.00172 PMID:30197590

Bagheri, M. (2014). Luxury consumer behavior in Malaysia: Loud brands vs. quiet brands. *Procedia: Social and Behavioral Sciences, 130*, 316–324. doi:10.1016/j.sbspro.2014.04.037

Bain & Company, Inc. (2019). *Luxury Goods Worldwide Market Study, Fall–Winter 2018.* Retrieved from https://www.bain.com/contentassets/8df501b9f8d6442eba00040246c6b4f9/bain_digest__luxury_goods_worldwide_market_study_fall_winter_2018.pdf

Becker, G. S., Murphy, K. M., & Werning, I. (2005). The equilibrium distribution of income and the market for status. *Journal of Political Economy, 113*(2), 282–310. doi:10.1086/427463

Belk, R. W. (1984). Three scales to measure constructs related to materialism: Reliability, validity, and relationships to measures of happiness. In T. Kinnear (Ed.), *Advances in Consumer Research* (Vol. 11, pp. 291–297). Provo, UT: Association for Consumer Research.

Belk, R. W. (1985). Materialism: Trait aspects of living in the material world. *The Journal of Consumer Research, 12*(3), 265–280. doi:10.1086/208515

Belk, R. W. (1996). Hyperreality and globalization: Culture in the age of Ronald McDonald. *Journal of International Consumer Marketing, 8*(3-4), 23–37. doi:10.1300/J046v08n03_03

Blumer, H. (1969). Fashion: From class differentiation to collective selection. *The Sociological Quarterly, 10*(3), 275–291. doi:10.1111/j.1533-8525.1969.tb01292.x

Boyd, D., & Ellison, N. (2008). Social network sites: Definition, history, and scholarship. *Journal of Computer-Mediated Communication, 13*(1), 210–230. doi:10.1111/j.1083-6101.2007.00393.x

Chang, L. D. M., Ling Tam, A. Y., & Suki, N. M. (2016). Moderating effect of races towards consumers' feeling of TCM usage. Handbook of Research on Leveraging Consumer Psychology for Effective Customer Engagement, 306-323.

Chang, L., & Arkin, R. M. (2002). Materialism as an attempt to cope with uncertainty. *Psychology and Marketing, 19*(5), 389–406. doi:10.1002/mar.10016

Chaudhuri, H. R., & Majumdar, S. (2006). Of diamonds and desires: Understanding conspicuous consumption from a contemporary marketing perspective. *Academy of Marketing Science Review, 2006*(11).

Chaudhuri, H. R., Mazumdar, S., & Ghoshal, A. (2011). Conspicuous consumption orientation: Conceptualisation, scale development and validation. *Journal of Consumer Behaviour, 10*(4), 216–224. doi:10.1002/cb.364

Chen, E. Y. I., Yeh, N.-C., & Wang, C. P. (2008). Conspicuous consumption: A preliminary report of scale development and validation. *Advances in Consumer Research. Association for Consumer Research (U. S.), 35*, 686–687.

Chu, S. C., Windels, K., & Kamal, S. (2016). The influence of self-construal and materialism on social media intensity: A study of China and the United States. *International Journal of Advertising, 35*(3), 569–588. doi:10.1080/02650487.2015.1068425

Churchill, G. A. Jr, & Moschis, G. P. (1979). Television and interpersonal influences on adolescent consumer learning. *The Journal of Consumer Research, 6*(1), 23–35. doi:10.1086/208745

Davis, M. (1992). Codes of ethics, professions, and conflict of interest: A case study of an emerging profession, clinical engineering. *Professional Ethics, A Multidisciplinary Journal, 1*(1/2), 179-195.

de Run, E. C., Butt, M., & Nee, C. Y. (2010). The influence of role models on young adults purchase. *Jurnal Kemanusiaan, 15*, 70–81.

Deci, E. L., & Ryan, R. M. (1995). Human autonomy: The basis for true self-esteem. In M. Kemis (Ed.), *Efficacy, agency, and self-esteem* (pp. 31–49). New York: Plenum.

Deloitte. (2017). *The new luxury consumers. Global Powers of Luxury Goods 2017.* Retrieved from: https://www2.deloitte.com/content/dam/Deloitte/global/Documents/consumer-industrial-products/gx-cip-global-powers-luxury-2017.pdf

Durvasula, S., Lysonski, S., & Watson, J. (Eds.). (2015). *Proceedings of the 1997 World Marketing Congress. A Cross-Cultural Examination of a Scale to Measure Trait Aspects of Vanity*. Springer.

Ekşi, O., & Candan, F. B. (2018). The effect of lifestyle on conspicuous consumption. *Current Debates in Business Studies*, (15), 109-125.

Escobar, A. (2016). The impact of the digital revolution in the development of market and communication strategies for the luxury sector (fashion luxury). *Central European Business Review, 5*(2), 17–36. doi:10.18267/j.cebr.149

Fitzmaurice, J., & Comegys, C. (2006). Materialism and social consumption. *Journal of Marketing Theory and Practice, 14*(4), 287–299. doi:10.2753/MTP1069-6679140403

Frank, R. H. (1985). *Choosing the right pond: Human behavior and the quest for status*. Oxford University Press.

Frenzen, J., & Nakamoto, K. (1993). Structure, cooperation, and the flow of market information. *The Journal of Consumer Research, 20*(3), 360–375. doi:10.1086/209355

Ger, G., & Belk, R. W. (1996). Cross-cultural differences in materialism. *Journal of Economic Psychology, 17*(1), 55–77. doi:10.1016/0167-4870(95)00035-6

Ger, G., & Belk, R. W. (1999). Accounting for materialism in four cultures. *Journal of Material Culture, 4*(2), 183–204. doi:10.1177/135918359900400204

Giovannini, S., Xu, Y., & Thomas, J. (2015). Luxury fashion consumption and Generation Y consumers: Self, brand consciousness, and consumption motivations. *Journal of Fashion Marketing and Management, 19*(1), 22–40. doi:10.1108/JFMM-08-2013-0096

Goh, K. Y., Heng, C. S., & Lin, Z. (2013). Social media brand community and consumer behavior: Quantifying the relative impact of user-and marketer-generated content. *Information Systems Research, 24*(1), 88–107. doi:10.1287/isre.1120.0469

Goldberg, M. E., & Gorn, G. J. (1978). Some unintended consequences of TV advertising to children. *The Journal of Consumer Research, 5*(1), 22–29. doi:10.1086/208710

Hajli, M. N. (2014). A study of the impact of social media on consumers. *International Journal of Market Research, 56*(3), 387–404. doi:10.2501/IJMR-2014-025

Hamilton, K. L., & Catterall, M. (2005). Towards a better understanding of the low income consumer. *Advances in Consumer Research. Association for Consumer Research (U. S.), 32*(1), 627–632.

Hani, A. (2019, August 8). Credit cards, personal loans landing Malaysians in debt trap. *The Malaysian Reserve*. Retrieved from https://themalaysianreserve.com/2019/08/08/credit-cards-personal-loans-landing-malaysians-in-debt-trap/

Hargittai, E. (2007). Whose space? Differences among users and non-users of social network sites. *Journal of Computer-Mediated Communication, 13*(1), 276–297. doi:10.1111/j.1083-6101.2007.00396.x

Hudders, L., & Pandelaere, M. (2012). The silver lining of materialism: The impact of luxury consumption on subjective well-being. *Journal of Happiness Studies, 13*(3), 411–437. doi:10.100710902-011-9271-9

Jang, K., Park, N., & Song, H. (2016). Social comparison on Facebook: Its antecedents and psychological outcomes. *Computers in Human Behavior, 62*, 147–154. doi:10.1016/j.chb.2016.03.082

Kamal, S., Chu, S. C., & Pedram, M. (2013). Materialism, attitudes, and social media usage and their impact on purchase intention of luxury fashion goods among American and Arab young generations. *Journal of Interactive Advertising, 13*(1), 27–40. doi:10.1080/15252019.2013.768052

Kamaruddin, A. R., & Mokhlis, S. (2003). Consumer socialization, social structural factors and decision-making styles: A case study of adolescents in Malaysia. *International Journal of Consumer Studies, 27*(2), 145–156. doi:10.1046/j.1470-6431.2003.00297.x

Kamineni, R. (2005). Influence of materialism, gender and nationality on consumer brand perceptions. Journal of Targeting. *Measurement and Analysis for Marketing, 14*(1), 25–32. doi:10.1057/palgrave.jt.5740167

Kapeller, J., & Schütz, B. (2015). Conspicuous consumption, inequality and debt: The nature of consumption-driven profit-led regimes. *Metroeconomica, 66*(1), 51–70. doi:10.1111/meca.12061

Kasser, T., Ryan, R. M., Couchman, C. E., & Sheldon, K. M. (2004). Materialistic values: Their causes and consequences. *Psychology and Consumer Culture: The Struggle for a Good Life in a Materialistic World, 1*(2), 11–28.

Kim, A. J., & Ko, E. (2012). Do social media marketing activities enhance customer equity? An empirical study of luxury fashion brand. *Journal of Business Research*, *65*(10), 1480–1486. doi:10.1016/j.jbusres.2011.10.014

Lange, F. A. (1873-75). *The History of Materialism* (B. Russell, Trans., 3rd ed.). New York: Arno Press.

Larsen, V., Sirgy, J. M., & Wright, N. D. (1999). Materialism: The construct, measures, antecedents, and consequences. *Academy of Marketing Studies Journal*, *3*(2), 78–110.

Lens, I., Pandelaere, M., & Warlop, L. (2010). Effects of Advertising Exposure on Materialism and Self-Esteem: Advertised Luxuries As a Feel-Good Strategy? *ACR North American Advances.*, *37*(1), 1–5.

Lim, W. M., Ng, W. K., Chin, J. H., & Boo, A. W. X. (2014). Understanding young consumer perceptions on credit card usage: Implications for responsible consumption. *Contemporary Management Research*, *10*(4), 287–302. doi:10.7903/cmr.11657

Mannion, C., & Brannick, T. (1995). Materialism and its measurement. *IBAR*, (16), 1-15.

Mat, A., Kori, N. L., Rahman, S. A., Munir, Z. A., & Bahry, N. S. (2016). Conspicuous consumption behaviour: A case study of luxury fashion consumers at selected malls in Kuala Lumpur, Malaysia. *Australian Journal of Basic and Applied Sciences*, *10*(11), 193–198.

McCay-Peet, L., & Quan-Haase, A. (2017). What is social media and what questions can social media research help us answer. The SAGE Handbook of Social Media Research Methods, 13-26.

Moav, O., & Neeman, Z. (2012). Saving rates and poverty: The role of conspicuous consumption and human capital. *Economic Journal (London)*, *122*(563), 933–956. doi:10.1111/j.1468-0297.2012.02516.x

Muntinga, D. G., Moorman, M., & Smit, E. G. (2011). Introducing COBRAs: Exploring motivations for brand-related social media use. *International Journal of Advertising*, *30*(1), 13–46. doi:10.2501/IJA-30-1-013-046

Nathan, R. J., Fook Chiun, D. C., & Suki, N. M. (2016). An online marketing strategies assessment for companies in airlines and entertainment industries in Malaysia. Handbook of Research on Leveraging Consumer Psychology for Effective Customer Engagement, 1-15.

Ordabayeva, N., & Chandon, P. (2010). Getting ahead of the Joneses: When equality increases conspicuous consumption among bottom-tier consumers. *The Journal of Consumer Research*, *38*(1), 27–41. doi:10.1086/658165

Ozimek, P., & Förster, J. (2017). The impact of self-regulatory states and traits on Facebook use: Priming materialism and social comparisons. *Computers in Human Behavior*, *71*, 418–427. doi:10.1016/j.chb.2017.01.056

Phan, M., Thomas, R., & Heine, K. (2011). Social media and luxury brand management: The case of Burberry. *Journal of Global Fashion Marketing*, *2*(4), 213–222. doi:10.1080/20932685.2011.10593099

Podoshen, J. S., & Andrzejewski, S. A. (2012). An examination of the relationships between materialism, conspicuous consumption, impulse buying, and brand loyalty. *Journal of Marketing Theory and Practice*, *20*(3), 319–334. doi:10.2753/MTP1069-6679200306

Podoshen, J. S., Li, L., & Zhang, J. (2011). Materialism and conspicuous consumption in China: A cross-cultural examination. *International Journal of Consumer Studies*, *35*(1), 17–25. doi:10.1111/j.1470-6431.2010.00930.x

Quoquab, F., Pahlevan, S., & Hussin, N. (2016). Counterfeit Product Purchase: What Counts—Materialism or Religiosity? *Advanced Science Letters*, *22*(5-6), 1303–1306. doi:10.1166/asl.2016.6739

Richins, M. L. (1987). Media, materialism, and human happiness. In W. Melanie & A. Paul (Eds.), *Advances in Consumer Research* (Vol. 14, pp. 352–356). Provo, UT: Association for Consumer Research.

Richins, M. L., & Dawson, S. (1992). A consumer values orientation for materialism and its measurement: Scale development and validation. *The Journal of Consumer Research*, *19*(3), 303–316. doi:10.1086/209304

Rindfleisch, A., Burroughs, J. E., & Denton, F. (1997). Family structure, materialism, and compulsive consumption. *The Journal of Consumer Research*, *23*(4), 312–325. doi:10.1086/209486

Roberts, J. A., Manolis, C., & Tanner, J. F. Jr. (2003). Family structure, materialism, and compulsive buying: A reinquiry and extension. *Journal of the Academy of Marketing Science*, *31*(3), 300–311. doi:10.1177/0092070303031003007

Rokeach, M. (1973). *The nature of human values*. New York: Free press.

Sandhu, S. K., & Paim, L. (2016). Consuming for status among Malaysian working women. *Journal of Emerging Economies & Islamic Research*, *4*(3).

Schiffman, L. G., & Kanuk, L. L. (2004). *Consumer behaviour* (8th ed.). Prentice-Hall Inc.

Schroeder, J. E., & Dugal, S. S. (1995). Psychological correlates of the materialism construct. *Journal of Social Behavior and Personality*, *10*(1), 243.

Schwedt, G., Chevalier, M., & Gutsatz, M. (2012). *Luxury retail management: How the World's top brands provide quality product and service support*. Hoboken, NJ: Wiley.

Scott, K. (2009). *Terminal materialism vs. instrumental materialism: Can materialism be beneficial?* (Doctoral dissertation). Oklahoma State University.

Segal, B., & Podoshen, J. S. (2013). An examination of materialism, conspicuous consumption and gender differences. *International Journal of Consumer Studies*, *37*(2), 189–198. doi:10.1111/j.1470-6431.2012.01099.x

Solomon, M. R. (1983). The role of products as social stimuli: A symbolic interactionism perspective. *The Journal of Consumer Research*, *10*(3), 319–329. doi:10.1086/208971

Sommer, R. (2017). Michael Kors - A Fashionable Trend. *Seeking Alpha*. Retrieved from https://seekingalpha.com/article/4133212-michael-kors-fashionable-trend

Srikant, M. (2013). Materialism in consumer behavior and marketing: A review. *Management & Marketing*, *8*(2), 329.

Suki, N. M. (2016). *Handbook of Research on Leveraging Consumer Psychology for Effective Customer Engagement.* https://www.igi-global.com/book/handbook-research-leveraging-consumer-psychology/149284

Sun, G., Wang, W., Cheng, Z., Li, J., & Chen, J. (2017). The intermediate linkage between materialism and luxury consumption: Evidence from the emerging market of China. *Social Indicators Research, 132*(1), 475–487. doi:10.100711205-016-1273-x

Tee, P. K., Gharleghi, B., & Chan, B. Y. F. (2013). Malaysian young consumer preferences in choosing international fashion brand. *Journal of Human and Social Science Research, 1*(1), 31–38.

Thoumrungroje, A. (2014). The influence of social media intensity and EWOM on conspicuous consumption. *Procedia: Social and Behavioral Sciences, 148,* 7–15. doi:10.1016/j.sbspro.2014.07.009

Trigg, A. B. (2001). Veblen, Bourdieu, and conspicuous consumption. *Journal of Economic Issues, 35*(1), 99–115. doi:10.1080/00213624.2001.11506342

Veblen, T. (1899). *The Theory of the Leisure Class: An Economic Study in the Evolution of Institutions.* Macmillan & Co.

Vogel, E. A., Rose, J. P., Roberts, L. R., & Eckles, K. (2014). Social comparison, social media, and self-esteem. *Psychology of Popular Media Culture, 3*(4), 206–222. doi:10.1037/ppm0000047

Wan-Ismail, W. N. A., Zakaria, N., & Abdul-Talib, A. N. (2016). Craving vs. Compulsion for Luxury Goods?: Trends and Patterns of Conspicuous Consumption Behavior in Asian Culture. In *Neuroeconomics and the Decision-Making Process* (pp. 287–297). IGI Global. doi:10.4018/978-1-4666-9989-2.ch015

Wang, X., Yu, C., & Wei, Y. (2012). Social media peer communication and impacts on purchase intentions: A consumer socialization framework. *Journal of Interactive Marketing, 26*(4), 198–208. doi:10.1016/j.intmar.2011.11.004

Wilcox, K., & Stephen, A. T. (2012). Are close friends the enemy? Online social networks, self-esteem, and self-control. *The Journal of Consumer Research, 40*(1), 90–103. doi:10.1086/668794

Wong, N. Y. (1997). Suppose you own the world and no one knows? In M. Brucks & D. MacInnis (Eds.), *Advances in consumer research* (Vol. 4, pp. 197–201). Provo, UT: Association for Consumer Research.

Yenicioglu, B., & Christodoulides, G. (2014). Branding in the age of digital connectivity. In *The Routledge companion to the future of marketing* (pp. 268–281). London: Sage.

Zhou, N., & Belk, R. W. (2004). Chinese consumer readings of global and local advertising appeals. *Journal of Advertising, 33*(3), 63–76. doi:10.1080/00913367.2004.10639169

Zhu, N. (2011). Household consumption and personal bankruptcy. *The Journal of Legal Studies, 40*(1), 1–37. doi:10.1086/649033

Chapter 5
A Study of Online Scams:
Examining the Behavior and Motivation Factors of Scammers and Victimization Consequences

Azlan Shah
Universiti Utara Malaysia, Malaysia

ABSTRACT

This chapter presents the overview of how the online fraud began; and how in starting to spread around the world. Mastering the motivation factor fraudster to do scamming. Also the perspectives of victim attitude, social media; the emerging trends of community attitudes and IT among public community among youngster or even among elders; the concept of motivation factors, by fraudsters; the characteristics of victim by dividing to gender and age stages; sustainable online media ;sustainable long hours of consuming internet; the importance of sustainable consumption, sustainability, and sustainable deterrence to avoid people being online scam victim. Mastering how this case working is essential for modern police organizations that seek to serve public and nation, reduce the loses are facing by victim in the future, strengthen strategy in combating online scam. It's also emphasize thoroughly the effect, and the consequences after victim got cheated by online. The chapter argues that mastering fraudster and victim attitude and knowledge to enhance the awareness and reduce online scam.

INTRODUCTION

Information and communication technology (ICT) have speeded up the development of the economy globally and enhanced the quality life for better life in this world. Internet technology has brought new ways of creating worldwide communication between people around the world. However, this accommodation was used by the opportunist as new space to take a chance to cheat the other sincere people out there for those use ICT to connecting with others throughout the world. Crime that arise nowadays was an online scam because it's like a virus that happen and attack so many people who are vulnerable since Internet has been use as a social media as medium to communicate. More research that delve into

DOI: 10.4018/978-1-7998-3042-9.ch005

aspect of consumer behavior and psychology in the digital economy is deemed necessary (Ling Chang, Ling Tam, & Suki, 2016; Nathan, Fook Chiun, & Suki, 2016; Suki, 2016).

The online scam has established very fast because in terms of the development of communication technological medium so that type crime was adapting by criminal to enable their activities involved. Such a crime may be committed thru the online communication are uninvited conversation through emails, chat rooms from personal computers, smart phones, Tablet applications, WhatsApp, Telegram, social media sites, and chatting forums (Hamin, Rosalili, & Rosli, 2018). Online Scam can be described of any deceitful activities or tactic that illicit money or other goods from a lay-man people by scammer group or personal. With the worldwide are more exposed and globalization of Internet, online scams have enlarged greater than before, and it's important to make a public more aware stay suspicion with people on the Internet that they never know who they really are.

There are a bundle types of online scams crime today reported throughout the world, but this paper will focus on Romance Swindle that related to Advance Fee Fraud and '419' Nigerian Letter Scam. Romance scams nowadays are take advantages of accelerate of Internet and Wi fi to cheating people who are using Internet and Media Social as platform to communicate each other's. However, scammers may also use social platform such as Facebook, WhatsApp's, Telegram and so many other social media platform or email to make contact. They have still been known to call their victims as a beginning entry. Usually this criminal using fake identity profiles that was designed to make victims confident to them. They maybe apply a fake name, or take on the others people identities of real without this real person permission. Usually they use the identity of trusted people such as military officer, engineer or professionals working overseas such as attached with oil and gas company. The modus operation is usually involved use fabricated identity background, scammer will claim they have high positioning in community and offering the victim be friendly especially with lonesome and desperate of love's women. After they get the trustworthiness and slowly become their online lover. And so, by the time when these online couple obtain and gain trust each other in the relationship, this criminal begin his tactic using so many of explanations and sweet talking to get the victim deliver their money into the love scammer's bank account, they will give several reason such as for buying the flight ticket, accidental hospitalize, business problem and so many more. This transaction of money will happen some many time until victim finally felt doubtful or realize that was not the true love connection after the victim finished her money in bank account.

Advance fee scam is case when the victims are persuaded confidently by criminal to get some amounts of money in the hope of gaining a much bigger profit. A type version on how these fraud working is an e-mail was sent to the victim, most often from African continent, seeking the other people to help to relocation large sums of money (normally in the tens of millions) out of the country, promising the investor or helper a percentage. The fraudster then started the tactic by making a request from victim for some amount of money that will be using to accelerate the process transaction, such as a bribe to bankers, custom officer, central bank officer or to pay certain fees such as processing or customs fees. The scholar has introduced and develop a model called "Scammers Persuasive Technique Model" to study and highpoint the process elaborates in the online cheating and they have identified that Near Win Phenomenon and Elaboration likelihood model that explain why people are becoming victimized in online scam, and in other cases people can be victimize on the second time. The researcher also studies about what the motivation and factors to the scammers to defraud the masses. They establish that most of scammers come from third world nations such as Nigeria.

In Malaysia perspective, online scam has raised from 10 years backward. This crime is more becoming as a menace to our economy since the victims' money has flowed out of this country to another country using by Western Union and Telegraphic Transfer wire provided by local bank. The victims only realized they have been cheated when the money gone. The victims have double hits of losses. Both financially and emotionally. Malaysia also not excluded from the Internet Scams, from study and case reported to Royal Malaysia Police shows that Malaysia people are vulnerable to online scam. Those scams are happened at Malaysia is job offer fraud, rent fraud, mule account fraud, internet auction scams advance fee fraud and online dating scams.

The case of Internet Scam happens in Malaysia, also happen in Singapore and Thailand and the other Asian countries, the losses reported was tremendously high when a victim losing their hard earn money just in eye blink. So government or authority agency need provide better understanding of the common online scamming methods. In Malaysia, the literacy on Internet can cover almost of people, this situation can make them danger exposed and can be reachable without boundaries. However, online scam is a crime that growing concern so many people in Malaysia. "Of the regions surveyed, Malaysia was the country, most vulnerable to internet scams. A further 46% of Malaysian respondents saying they know a friend or family member who has been scammed online," rendering to a declaration by Telenor.

Malaysians were also easily can be a victims of Internet scammers, where a criminal constructs a counterfeit identity an online dating platform to bring about money from victim. Something that involve a huge amount of money. Because Internet are easy tool to put anything about the information there so that also easy to these scammers to find fake information. Educated people also even can be a victim of online scams, everybody can be a victim without care about what their gender, occupation or age status. One of the solution that can be taken by public is don't entertain on a link in an unfamiliar email and don't respond to any unknown messages that we didn't know the source validity. These articles also from many scholars are recommended to gain more awareness campaign and strengthened the enforcement agency that linked to this crime. This problem is never stopping and continuingly since we still have the ICT and people who are greedy.

HISTORY OF ONLINE SCAM

Online scam has grown from 10 years back. The criminal uses the accommodation of e-mail, messenger and Facebook to hook the victim. The massive growth of knowledge in "information and communication technologies (ICTs)" and the popularity of the using internet given an alternative best place for loving events without boundaries. The online romance swindle that started since around year 2008 and has its roots in a paper-mail based fraud before scammers using the post office as a medium to send the fake lover letters. (Whitty & Buchanan, 2012). Internet lover finders found exhilaration when they interact and communicate with other people throughout new digital mediums such as online platform. (Rege, 2009). Both scammers and victim do not need to see each other in the real world when the communicate, but the success of communication has driven the cybercrime, such as romance scam and an advance fee fraud. "Cybercrime was defined as dishonesty of advance fee fraud schemes which use fabricated identity to approach and starting a romantic relationship with their victim targets with the purpose of swindling their victim sums large of money" (Koon, 2013). E-mail also create a space to enables the fraudster to be communicated to a huge number of people with the help of e-mail lists, which can be well targeted and relatively easy to obtain. (Chang, 2008)

Online scam has generated a great loss throughout the world, especially for the people from developing country in term of money illicitly by scammers. “As reported by UK Office of Fair Trading showing a dramatic increase from 2006 when the UK consumers lose approximately £3.5 billion to scams each year, with the average amount lost per scam being £850”. (Whitty & Buchanan, 2012). The scammers also have used the word that convinced the victim with empty promises, but reassuring until the victim will hand over their money. The fraud will stop only when the victim know and understand that they have been scammed and illicit to give money. (Whitty, 2013). (Rege, 2009) argue the scammer communicate with victim and from there they successfully build a strong bond with them that can last from 3 to 6 months. After got the victim trustworthiness they starting creating a story of a tragic or desperate circumstance such as theft of personal documents during travel, unexpected hospital funds, or travel expenses and finally request money from victims by. A lot of money have been sent several time before the scam is exposed and realize by victim they have been cheated.

Another factor is, the scammer also shows the religious attitude, always take care and concern just like an charming lover and using the sweet word until slowly gave many reasons to make the victim felt sympathy and influence her to give money to help. As mention (Whitty, 2018) many of those criminal belong a high skill in networking, have learn about how to deceiving and persuasion technique, they also learn about Machiavellianism technique. In most cases of the scam seek to obtain an urgent response from victims, so they didn’t provide so much time to victim to think rationally. This is how the scammer are playing with psychological aspect to push and gives victims less time to validate the information that given to them before, and may pressure them into taking the way in shortcuts of decision making without refer to someone else.(Chang, 2008). So victim have a limited time to validate the information, so it easy to scammers to manipulate victim minds.

Persuasive Technique Using by Fraudster

Past studies have discussed about the cause of online scam in term of how the persuasive technique was using by scammer. There is limited research that have intensive focus on the persuasive techniques using by the online swindlers. However, this is very crucial for us to recognize the psychology of the cyber fraudster in order to improve detection and prevention measure can be taken one step ahead from these criminal (Whitty, 2018). This is important to know what they think and how they move in the way to cheat their victim. Since no solid theory have been draw to study and understanding about online fraud and instead scholars tend to taking the theories developed by social psychologists and adapt these online scam frauds. First is the failure by victim in decision making when the scammers create the situation and and push them to action for example when they are forced, some cases where the scammers are telling that they come from the government and authority department just to convince the victim to make they believe that they are dealing with the right people. “As (Chang, 2008) have mentioned, there are six basic principles relying on tendency how victim can cooperate with is they are highly likely to persuade or influence by others, being liking, reciprocation, commitment/consistency, scarcity, social recommendation, and validation by authority”. All these techniques are using by fraudster to convince the victim when they scamming.

Another persuasive technique is reciprocal; it happens in Romance Scam or Advance Fee Fraud when the scammer can persuade the victim with promise to give some gift and because of that in order to receive something back (Rege, 2009). For example, scammer will ask victim to pay some amount the they will believe they will get back their money plus with interest. It always happens in case when victim was contacted by somebody act as authority officer said the parcel posted to victim carried a lot of cash money, jewelry and expensive goods. It gives the motivation to victim to believe they will gain the profit and make the payment without thinking twice. Psychological encouragements used in online scam, such as validity of authority and expert confluence such as from enforcement agency, mimicking and referencing persons / organizations, providing partial proof/legitimacy, reasoning, giving in return, forming limitation and implying insufficiency. (Chang & Chong, 2010). Online criminals in the execution of the Nigerian scam were persistent and spent a lot of time to actively communicating with the victim, to the process make the victim melting and to gain her trust. (Miladinovic-Bogavac, 2017).

Scholar also found that the factor contribute victimization is near win phenomenon. The fake persona will influence victim to believe that if they reciprocate to cooperation to send some amount of money, they will raise the good rewards, after some victims are successfully persuaded they will draw into the trap and find it hard to exit and accepting their fate. The victim also found that they are more likely to have low self-control. The study also believe that consequences are impact to victim life. (Whitty, 2015) argue that the victim was double trouble, hard earn money losses and love broke (loss of fake bond). The victim is often not to report the cases because they are shy and feeling fooled and blame themselves. Victim will fell psychological effect can include dishonor, guilty, humiliation, desperation, feeling suicidal, sorrow, anxiety and loss of trust to others. Support system such a family and friend often blame the victim for the financial losses and victim also feel that the society will think that they are stupid and greedy. Some victim was experience post-traumatic stress, it like the addiction on internet conversation with the scammers. On other cases victim have went to Ghana to meet their fake persona and was kidnapped to get the ransomed.

Victim also faced the denial syndrome that they can't believe that the scammer is fake and was not real, because they have the real feeling when they communicate. The denial syndrome can contribute potentially to re-victimize on second wave of scams. Some were giveaway the past like nothing is happen, some of them desperately pay money just to continue that they believe is true relationship. However, some victim is so frustrated until they decided to not subscribe online dating plaform anymore, while others victim had decided to end up overall on connections. Fascinatingly, there also have the victim had continued using the online dating sites with the hope they will fine their true love although they all know they were possible scammed again.

The tactic using by this criminal usually involved using fake name and background profile, targeted who are isolated and desperate of love's person and pretend to be lover persona to victim. (Diana, Tobi, & Masrom, 2015). Then, with the long process of conversation and persuasive technique were use, scammer successfully obtained in the relationship the love criminal starting to persuade with certain to make the victim banking their money (normally by online banking system) to the mule bank account. This deal may happen several times until the victim get doubtful feeling or their money were finish and felt that persona was fake and just cheating their relationship only.

Koon (2013) "also added these scammers uses fake persona usually is western identity to attract Asian victim and vice versa and them can be a male, female or youngsters too". "One case that was reported on November 21, 2012 which the victim was a bank customer services officer had lost around Ringgit Malaysia RM61,200.00 of her mother's savings to a man she befriended on Facebook". (Diana et al., 2015).

"Malaysia been claimed as a country that keep network of Nigerian love scam. It is also reported that hundreds of American women are being trapped by love scammer based in Malaysia. Most Internet love scammers which based on Malaysia also had been reported to take advantage on the advancement of Malaysia ICT infrastructure and banking system which facilitate them to use internet smoothly and make international transfer quickly via bank transaction services." "Scammers impersonate clients requesting wire transfers of funds into a new or foreign bank account, which is actually the fraudsters' account. The amounts stolen this way can reach up to several hundred thousand dollars." (Werner, 2017). All of this provide very comfort environment to these scammers compare than which operate in their own origin country.

Otherwise Malaysia also aimed to become a global education hub. This opportunity was using by these African coming to Malaysia to register visa as a student. But most of them just pretend to be a student, but on other side they working close with the scammers syndicate to cheating local people.

Royal Malaysia Police (RMP) also has reported that they have done a lot of arrest, most of suspect are Nigerian, but surprisingly, the authority also manages to catch a local Malaysia woman that also stay and involved with these group of cyber cheating. Most of Malaysia women has been detained because of their involvement as a mules account. An investigation found that these woman has been knowing the syndicate nor have stay with the for several time.

This is why we believe that the importantly research need to doing in term of what the cause and the consequences among woman in Malaysia more vulnerable to be a victim in online scam such as love scam and advance fee fraud. As cybercriminals nowadays continue to develop in many ways to swindle people money, there have changed the modus operation quickly after they know their style has been knowing by public. So the computer users need to become even more attentive and cautious in their daily practices (Werner, 2017).

Romance Scam

"Online romance Scams or Love Scam, or 'sweetheart swindles', are an emotionally upsetting category of online scam, as scammers using the nice word to make their victims believe they have strong feelings for them just to persuade victim to continue communicate with them". (Rege, 2009). They act as a pious person and try to convince the victim, that final aim to lure the victim to hand over the money via mule account or thru other financial service, for example online banking or western union services. However, this process is going through three weeks to three months for the scammer to build strong relationship between them. They build the trustworthiness and make the victim of perceived they are really in real love, although they have never seen each other though in real life or thru online webcam chatting. The scammer just sends the text every day to showing they are really concerned about the victim. As mention by (Miladinovic-Bogavac, 2017) The scammer will use the simple English word that using by common people to be easy read and understand by people all over the world to whom the message were send. As we know language also a main role to make sure the two ways communication will successful. Usually these scammer using easy language weather they know that word are written not in proper grammar.

Advance Fee Fraud

The topic of advance fee fraud is very crucial to study because it's a spread phenomenon that need awareness among internet users in terms of safety, reliance, and financial loss.(Chang, 2008). "All forms of advance fee fraud offer an incentive to the recipient in the form of monetary award or reward. Many of these monetary incentives are offered as a form of reciprocation". (Rege, 2009). This style of scam also originally come from an African country, that stated and cheat the victim by promising them a large sum of money for example, for military contract, heritage the welfare property, booty gains from war, and a large money in the bank that cannot be withdrawn. A normal version of the online scam is an e-mail, most often from African continent such as Nigeria, these criminal seeking an investor to help in transfer large sums of money (usually in tens of millions) out of the country, promising the investor a share. (Chang, 2008) . These e-mails are usually attached with fake official letter were claiming to be a government, bank official or civil custom officer. (Ahmed & Oppenheim, 2006).

The criminal then asking for a sum of money that is essential in smoothing the process fees or to pay to other authority agency such as custom officer or central bank to release the money. They also give a several reason to release the money such as large sum of money are stuck at airport so victim will be contacted by member of syndicate said that the money was under victim name and this case regulate under Anti Money Laundering and Terrorism Act. A victim will have convinced or scared by the scammer to get the money nor property and will reciprocate if they willing to help. So victim started bank in the money to the scammers, usually using the online banking facilities and other financial remittance provider that nearby and easy to reach by the victim. Usually they are asking to bank in small amount and after that with several reason the amount and frequency to bank in money will increase. (Chang & Chong, 2010).

At this stage victim are still believe with the scammer that they will get to profit and keep it secret from their family knowledge, until finally they found they have been cheated when they losing the money or they lost contact with the scammers. Advance fee fraud also attack the desperate person who are needed loan in urgently. These scams, a con artist offers a "guaranteed" loan as long as the victim pays a special fee in advance. The advanced fee fraudster will tell the victim they can secure a loan from a legitimate lending institution, such as a bank. In reality, they have no power to get a loan for. Instead, they steal the fee and disappear. Advance fee fraudsters often ask for a percentage of the gross loan amount for payment of their required fee. So after victim bank in the money, this scammer will cut off or block the conversation between them. After all this happen, victim have realise that they have been cheating.

FUTURE RESEARCH DIRECTIONS

"A number of cybercrime typologies have been developed during this period, but none have been universally embraced by researchers working in the field". (Reyns, 2015). This scarce paper discussed about this type of crime. Another field that can be explore by researcher is about how the scammers can manipulate the new technology such as software for example VOIP system. The authority also need to inform online consumer and public out there of the tactic using by advance fee fraudsters. Considering the current and widespread problem of advance fee-fraud e-mails, this information is crucial for internet users to improve their knowledge and awareness in identifying fraudulent schemes and avoiding them.

The new aspect can be explored is how the early prevention can be taken, to guide the community about the online scam, this effort can start since primary school until university student. Security measure also can be taken such as give a talk to senior citizen about the modus operandi online scam, because as we know, the baby boomers' generation are not IT savvy. They also very high respect to the authority agency, so when the scammer uses this tactic, so they will alert very well.

As mention by (Reyns, 2015), more study is essential to exploring these crimes from a criminal psychology, technique use and victimization perspective. It because we need to know how victim can be manipulating until they can be cheated. This is one step ahead of prevention, because it was not easy to combatting this crime with just study how the criminal work and how they operated.

One of the best ways to battle borderless online scam is to help people take one steps ahead with knowledge thru campaigns to prevention measure. Also these criminal have been caught up in the fraud in the first place to charge them in court. Educating businesses and public consumers is a crucial part in the way to containing such scams.

CONCLUSION

This chapter highlighted the overview of the critical impact the online scam has on its victims physically and emotionally. We also study about what the motivation factor of criminal when they are trying take advantages in cyberspace during swindle their victims. "Unlike victims of other scams, most of the victims in this study experienced a 'double hit' of the loss of money and a relationship". (Buchanan & Whitty, 2014). Online scam is a continuous threat, and just because it doesn't represent a physical threat in the form of someone trying to break into your home, it can be just as damaging.

This online scam is a new challenge for IT professionals, businesses, employees, and individuals in public. Authority that govern the Internet also need to take the prevention in term online security more seriously and need stern action to empowered the law that we have currently. Most people can be a victims of advance fee loan scams and romance scam when they are unable to identify the sources of information that they have receive thru internet.

Routine activities theory also said about the habit of people in consuming the internet also could expose potential victims to cyber criminals. (Mesch & Dodel, 2018). Routine Internet activities are also having tendency to vulnerable of cyber victimization. We also can suggest to the authority who have control the Internet such Multimedia Commission Malaysia to educate internet consumer such as pop up message about scam alert. The other way can be taken is to take the stern action such as block the page or email involving scam and fake identity use by scammers.

Elders citizen need to be inform about this tactic and what is the online scam because are often at greater risk of becoming victims of online fraud. Prevention among elderly friend or relative, a seminar or talk to them about the risks of online fraud and let them know that they can always ask their nearby family if they are unsure about something. However as explain by (Whitty, 2017) prevention and awareness raising programs among middle age and youngster also need to do because this group age also are vulnerable to be a victim of cybercriminal. We need to explain public community how this illegal activity operate that promote risks or how to avoid to be a victim to this online scam. So we hope by the aggressive campaign and promotion about what of the typology of scam can reduce the cases in future. The law enforcement agency also need to be supply with this information so can be value added knowledge in their future investigation during combatting the Internet Scam.

REFERENCES

Ahmed, T., & Oppenheim, C. (2006). Experiments to identify the causes of spam. *Aslib Proceedings*, *58*(3), 156–178. doi:10.1108/00012530610701013

Buchanan, T., & Whitty, M. T. (2014). The online dating romance scam: Causes and consequences of victimhood. *Psychology, Crime & Law*, *20*(3), 261–283. doi:10.1080/1068316X.2013.772180

Chang, J. J. S. (2008). An analysis of advance fee fraud on the internet. *Journal of Financial Crime, 15*(1), 71–81. doi:10.1108/13590790810841716

Chang, J. J. S., & Chong, M. D. (2010). Psychological influences in e-mail fraud. *Journal of Financial Crime, 17*(3), 337–350. doi:10.1108/13590791011056309

Chang, L. D. M., Ling Tam, A. Y., & Suki, N. M. (2016). Moderating effect of races towards consumers' feeling of TCM usage. Handbook of Research on Leveraging Consumer Psychology for Effective Customer Engagement, 306-323.

Diana, S., Tobi, S. N., & Masrom, M. (2015). *Cybercrime over Internet Love Scams in Malaysia : A Discussion on the Theoretical Perspectives, Connecting Factors and Keys to the Problem.* doi:10.5296/jmr.v7i2.6938

Hamin, Z., Rosalili, W., & Rosli, W. (2018). Cloaked By Cyber Space : A Legal Response to the Risks of Cyber Stalking in Malaysia. doi:10.5281/zenodo.1467931

Koon, T. H. (2013). *Preying on Lonely Hearts : A Systematic Deconstruction of an Internet Romance Scammer's Online Lover Persona.* Academic Press.

Mesch, G. S., & Dodel, M. (2018). Low Self-Control, Information Disclosure, and the Risk of Online Fraud. *The American Behavioral Scientist, 62*(10), 1356–1371. doi:10.1177/0002764218787854

Miladinovic-Bogavac, Z. (2017). Business scam in saber space. *Ekonomika (Nis), 63*(4), 97–104. doi:10.5937/ekonomika1704097M

Nathan, R. J., Fook Chiun, D. C., & Suki, N. M. (2016). An online marketing strategies assessment for companies in airlines and entertainment industries in Malaysia. Handbook of Research on Leveraging Consumer Psychology for Effective Customer Engagement, 1-15.

Rege, A. (2009). What's Love Got to Do with It? Exploring Online Dating Scams and Identity Fraud. *International Journal of Cyber Criminology.*

Reyns, B. W. (2015). A routine activity perspective on online victimisation. *Journal of Financial Crime, 22*(4), 396–411. doi:10.1108/JFC-06-2014-0030

Suki, N. M. (2016). *Handbook of Research on Leveraging Consumer Psychology for Effective Customer Engagement.* https://www.igi-global.com/book/handbook-research-leveraging-consumer-psychology/149284

Werner, R. R. (2017). How to Protect Against Common Cyberattacks and Insure Against Potential Losses. (cover story). *The CPA Journal, 87*(3), 16. Retrieved from http://search.ebscohost.com.proxy.cecybrary.com/login.aspx?direct=true&db=f5h&AN=121733191&site=ehost-live&scope=site

Whitty, M. T. (2013). The Scammers Persuasive Techniques Model: Development of a Stage Model to Explain the Online Dating Romance Scam. *British Journal of Criminology.* doi:10.1093/bjc/azt009

Whitty, M. T. (2015). *Mass-marketing fraud: A growing concern.* Academic Press.

Whitty, M. T. (2017). Do You Love Me? Psychological Characteristics of Romance Scam Victims. *Cyberpsychology, Behavior, and Social Networking.* doi:10.1089/cyber.2016.0729 PMID:28657792

Whitty, M. T. (2018). 419 – It's just a Game : Pathways to Cyber- Fraud Criminality emanating from West Africa. doi:10.5281/zenodo.1467848

Whitty, M. T., & Buchanan, T. (2012). The Online Romance Scam: A Serious Cybercrime. *Cyberpsychology, Behavior, and Social Networking*, *15*(3), 181–183. doi:10.1089/cyber.2011.0352 PMID:22304401

Chapter 6
The Affective Economy and Online Fan Communities:
A Case Study of Johnny & Associates

Nur Aliah Mansor
https://orcid.org/0000-0001-7485-594X
Universiti Malaysia Kelantan, Malaysia

Zam Zuriyati Mohamad
https://orcid.org/0000-0003-0222-0480
Universiti Tunku Abdul Rahman, Malaysia

Rizalniyani Abdul Razak
https://orcid.org/0000-0002-3200-1388
Universiti Tunku Abdul Rahman, Malaysia

Norrina Din
https://orcid.org/0000-0002-1347-5895
Universiti Teknologi MARA, Malaysia

Arbaiah Abdul Razak
https://orcid.org/0000-0003-4442-1686
Independent Researcher, Malaysia

ABSTRACT

This chapter explores participation and co-production in affective media experiences in Johnny & Associates' online fan communities. Johnny & Associates is a Japanese all-male talent management company established in the 1960s. As a pioneer in the idol industry, Johnny & Associates and artists under its management have been highly influential in the contemporary Japanese entertainment industry. These artists are collectively known as Johnny's idols or Janīzu. Much of the data are collected through participant-experiencer and interviews. The originality of this case study stems mainly from the empirical data for Johnny & Associates, Janīzu, and the global fan base during Johnny & Associates' transition to a social media platform. This chapter analyses marketing strategy, audience awareness, and behaviour in relation to a mass media phenomenon. The complex interaction among Johnny & Associates, Janīzu, and fans generates tensions and contradictions that mirror the modern mediated life.

DOI: 10.4018/978-1-7998-3042-9.ch006

INTRODUCTION

Japan is the second largest music market in the world, and its music is completely produced by local artists (IFPI, 2014). One branch of Japan's contemporary music scene is the idol industry. Johnny's idols, or Janīzu, is the term for artists represented by a Japanese all-male talent management company, Johnny & Associates. The term Janīzu, or Johnny's idols, is preferred to the term celebrity. Also, the term idol fits this popular subculture. Since different definitions of idol appear in the literature, this paper uses Hiroshi Aoyagi's (2005) concept of idols as "all-round popular talents" who sing, dance, act in dramas, and appear in commercials. While idols' performance is often ridiculed as artless or "bubble-gum," their popularity is an unmistakable phenomenon in Japanese society. The word idols is mostly relevant to young performers who sing, pose for photographs, and appear frequently in the Japanese media. However, the phenomenal popularity of Janīzu did not come overnight. The idols had to hone their skills in dancing, singing, and acting to please the audience. As the performers are trained to be observant of audience responses, they can handle unexpected situations by utilizing their resources. Also, during the global music crisis, Janīzu enjoyed unprecedented popularity and achieved impressive CD sales targets in the Japanese market.

More research that delve into aspect of consumer behavior and psychology in the digital economy is deemed necessary (Ling Chang, Ling Tam, & Suki, 2016; Nathan, Fook Chiun, & Suki, 2016; Suki, 2016). By way of a case study, this study focuses on commodification of Janīzu and how female fans experience the highly constructed personas of Janīzu. A range of specific affective dimensions in Johnny's fandom such as maternal feelings, shōnen, relatability, uncool-ness, and sexuality will be discussed. This chapter aims to advance the understanding of the interrelationships between the roles of affective components in marketing and how marketers use the affective component in their strategic marketing decisions.

The discussion draws upon ethnographic research conducted between November 2013 and March 2014 and 11 in-depth interviews with members of Johnny's English-speaking online fan communities on LiveJournal.

BACKGROUND

The affective economy refers to an understanding of the emotional relationship that the consumer has toward exposure to a product and purchase decision (Jenkins, 2006). Affect involves stimulation, drives, motivations, emotions, feelings, sensations, or that which is experienced in a lived and embodied place and time (McStay, 2013). In short, it is corporeal. Affect is an umbrella term for a set of more specific mental processes, including emotions, moods, and possibly attitudes. Thus, affect might be considered a general category for mental feeling processes, rather than a particular psychological process per se (Bagozzi et al., 1999). In the context of this case study, affect also refers to emotional experience, the feeling of ease, well-being, satisfaction, excitement, passion, and even the sense of connectedness or community (Hardt, 1999, p. 96). Rather than defining affect philosophically, this case study defines the term from a marketing perspective.

Scholars who study marketing have viewed the affective economy as the desire to link brand meaning to symbolic consumption. This means that advertising involves a delicate balance between consumer passion and rationality expressed in terms of a movement among visual play, emotion, passion, nonsense, and a call to order (Oswald, 2010). In regard to the social media environment, affective intensity creates a sense of being desirable and having importance and a sense of making things matter (Paasonen, 2018).

Celebrity is central to affective activities. Affective activism is often mentioned in fan studies literature due to fans' connection with the celebrity. Fan labor activities relate to affective activities undertaken freely and willingly that produce value for the user (unpaid labor) (Coté & Pybus, 2007; Jarrett, 2003; Terranova, 2000; Martens, 2011). Audiences are described not as passive consumers, but as active, emotionally engaged, and socially networked users (Jenkins, 2006). Commodified affective fan activism includes active promoters for the artists, creating content on fan sites, and creating content for advertisers/management (Baym & Burnett, 2009; Yang, 2009).

Previous research in fan-related activities shows that affective activities allow fans to gain cultural capital, establish social connections with the celebrities and feel close to them, and channel their knowledge through "collective intelligence" (Jenkins, 2006; Baym & Burnett, 2009). Fans' affective activities also build "affective labor," which produces social network forms of community within their social group (i.e., their relationship with other fans) (Hardt, 1999, p. 96). This, however, does not necessarily generate economic return for the fan.

While such participation seems like a form of empowerment, it is also a way for agencies to exploit fans' labor to create commodified cultural products which they in turn can sell back to the fans who helped shape them (Martens, 2011). In a previous study on the star-making process of a Chinese idol, Li Yuchun, the fans were involved in affective activities by being active promoters of Li. Her fans voted during the show, actively promoted her albums, and bought multiple copies of her album. However, her fans felt exploited when Yuchun's management company read their comments on forums and repackaged Li according to the fans' comments, including their stated desire to see Yuchun be more involved with her music/album production (Yang, 2009). This chapter aims to advance the understanding of the interrelationship between the role of affect and its influence on fans' consumption.

JANĪZU AS A COMMODITY

Janīzu as Hardworking and Relatable Idols

Rather than charisma, a core characteristic in the marketing of Janīzu is the boy-next-door image (Glasspool, 2012; Nagaike, 2012). An idol has to be relatable, and Janīzu's star quality takes a long time to build. The Shōnen Club (Boys Club) television program plays an important role in shaping the idols as hardworking, relatable, and "uncool" idols. The Shōnen Club was aired twice a month by the NHK television channel. In 1998, Hideaki Takizawa of Tackey & Tsubasa, leader of the Johnny's Junior faction at that time, kick-started the program. Today, the Shōnen Club features the most recent Johnny's group to make its debut and Johnny's Junior. They generally sing from an enormous track list created by the Seniors and compete against each other in variety-like game segments, allowing fans to see their individualism. The Shōnen Club often airs clips of the Juniors from their early days, thereby showing how much they have grown as idols.

Another important element of building this image is attributed to portrayal of hardworking idols on variety shows and concert backstage documentary DVDs. JOHNNY'S WORLD: Top of the J-Pops, a television documentary, follows Ryosuke Yamada learning to walk a tightrope. The learning process is narrated until the first day of the performance. On observing this process, one of the Juniors said:

Some people find it too tough, and it is hard, but it's how you make your dream a reality. If you give up now, you give up on the dream. (JOHNNYS' World: Top of the J-Pops, 2013)

Koichi Domoto of KinKi Kids reflects his own journey building up his career as an idol in the same television documentary. He said:

We were trained since kids. It taught us to be brave, to stand strong. What happens after that is gradually you learn to go further on your own. Not everyone does, of course, that's where you see the difference

Janīzu anticipate their singing debut, which they refer to as their CD debut; only then are they considered to have officially made their debut in the Japanese entertainment industry. However, the biggest avenue for them to be recognized by the public and found by overseas fans is through their appearance on various television programs.

During the interviews with fans, they noted various ways they could enjoy their favorite Janīzu. Because Janīzu are multi-talented with careers in many areas of the entertainment business, fans have many ways to enjoy their idols. For example, TOKIO was the first group of Janīzu to debut as a band. The five members of the band - leader and guitarist Shigeru Joshima, bassist Tatsuya Yamaguchi, keyboardist Taichi Kokubun, drummer Masahiro Matsuoka, and frontman Tomoya Nagase, did not have choreographed dance routines to their songs. However, TOKIO had the same career path as their Seniors. Their weekly variety program titled The! Tetsuwan! DASH!! is performed while the five members carry out labor-intensive work such as carpentry to help local communities across Japan with conservation projects. On the program, they wear white crewneck T-shirts and overalls and wrap their heads in a white towel for wiping sweat away and don safety helmets. Their image on the show is in sharp contrast to their on-stage persona where they dress smartly in power suits. Variety programs are essential in Japan to market the idols as being relatable to their fans and the general audience. This creates a breed of idols known as real-life idols.

The image of Janīzu in popular dramas is very much constructed by television producers with a script that is likely agreed on with Johnny & Associates. This observation is in line with David Marx's assessment of Japanese talent agencies and their business principles (Marx, 2012). He suggested that these agencies "exert strong control over the entertainment" industry ecosystem (p. 41-46). In contrast, variety programs have a more laid-back approach when using the idols. For this reason, they play a crucial part in showcasing the human side of Janīzu. A few examples of variety programs mentioned by the study participants that attracted them into fandom are TOKIO's The! Tetsuwan! DASH!!, V6's Gakkō e Ikō, and the Shōnen Club.

All fans from the interviews also shared that they are attracted to Janīzu because they are hardworking. The fans described the hardworking nature of the idols as follows:

Not necessarily "handsome" or naturally talented but somebody who works hard and can make the most of their looks and abilities. (Fan #7, research interview, 2013)

I deeply admire his professionalism and how he always seem to put in 150% effort (or even more) in everything he does. On top of that, because Kame is my age, I see him as my role model. (Fan #10, research interview, 2013)

October 2005 when I watched hana Yori dango Japan version while comparing with the Taiwan version, Matsuda shota was awesome (still my fav) and domyouji was a darling (he still is to me). And then in 2007 Toma was in the second season first episode and he just rox big time!! Mid2007 I was suicidal and found the web page on Toma and that's where all of it seriously started. (Fan #5, research interview, 2013)

Based on the interviews with fans, the life experiences of Janīzu and fans are similar. Additionally, without exception, every interviewee revealed that the idols played a significant part during a difficult time in their lives. The fans admitted that as they faced serious problems at various stages of their lives, such as the death of a loved one or work or college troubles, the idols cheered them up. The fans also pointed out that they could relate to the idols' own struggles and how they worked through them was inspirational. This finding supports Rajagopalan's (2011) statement that a celebrity is a catalyst in fans' emotional transformation from a state of misery and hardship to contentment and emotional well-being. He presented a case of Russian online fans navigating losses and hardships through emotional support from a Hindi superstar, Shah Rukh Khan.

The idols are seen as very hardworking even from an early age. They are signed up as Juniors when they are between 6 and 12 years old and debut as soon as management thinks they are ready to launch. Based on the fans' quotations above, they feel that Janīzu seem to lose their childhood, and it is clear that the idols seem to experience a very different upbringing from their fans. The majority of the fans encountered Janīzu in their early 20s while in college. As soon as they started working, they claimed that they used Janīzu's life experiences and work ethic as a point of reference to overcome workplace difficulties and real-life situations. As the fans grow older at the same time as their idols, they encounter the same experiences and problems as the idols. These parallel experiences seem to make the fans' transition from college to working life easier as the circumstances create the illusion that they are growing up with their idols.

These findings are aligned with Stevenson's (2009) research suggesting that this interaction is evidence of an intimate relationship between fan and idol. This is achieved through fans' immersion in the music and the artist's life over the years. Stevens (2011) studied David Bowie's fans, who had been fans since they were teenagers. Their fandom occupying many years of their lives and their relationship with Bowie developed over time. His fans considered him to be a survivor of cultural change, which provided them with hope to be able to adapt to a fast-changing society.

Likewise, the idols are not afraid to show their emotional or vulnerable sides. A few examples are Sho Sakurai of Arashi who is afraid of heights, Ryuhei Maruyama of Kanjani Eight who battles weight gain, and A.B.C-Z who compares their popularity to another Johnny's group of the same age, Kis-My-Ft2. Consequently, because fans can relate to these down-to-earth personal qualities, they idolize the idols for their off-stage attributes first rather than their musical talents.

Building Boys-Next-Door Image Through Seishun Dorama (Youth Television Drama Series)

Many young Japanese talents make their acting debut through youth-oriented drama series (seishun dorama), and as Johnny's Juniors join early, Johnny & Associates makes good commercial use of their youthfulness (shōnen). High school settings are vital to this genre and dorama production. Seishun dorama themes revolve around friendship, first loves, and dreams, which many viewers can relate to (Iwabuchi, 2004). Kinpachi-sensei, a famous dorama, has starred members of the Tanokin Trio, Shunsuke Kazama, KAT-TUN, and Hey! Say! JUMP. Seishun doramas cultivate transnational imagination and a self-reñection toward one's own culture and society (Iwabuchi, 2004), and they have successfully transcended across international audiences. Iwabuchi's assertion is reflected in several fans' discovery stories of Janīzu from seishun dorama, as follows:

Anyway, when I heard of Hokuto and Yugo's new drama Bakaleya, I just had to watch it. After watching that drama, my bias quickly changed from Nakaken to Hokuto XD. (Fan #11, research interview, 2013)

So, I have this friend whom I share our interests with each other even when we are in different fandoms; we're open to new things. She just finished watching Nobuta wo Produce around Feb 2008 and found Yamapi's character really cute. She started googling around and realized that Kame is very pretty. Both of us love pretty boys. So, she ended up sharing (spamming) with me Kame's pretty pictures for a month, before I finally caved and decided that Kame is really an ikemen and ikemen is really good as a stress reliever (laughs). (Fan #10, research interview, 2013)

Shiritsu Bakaleya Koukou (Bakaleya) and Nobuta wo Produce are popular seishun doramas starring Johnny's idols. In fact, the majority of participants in the study encountered Janīzu from the popular drama Hana Yori Dango starring Jun Matsumoto of Arashi. Hana Yori Dango is based on a popular shōjo (girls) manga. Matsumoto, who plays Tsukasa Domyōji, is a high-school student from an upper-class family who falls in love with a student from a working-class family. Tsukasa Domyōji's naivety and his strong feeling for the girl attracts the female audiences to the actor who plays the character (Harris & Ferris, 2011). The young audience also feels an intense sympathy toward another Romeo and Juliet character (Iwabuchi, 2004). This leads to the discovery of his idol group, Arashi.

The interviews with fans revealed that those who were drawn to the Japanese popular media content through a dorama would eventually watch more doramas. This leads them to discover other young actors such as Toma Ikuta, Tomohisa Yamashita, and Kazuya Kamenashi of KAT-TUN. This again supports Iwabuchi's (2004) assertion that the dorama plays an important role in spreading the Japanese popular culture. The fans who searched on the Internet for information about these actors were all directed to the same place, namely, Johnny & Associates.

The idols wear high school uniforms in doramas. In 2014, one of Johnny's Juniors from Bakaleya dorama, Hokuto Matsumura, also starred in SHARK. Aside from Matsumura and Iwamoto, SHARK starred a different line-up of Johnny's Juniors. SHARK is a dorama about a five-member band that wants to change the world with their music; they dream of making their major debut. In contrast to his school image in Bakaleya, Matsumura was styled in black and leather rock clothing to emphasize a mature image and position himself as a "cool" idol among fans.

Matsumura's transformation is just one example of capturing fans' feelings of growing up with the idol. Fans can see and feel the Junior (and idols) from the high school, college, working, and having-a-family aspects of the idols' life on the screen. Johnny & Associates also holds coming-of-age ceremonies at Meiji Shrine, Tokyo. The ceremonies are usually swarmed by fans.

Jason Karlin made the case quite well when he described Japanese idol fans as having a "motherly gaze" because they have been following the idol's career since the idol was a Junior. As a result, the fans adopt these idols into their family (Karlin, 2012). All the fans' feelings of being equals, motherly, or an older sibling are attributed to the construction of a real-life type of idol. Karlin's "motherly gaze" is another face of affective labor (Hardt, 1999). Female fans derive their pleasure from supporting and encouraging the success of their idols. By enacting complete control over the transformation of the idols, from boys to men, through television doramas and album releases, Johnny & Associates can market relatable idols and sell the idols themselves.

Transformation From Boys to Men Through Female Magazines

Janīzu are expected to maintain a youthful shōnen image, despite their actual age; hence, idols smile with bared teeth and clear, sparkling eyes to display marketable cuteness. This is illustrated by their appearance on the covers of idol magazines. The pictures are often digitally enhanced to make lips pinker and eyes sparkle with stars on top of the idols' invariably slender, stylishly dressed figures against a brightly colored background (Glasspool, 2012).

The success and popularity that Janīzu enjoy with female audiences is no doubt attributed to their looks and sex appeal, often labeled by fans and media as ikemen (pretty boy). Janīzu occasionally have long hair, are always clean shaven, and have lean bodies. In concerts, they often wear costumes that cross gender boundaries, such as form-fitting suits, with huge flowers, feathers, and sequins sewn to their costumes. One of the most notable of Johnny's jokes among fans and the idols themselves refers to Arashi's transparent costume, made from clear plastic, under which the group wore only white shorts. They wore the costumes when promoting their debut single A•RA•SHI between 1999 and 2000.

In contrast to their shōnen image, the idols are aware that they are viewed as sex objects and often play upon this construction. Almost every year, one of Janīzu pose nude for an appearance in an.an, one of Japan's most popular women's magazines. The picture exists purely as an example of sexually desirable masculinity for the visual pleasure of the magazine's readership, which is entirely composed of females. The feature is sexually explicit, incorporating staged sexual positions with female, Caucasian models, fondling of the female breasts, or posing in a shower. However, an.an's annual sex issues have always caused shocks and scandals among readers through images of eroticized male bodies and nude shots of Janīzu, thus prompting readers to project their own images onto the pictures. Although their ideal image has been described as boyish and youthful, this idealization has been challenged with Janīzu appearances in women's magazines like an.an. This idea is in line with Sigmund Freud's psychoanalysis theory (1926), which suggests a role for unconscious wishes and desires, where, in this case, the images attract the reader to escape from her world and enter a world of fantasy and daydreams. These images signify appropriate symbolic terms that are related to the consumers' unconscious desires. Thus, this raises an issue of the extent to which these variations of Janīzu image representations are interpreted by fans and how such interpretations influence fans' consumption.

Fans expressed their desire to idealize the sexual appeal of the idols as follows:

Matsumura Hokuto is my number 1:D he doesn't have an official group though but goes by HokuJe together with Jesse:) I love that pair. The reason he is my favorite is because he is flirty and eroi. X) It's like the main reason that I'm in the Johnny's fandom in the first place... give me hip rolls or go home. (Fan #11, research interview, 2013)

Why Matsujun from Arashi is my fav? Bcos when he was younger, he wriggled and shakes like nobody business!!! Now he do it lesser oh why they all grow up!!! And he is my darling domyouji!! (Fan #5, research interview, 2013)

Surprisingly, the sexiness of Janīzu is not discussed openly by many in the interviews. Only two fans said that the idols dance routine is choreographed so the fans can enjoy the idols' bodies. This finding is similar to Darling-Wolf's (2004) study of SMAP, whose choreography is designed to please the female audience.

In many of Janīzu television dramas, scenes in which they take showers are among the most anticipated. Janīzu are allowed to cross boundaries such as posing nude for the magazine as well as showing their sex appeal on television as long as their actions are authorized by Johnny & Associates. The management terminated the contract of Koki Tanaka, a former member of KAT-TUN in October 2013, when a full-frontal photo of him made the tabloids' front cover. Previously, Tanaka had played the bad boy image in the group, but in reality the bad boy act was not well received by the management.

Even though they are aware that they represent the ultimate fan fantasy, not all Janīzu are comfortable with their sexual objectification. In the variety show Himitsu no Arashi-chan (2012) that aired on May 10, 2012, Satoshi Ohno of Arashi stated that for his 2008 Maō television drama, the script required him to perform in two shower scenes which he actually hated doing. He also referred to another member of the group, Jun Matsumoto, who usually acted as a leading man in romantic dramas such as Hana Yori Dango as being much more adept in doing shower scenes. Ohno, who is very reserved in terms of his actions and words, constructed an authentic identity unique among Janīzu.

In a different television program, Arashi ni Shiyagare, which aired on November 13, 2010, the other members of Arashi expressed having a difficult time adjusting to being alone at home after performing to 70,000 fans at the Tokyo Dome a few hours earlier. Ohno said that he felt the most real when he is at home, absorbed in his drawing, and said that television appearances are a sharp contrast to his actual life and his television appearances feel like a dream. Ohno is an example of tensions that exist between what Johnny & Associates wants the idol to be and the idols' struggles to stay real.

The intensity of Johnny's fans' association with their idols is similar to the relationship of many East Asian celebrities with their fans. For example, the Hong Kong celebrity Jackie Chan was marketed by his former talent agency as everybody's Jackie, especially to his Japanese female audience (Morimoto, 2013). Chan, who is a popular star in action movies, was not allowed to be involved in any romantic movie projects until his contract with his former agency ended and he had established his own production company. It is not clear who is to blame here, the idols, the fans, or the marketing, but it nonetheless highlights the complex relationship between the idols and their fans.

IDOL-FAN RELATIONSHIP

In Japan's entertainment industry, idols are regarded as dream sellers, and the fans buy into their fantasy, devouring as much of this dream commodity as they can. The following further illustrates how the intensity of Janīzu-fan relationships is formed. First, one of the fans asked one of the idols, Yuya Takaki of Hey! Say! JUMP, in the JOHNNYS' World documentary how he regarded his fans: His response was "as my girlfriend" (JOHNNYS' World: Top of the J-Pops, 2013). Janīzu always have pet names for their fans and the names are only known among the fan's circle. For instance, Subaru Shibutani has named Kanjani Eight fans as eighters although this is not to be mistaken with the official Janīzu fan club, Johnny's Family Club. Likewise, Junta Nakama of Johnnys' WEST often writes to an imaginary fan named JasMine on his blog on Johnny's Web, Johnny's mobile site.

Fans who were interviewed said that they liked the fact that Janīzu pay attention to the fans. They feel like they are part of something important, as expressed in the following excerpts:

My love for him only grew after I got to meet him, and now I write to him every now and then on his radio show or through j-net promotions and I hope that he still remembers me (he at least said he did on his radio show). (Fan #3, research interview, 2013)

So that fans can feel they're a part of something. Which is much of what the appeal is, I think. When fans have so many different ways to enjoy their idols, they become a bigger part of their life, which is what keeps their love going strong. (Fan #6, research interview, 2013)

In idol magazines such as Duet and Wink Up, as well as television interviews, Janīzu are often asked questions about their type of woman, ideal date, and other questions that highlight their romantic side. On television programs and during concerts, Kazunari Ninomiya of Arashi often flashes flirty winks to appeal to the female audience. Although the majority of Janīzu songs are based on love themes, each group has at least one serenade song often dedicated to their fans, such as Hey! Say! JUMP's Romeo and Juliet. These findings are consistent with Duran Duran's fans, where the fans embedded the love song into their own fantasies; the fans wanted to see themselves as the woman for whom the singer was expressing such yearning (Anderson, 2012).

Kimura Takuya of SMAP fame has always insisted that he is a "public property" (Galbraith & Karlin, 2012). In East Asia, this is taken seriously to the point that if a celebrity gets married or even starts to date, the fans are entitled to a "rebate." An uproar from fans always follows a marriage announcement. Takuya himself married a fellow female Japanese idol in 2000. His marriage announcement also included news of his girlfriend's pregnancy. Nevertheless, he has never mentioned his wife or children in media interviews. With the exception of Takuya, all other Johnny's idols get married after they have passed the peak of their popularity. Kitagawa has to approve of the marriage as a business strategy and partly because Kitagawa serves as a father figure to the idols. Despite his approval, their marriage would not be announced by their agency, and it is never mentioned in their biography on the Johnny & Associates official website. Usually, the celebrity and spouse will hold a press conference to announce their news to the media. After the marriage, however, they do not mention their marriage during events or concerts so that they look like they are not involved in any romantic relationship. The fans know about the marriage but choose not to think about it.

When an idol does get involved with a woman, usually in secret, the Japanese media, especially the red tops, go crazy. Even the idols who attend gōkōn (group blind dates) are stalked by the paparazzi, so it is clear that the media treat them differently, and the "scoop" is often not as it seems. However, it is not exclusive to Janīzu to have a scandal-free image in Japan. The most extreme case in Japan's idol scene was when AKB48's Minami Minegishi shaved her head to apologize to fans when the news of her dating another celebrity leaked in January 2013. Head-shaving symbolizes an act of penance in Japanese culture. Still, her actions caused an uproar as the video was uploaded to AKB48's official YouTube channel where she apologized to her fans. It is rumored among the AKB48 online fan communities that her management had suggested Minegishi's action.

The most intense reactions by the Johnny & Associates management team following an idol marriage was to Jin Akanishi's marriage in February 2012; the reaction indicates how tightly Johnny & Associates controls everything. Akanishi married a fellow Japanese actress in 2012, but he failed to notify Johnny

& Associates about his nuptials. The agency then canceled his United States music activities and his Japanese tour. Akanishi's scandal is an indication of how tightly Johnny & Associates management controls its idols' images. Consequently, both male and female idols in Japan are expected to remain (or seem to remain) single and available for fan fantasies. Their public image is supposed to reconcile with chaste shōnen (young boys) or shōjo (young girls). Fans have linked idols to single and chaste shōnen based on their desire. This has formed a highly complex idol-fan relationship. Having discussed the idols' image construction, the following section examines Johnny's fangirls' role in supporting Janīzu careers.

AFFECTIVE WORKS OF JOHNNY'S FANGIRLS

This section provides descriptive background of the research participants to understand the type of fan who engages and participates in Johnny's fan culture. Before we can understand whether and how the fans are aware of being exploited by the commercial agency, we must first understand how the fans use Internet technologies for their media consumption. It is important to note the Internet's significance to overseas Johnny's fans in their media consumption within the fandom. It is also important to study the fans from "below" a grassroot cultural approach that considers them from the perspective of consumers themselves to permit understanding of the role they play in the consumption but also production of Johnny & Associates (Turner, 2004). Access to Japanese celebrity culture outside of Japan is difficult to attain if a fan does not live in a major metropolitan area that carries imported Japanese cultural goods or in a country that imports Japanese television programming and, even then, access is quite limited. As a result of this lack of physical access, the Internet is the gateway for Johnny's media consumption (Pradhan, 2010), where LiveJournal is considered a hub for Johnny's-related media. Not only is the physical unavailability overcome by the Internet, but television shows, doramas and commercials, radio shows, magazines, J-webs, and photos are all available in digital form.

Johnny's fangirls or JE fangirls (Johnny's Entertainment) is the common name by which fans address themselves. The fans who were interviewed shared similar profiles. They were professionals who had a stable monthly income and fixed working hours. These types of fans stated that they were involved in fandom activities within working hours. There were also fans who are studying in graduate schools on a full-time or part-time basis; one is working in shifts and arranges her time for fan-related online activities, such as downloading and posting concert updates around classes and work shifts. The majority of fans considers Johnny's fandom a significant part of themselves.

The existence of Internet technologies allows fans to bypass traditional media networks to obtain information directly. Fans manage web sites, LiveJournal blogs and communities, Tumblr, and Twitter accounts to provide news and information to their fandoms. Johnny's LiveJournal online communities hold a unique position as they are built on fan-generated contents. On LiveJournal communities, fans can create their personal blog, as well as contribute to the communities, thus creating and amassing information. Johnny & Associates never intended to target the overseas market. Therefore, Johnny's LiveJournal online communities create user-generated content (UGC) to reach a significant audience. All the acts in the community are voluntary. UGC might represent both the expression of customer complaints and brand fan dedication (Burmann, 2010).

Fans use the online communities to praise and critique the Johnny's-related brand. They also take upon themselves the work of marketing and branding Johnny's, as follows:

I didn't like how Western/English language fans were always trashing JE music!! This is good music if you just get rid of American preconceptions of what "good" music is. So, I wanted to give fangirls a different vocabulary for music and a different frame of reference. (Fan #7, research interview, 2013)

The responses I get are always interesting. It's enough to make me wish somebody from Arashi's team really was reading through to see how fangirls respond to their music. (Fan #7, research interview, 2013)

And then after that I started buying TV navi magazine pretty regularly. They have a 1-page interview each month on Ueda and Nakamaru's radio show. I love that radio show. No one really scans the magazines so I'll buy and scan them. The Ueda fandom has always been rather small, so the mentality then was to buy photos/doujinshi/magazines so as to keep and share with more people. (Fan #10, research interview, 2013)

Lately I've been trying to find time to translate scans, been doing a few but I don't have as much time for that as I might want. I don't want it to start to feel like a job. Considering all the other missions I've set myself on doing I might have less time translating. More of late, when I decided to start contributing to dramawiki, I started creating pages for most Johnny's boys that didn't have one (mostly Juniors). I've created some drama pages also but they require more work and time so I haven't done as many of those. Dramawiki is fun, and it was always the site I turned to since the beginning of my fangirling. (Fan #11, research interview, 2013)

Fans are reworking the commercial brand from the agency through creation of their own work – fan fiction, fan work, and fan art. Fans also are drawing attention to their favourite idols by making more information available on the Internet and also in English. One fan even shows a keen interest in the performance and musical aspects of Janīzu where she often updates her personal LiveJournal with screenshots from the Shōnen Club and various Japanese music shows that feature Janīzu. She created a LiveJournal community to review Johnny's music to give her own interpretation of the music.

Another example of affective fan work done by Johnny's fangirls is sending mass postcards for KAT-TUN. Following Koki Tanaka's dismissal in 2013, KAT-TUN was left with four members. In October 2013, members of KAT-TUN's LiveJournal online community started a project, where fans of each country were to send postcards to KAT-TUN each month. The post was described as follows:

Never could we imagine that it would be in such moment and under such circumstances that we would be presenting this idea. Then again - now is the moment, when our boys KAT-TUN need our support more than ever, need to know that they are still loved by us – their hyphens.

The postcard is custom made with the KAT-TUN member's photo or art, name of the country of the sender, and the project logo created by fans and includes International Hyphens Support KAT-TUN as the motto. The objective of the project is to show support to KAT-TUN and show Johnny & Associates that Janīzu have many fans all over the world. Fans from Russia, the United States, Malaysia, Kazakhstan, Czech Republic, and Moldova participated in the postcard-sending project. Since the one-way nature of Johnny's artist-fan interaction is still in place, some Johnny's fangirls send snail mail regularly to show support for their idols. Snail mail is one way to sustain social bonds not only between fans from various locations (Galuszka, 2015) but also between fans and artists. Johnny's fangirls can send their fan letters to Johnny's Family Club building in Shinjuku. However, "building" is an exaggeration. The Shinjuku's Johnny's Family club refers to a physical place; a basement that displays Janīzu's awards, signed posters, signed CDs, and message cards to fans–it is a Janīzu's museum with free entrance.

Even though Johnny's fangirls want to be noticed by the agency, they also show contradictions. On New Year's Day 2014, TOKIO's variety program aired a segment in which they tried tasting realistic-looking objects made from chocolate such as shoes, door handles, and photo frames. Johnny's fangirls had made animated gifs and posted them on Tumblr. Although this was not their intention, the animated gifs caught the attention of the Internet and went viral overnight.

However, some fans were displeased by the sudden attention received by Janīzu on the Internet:

Tokio is now famous overseas and the agency might come down on international fandom.... if this somehow links back to je fandom and all our sharing sites, it could get really bad quick... this whole thing is just making me feel very protective for some reason...they are not TOKIO anymore, they're nameless funny faces. (Fan #3, Twitter, January 2014)

This fan conveyed her uneasiness with the sudden attention that TOKIO received. This situation may lead the agency to international fandom, and the consequence is that the agency might shut down the community, a situation that Johnny's fangirls would like to avoid. On one side, the fans want to be recognized by the agency; however, yet another conflict is the attention that they receive and feeling protective of the community. This is just an example of the complicated dynamics between fans and the agency.

In a similar vein, in regard to SMAP's disbandment, the group's Japanese fans launched a campaign that encouraged the purchase of the tune, Sekai ni Hitotsu Dake no Hana, to stop SMAP from disbanding (Kyodo, 2016). As a result, the single topped the Oricon, with 2.6 million copies sold, nearly reaching the campaign's goal of 3 million copies. Even though the fan's efforts did not stop the group from disbanding, this circumstance illustrates the agency's monetary gain from fans' affective work.

All the above examples are consistent with Jenkins' (2015) research of the Harry Potter Alliance audience. Jenkins used a mechanism similar to fan groups' letter-writing and "save the show" campaigns, which moved the audience from engagement within participatory culture to involvement in political life. Fans are no longer just active producers who collaboratively produce fan works, such as fan fiction, fan art, and subtitling or translation services for foreign texts. Fans are mobilized as active participants in social and political movements because they are united by a common factor: their consumption of popular culture (Chin & Morimoto, 2013). They become promoters of and collaborators with their favorite brands (Yang, 2009; Hamilton & Hewer, 2010; Baym & Burnett, 2009). Although their direct and indirect appeals to Johnny & Associates can be seen as positive acts to support their favorite artists, the appeals can also be interpreted as contradictory to Johnny & Associates' business decisions. This reveals the other side of the coin of prosumers, which are resisters and anti-fans of the brand (Hamilton & Hewer, 2010; Gray, 2003). This is in line with Gray's (2003) argument that "fan studies have taken us to one end of a spectrum of involvement with a text, but we should also look at the other end to those individuals spinning around a text in its electron cloud, variously bothered, insulted or otherwise assaulted by its presence" (p. 70). Therefore, Johnny's fangirls' affective works illustrate a correlation between loving and disliking Johnny & Associates' products and brands.

CONCLUSION

This chapter presents and considers field data in the form of fan testimonials. The chapter aims to answer this question, "What are the commodification processes carried out for artists of Johnny & Associates?" To answer, the chapter explores the strong affective emotional response of fans through their response to Johnny & Associates' information management practices.

The chapter outlines how the image created for and by the celebrity is consumed by fans on the Japanese side of the business. The frequent appearance of Janīzu on television adds to the perception that they are simply a next-door neighbor. The multi-personas of Janīzu and the tensions that the idols experience to stay real with what the management implies and what is expected from them also is explored. Janīzu as the ultimate female fan fantasy, along with the complex relationship between the idols and their fans, is discussed.

Finally, the most significant finding to emerge from this chapter is the agency's highly evolved marketing strategy and how it operates, particularly in generating the idols' public image. This highly constructed image is how the agency tries to increase the fan base, its desire and demand for more products. The agency commodifies elements of the idols' youth (shōnen) and real-self authenticity to further capitalize on the emotional intimacy between fans and idols.

REFERENCES

Anderson, T. (2012). Still kissing their posters goodnight: Female fandom and the politics of popular music. *Participations*, *9*(2), 239–264.

Aoyagi, H. (2005). *Islands of eight million smiles: idol performance and symbolic production in contemporary Japan*. Cambridge: Harvard University Asia Center. doi:10.2307/j.ctt1tm7fbd

Bagozzi, R. P., Gopinath, M., & Nyer, P. U. (1999). The role of emotions in marketing. *Journal of the Academy of Marketing Science*, *27*(2), 184–206. doi:10.1177/0092070399272005

Baym, N. K., & Burnett, R. (2009). Amateur experts: International fan labour in Swedish independent music. *International Journal of Cultural Studies*, *12*(5), 433–449. doi:10.1177/1367877909337857

Chang, L. D. M., Ling Tam, A. Y., & Suki, N. M. (2016). Moderating effect of races towards consumers' feeling of TCM usage. Handbook of Research on Leveraging Consumer Psychology for Effective Customer Engagement, 306-323.

Chin, B., & Morimoto, L. (2013). Towards a theory of transcultural fandom. *Participations*, *10*(1), 92–108.

Coté, M., & Pybus, J. (2007). Learning to immaterial labour 2.0: MySpace and social networks. *Ephemera*, *7*(1), 88-106.

Darling-Wolf, F. (2004). Virtually multicultural: trans-Asian identity and gender in an international fan community of a Japanese star. *New Media & Society*, *6*(4), 507–528. doi:10.1177/146144804044332

Freud, S. (1926). Psycho-analysis. *To Theories Of*, 11.

Galbraith, P. W., & Karlin, J. G. (2012). *Idols and celebrity in Japanese media culture*. Hampshire: Palgrave Macmillan. doi:10.1057/9781137283788

Glasspool, L. (2012). From boys next door to boys' love: Gender performance in Japanese male idol media. In *Idols and celebrity in Japanese media culture* (pp. 113–130). Hampshire: Palgrave Macmillan. doi:10.1057/9781137283788_6

Gray, J. (2003). New audiences, new textualities: Anti-fans and non-fans. *International Journal of Cultural Studies*, *6*(1), 64–81. doi:10.1177/1367877903006001004

Hamilton, K., & Hewer, P. (2010). Tribal mattering spaces: Social-networking sites, celebrity affiliations, and tribal innovations. *Journal of Marketing Management*, *26*(3-4), 271–289. doi:10.1080/02672571003679894

Hardt, M. (1999). Affective labor. *Boundary 2*, *26*(2), 89-100.

Harris, S. R., & Ferris, K. O. (2011). *Stargazing: Celebrity, fame, and social interaction*. Routledge.

Himitsu no Arashi-chan. (2012b). Tokyo: Tokyo Broadcasting System.

IFPI. (2014). *IFPI digital music report 2014: lighting up new markets*. Retrieved from https://www.ifpi.org/downloads/Digital-Music-Report-2014.pdf

Iwabuchi, K. (2004). *Feeling Asian modernities: Transnational consumption of Japanese TV dramas* (Vol. 1). Aberdeen: Hong Kong University Press.

Jarrett, K. (2003). Labour of love: An archaeology of affect as power in e-commerce. *Journal of Sociology (Melbourne, Vic.)*, *39*(4), 335–351. doi:10.1177/0004869003394002

Jenkins, H. (2006). *Convergence culture: where old and new media collide*. New York: New York University Press.

Jenkins, H. (2015). "Cultural acupuncture": Fan activism and the Harry Potter alliance. In L. Geraghty (Ed.), *Popular media cultures* (pp. 206–229). Basingstoke: Springer. doi:10.1057/9781137350374_11

Johnnys' World. (2013). *Top of the J-Pops*. Tokyo: NHK World. [Television documentary]

Karlin, J. G. (2012). Through a looking glass darkly: television advertising, idols, and the making of fan audiences. In *Idols and celebrity in Japanese media culture* (pp. 72–93). Hampshire: Palgrave Macmillan. doi:10.1057/9781137283788_4

Kyodo. (2016). 2003 SMAP single tops chart after massive purchases by fans fearing group's breakup. *The Japan Times*. Retrieved from https://www.japantimes.co.jp/culture/2016/01/24/music/2003-smap-single-tops-chart-massive-purchases-fans-fearing-groups-breakup/#.Wy9me1UzZ0w

Martens, M. (2011). Transmedia teens: Affect, immaterial labor, and user-generated content. *Convergence*, *17*(1), 49–68. doi:10.1177/1354856510383363

Marx, D. W. (2012). The Jimusho system: understanding the production logic of the Japanese entertainment industry. In *Idols and celebrity in Japanese media culture* (pp. 35–55). Hampshire: Palgrave Macmillan. doi:10.1057/9781137283788_2

McStay, A. (2013). *Creativity and advertising: Affect, events and process*. London: Routledge. doi:10.4324/9780203492208

Morimoto, L. (2013). Trans-cult-ural fandom: Desire, technology and the transformation of fan subjectivities in the Japanese female fandom of Hong Kong stars. *Transformative Works and Cultures,* (14).

Nagaike, K. (2012). Johnny's idols as icons: Female desires to fantasize and consume male idol images. In *Idols and celebrity in Japanese media culture* (pp. 97–112). Hampshire: Palgrave Macmillan. doi:10.1057/9781137283788_5

Nathan, R. J., Fook Chiun, D. C., & Suki, N. M. (2016). An online marketing strategies assessment for companies in airlines and entertainment industries in Malaysia. Handbook of Research on Leveraging Consumer Psychology for Effective Customer Engagement, 1-15.

Oswald, L. R. (2010). Marketing hedonics: Toward a psychoanalysis of advertising response. *Journal of Marketing Communications*, *16*(3), 107–131. doi:10.1080/13527260802503638

Paasonen, S. (2018). Affect, data, manipulation and price in social media. *Distinktion: Journal of Social Theory*, 1-16.

Pradhan, J. (2010). It's My Passion, That's My Mission to Decide, I'm Going Worldwide: the Cosmopolitanism of Global Fans of Japanese Popular Culture (Master of Arts). University of Massachusetts Amherst.

Rajagopalan, S. (2011). Shahrukh Khan as media text: Celebrity, identity and emotive engagement in a Russian online community. *Celebrity Studies*, *2*(3), 263–276. doi:10.1080/19392397.2011.609333

Stevens, C. S. (2011). Touching the audience: Music and television advertising in Japan. *Japanese Studies*, *31*(1), 37–51. doi:10.1080/10371397.2011.560260

Stevenson, N. (2009). Talking to Bowie fans: Masculinity, ambivalence and cultural citizenship. *European Journal of Cultural Studies*, *12*(1), 79–98. doi:10.1177/1367549408098706

Suki, N. M. (2016). *Handbook of Research on Leveraging Consumer Psychology for Effective Customer Engagement*. https://www.igi-global.com/book/handbook-research-leveraging-consumer-psychology/149284

Terranova, T. (2000). Free labor. In *Digital Labor* (pp. 41–65). Routledge.

Yang, L. (2009). All for love: The Corn fandom, prosumers, and the Chinese way of creating a superstar. *International Journal of Cultural Studies*, *12*(5), 527–543. doi:10.1177/1367877909337863

Zhou, E. L. (2013). Displeasure, star-chasing and the transcultural networking fandom. *Participations*, *10*(2), 139–167.

Chapter 7
Antecedents, Motivations, and Consequences of Electronic Word-of-Mouth Communication for Consumers:
A Comprehensive Understanding

Raife Meltem Yetkin Özbük
https://orcid.org/0000-0002-2014-1850
Akdeniz University, Turkey

ABSTRACT

The advent of internet-based technologies and social media has drastically affected how people communicate and share information. Electronic word-of-mouth (E-WOM) communication is one of those communication methods, and it has attracted the attention of scholars because of its effects on the consumer's decision-making process. However, there is a fragmentation of the E-WOM communication literature because of the broad range of platforms and different E-WOM formats. Therefore, the purpose of this chapter is to provide a comprehensive understanding of the antecedents, motivations, and consequences of E-WOM communication for consumers in the digital economy.

INTRODUCTION

The developments in internet-based technologies and the popularity of social media platforms have led to a transformation in how consumers communicate with each other about a product, service, brand, or experience in the digital economy. Electronic word-of-mouth (E-WOM) communication as a digitalized form of traditional word-of-mouth (WOM) is one of these ways. E-WOM may be in written format such as online reviews (Casaló, Flavián, Guinalíu, & Ekinci 2015; Park & Lee 2009a), e-mails (Phelps, Lewis, Mobilio, Perry, & Raman 2004) or in verbal format similar to traditional WOM such as online videos (Hautz, Füller, Hutter, & Thürridl 2014). E-WOM communication may occur on various platforms such

DOI: 10.4018/978-1-7998-3042-9.ch007

as firms' web sites (Filieri 2015), online retailing platforms (Zhao, Yang, Narayan, & Zhao 2013), brand communities, independent web sites, consumer blogs, or social networking sites (Koo 2015).

The fragmentation of the E-WOM communication literature because of the broad range of platforms and different E-WOM formats causes the need for an extant study to show why and when consumers engage in E-WOM communication, why consumers receive E-WOM messages and how these messages affect them in the digital economy. More research that delved into the aspect of consumer behavior and psychology in the digital economy is deemed necessary (Chang, Ling Tam, & Suki, 2016; Nathan, Fook Chiun, & Suki, 2016; Suki, 2016). Accordingly, the purpose of this study is to provide a comprehensive understanding of the antecedents, motivations, and consequences of E-WOM for consumers in the digital economy.

BACKGROUND

E-WOM is defined as "any positive or negative statement made by potential, actual, or former customers about a product or company, which is made available to a multitude of people and institutions via the Internet" (Hennig-Thurau, Gwinner, Walsh, & Gremler, 2004: 39). There are different terms used for E-WOM in various disciplines (Clow & Donald, 2012: 276; King, Racherla, & Bush, 2014) such as online reviews (Chiou, Hsiao, & Chiu, 2018; Esmark Jones, Stevens, Breazeale, & Spaid, 2018), online product reviews (Floyd, Freling, Alhoqail, Cho, & Freling, 2014; Lee & Shin, 2014), online recommendations (Prendergast, Paliwal, & Chan, 2018), online word of mouth (Schmit & Thierry, 2018; Tang, 2017; Tang, 2016), online buzz (Lee, Lee, Kim, & Lee, 2013), online viral marketing (Koch & Benlian, 2015), or online consumer reviews (Filieri, Hofacker, & Alguezaui, 2018; Filieri, McLeay, Tsui, & Lin, 2018).

The properties of E-WOM communication are explained by discussing the components of E-WOM communication and their differences from traditional WOM communication. Similar to traditional WOM communication, E-WOM communication is composed of the sender, receiver, and message. However, overall, there are two important differences between traditional WOM and E-WOM. First, E-WOM occurs via an Internet or web-based platform. Second, in E-WOM, there is no direct feedback from the message receiver to the message sender in all communications. Third, message senders of E-WOM communication are the people who provide E-WOM (Ismagilova, Dwivedi, Slade, & Williams, 2017). They are generally anonymous; they have nicknames and no relationship with the message receiver (Park, Lee, & Han, 2007).

In traditional WOM, the consumers, as message senders, share their opinions with other consumers after the time has passed over their positive or negative experiences. However, in E-WOM communication, they can immediately share their opinions while they are experiencing a product or service (Berger & Schwartz, 2011). Additionally, even if the message sender and receiver are distant from each other, they can easily exchange information via internet or web-based platforms in E-WOM communication (Park et al., 2007; Steffes & Burgee, 2009). The credibility of the message sender (source credibility), i.e., the information seeker's perceptions of the source's expertise (Schiffman & Wisenblit, 2019), has positive effects on information adoption of the message received (Zhang & Watts, 2008) and attitudes toward information usefulness (Sussman & Siegal, 2003). For example, online reviews of experienced consumers are found as more useful by other reviewers (Casaló et al., 2015; Cheng & Ho, 2015; Filieri, 2015).

Message receivers of E-WOM communication are the people who actively engage in searching for and receiving information online. They are divided into two groups: pure receivers and resenders. Pure receivers only search and receive information. If they resend the information to others via different E-WOM engagement, they are called as resenders. Resenders are both message receivers and senders of E-WOM communication (Huang, Cai, Tsang, & Zhou, 2011). Message receivers are prospective consumers (He & Bond, 2013). In traditional WOM, a message sender may contact a few message receivers and message sender should be at the same place with the receiver. However, in E-WOM, numerous receivers may simultaneously deliver the opinions of the message sender (Park et al., 2007) at any time and place (Luo & Zhong, 2015). Additionally, the message receiver can easily respond to the message sender in traditional WOM (López & Sicilia, 2014). However, the responsiveness of the receiver in E-WOM communication depends on the platform's permission. Finally, the degree of intimacy and frequency of contacts between the receiver and the sender are strong in traditional WOM (Dellarocas, 2003). Traditional WOM emerges from a sender who is known by the message receiver, so the credibility of the sender and the message are known to the receiver (Steffes & Burgee, 2009). However, there is almost no relationship between the message sender and receiver in E-WOM communication (Park et al., 2007).

E-WOM messages have different characteristics. They can be in the written format, such as online reviews, blog articles, e-mails, or in the verbal format, such as videos. Messages of E-WOM communication are more persistent and accessible than messages of traditional WOM (Hung & Li, 2007; Lee, Park, & Han, 2008). Thus, they are in higher volume compared to traditional WOM (Chatterjee, 2001; Pan & Zhang, 2011). Different characteristics of E-WOM messages such as valence, volume, content, and format are studied by many researchers.

Valence is one of the most frequently studied E-WOM characteristics due to its effects on consumers and firms. Valence is related to the E-WOM communication direction and shows whether the message is positive or negative. Consumers may perceive E-WOM messages as useful (Casaló et al., 2015; Pan & Zhang, 2011; Purnawirawan, Eisend, Pelsmacker, & Dens, 2015; Schlosser, 2011), trustable (Benedicktus, Brady, Darke, & Voorhees, 2010; Pan & Chiou, 2011) or persuasive (Chakravarty, Liu, & Mazumdar, 2010) according to the valence of the message. Similarly, consumers' purchase intentions are affected by the E-WOM message communication direction (Wang, Yu, & Wei, 2012). Firms also benefit from E-WOM message valence while they are predicting new product performance (Parthasarathy & Forlani, 2010), market structure (Lee & Bradlow, 2011; Netzer, Feldman, Goldenberg, & Fresko, 2012; Tirunillai & Tellis, 2012; van Noort & Willemsen, 2012) or sales (Chevalier & Mayzlin, 2006; Chintagunta, Gopinath, & Venkataraman, 2010; Duan, Gu, & Whinston, 2008; Ho-dac, Carson, & Moore, 2013).

Volume is another E-WOM characteristic that is also effective in the persuasiveness of consumers, their product choice, and the sales of a firm. E-WOM volume is the cumulative number of online product reviews at a certain time (Chintagunta et al., 2010). For example, Khare, Labrecque, & Asare (2011) mentioned that the volume of online reviews is effective on the persuasiveness of consumers. Additionally, Huang & Chen (2006) discussed that in addition to sales volume and reviewer's expertise, online reviews' volume impacts consumer's product choice. Finally, there is a relationship between the sales volume and the product reviews' volume (Yang, Kim, Amblee, & Jeong, 2012; Zhang, Ma, & Cartwright, 2013). Variance in E-WOM ratings is also effective in the firm's sales. For example, consumers remove the products with high variances in online ratings from their consideration sets (Wang, Liu, & Fang, 2015).

Consumers may read multiple reviews when selecting products. Online review sets with positive and negative balances (the number of positive reviews is higher than or lower than the number of negative reviews, respectively) are found to be more useful than neutral review sets (the number of positive reviews is equal to the number of negative reviews) (Purnawirawan, De Pelsmacker, & Dens, 2012).

Content and format of E-WOM communication are also effective in the decision-making process of consumers (Ludwig et al., 2012). For example, the content of online reviews such as more information based vs more story-based is effective in persuading consumers (Hamby, Daniloski, & Brinberg, 2015). Additionally, when a review includes the reviewer's emotions, the rationality of and perceived usefulness of a review decrease (Kim & Gupta, 2012). Recent online reviews rather than old ones are found as more useful (Jin, Hu, & He, 2014).

Different characteristics of message senders, message receivers, and E-WOM messages hosted on a broad range of platforms cause fragmentation in E-WOM communication literature. Therefore, there is a need for an extant study to answer the following research questions:

RQ1: What are the antecedents of E-WOM communication?
RQ2: What are the motivations of consumers for sending and receiving E-WOM messages?
RQ3: What are the effects of E-WOM communication on the message receivers?

ANTECEDENTS OF E-WOM COMMUNICATION

Antecedents of E-WOM communication affect E-WOM engagement behavior (Jeong & Jang, 2011). Many researchers mentioned that limited research has been conducted on the antecedents of E-WOM behavior (Boo & Kim, 2013; Cheung & Lee, 2012; Liang, Ekinci, Occhiocupo, & Whyatt, 2013). While some antecedents such as satisfaction, dissatisfaction, or e-loyalty depend on the firm's performance, some antecedents such as prior E-WOM experience, online communication familiarity, involvement, risk-taking, posting frequency are only existed at the personal level. The following answers to the RQ1: What are the antecedents of E-WOM communication?

Satisfaction or dissatisfaction is one of the antecedents of E-WOM communication. After positive experiences, satisfied customers often engage in positive E-WOM along with other behavioral intentions. For example, service quality and satisfaction affect the revisit of the website, purchase intention, and positive E-WOM behavior (Gounaris, Dimitriadis, & Stathakopoulos, 2010). Jeong & Jang (2011) mentioned that satisfactory restaurant experiences related to food quality, service quality, atmosphere, and price fairness trigger positive E-WOM engagement. Service recovery is one of the alternatives to re-obtain customer satisfaction within the firms. Thus, consumers who are satisfied with the compensation efforts of firms have positive post-recovery satisfaction and trust which then turns into positive E-WOM behavior (Lii & Lee, 2012). Gohary, Hamzelu, & Alizadeh (2016) mentioned that firms could make their customers more satisfied by including them in the service failure recovery process, and this results in an increase in the positive E-WOM behavior. On the other hand, as a result of service failure (Lin, Wang, & Chang, 2011), dissatisfaction (Gebauer, Füller, & Pezzei, 2013) determines negative E-WOM engagement.

Satisfaction does not always affect positive E-WOM behavior directly. E-loyalty acts as a mediator between satisfaction and positive E-WOM behavior (Hsu, Wang, & Chih, 2015). E-loyalty also determines E-WOM behavior. For example, the quality and characteristics of the website affect e-loyalty that then leads to positive E-WOM engagement (Kumar Roy, M. Lassar, & Butaney, 2014; Srinivasan, Anderson, & Ponnavolu, 2002).

E-WOM engagement behavior is also explained by personal differences. For example, prior E-WOM experience is effective on negative online posting behavior (Boo & Kim, 2013). Additionally, familiarity with online communication technologies has a positive relationship with E-WOM engagement behavior (Boo & Kim, 2013; Liang et al., 2013). Online review posting frequency is another antecedent. For example, Moe & Schweidel (2012) mentioned that while infrequently posting consumers write similar to the previous reviewers, frequently posting consumers write online reviews different from the previous ones to differentiate themselves from previous reviewers and ratings. Finally, consumers' involvement is positively associated with E-WOM behavior (Alhidari, Iyer, & Paswan, 2015).

MOTIVATIONS OF E-WOM COMMUNICATION

There is a cause-effect relationship between antecedents and motivations of E-WOM behavior. Antecedents of E-WOM behavior motivate consumers to engage in E-WOM communication (Jeong & Jang, 2011). Similar to the antecedents of E-WOM behavior, motivations of E-WOM behavior took limited attention in the literature (Gonçalves, Silva, & Martins, 2018). Different authors mentioned about different motivations of E-WOM behavior and called motivations under different names such as altruism, concern for others, or desire to help the company. Therefore, similar motivations are examined under the main headings in this chapter. The following sections answer the RQ2: What are the motivations of consumers for sending and receiving E-WOM messages?

Motivations of E-WOM Senders

Motivations of E-WOM senders are grouped into five headings: altruism, personal benefits, expressing feelings, social benefits, and economic benefits. The studies examined E-WOM senders' motivations are summarized in Table 1.

Table 1. Motivations of E-WOM Senders

Studies	Motivations										
	Altruism	Personal benefits						Expressing Feelings		Social Benefits	Economic Benefits
		Self-enhancement	Personal growth	Hedonic benefits	Empowerment	Advice seeking	Self-presentation	Positive feelings	Negative feelings		
Gonçalves et al. (2018)	✓	✓		✓	✓					✓	
Hennig-Thurau et al. (2004)	✓	✓				✓			✓	✓	✓
Ho & Dempsey (2010)	✓		✓				✓			✓	
Jeong & Jang (2011)	✓							✓			
Phelps et al. (2004)				✓						✓	
Presi, Saridakis, & Hartmans (2014)	✓	✓							✓		✓
Teichmann, Stokburger-sauer, Plank, & Strobl (2015)	✓	✓		✓		✓	✓				
Yoo & Gretzel (2008)	✓	✓		✓				✓	✓	✓	

Altruism

Altruism is defined as the desire to help others (Piliavin & Charng, 1990). It is other-oriented and intrinsic motivation (Teichmann et al., 2015). An altruistic reviewer obtains utility from adding more information to other people or parties (Ye Hu & Li, 2011). Altruism is found as a strong motivator (Presi et al., 2014; Yoo & Gretzel, 2008), and many studies mentioned that there is a positive relationship between altruism and E-WOM behavior (Hennig-Thurau et al., 2004; Ho & Dempsey, 2010). However, Teichmann et al. (2015) found that altruism has negative impacts.

Altruism is closely related to concern for others in the E-WOM literature (Hennig-Thurau et al., 2004; Ho & Dempsey, 2010). For example, Gonçalves et al. (2018) mentioned that the motivation of "helping other travelers" triggers online review writing behavior in the hotel industry. Similarly, a desire to help the company (Jeong & Jang, 2011) and desire to assist the platform (Hennig-Thurau et al., 2004) are related to altruism based on the object. Furthermore, both positive and negative experiences trigger consumers to engage in E-WOM behavior with altruistic motivations. For instance, Jeong & Jang (2011) mentioned that concern for others and helping restaurant companies are the motives of consumers to engage in positive E-WOM after a positive restaurant experience. On the other hand, Presi et al. (2014) demonstrated that altruistic motivations are strong drivers in engaging negative user-generated content.

Personal Benefits

Engaging in E-WOM on the Internet brings personal benefits to the consumers. The motivations related to personal benefits are self-enhancement, personal growth, hedonic benefits, empowerment, advice seeking, and self-presentation.

Self-Enhancement

Self-enhancement is the need to feel good and seeking positive evaluations from others. Therefore, individuals like to present themselves favorably to others and to improve self-concept (Baumeister, 1982; Gregg, Hepper, & Sedikides, 2011). It is self-oriented and extrinsic motivation (Teichmann et al., 2015). Self-enhancement is a strong motivator for engaging in E-WOM behavior (Hennig-Thurau et al., 2004; Presi et al., 2014; Yoo & Gretzel, 2008). Positive self-enhancement is related to extraversion and expressing positive feelings in many studies (e.g., Hennig-Thurau et al., 2004; Hu & Kim, 2018; Yoo & Gretzel, 2008). Gonçalves et al. (2018) discussed self-enhancement under personal motivations by emphasizing that consumers feel good when they share their successful experiences. Teichmann et al. (2015) mentioned that self-enhancement is related to opinion leadership; that is, consumers have self-oriented purposes of participating in online communities.

Personal Growth

Personal growth motivator is defined as "active, intentional engagement in the process of personal growth" (Robitschek, 1998). Ho & Dempsey (2010) mentioned that personal growth might be a potential motivator for E-WOM behavior by forwarding information and help consumers to develop expertise and knowledge. They examined young adults' email forwarding behavior using surveys but found a negative relationship between personal growth and E-WOM engagement behavior.

Hedonic Benefits

Hedonic benefits are important motivators for consumers and related to enjoyment, fun, entertainment, amusement (Nambisan & Baron, 2007; Teichmann et al., 2015; Wang & Fesenmaier, 2004). Consumers post E-WOM based on their hedonic benefits. For example, Phelps et al. (2004) mentioned that consumers' motivations to engage in E-WOM via passing e-mails are related to their desires for fun or entertainment.

Enjoyment is a self-oriented and intrinsic motivator and positively affect E-WOM engagement behavior (Teichmann et al., 2015). Enjoyment is also related to positive self-enhancement. For example, Yoo & Gretzel (2008) analyzed the motivation of posting online reviews and found that the motivations of enjoyment, expressing positive feelings, and self-enhancement are combined under one factor and labeled it as enjoyment/positive self-enhancement. Similarly, Gonçalves et al. (2018) found that men are motivated to write travel websites for personal motivations to have some fun.

Empowerment

Consumer empowerment is another motivator related to personal benefits. Wright, Newman, & Dennis (2006) mentioned that consumers feel empowered when they can have enjoyment in the consumption process. Therefore, consumer empowerment is also related to E-WOM behavior. For example, Gonçalves et al. (2018) mentioned that consumer empowerment is effective in E-WOM engagement when consumers believe that their opinions are important for hotel management to improve service quality. Similarly, Bronner & de Hoog (2011) discussed that consumer empowerment is aimed at quality assurance.

Advice Seeking

Consumers also post E-WOM to seek advice about resolving their problems. Advice seeking is a post-purchase motivation to acquire the skills necessary to better understand the functioning of the product (Hennig-Thurau et al., 2004). It is a self-oriented and extrinsic motivation (Teichmann et al., 2015).

Self-Presentation

Self-presentation is another motivation in engaging E-WOM communication. Teichmann et al. (2015) mentioned that self-presentation is related to recognition by others in an online environment, promoting themselves, or putting information about themselves online. People with higher self-presentation motives tend to engage in E-WOM communication. Similarly, Ho & Dempsey (2010) discussed the need to be individualistic is positively related to online content forwarding behavior.

Expressing Feelings

Positive Feelings

Satisfactory consumption experiences motivate consumers to express their positive feelings (Sundaram, Kaushik, & Webster, 1998) and to engage in positive E-WOM communication. Yoo & Gretzel (2008) also mentioned that expressing positive feelings is related to a sender's positive affect and psychological benefits. Additionally, Jeong & Jang (2011) discussed that satisfactory restaurant experiences trigger E-WOM communication with the motivation of positive feeling expression or the need to help the restaurant. Therefore, it is expected that the expression of positive feelings is closely related to altruism motivation.

Negative Feelings

Negative feelings are emerged from dissatisfying consumption experiences and expressing negative feelings is a motivator of negative E-WOM engagement (Hennig-Thurau et al., 2004). Those feelings include negative emotions, such as frustration or anger. Expressing negative feelings aims at anxiety reduction or warning/helping others (Sundaram et al., 1998). On the other hand, Presi et al. (2014) inspected the user-generated content behavior of the dissatisfied consumer and distinguished venting from altruism. They mentioned that venting is closely related to vengeance. Yoo & Gretzel (2008) found that motives for expressing negative feelings are stronger for males rather than females.

Social Benefits

Social benefits motivate consumers to engage in E-WOM communication because the participation and integration of social communities provide consumers to receive social benefits by being a community membership (Hennig-Thurau et al., 2004). Social benefits can also be gained by social connections. For example, Phelps et al. (2004) mentioned that people are motivated by the desire for social connections while they are forwarding e-mails as a way of E-WOM communication. E-WOM engagement provides consumers to organize themselves and voice their opinions collectively over the companies (Yoo & Gretzel, 2008). On the other hand, Ho & Dempsey (2010) discussed the need to be part of a group as a potential motivator of E-WOM communication behavior, but they found that the need to belong to a community did not significantly affect online content forwarding behavior. Gonçalves et al. (2018) also found no relationship between social benefit and online hotel review writing behavior.

Economic Benefits

Economic benefits are described as economic incentives for writing online reviews such as free-entry coupons, discounts (Jeong & Jang, 2011). They are considered as a sign of appreciation by the E-WOM sender (Hennig-Thurau et al., 2004). Especially, consumers having negative experiences expect financial compensation such as money back, and economic motivations are strong drivers for creating user-generated content after bad experiences (Presi et al., 2014).

Motivations of E-WOM Receivers

Motivations of E-WOM receivers are grouped into four headings: altruism, personal benefits, social benefits, and economic benefits. The studies examined E-WOM receivers' motivations are summarized in Table 2.

Altruism

Similar to E-WOM engagement motivations, consumers receive E-WOM with altruistic motivations. For example, Burton & Khammash (2010) mentioned that site involvement is an important motivator for women consumers in reading reviews posted on consumer-opinion portals. Site involvement includes the "administrative duties" for the website. In other words, consumers are motivated by helping the management team of a website by examining review accuracy and availability. Furthermore, consumers

Table 2. Motivations of E-WOM Receivers

Studies	Motivations									
	Altruism	Personal Benefits							Social Benefits	Economic benefits
		Risk Reduction	Saving Time/Money/ Effort	Reducing Dissonance	Obtaining information	Personal Growth	Hedonic Benefits	Empowerment		
Burton & Khammash (2010)	✓	✓	✓	✓	✓	✓	✓	✓	✓	✓
Hennig-Thurau, Walsh, & Walsh (2003)		✓	✓	✓	✓				✓	✓
Huang & Yang (2008)		✓	✓		✓		✓		✓	
Goldsmith & Horowitz (2006)		✓	✓		✓		✓		✓	
Khammash & Griffiths (2011)	✓	✓	✓	✓	✓	✓	✓	✓	✓	✓
Kim, Mattila, & Baloglu (2011)		✓	✓						✓	
You, Lee, Lee, & Kang (2013)					✓		✓		✓	

can also offer general help to the site management team (Khammash & Griffiths, 2011). Therefore, site administrative duties are closely related to the altruistic motives of consumers.

Personal Benefits

Several motivations of E-WOM receivers are grouped under personal benefits. These motivations are risk reduction, saving time/money/effort, reducing dissonance, obtaining information, personal growth, hedonic benefits, and empowerment.

Risk Reduction

Consumers try to reduce their purchasing risks by reading online reviews. Thus, they benefit from others' experiences before buying a good or use a service or to get the help of other consumers to decide on the right product or service (Hennig-Thurau et al., 2003). For example, Huang & Yang (2008) mentioned that consumers reduce the risk of buying the wrong books by reading a wide variety of internet book reviews. Online reviews may include good or bad experiences. Thus, a motive to reduce risk in a buying decision is strongly linked to reading positive or negative reviews (Khammash & Griffiths, 2011).

By conducting research for identifying motivations for reading online customer reviews, Burton & Khammash (2010) found that risk reduction motivation is the most common driver behind reading behavior. Similarly, Goldsmith & Horowitz (2006) conducted a survey with 309 consumers and demonstrated that consumers seek others' opinions to reduce their risks. Furthermore, a risk reduction motivator is substantial for female consumers regardless of their expertise levels (Kim, Mattila, & Baloglu, 2011).

Saving Time/Money/Effort

Consumers spend time to find the product they are willing to buy because they want to make better buying decisions. Reading online reviews help consumers to save decision-making time (Hennig-Thurau et al., 2003; Khammash & Griffiths, 2011). In other words, they can easily get different and opposing views about a product or service from online opinions. Consumers also save money and effort in addition to the time while reading online reviews. For example, Goldsmith & Horowitz (2006) stated that consumers find lower prices and compare others' opinions to save money by reading online reviews. Furthermore, Kim et al. (2011) conducted a survey with 781 travelers in Las Vegas, conducted factor analysis, and found a factor called "convenience and quality". This factor is closely related to getting information in the fastest and easiest way, saving time, finding the lowest prices. Huang & Chen (2006) also discussed that decreased search time and reduced risk via reading online reviews help consumers to believe that they make the right purchase. On the other hand, sometimes, reading online reviews may increase the time people spent because they may elaborate on the details in the online review about the product (Burton & Khammash, 2010).

Reducing Dissonance

Dissonance reduction is a post-purchase motivator for reading online reviews (Burton & Khammash, 2010). Online reviews help consumers to believe that they make the right choice, so reduce their dissonance (Khammash & Griffiths, 2011). Consumers are seeking praises for the product they choose in the online environment (Burton & Khammash, 2010) or willing to see they are not alone with this problem in their product choices (Hennig-Thurau et al., 2003). Dissonance reduction motivation is also related to risk reduction or time/money/effort saving because as Kotler & Armstrong (2011, p. 151) stated that consumers are willing to reduce their dissonance when they are highly involved with an expensive, risky, time-consuming purchases.

Obtaining Information

While consumers are evaluating product quality of a product, they tend to seek information from other consumers rather than benefiting from their own experiences in the same product category because seeking information from other consumers facilitates their learning process about the product (Zhao et al., 2013). Consumers read online reviews with the motivation of obtaining information before or after their purchases (Burton & Khammash, 2010). For example, they want to learn the functioning of the product or seeking for learning about the products in the market place (Hennig-Thurau et al., 2003; Khammash & Griffiths, 2011). They can also get new ideas or learn something new while reading online reviews (You et al., 2013). Obtaining information is related to the information need for cognition. Huang & Yang (2008) mentioned that consumers with a high need for cognition motivation tend to read online reviews more and to get more pleasure.

Personal Growth

Self-improvement is closely related to the personal growth motivator of online reading. For example, Burton & Khammash (2010) demonstrated that consumers read online reviews to broaden their horizons and improve their language skills, which are two sub-components of the motive of "self-improvement". Those motives are also mentioned in the study of Khammash & Griffiths (2011) as emergent motives under self-involvement motivation.

Hedonic Benefits

People sometimes read online reviews to acquire some hedonic benefits. For example, Huang & Yang (2008) mentioned that reading online reviews is not just for the right book purchase; consumers may also get hedonic benefits such as feeling pleasure. Reading online reviews may sometimes be cool or fun (Goldsmith & Horowitz, 2006). You et al. (2013) found an entertainment dimension as one of the online review reading motivations. Accordingly, people read online reviews to get some fun, to kill time and to relieve boredom. Similarly, Khammash & Griffiths (2011) mentioned hedonic benefits under self-involvement motives such as fun, enjoyment, curiosity, compulsive habit, and boredom.

Empowerment

Consumer empowerment motivation triggers reading behavior. Burton & Khammash (2010) identified three motives within the consumer empowerment theme, namely, trusted product opinion, average/non-expert product opinion, unique product experience. In other words, consumers gain empowerment by reading online reviews from a trusted source, from average/non-expert reviewers like themselves, or by reading the unique product experiences of other consumers. Khammash & Griffiths (2011) showed that while finding non-expert opinion motivates people for reading positive online reviews, seeking unique consumer experiences or trusted opinions motivates for reading negative ones.

Social Benefits

Various social benefits motivate consumers to read online reviews. First, people like and enjoy being part of a community on the internet. This motivation is mentioned as "belonging to a virtual community" in many studies (Burton & Khammash, 2010; Hennig-Thurau et al., 2003; Khammash & Griffiths, 2011). Consumers may be influenced by others, and they can also think that belonging to a virtual community or being popular among friends is cool (Goldsmith & Horowitz, 2006). When consumers belong to a virtual community, they may read from preferred authors. They may also read to inform third parties, to understand people, or to encourage reciprocal reading (Burton & Khammash, 2010). Second, they can gain "social utility" by presenting themselves to others, be social with others, or be attractive to others (You et al., 2013). Third, people tend to change their purchasing behavior in line with the values and the behavior of their virtual community and are motivated to see how other people think of a product in the same way. While Hennig-Thurau et al. (2003) labeled this motivation "determination of social position", Huang & Yang (2008) called it "social orientation". This motivation is closely related to the reduction of dissonance. The study mentioned above by Kim et al. (2011) also found a factor called "social reassurance", which consists of the motivations such as belonging to a virtual community and social orientation.

Economic Benefits

Economic benefit or remuneration is a potential motivator for consumers to read online reviews. Consumers may expect to get a reward for reading and evaluating online contributions. Burton & Khammash (2010) found that remuneration is more effective as a motivator for younger rather than older website users. Hennig-Thurau et al. (2003) showed that there is a weak negative relationship between remuneration motive and willingness to read. Similarly, Khammash & Griffiths (2011) found that remuneration negatively impacts the total time spent on reading reviews online.

CONSEQUENCES OF E-WOM COMMUNICATION TO RECEIVERS

Receiving E-WOM messages has some effects and changes in consumers, such as changes in perceptions, information adoption and dissemination, forming attitudes, product choice, and purchase intention. Thus, the following section answers RQ3: What are the effects of E-WOM communication on the message receivers?

Perceptions of Receivers

Perception is defined as "the process by which individuals select, organize, and interpret stimuli into a meaningful and coherent picture of the world" (Schiffman & Wisenblit, 2019, p. 76). Perception of the persuasiveness, helpfulness, or trustworthiness of information provided by others via E-WOM helps readers to learn, make a decision, act, or react.

Perceived Persuasion

One of the aims of online reviews is to persuade consumers to choose/purchase the product because the persuasiveness of online reviews changes the consumers' behavior (Mafael, Gottschalk, & Kreis, 2016). Perceived persuasion of online reviews differs according to the valence of online reviews and the readers' intention to use the product. For example, Zhang, Craciun, & Shin (2010) discussed that when consumers evaluate products with promotion consumption goals, they perceive positive reviews to be more persuasive than negative ones. However, if they evaluate products with prevention consumption goals, they perceive negative reviews to be more persuasive than positive ones.

A format of online reviews such as narrative or informative is also effective on perceived persuasion (Hamby et al., 2015). Further, the reviews of anonymous or similar consumers have higher persuasive effects on readers rather than dissimilar consumers (Naylor, Lamberton, & Norton, 2011). Besides, the volume of online reviews has different effects on perceived persuasion (Khare et al., 2011). The study of Chakravarty et al. (2010) with moviegoers showed that online reviews persuade infrequent moviegoers more than frequent goers, and negative online reviews persuade consumers more than positive ones.

Perceived Usefulness/Helpfulness

Perceived helpfulness of E-WOM is defined as "the extent to which a consumer perceives a product review to be useful in performing his/her shopping tasks" (Pan & Zhang, 2011). Similarly, perceived usefulness of online reviews is defined as "the degree to which consumers believe that online reviews would facilitate their purchase decision-making process" (Park & Lee, 2009a, p. 334). The studies conducted their research with secondary data mentioned about perceived usefulness as the useful votes of online review (Chen & Lurie, 2013; Cheng & Ho, 2015; Wu, 2013). Perceived usefulness/helpfulness takes the attention of researchers because of its impact on product choice (Bigné, Caplliure, & Miquel, 2016; Chen & Lurie, 2013) or purchase decisions (Agnihotri & Bhattacharya, 2016;

Park & Lee, 2009b). Some models have been developed with artificial intelligence to predict the number of useful votes of an online review (Singh et al., 2017) and in some studies, the perceived usefulness/helpfulness of online reviews are equivalent to online review's quality (Felbermayr & Nanopoulos, 2016) or value (Chen & Lurie, 2013).

There are many variables effective on the perceived usefulness/helpfulness. First, the researchers discussed the effects of the valence of online reviews on perceived usefulness/helpfulness. Negative reviews were found to be more useful/helpful due to the negativity bias (Casaló et al., 2015; Purnawirawan et al., 2015). Contrary to these findings, some studies discussed that positive reviews are as useful/helpful as negative reviews (Wu, 2013), and even positive reviews are more useful/helpful than negative reviews (Pan & Zhang, 2011). Further, Schlosser (2011) mentioned that extremely positive and extremely negative reviews are more useful/helpful than neutral reviews.

How the perceived usefulness/helpfulness of positive and negative online reviews changes for different situations has become a matter of concern to researchers. Positive reviews of expert reviewers are perceived to be more useful/helpful (Casaló et al., 2015). Moreover, as the consumers may read multiple reviews when selecting products, review sets with positive and negative balances (the number of positive reviews is higher than or lower than the number of negative reviews, respectively) are found to be more useful than neutral review sets (the number of positive reviews is equal to the number of negative reviews). However, there is no difference between the review sets with positive and negative balances (Purnawirawan et al., 2012). Further, the rationality of a review decreases when a reviewer expresses his/her emotions in a review, which in turn decreases the perceived usefulness of the review. Beyond the valence of online reviews, perceived usefulness/helpfulness of online reviews are higher for consumers who read many reviews including similar emotions than for consumers who read many reviews including no emotions (Kim & Gupta, 2012). Additionally, the reviewer's rationality and reliability perceived by readers have positive effects on the perceived usefulness of online reviews (Folse, Porter, Godbole, & Reynolds, 2016).

The information quality and source credibility are other variables affecting the usefulness/helpfulness of online reviews in addition to the valence of online reviews (Cheng & Ho, 2015). Product rankings and consumer ratings also have a significant impact on the perceived usefulness/helpfulness of online reviews (Filieri, 2015). Further, recent online reviews are more useful/helpful than out-dated online reviews (Jin, Hu, & He, 2014), and long online reviews are more useful/helpful than short ones (Filieri, 2015; Pan & Zhang, 2011). The reviews of experiential products and familiar products are also more useful/helpful than the reviews of search products and unfamiliar products (Casaló et al., 2015; Pan & Zhang, 2011). Moore (2015) mentioned that online reviews with explanations are more useful/helpful for functional products than hedonic ones.

Furthermore, the consumers who read online reviews from mobile devices found online reviews less useful (März, Schubach, & Schumann, 2017). On the other hand, the information quantity (Filieri, 2015) and picture (Casaló et al., 2015) in an online review do not have significant impacts on perceived usefulness.

Perceived Trustworthiness

The tie strength between message sender and receiver significantly affects the perceived trust of consumers in online information. Consumers perceive either positive or negative reviews for experience goods or credential goods to be trustful as long as the tie strength between the message sender and the receiver is strong. However, all else being equal, negative information for experience goods rather than credence goods are perceived as more trustworthy (Pan & Chiou, 2011). Reimer & Benkenstein (2016) mentioned that the trustfulness of online review acts as a mediator in the relationship between the valence of online review and purchase intention. Moreover, online consumers had higher levels of trust and greater purchase intentions for familiar brands than unfamiliar brands; for high consensus information than low consensus information; for online retailers with the physical store than online retailers with no physical store (Benedicktus et al., 2010).

Information Adoption and Dissemination

Consumers adopt information based on the quality, authority, authenticity, and interestingness of the message (Huang et al., 2011). Additionally, source credibility, product rankings, and consumer ratings have an important impact on the perceived usefulness of online reviews, which positively affects information adoption (Filieri, 2015). Similarly, consumers disseminate the message depending on the quality, authority, authenticity, and interestingness of the message. As these characteristics in a message become high, the readers easily accept the information in E-WOM, which has a significant impact on consumer's resending intention (Huang et al., 2011). Also, resending intention depends on consumer's tie with the message source, involvement with the product, message context, and message channel (Chiu et al., 2014). However, consumers are more likely to share their opinions by traditional WOM rather than by E-WOM (social media) because of the perceived social risk (Eisingerich, Helen, Liu, Michael, & Bell, 2015).

Receivers' intention to disseminate information also depends on the strength of the social ties between the message sender and him/her. When the ties are strong between them (compared to weak ties), the impact of E-WOM is higher (Groeger & Buttle, 2014), and people exchange much and similar information with each other (Lee et al., 2013).

Attitudes of Consumers

Attitude is defined as "a person's relatively consistent evaluations, feelings, and tendencies toward an object or idea" (Kotler & Armstrong, 2011, p. 174). E-WOM helps consumers to form attitudes (Schiffman & Wisenblit, 2019, p. 142) toward the product (Martin & Lueg, 2013; Pan & Zhang, 2011; Wang, Yu, & Wei, 2012), service (Purnawirawan et al., 2012; Lu Zhang & Hanks, 2018) or brand (Eisingerich et al., 2015; Koo, 2015). In this relationship, E-WOM characteristics have an important role in consumers' product evaluation. The valence of E-WOM is an important determinant in attitude formation and change. The effects of negative E-WOM are greater than the effects of positive E-WOM on attitude formation and change (Lee & Ro, 2016). In addition, tie strength and product type are important moderators in the relationship between negative E-WOM and attitudes (Koo, 2015). The variance of E-WOM is another determinant. For example, Park & Park (2013) mentioned that consumer's evaluation of a product depends on the variance in product ratings and the consumers' performance expectations from the product.

Personal characteristics are also effective in the relationship between E-WOM and attitude. For example, Pang & Qiu (2016) showed that online review chunking affects product attitude, and consumer's motivation to think, i.e., a tendency to engage in information-processing activities, acts as a moderator in this relationship. Zhang & Hanks (2018) mentioned that customers high in cosmopolitanism, who perceive themselves as citizens of the world rather than of the nation, tend to have a more positive attitude towards a service provider after reading positive online reviews written by reviewers with different ethnic backgrounds.

Product Choice

One of the influences of E-WOM on consumers is the product/service choice. A product's sales volume, online reviews' volume, and the message sender have impacts on the product choice of consumers. Online reviews of inexpert consumers are more effective than expert consumers' reviews in product choices (Huang & Chen, 2006). However, Kostyra, Reiner, Natter, & Klapper (2016) mentioned that online reviews' volume does not have a direct impact on product choice. They cited that online reviews' volume acts as a mediator in the relationship between the valence of online reviews and product choice of consumers.

Including a cue about the consumption of the product in the online review enhances the probability of this product choice (Chen & Lurie, 2013). Furthermore, when a reviewer writes an online review in an explanatory manner, the reader easily predicts the attitude of the writer towards a product, and the perceived helpfulness of this review increases, which in turn affects product choice (Moore, 2015). However, E-WOM leads to spending more time on the choice task of consumers (Gupta & Harris, 2010). Thus, while consumers who use the internet rely on product ratings in their product choices, consumers who do not use the internet rely on traditional WOM. In addition, consumers tend to behave opposite to the recommendation when they encounter with a recommendation that contradicts with their initial impression about a product (Fitzsimons & Lehmann, 2004).

Purchase Intention

Consumers often read online reviews before they purchase goods and services (Gottschalk & Mafael, 2017). Consumers have higher purchase intentions when they perceive E-WOM as useful or helpful (Park & Lee, 2009a), and credible (Reimer & Benkenstein, 2016). Further, source credibility, source experience, and evidence in online reviews have positive effects on E-WOM usage, which positively affects the purchase intentions of consumers (Martin & Lueg, 2013). Recent online reviews rather than old ones (Jin et al., 2014) and detailed online reviews rather than general ones (Jiménez & Mendoza, 2013) have significant effects on the purchase intentions of consumers.

FUTURE RESEARCH DIRECTIONS

In the digital economy, understanding the antecedents, motivations, and consequences of E-WOM communication for consumers is much more difficult due to a broad range of platforms and different E-WOM formats. Therefore, this chapter provided a comprehensive understanding of the E-WOM communication literature and insights about future research opportunities and emerging trends.

The antecedents of E-WOM communication can be analyzed under two groups: (1) the antecedents such as satisfaction, dissatisfaction and e-loyalty which mainly depend on the firm's performance; (2) the antecedents due to the personal differences such as prior E-WOM experience, familiarity with online communication technologies, and consumer's involvement. Regarding the first group of the antecedents, firms should deliver high service quality to their customers, manage service failure situations, and proactively offer service recovery to satisfy their customers, and therefore, they can increase their positive online reviews. Researchers mentioned that to date, only a limited number of studies have been conducted on the antecedents of E-WOM behavior (Boo & Kim, 2013; Cheung & Lee, 2012; Liang, Ekinci, Occhiocupo, & Whyatt, 2013). Therefore, future studies on the antecedents of E-WOM are recommended.

Antecedents motivate consumers to engage in E-WOM behavior. Altruism, personal benefits, expressing feelings, social benefits, and economic benefits are the motivations of E-WOM senders. Among these motivations, social benefits can be gained by being a community membership (Hennig-Thurau et al., 2004), building social connections (Phelps et al., 2004), and voicing collectively (Yoo & Gretzel, 2008). However, some studies mentioned that social benefits are not related to E-WOM engagement (Gonçalves et al., 2018; Ho & Dempsey, 2010). Thus, there is a need to understand the relationship between social benefits and E-WOM engagement behavior. Economic incentives may also be the motivation for engaging in E-WOM communication (Hennig-Thurau et al., 2004; Presi et al., 2014). Therefore, firms may use economic incentives to promote E-WOM engagement after the positive experiences of their consumers.

The motivations of E-WOM receivers are similar to E-WOM senders' motivations. Although altruism has been studied extensively among E-WOM sending motivations (Gonçalves et al., 2018; Hennig-Thurau et al., 2004; Ho & Dempsey, 2010; Jeong & Jang, 2011; Presi et al., 2014; Teichmann et al., 2015; Yoo & Gretzel, 2008), it has received little attention within the motivations of E-WOM receivers (Burton & Khammash, 2010; Khammash & Griffiths, 2011). Thus, a future study that identifies and investigates consumers who read E-WOM with altruistic motives would be fascinating. Furthermore, there are contradictory results about the effect of E-WOM reading (search time) on decision-making time. While Burton & Khammash (2010) mentioned that reading online reviews makes decision-making hard because of the details in E-WOM, others discussed that reading online reviews saves decision-making time (Hennig-Thurau et al., 2003; Khammash & Griffiths, 2011). Additionally, people may also read E-WOM to kill time (You et al., 2013). Thus, further research should be undertaken to investigate the relationship between search time and decision-making time. Economic benefits are also potential motivators for E-WOM receivers (Burton & Khammash, 2010). However, studies showed that there is a weak and negative relationship between remuneration and reading behavior (Hennig-Thurau et al., 2003; Khammash & Griffiths, 2011). Firms should be cautious while encouraging their customers to read online reviews by providing them with economic benefits.

This chapter answered the research questions regarding customer decision-making behavior in B2C market settings. However, the role of E-WOM communication in B2B settings remains understudied. Therefore, future studies should examine the antecedents, motivations and consequences of E-WOM communication for customers in a B2B context.

CONCLUSION

Advancements in internet-based technologies have resulted in fundamental changes in how consumers communicate with each other about a product, service, brand, or experience. Thus, traditional WOM has transformed into E-WOM, specifically as online reviews (Casaló et al., 2015; Park & Lee, 2009a), e-mails (Phelps et al., 2004) or online videos (Hautz et al., 2014). E-WOM hosts on different platforms such as firms' websites (Filieri, 2015), online retailing platforms (Zhao et al., 2013), brand communities, independent Websites, consumer blogs, or social networking sites (Koo, 2015).

Similar to WOM, E-WOM has mainly three components: message sender, message receiver, and the message itself. However, the important role of the internet or web-based technologies in E-WOM affects those components. Message senders are anonymous (Park et al., 2007), and they can immediately share their opinions with others (Berger & Schwartz, 2011). On the other hand, there are numerous message receivers of one message at any time and place (Luo & Zhong, 2015). Message sender and receiver can be distant from each other (Park et al., 2007; Steffes & Burgee, 2009). Additionally, the messages are persistent (Hung & Li, 2007; Lee et al., 2008) and high in volume (Chatterjee, 2001; Pan & Zhang, 2011).

Satisfaction (Gohary et al., 2016; Gounaris et al., 2010; Jeong & Jang, 2011; Lii & Lee, 2012), dissatisfaction (Gebauer et al., 2013), and e-loyalty (Hsu et al., 2015; Kumar et al., 2014; Srinivasan et al., 2002) are the antecedents that depend on the firm's performance since service quality, service failure and service recovery are closely related to them. Antecedents due to the personal differences are prior E-WOM experience (Boo & Kim, 2013), E-WOM posting frequency (Moe & Schweidel, 2012), familiarity with online communication technologies (Boo & Kim, 2013; Liang et al., 2013), and consumer's involvement (Alhidari et al., 2015).

The E-WOM communication motivation literature showed that similar motivations were named differently in the studies. Therefore, by providing a comprehensive framework for motivations of E-WOM senders, motivations are grouped into five: altruism, personal benefits, expressing feelings, social benefits, and economic motivations. Altruism is closely related to concern for others (Hennig-Thurau et al., 2004; Ho & Dempsey, 2010), desire to help the company (Jeong & Jang, 2011) and desire to assist the platform (Hennig-Thurau et al., 2004). Personal benefits include the motivations as self-enhancement (Gonçalves et al., 2018; Hennig-Thurau et al., 2004; Presi et al., 2014; Teichmann et al., 2015; Yoo & Gretzel, 2008), personal growth (Ho & Dempsey, 2010), hedonic benefits (Gonçalves et al., 2018; Phelps et al., 2004; Teichmann et al., 2015; Yoo & Gretzel, 2008), empowerment (Gonçalves et al., 2018), advice seeking (Hennig-Thurau et al., 2004; Teichmann et al., 2015), self-presentation (Ho & Dempsey, 2010; Teichmann et al., 2015). The motivation for expressing feelings may be positive feelings (Jeong & Jang, 2011; Yoo & Gretzel, 2008) or negative feelings (Hennig-Thurau et al., 2004; Presi et al., 2014; Yoo & Gretzel, 2008).

Similar motivations were also discussed for E-WOM receivers in the literature. Altruism is related to site involvement (Burton & Khammash, 2010) and offering general help to the site management team (Khammash & Griffiths, 2011). Obtaining personal benefits includes risk reduction, saving time/money/effort, reducing dissonance, obtaining information, personal growth, hedonic benefits, and empowerment. Social benefits are emphasized intensively in the studies as a message receiver motivator (Burton & Khammash, 2010; Hennig-Thurau et al., 2003; Huang & Yang, 2008; Goldsmith & Horowitz, 2006; Khammash & Griffiths, 2011; Kim et al., 2011; You et al., 2013). Economic benefits are also effective for E-WOM receivers (Burton & Khammash, 2010).

Receiving E-WOM affects consumers and causes some changes in their perceptions, attitudes, and behavior. The consequences of E-WOM for consumers can be examined in five groups. First, the different characteristics of the message, sender, and receiver affect the perception of consumers, such as perceived persuasion, perceived usefulness/helpfulness, and perceived trustworthiness of E-WOM. Second, they may adopt or disseminate information. Third, they might form attitudes toward the product, service or brand; or their attitudes can change. Fourth, E-WOM could affect consumers' product choices. Finally, E-WOM may increase or decrease purchase intentions.

REFERENCES

Agnihotri, A., & Bhattacharya, S. (2016). Online review helpfulness: Role of qualitative factors. *Psychology and Marketing*, *33*(11), 1006–1017. doi:10.1002/mar.20934

Alhidari, A., Iyer, P., & Paswan, A. (2015). Personal level antecedents of eWOM and purchase intention, on social networking sites. *Journal of Customer Behaviour*, *14*(2), 107–125. doi:10.1362/147539215X14373846805707

Baumeister, R. F. (1982). Self-esteem, self-presentation, and future interaction: A dilemma of reputation. *Journal of Personality*, *50*(1), 29–45. doi:10.1111/j.1467-6494.1982.tb00743.x

Benedicktus, R. L., Brady, M. K., Darke, P. R., & Voorhees, C. M. (2010). Conveying trustworthiness to online consumers: Reactions to consensus, physical store presence, brand familiarity, and generalized suspicion. *Journal of Retailing*, *86*(4), 322–335. doi:10.1016/j.jretai.2010.04.002

Berger, J., & Schwartz, E. M. (2011). What drives immediate and ongoing word of mouth? *JMR, Journal of Marketing Research*, *48*(5), 869–880. doi:10.1509/jmkr.48.5.869

Bigné, E., Caplliure, E. M., & Miquel, M. J. (2016). eWOM on travel agency selection: Specialized versus private label. *Psychology and Marketing*, *33*(12), 1046–1053. doi:10.1002/mar.20938

Boo, S., & Kim, J. (2013). Comparison of negative eWOM intention: An exploratory study. *Journal of Quality Assurance in Hospitality & Tourism*, *14*(1), 24–48. doi:10.1080/1528008X.2013.749381

Bronner, F., & de Hoog, R. (2011). Vacationers and eWOM: Who posts, and why, where, and what? *Journal of Travel Research*, *50*(1), 15–26. doi:10.1177/0047287509355324

Burton, J., & Khammash, M. (2010). Why do people read reviews posted on consumer-opinion portals? *Journal of Marketing Management*, *26*(3–4), 230–255. doi:10.1080/02672570903566268

Casaló, L. V., Flavián, C., Guinalíu, M., & Ekinci, Y. (2015). Avoiding the dark side of positive online consumer reviews: Enhancing reviews' usefulness for high risk-averse travelers. *Journal of Business Research*, *68*(9), 1829–1835. doi:10.1016/j.jbusres.2015.01.010

Chakravarty, A., Liu, Y., & Mazumdar, T. (2010). The differential effects of online word-of-mouth and critics' reviews on pre-release movie evaluation. *Journal of Interactive Marketing*, *24*(3), 185–197. doi:10.1016/j.intmar.2010.04.001

Chang, L. D. M., Ling Tam, A. Y., & Suki, N. M. (2016). Moderating effect of races towards consumers' feeling of TCM usage. Handbook of Research on Leveraging Consumer Psychology for Effective Customer Engagement, 306-323.

Chatterjee, P. (2001). Online reviews: Do consumers use them? *Advances in Consumer Research. Association for Consumer Research (U. S.)*, *28*, 129–133.

Chen, J., Teng, L., Yu, Y., & Yu, X. (2016). The effect of online information sources on purchase intentions between consumers with high and low susceptibility to informational influence. *Journal of Business Research*, *69*(2), 467–475. doi:10.1016/j.jbusres.2015.05.003

Chen, Z., & Lurie, N. H. (2013). Temporal contiguity and negativity bias in the impact of online word of mouth. *JMR, Journal of Marketing Research*, *50*(4), 463–476. doi:10.1509/jmr.12.0063

Cheng, Y. H., & Ho, H. Y. (2015). Social influence's impact on reader perceptions of online reviews. *Journal of Business Research*, *68*(4), 883–887. doi:10.1016/j.jbusres.2014.11.046

Cheung, C. M. K., & Lee, M. K. O. (2012). What drives consumers to spread electronic word of mouth in online consumer-opinion platforms. *Decision Support Systems*, *53*(1), 218–225. doi:10.1016/j.dss.2012.01.015

Chevalier, J. A., & Mayzlin, D. (2006). The effect of word of mouth on sales: Online book reviews. *JMR, Journal of Marketing Research*, *43*(3), 345–354. doi:10.1509/jmkr.43.3.345

Chintagunta, P. K., Gopinath, S., & Venkataraman, S. (2010). The effects of online user reviews on movie box office performance: Accounting for sequential rollout and aggregation across local markets. *Marketing Science*, *29*(5), 944–957. doi:10.1287/mksc.1100.0572

Chiou, J. S., Hsiao, C. C., & Chiu, T. Y. (2018). The credibility and attribution of online reviews: Differences between high and low product knowledge consumers. *Online Information Review*, *42*(5), 630–646. doi:10.1108/OIR-06-2017-0197

Chiu, H. C., Pant, A., Hsieh, Y. C., Lee, M., Hsioa, Y. T., & Roan, J. (2014). Snowball to avalanche: Understanding the different predictors of the intention to propagate online marketing messages. *European Journal of Marketing*, *48*(7/8), 1255–1273. doi:10.1108/EJM-05-2012-0329

Clow, K., & Donald, B. (2012). *Integrated Advertising, Promotion and Marketing Communications*. Essex: Pearson.

Dellarocas, C. (2003). The digitization of word of mouth: Promise and challenges of online feedback mechanisms. *Management Science*, *49*(10), 1407–1424. doi:10.1287/mnsc.49.10.1407.17308

Duan, W., Gu, B., & Whinston, A. B. (2008). The dynamics of online word-of-mouth and product sales- An empirical investigation of the movie industry. *Journal of Retailing*, *84*(2), 233–242. doi:10.1016/j.jretai.2008.04.005

Eisingerich, A. B., Helen, H., Liu, Y., Michael, H., & Bell, S. J. (2015). Why recommend a brand face-to-face but not on Facebook? How word-of-mouth on online social sites differs from traditional word-of-mouth. *Journal of Consumer Psychology*, *25*(1), 120–128. doi:10.1016/j.jcps.2014.05.004

Esmark Jones, C. L., Stevens, J. L., Breazeale, M., & Spaid, B. I. (2018). Tell it like it is: The effects of differing responses to negative online reviews. *Psychology and Marketing*, *35*(12), 891–901. doi:10.1002/mar.21142

Felbermayr, A., & Nanopoulos, A. (2016). The role of emotions for the perceived usefulness in online customer reviews. *Journal of Interactive Marketing*, *36*, 60–76. doi:10.1016/j.intmar.2016.05.004

Filieri, R. (2015). What makes online reviews helpful? A diagnosticity-adoption framework to explain informational and normative influences in e-WOM. *Journal of Business Research*, *68*(6), 1261–1270. doi:10.1016/j.jbusres.2014.11.006

Filieri, R., Hofacker, C. F., & Alguezaui, S. (2018). What makes information in online consumer reviews diagnostic over time? The role of review relevancy, factuality, currency, source credibility and ranking score. *Computers in Human Behavior*, *80*, 122–131. doi:10.1016/j.chb.2017.10.039

Filieri, R., McLeay, F., Tsui, B., & Lin, Z. (2018). Consumer perceptions of information helpfulness and determinants of purchase intention in online consumer reviews of services. *Information & Management*, *55*(8), 956–970. doi:10.1016/j.im.2018.04.010

Fitzsimons, G. J., & Lehmann, D. R. (2004). Reactance to recommendations: When unsolicited advice yields contrary responses. *Marketing Science*, *23*(1), 82–94. doi:10.1287/mksc.1030.0033

Floyd, K., Freling, R., Alhoqail, S., Cho, H. Y., & Freling, T. (2014). How online product reviews affect retail sales: A meta-analysis. *Journal of Retailing*, *90*(2), 217–232. doi:10.1016/j.jretai.2014.04.004

Folse, J. A. G., Porter, M. III, Godbole, M. B., & Reynolds, K. E. (2016). The effects of negatively valenced emotional expressions in online reviews on the reviewer, the review, and the product. *Psychology and Marketing*, *33*(9), 747–760. doi:10.1002/mar.20914

Gebauer, J., Füller, J., & Pezzei, R. (2013). The dark and the bright side of co-creation : Triggers of member behavior in online innovation communities. *Journal of Business Research*, *66*(9), 1516–1527. doi:10.1016/j.jbusres.2012.09.013

Gohary, A., Hamzelu, B., & Alizadeh, H. (2016). Please explain why it happened! How perceived justice and customer involvement affect post co-recovery evaluations: A study of Iranian online shoppers. *Journal of Retailing and Consumer Services*, *31*, 127–142. doi:10.1016/j.jretconser.2016.03.013

Goldsmith, R. E., & Horowitz, D. (2006). Measuring motivations for online opinion seeking. *Journal of Interactive Advertising*, *6*(2), 2–14. doi:10.1080/15252019.2006.10722114

Gonçalves, H. M., Silva, G. M., & Martins, T. G. (2018). Motivations for posting online reviews in the hotel industry. *Psychology and Marketing*, *35*(11), 807–817. doi:10.1002/mar.21136

Gottschalk, S. A., & Mafael, A. (2017). Cutting through the online review jungle— Investigating selective eWOM processing. *Journal of Interactive Marketing*, *37*, 89–104. doi:10.1016/j.intmar.2016.06.001

Gounaris, S., Dimitriadis, S., & Stathakopoulos, V. (2010). An examination of the effects of service quality and satisfaction on customers' behavioral intentions in e-shopping, 24(2), 142-156. *Journal of Services Marketing*. doi:10.1108/08876041011031118

Gregg, A. P., Hepper, E. G., & Sedikides, C. (2011). Quantifying self-motives: Functional links between dispositional desires. *European Journal of Social Psychology*, *41*(7), 840–852. doi:10.1002/ejsp.827

Groeger, L., & Buttle, F. (2014). Word-of-mouth marketing: Towards an improved understanding of multi-generational campaign reach. *European Journal of Marketing*, *48*(7–8), 1186–1208. doi:10.1108/EJM-02-2012-0086

Gupta, P., & Harris, J. (2010). How e-WOM recommendations influence product consideration and quality of choice: A motivation to process information perspective. *Journal of Business Research*, *63*(9–10), 1041–1049. doi:10.1016/j.jbusres.2009.01.015

Hamby, A., Daniloski, K., & Brinberg, D. (2015). How consumer reviews persuade through narratives. *Journal of Business Research*, *68*(6), 1242–1250. doi:10.1016/j.jbusres.2014.11.004

Hautz, J., Füller, J., Hutter, K., & Thürridl, C. (2014). Let users generate your video ads? The impact of video source and quality on consumers' perceptions and intended behaviors. *Journal of Interactive Marketing*, *28*(1), 1–15. doi:10.1016/j.intmar.2013.06.003

He, S. X., & Bond, S. D. (2013). Word-of-mouth and the forecasting of consumption enjoyment. *Journal of Consumer Psychology*, *23*(4), 464–482. doi:10.1016/j.jcps.2013.04.001

Hennig-Thurau, T., Gwinner, K. P., Walsh, G., & Gremler, D. D. (2004). Electronic word-of-mouth via consumer-opinion platforms: What motivates consumers to articulate themselves on the Internet? *Journal of Interactive Marketing*, *18*(1), 38–52. doi:10.1002/dir.10073

Hennig-Thurau, T., Walsh, G., & Walsh, G. (2003). Electronic word-of-mouth: Motives for and consequences of reading customer articulations on the internet. *International Journal of Electronic Commerce*, *8*(2), 51–74. doi:10.1080/10864415.2003.11044293

Ho, J. Y. C., & Dempsey, M. (2010). Viral marketing : Motivations to forward online content ☆. *Journal of Business Research*, *63*(9–10), 1000–1006. doi:10.1016/j.jbusres.2008.08.010

Ho-dac, N. N., Carson, S. J., & Moore, W. L. (2013). The effects of positive and negative online customer reviews : Do brand matter? *Journal of Marketing*, *77*(6), 37–53. doi:10.1509/jm.11.0011

Hsu, L., Wang, K., & Chih, W. (2015). Effects of web site characteristics on customer loyalty in B2B e-commerce : Evidence from Taiwan. *Service Industries Journal*, *33*(11), 1026–1050. doi:10.1080/02642069.2011.624595

Hu, Ye., & Li, X. (2011). Context-dependent product evaluations : An empirical analysis of internet book reviews. *Journal of Interactive Marketing*, *25*(3), 123–133. doi:10.1016/j.intmar.2010.10.001

Hu, Y., & Kim, H. J. (2018). Positive and negative eWOM motivations and hotel customers' eWOM behavior: Does personality matter? *International Journal of Hospitality Management*, *75*, 27–37. doi:10.1016/j.ijhm.2018.03.004

Huang, J. H., & Chen, Y. F. (2006). Herding in online product choice. *Psychology and Marketing*, *23*(5), 413–428. doi:10.1002/mar.20119

Huang, M., Cai, F., Tsang, A. S. L., & Zhou, N. (2011). Making your online voice loud: The critical role of WOM information. *European Journal of Marketing*, *45*(7), 1277–1297. doi:10.1108/03090561111137714

Huang, Y. K., & Yang, W. I. (2008). Motives for and consequences of reading internet book reviews. *The Electronic Library*, *26*(1), 97–110. doi:10.1108/02640470810851770

Hung, K. H., & Li, S. Y. (2007). The influence of eWOM on virtual consumer communities: Social capital, consumer learning, and behavioral outcomes. *Journal of Advertising Research*, *47*(4), 485–495. doi:10.2501/S002184990707050X

Ismagilova, E., Dwivedi, Y. K., Slade, E., & Williams, M. D. (2017). *Electronic Word of Mouth (eWOM) in the Marketing Context A State of the Art Analysis and Future Directions*. Springer.

Jeong, E. H., & Jang, S. C. S. (2011). Restaurant experiences triggering positive electronic word-of-mouth (eWOM) motivations. *International Journal of Hospitality Management*, *30*(2), 356–366. doi:10.1016/j.ijhm.2010.08.005

Jiménez, F. R., & Mendoza, N. A. (2013). Too popular to ignore: The influence of online reviews on purchase intentions of search and experience products. *Journal of Interactive Marketing*, *27*(3), 226–235. doi:10.1016/j.intmar.2013.04.004

Jin, L., Hu, B., & He, Y. (2014). The recent versus the out-dated: An experimental examination of the time-variant effects of online consumer reviews. *Journal of Retailing*, *90*(4), 552–566. doi:10.1016/j.jretai.2014.05.002

Khammash, M., & Griffiths, G. H. (2011). "Arrivederci CIAO.com, Buongiorno Bing.com" - Electronic word-of-mouth (eWOM), antecedences and consequences. *International Journal of Information Management*, *31*(1), 82–87. doi:10.1016/j.ijinfomgt.2010.10.005

Khare, A., Labrecque, L. I., & Asare, A. K. (2011). The assimilative and contrastive effects of word-of-mouth volume: An experimental examination of online consumer ratings. *Journal of Retailing*, *87*(1), 111–126. doi:10.1016/j.jretai.2011.01.005

Kim, E. E. K., Mattila, A. S., & Baloglu, S. (2011). Effects of gender and expertise on consumers' motivation to read online hotel reviews. *Cornell Hospitality Quarterly*, *52*(4), 399–406. doi:10.1177/1938965510394357

Kim, J., & Gupta, P. (2012). Emotional expressions in online user reviews: How they influence consumers' product evaluations. *Journal of Business Research*, *65*(7), 985–992. doi:10.1016/j.jbusres.2011.04.013

King, R. A., Racherla, P., & Bush, V. D. (2014). What we know and don't know about online word-of-mouth: A review and synthesis of the literature. *Journal of Interactive Marketing*, *28*(3), 167–183. doi:10.1016/j.intmar.2014.02.001

Koch, O. F., & Benlian, A. (2015). Promotional tactics for online viral marketing campaigns: How scarcity and personalization affect seed stage referrals. *Journal of Interactive Marketing*, *32*, 37–52. doi:10.1016/j.intmar.2015.09.005

Koo, D. (2015). The strength of no tie relationship in an online recommendation: Focused on interactional effects of valence, tie strength, and type of service. *European Journal of Marketing*, *49*(7/8), 1163–1183. doi:10.1108/EJM-01-2014-0022

Kostyra, D. S., Reiner, J., Natter, M., & Klapper, D. (2016). Decomposing the effects of online customer reviews on brand, price, and product attributes. *International Journal of Research in Marketing*, *33*(1), 11–26. doi:10.1016/j.ijresmar.2014.12.004

Kotler, P., & Armstrong, G. (2011). *Principles of Marketing*. Academic Press.

Kumar Roy, S., & Lassar, M., W., & Butaney, G. (2014). The mediating impact of stickiness and loyalty on word-of-mouth promotion of retail websites. *European Journal of Marketing*, *48*(9/10), 1828–184. doi:10.1108/EJM-04-2013-0193

Lee, E. J., & Shin, S. Y. (2014). When do consumers buy online product reviews? Effects of review quality, product type, and reviewer's photo. *Computers in Human Behavior*, *31*(1), 356–366. doi:10.1016/j.chb.2013.10.050

Lee, H., Lee, D., Kim, T., & Lee, J. (2013). The moderating role of socio-semantic networks on online buzz diffusion. *Journal of Business Research*, *66*(9), 1367–1374. doi:10.1016/j.jbusres.2012.02.038

Lee, J., Park, D. H., & Han, I. (2008). The effect of negative online consumer reviews on product attitude: An information processing view. *Electronic Commerce Research and Applications*, *7*(3), 341–352. doi:10.1016/j.elerap.2007.05.004

Lee, S. H., & Ro, H. (2016). The impact of online reviews on attitude changes: The differential effects of review attributes and consumer knowledge. *International Journal of Hospitality Management*, *56*, 1–9. doi:10.1016/j.ijhm.2016.04.004

Lee, T., & Bradlow, E. (2011). Automated marketing research using online customer reviews. *JMR, Journal of Marketing Research*, *48*(5), 881–894. doi:10.1509/jmkr.48.5.881

Liang, S. W. J., Ekinci, Y., Occhiocupo, N., & Whyatt, G. (2013). Antecedents of travellers' electronic word-of-mouth communication. *Journal of Marketing Management*, *29*(5–6), 584–606. doi:10.1080/0267257X.2013.771204

Lii, Y., & Lee, M. (2012). The joint effects of compensation frames and price levels on service recovery of online pricing error. *Managing Service Quality*, *22*(1), 4–20. doi:10.1108/09604521211198083

Lin, H. H., Wang, Y. S., & Chang, L. K. (2011). Consumer responses to online retailer's service recovery after a service failure: A perspective of justice theory. *Managing Service Quality*, *21*(5), 511–534. doi:10.1108/09604521111159807

López, M., & Sicilia, M. (2014). Determinants of E-WOM influence: The role of consumers' internet experience. *Journal of Theoretical and Applied Electronic Commerce Research*, *9*(1), 28–43. doi:10.4067/S0718-18762014000100004

Ludwig, S., de Ruyter, K., Friedman, M., Brüggen, E. C., Wetzels, M., & Pfann, G. (2012). More than words: The influence of affective content and linguistic style matches in online reviews on conversion rates. *Journal of Marketing*, *77*(1), 87–103. doi:10.1509/jm.11.0560

Luo, Q., & Zhong, D. (2015). Using social network analysis to explain communication characteristics of travel-related electronic word-of-mouth on social networking sites. *Tourism Management*, *46*, 274–282. doi:10.1016/j.tourman.2014.07.007

Mafael, A., Gottschalk, S. A., & Kreis, H. (2016). Examining biased assimilation of brand-related online reviews. *Journal of Interactive Marketing*, *36*, 91–106. doi:10.1016/j.intmar.2016.06.002

Martin, W. C., & Lueg, J. E. (2013). Modeling word-of-mouth usage. *Journal of Business Research*, *66*(7), 801–808. doi:10.1016/j.jbusres.2011.06.004

März, A., Schubach, S., & Schumann, J. H. (2017). "Why Would I Read a Mobile Review?" Device compatibility perceptions and effects on perceived helpfulness. *Psychology and Marketing*, *34*(2), 119–137. doi:10.1002/mar.20979

Moe, W. W., & Schweidel, D. A. (2012). Online product opinions: Incidence, evaluation, and evolution. *Marketing Science, 31*(3), 372–386. doi:10.1287/mksc.1110.0662

Moore, S. G. (2015). Attitude predictability and helpfulness in online reviews: The role of explained actions and reactions. *The Journal of Consumer Research, 42*(1), 30–44. doi:10.1093/jcr/ucv003

Nambisan, S., & Baron, R. A. (2007). Interactions in virtual customer environments: Implications for product support and customer relationship management. *Journal of Interactive Marketing, 21*(2), 42–62. doi:10.1002/dir.20077

Nathan, R. J., Fook Chiun, D. C., & Suki, N. M. (2016). An online marketing strategies assessment for companies in airlines and entertainment industries in Malaysia. Handbook of Research on Leveraging Consumer Psychology for Effective Customer Engagement, 1-15.

Naylor, R. W., Lamberton, C. P., & Norton, D. A. (2011). Seeing ourselves in others: Reviewer ambiguity, egocentric anchoring, and persuasion. *JMR, Journal of Marketing Research, 48*(3), 617–631. doi:10.1509/jmkr.48.3.617

Netzer, O., Feldman, R., Goldenberg, J., & Fresko, M. (2012). Mine your own business: Market-structure surveillance through text mining. *Marketing Science, 31*(3), 521–543. doi:10.1287/mksc.1120.0713

Pan, L. Y., & Chiou, J. S. (2011). How much can you trust online information? Cues for perceived trustworthiness of consumer-generated online information. *Journal of Interactive Marketing, 25*(2), 67–74. doi:10.1016/j.intmar.2011.01.002

Pan, Y., & Zhang, J. Q. (2011). Born unequal: A study of the helpfulness of user-generated product reviews. *Journal of Retailing, 87*(4), 598–612. doi:10.1016/j.jretai.2011.05.002

Pang, J., & Qiu, L. (2016). Effect of online review chunking on product attitude: The moderating role of motivation to think. *International Journal of Electronic Commerce, 20*(3), 355–383. doi:10.1080/10864415.2016.1121763

Park, C., & Lee, T. M. (2009a). Antecedents of online reviews' usage and purchase influence: An empirical comparison of U.S. and Korean consumers. *Journal of Interactive Marketing, 23*(4), 332–340. doi:10.1016/j.intmar.2009.07.001

Park, C., & Lee, T. M. (2009b). Information direction, website reputation and eWOM effect: A moderating role of product type. *Journal of Business Research, 62*(1), 61–67. doi:10.1016/j.jbusres.2007.11.017

Park, D. H., Lee, J., & Han, I. (2007). The effect of on-line consumer reviews on consumer purchasing intention: The moderating role of involvement. *International Journal of Electronic Commerce, 11*(4), 125–148. doi:10.2753/JEC1086-4415110405

Park, S. B., & Park, D. H. (2013). The effect of low- versus high-variance in product reviews on product evaluation. *Psychology and Marketing, 30*(7), 543–554. doi:10.1002/mar.20626

Parthasarathy, M., & Forlani, D. (2010). Do satisfied customers bad-mouth innovative products? *Psychology and Marketing, 27*(12), 1134–1153. doi:10.1002/mar.20377

Phelps, J. E., Lewis, R., Mobilio, L., Perry, D., & Raman, N. (2004). Viral marketing or electronic word-of-mouth advertising: Examining consumer responses and motivations to pass along email. *Journal of Advertising Research*, *44*(4), 333–348. doi:10.1017/S0021849904040371

Piliavin, J. A., & Charng, H.-W. (1990). Altruism: A review of recent theory and research. *Annual Review of Sociology*, *16*(1), 27–65. doi:10.1146/annurev.so.16.080190.000331

Prendergast, G., Paliwal, A., & Chan, K. K. F. (2018). Trust in online recommendations: An evolutionary psychology perspective. *International Journal of Advertising*, *37*(2), 199–216. doi:10.1080/02650487.2016.1239879

Presi, C., Saridakis, C., & Hartmans, S. (2014). User-generated content behaviour of the dissatisfied service customer. *European Journal of Marketing*, *48*(9/10), 1600–1625. doi:10.1108/EJM-07-2012-0400

Purnawirawan, N., De Pelsmacker, P., & Dens, N. (2012). Balance and sequence in online reviews: How perceived usefulness affects attitudes and intentions. *Journal of Interactive Marketing*, *26*(4), 244–255. doi:10.1016/j.intmar.2012.04.002

Purnawirawan, N., Eisend, M., De Pelsmacker, P., & Dens, N. (2015). A Meta-analytic investigation of the role of valence in online reviews. *Journal of Interactive Marketing*, *31*, 17–27. doi:10.1016/j.intmar.2015.05.001

Reimer, T., & Benkenstein, M. (2016). Altruistic eWOM marketing: More than an alternative to monetary incentives. *Journal of Retailing and Consumer Services*, *31*, 323–333. doi:10.1016/j.jretconser.2016.04.003

Robitschek, C. (1998). Personal growth initiative: The construct and its measure. *Measurement & Evaluation in Counseling & Development*, *30*(4), 183–198. doi:10.1080/07481756.1998.12068941

Schiffman, L. G., & Wisenblit, J. (2019). *Consumer Behavior* (12th ed.). Pearson.

Schlosser, A. E. (2011). Can including pros and cons increase the helpfulness and persuasiveness of online reviews? The interactive effects of ratings and arguments. *Journal of Consumer Psychology*, *21*(3), 226–239. doi:10.1016/j.jcps.2011.04.002

Schmit, V., & Thierry, B. (2018). The online-word-of-mouth: Research perspectives on multicriteria rating. *Le Travail Humain*, *81*(3), 227–246. doi:10.3917/th.813.0227

Singh, J. P., Irani, S., Rana, N. P., Dwivedi, Y. K., Saumya, S., & Kumar Roy, P. (2017). Predicting the "helpfulness" of online consumer reviews. *Journal of Business Research*, *70*, 346–355. doi:10.1016/j.jbusres.2016.08.008

Srinivasan, S. S., Anderson, R., & Ponnavolu, K. (2002). *Customer loyalty in e-commerce : an exploration of its antecedents and consequences*. Academic Press.

Steffes, E. M., & Burgee, L. E. (2009). Social ties and online word of mouth. *Internet Research*, *19*(1), 42–59. doi:10.1108/10662240910927812

Suki, N. M. (2016). *Handbook of Research on Leveraging Consumer Psychology for Effective Customer Engagement*. https://www.igi-global.com/book/handbook-research-leveraging-consumer-psychology/149284

Sundaram, D. S., Kaushik, M., & Webster, C. (1998). Word-of-mouth communications: A motivational analysis. *Advances in Consumer Research. Association for Consumer Research (U. S.).*

Sussman, S. W., & Siegal, W. S. (2003). Informational influence in organizations: An integrated approach to knowledge adoption. *Information Systems Research, 14*(1), 47–65. doi:10.1287/isre.14.1.47.14767

Tang, L. (2017). Mine your customers or mine your business: The moderating role of culture in online word-of-mouth reviews. *Journal of International Marketing, 25*(2), 88–110. doi:10.1509/jim.16.0030

Tang, M. C. (2016). The effect of online word of mouth on fantasy readers' preference stability: The moderating role of involvement and knowledge. *Library & Information Science Research, 38*(4), 292–300. doi:10.1016/j.lisr.2016.11.003

Teichmann, K., Stokburger-sauer, N. E., Plank, A., & Strobl, A. (2015). Motivational drivers of content contribution to company- versus consumer-hosted online communities. doi:10.1002/mar

Tirunillai, S., & Tellis, G. J. (2012). Does chatter really matter? Dynamics of user-generated content and stock performance. *Marketing Science, 31*(2), 198–215. doi:10.1287/mksc.1110.0682

van Noort, G., & Willemsen, L. M. (2012). Online damage control: The effects of proactive versus reactive webcare interventions in consumer-generated and brand-generated platforms. *Journal of Interactive Marketing, 26*(3), 131–140. doi:10.1016/j.intmar.2011.07.001

Wang, F., Liu, X., & Fang, E. (2015). User Reviews Variance, Critic Reviews Variance, and Product Sales: An Exploration of Customer Breadth and Depth Effects. *Journal of Retailing, 91*(3), 372–389. doi:10.1016/j.jretai.2015.04.007

Wang, X., Yu, C., & Wei, Y. (2012). Social Media Peer Communication and Impacts on Purchase Intentions: A Consumer Socialization Framework. *Journal of Interactive Marketing, 26*(4), 198–208. doi:10.1016/j.intmar.2011.11.004

Wang, Y., & Fesenmaier, D. R. (2004). Towards understanding members' general participation in and active contribution to an online travel community. *Tourism Management, 25*(6), 709–722. doi:10.1016/j.tourman.2003.09.011

Wright, L. T., Newman, A., & Dennis, C. (2006). Enhancing consumer empowerment. *European Journal of Marketing, 40*(9–10), 925–935. doi:10.1108/03090560610680934

Wu, P. F. (2013). In search of negativity bias: An empirical study of perceived helpfulness of online reviews. *Psychology and Marketing, 30*(11), 971–984. doi:10.1002/mar.20660

Yang, J., Kim, W., Amblee, N., & Jeong, J. (2012). The heterogeneous effect of WOM on product sales: Why the effect of WOM valence is mixed? *European Journal of Marketing, 46*(11), 1523–1538. doi:10.1108/03090561211259961

Yoo, K. H., & Gretzel, U. (2008). What motivates consumers to write online travel reviews? *Information Technology & Tourism, 10*(4), 283–295. doi:10.3727/109830508788403114

You, K. H., Lee, S. A., Lee, J. K., & Kang, H. (2013). Why read online news? The structural relationships among motivations, behaviors, and consumption in South Korea. *Information Communication and Society*, *16*(10), 1574–1595. doi:10.1080/1369118X.2012.724435

Zhang, J. Q., Craciun, G., & Shin, D. (2010). When does electronic word-of-mouth matter? A study of consumer product reviews. *Journal of Business Research*, *63*(12), 1336–1341. doi:10.1016/j.jbusres.2009.12.011

Zhang, L., & Hanks, L. (2018). Online reviews: The effect of cosmopolitanism, incidental similarity, and dispersion on consumer attitudes toward ethnic restaurants. *International Journal of Hospitality Management*, *68*, 115–123. doi:10.1016/j.ijhm.2017.10.008

Zhang, L., Ma, B., & Cartwright, D. K. (2013). The impact of online user reviews on cameras sales. *European Journal of Marketing*, *47*(7), 1115–1128. doi:10.1108/03090561311324237

Zhang, W., & Watts, S. A. (2008). Capitalizing on content : Information adoption in two online communities. *Journal of the Association for Information Systems*, *9*(2), 73–94. doi:10.17705/1jais.00149

Zhao, Y., Yang, S., Narayan, V., & Zhao, Y. (2013). Modeling consumer learning from online product reviews. *Marketing Science*, *32*(1), 153–169. doi:10.1287/mksc.1120.0755

Chapter 8
Examining Perceived Value Influence Mobile Game Addiction:
A Case of Turkish Young Adults

Seda Yildirim
Tekirdag Namık Kemal University, Turkey

ABSTRACT

This study aimed to investigate mobile game addiction through perceived game value. According to this aim, the relationship between mobile game addiction and consumption values was tested. From 500 e-survey forms, 386 forms were accepted for analysis. To measure perceived value, Sheth, Newman, and Gross's consumption values model was adapted. Lemmens, Valkenburg, and Peter's game addiction model were used in this study to measure mobile game addiction. With the help of canonical correlation analysis, it was tested whether there was a significant relationship between perceived value and mobile game addiction. Consequently, it was found that perceived values were significantly related to mobile game addiction. Especially, functional, emotional, and conditional values had a strong correlation with mobile game addiction. This study provides some evidence that perceived game value can influence game addiction.

INTRODUCTION

The rise of mobile game market can't be ignored that every developments in mobile game market attracts new global and leading brands (Jiang et.al., 2015). For example, game market had $99.6 billion (Bn) in revenues by 2016 and mobile gaming had higher revenue than PC games globally at the same year. Concole gaming had $30.8 Bn, PC gaming had 31.9 Bn and mobile gaming had $36.9 Bn in the share of total gaming industry in 2016 (CGA, 2016). In 2018, mobile gaming market became the biggest gaming market globally. With the help of mobile devices such as smartphone, there have been 2.2. billion players in mobile gaming market (Newzoo, 2018). Then, the birth and growth of mobile game is

DOI: 10.4018/978-1-7998-3042-9.ch008

related with mobile phone. Because mobile games got available when second generation (2G) mobile phones appeared in the market. 3G expanded mobile game market through its new technology. Nowadays, 4G is serving in mobile communication industry and mobile games can be bought and played by more people globally (Kim, 2013:43).

The definition of mobile game is mainly based on mobile devices such as smartphones. In other words, the literature generally defined mobile games as one type of game that can be played by mobile phones or devices (Mäyrä, 2015:1). In this context, the history showed that Tetris was the first mobile device that people played a video game. The first mobile games were variant of Tetris. Then, Nokia presented Snake game with phones and mobile games firstly joined into mobile phone platform (Handjam, n.d.). According to Kaye (2014), the historical development of mobile games can be explained as Table 1.

It is a fact that mobile phones or smartphones has accelerated the development of mobile gaming industry. Especially, players can be more satisfied with video games of mobile devices recently (Kim, 2013). Understanding players' intention to online games is the big dilemma for researchers. Because researchers can find different results when they investigate online game addiction or online game play-

Table 1. A Brief History of Mobile Games

Years	Important Events
1997	The world meets the first mobile game through Nokia – SNAKE by 1997.
1999	Gameloft begins making mobile games for phones/smartphones.
2000	Jamdat is founded and begins to make mobile games.
2001	The year of 2001 makes new opportunities for mobile gaming industry. Java One Conference in 4th June provides J2ME for phones. Then, Sonic the Hedgehog joins into mobile gaming industry by June 2001 and Brew joins into mobile gaming industry by September 2001.
2002	Nokia 3410 and Siemens M50 get J2ME.
2003	Nokia N-Gage gives Splinter Cell in December 2003. In June 2003, Jamdat Bowling becomes so popular mobile game in US gaming market.
2004	Prince of Persia: The Sands of Time gets into mobile platform in January 2004. Motorola Razr gets so popular by 2004.
2005	EA mobile buys Jamdat for $680m in December 2005. Sorrent and Macrospace signs for a merger and creates GluMobile in June 2005.
2006	The Gizmondo (handheld game console) goes bankrupt in February 2006. Digital Chocolate (mobile game makers) gets $22.5m.
2007	Steve Jobs introduced iphone to the market and it firstly goes on sale in the US. By September 2007, iphone users meet Tap Tap Revolution for the first time.
2008	Android market welcomes in 2008 and APP store opens with 500 apps by July 2008.
2009	Developers begin to sell App Purchases with Apple. In April 2009, Doodle Jump joins into mobile gaming market and Angry Birds occurs by December 2009.
2010	The Pure Android Nexus One goes on sale by Google in 2010. Ipad goes on sale in April 2010. Flight control and Plants vs Zombies get into App Store in February 2010. Infinity Blade gets into App Store in December 2010.
2011	The Ipad 2, The Samsung Galaxy S2 and Kindle Fire (Amazon) tablet join into the mobile market.
2012	Nexus 7 tablet is released by Google and Ipad Mini tablet is released. Candy Crush Saga is released on İOS.
2013	HTC One (Blackberry Z10) launches. EA releases Plants and Zombies 2.

Source: adapted from Kaye, 2014:5-10

ing behavior. To discover why people get addicted to mobile games, firstly, we should understand why they love mobile games. For example, Koo (2009) explained the relationships between playing online game intention and some experiential motives as "concentration, perceived enjoyment, escape behavior, epistemic curiosity, social affiliation and control behavior". He found out perceived enjoyment, escape behavior and social affiliation had a significant effect on intention to play online game.

Wu et.al. (2010) studied the relationships between gratifications (achievement, enjoyment, social interaction), presence (spatial and social), service mechanisms (fairness, security, incentive), continuance motivation and proactive stickiness. They found gratification and service mechanism had a significant effect on intention to continue playing game and so this was an important indicator for being proactive stickiness to online games. Liu and Li (2011) studied the relationships between "perceived ease of use, perceived usefulness, perceived enjoyment, cognitive concentration, use context, attitude and behavioral intention" for mobile games. They found perceived usefulness and perceived enjoyment had an effect on attitude of mobile games and they found perceived usefulness, perceived enjoyment and cognitive concentration had a positive effect on playing mobile game. Liang and Yeh (2009) studied on indicators (playfulness, situational effect task, attitude, subjective norm and ease of use) for intention to use mobile game. They determined subjective norm and perceived playfulness had an effect on using mobile game when user had no other tasks.

2000s brings people to much more opportunities with mobile devices such as mobile phones, smartphones, tablets etc. With higher technologic development such as "3G and handheld technologies" the number and usage of mobile devices is getting higher and also mobile gaming is the most profitable market now (Liu and Li, 2011:890). Being independent from a specific place, mobile games are always available for users and this is a big advantage for mobile devices (Liang and Yeh, 2009:51). Innovative mobile devices and smartphones have made more attractive mobile games for consumers recently. In this point, game market had a new competitor as mobile gaming that new challenges will occur in a mobile gaming industry in the future. On the other side, mobile devices can sometimes influence people negatively. People may get away from society in a real life or get some mental illnesses when they become addicted to mobile devices and its facilities such as games or social media platforms, The literature gives so many example and cases about technology addiction or mobile phone addiction. Game addiction is known term for a long time but the conceptualization of mobile game addiction has some gaps.

More research that delve into aspect of consumer behavior and psychology in the digital economy is deemed necessary (Ling Chang, Ling Tam, & Suki, 2016; Nathan, Fook Chiun, & Suki, 2016; Suki, 2016). Accordingly, this study investigates the relationship between perceived value and mobile game addiction. In addition, it is expected to explain mobile game addiction through perceived values. With providing empirical findings, it is thought to guide future studies and give new information for policy makers in a game market.

FROM GAME PLAYING BEHAVIOR TO GAME ADDICTION

The internet world provides the dream of global world today and it makes everything more accessible. However internet is seen as a big threat for young adults and children today. Young generation has been influenced by the information technology that the latest studies show that "one of every three teens is engaged via their mobile phones/cell phones/smartphone (De la Puente and Balmori, 2007:2). Like as reaching internet easily via mobile devices, playing online game behavior is now changed into playing mobile game behavior. Dieckmann (1999) indicated that mobility increased playing game behavior. Koo (2009) summarized behavioral studies of games with three basic approaches as *"attractive functions of virtual world, psychology and cognitive and perceptual factors"*. This study will keep third approach that the influence of perceptual factors on playing mobile games will be investigated.

According to literature, "Technology Acceptance Model (TAM) which is developed by Davis (1989)" is mostly used to determine behavioral attitudes for technological devices. Hsu and Lu (2007) investigated online game players' attitude through TAM approach and they found out customer loyalty was related with perceived enjoyment, social norms and preference. Chen et.al.(2007) employed TAM model to explain mobile social games and they determined that perceived enjoyment and perceived ease of use were dominant factors for playing mobile social game behavior. Nguyen (2015) determined the strong effect of perceived enjoyment on playing mobile game behavior via TAM model. Jiang et.al.(2015) studied on mobile game adoption and they determined "perceived usefulness, perceived entertainment, economic cost and subjective norm" were effected on mobile game adoption behavior.

Excessive playing online games may cause troubles for players or users. Some researchers said that online game addiction is not really addiction. For example, Ahn and Randall (2007) examined that some MMORPG (Massively Multiplayer Online Role Playing Games) players were excessive players but not addicted people. Wood (2008) determined that excessive online playing behavior would be a problematic behavior in the long term. Ng and Wiemer-Hastings (2005)'s study showed that some of MMORPG players were excessive players that they spent too much time for playing but not addicted. Tavormina and Tavormina(2017) examined that excessive playing behavior may cause addiction and problems. The attention should be given to excessive playing behavior and future causes such as being addicted and having social and psychological problems should be investigated (Schwartz, 2013). Woog (2016) determined that excessive game play behavior caused game addiction. He suggested reducing playing time and amount of game play can prevent addiction.

After investigating intention to play mobile game, the main question can be why playing game may be dangerous for users. In this point, excessive usage of mobile devices and excessive behavior of playing mobile games may result as bad habits. Although studies on gaming addiction has a long history, 2000s brings new approach for game addiction (Kuss,2013:127). Especially, online games and mobile games are so popular in todays and addiction to online games or mobile games are threat for youngers (Karapetsas et.al.,2014; Ku et.al.,2014;). During last decade, people became more close to technology and they began to spend much more time with their mobile devices (Anderson et.al.,2007). Accordingly, usage of mobile devices has changed people's habits over the time and the most dangerous problem of addiction disguised as technology addiction (Griffiths,1995). Internet addiction, game addiction and mobile phone addiction have been investigated by researchers recently to understand addiction of technology (Young,1996; Griffiths,1995; Griffiths 2000; Davis, 2001; Wan and Chiou,2006; Charlton and Danforth,2007; Young,2009; Beranuy et.al.,,2013). Game addiction can be defined as problematic usage of computer and video games (Lemmens, Valkenburgve Peter, 2009). When gaming behavior passes over "sleep, diet or socializing (Young,2004)", the addiction comes out in the open.

It can be said that younger are seen as the first to be addicted to online / mobile games as much as internet. In this point, game addiction is investigated under clinical approach at first (Baysak et.al.,2016:21). Patients who have problems because of excessive computer use are seeing by clinicians in the United States (Woog, 2016:272). However, there is a conflict for defining game addiction between clinicians and academicians. Some researchers investigated game addiction based on pathological theories and some of them investigated game addiction by behavioral theories (Lemmens, 2010). Griffiths (2015) summarized the development of game addiction studies and he determined that researches have been updated by 2000s. The number of studies on problematic /excessive and addictive game playing behavior increased as much as its methodology. 1970s gave the first video games and 1980s showed the first reports of video game addiction.

By 2000s, studies on game addiction almost reached the peak (Griffiths, 2015:1). However, there are still gaps in defining or measuring game addiction based on data, measures, sampling, methods etc. (Sepehr and Head, 2013) when game market is growing day-to-day. For example, Vollmer, Randler, Horzum and Ayas (2014) investigated relationships between computer game addiction, computer game usage time, age, gender, BIG-5 personality, and chronotype in Turkey. The study found that there were significant relationships between computer game addiction and play time and chronotype. In addition, the study showed that male students and evening players had higher game addictions scores. Wood (2008) investigated video game addiction through four case studies. The study determined people who were mostly excessive video game player, had also some symptomatic problems and couldn't manage their time effectively.

Zorbaz, Ulas and Kizildag (2015) investigated the relationship between video game addiction and interfamily relationships. According to results, the study found that male students had higher game addiction scores. The study suggested that family could prevent video game addiction for primary school students. Brian and Wiemer-Hastings (2005) found that users of massively multiplayer online role playing games (MMORPGs) weren't called as addicted although they were excessive players and spent so much time in online playing. In fact, excessive playing behavior is one step away from game addiction that there are some difficulties in determining game addiction. While digital game market is keeping its rising trend, people have some troubles in keeping the balance between virtual life and actual life. Especially, young adults and children are closer to negative outcomes of virtual life such as game addiction (Fisher, 1994; Chiu et.al., 2004; Nalwa and Anand, 2004; Skoric et.al.,2009; Zorbaz et.al.,2015). With this study, it is aimed to explain mobile game addiction of young adults through perceived value in Turkey. The study keeps marketing perspective to explain game addiction and it includes consumption values theory to explain game addiction.

PERCEIVED VALUE

Values are thought as almost the most important thing that influence human life and also influence consumer preferences (Kayabaşı et.al., 2012:1327). For products, values are generally defined as benefits that influence consumer decision making (Lim et.al., 2012:210) and perceived benefits and attributes of products examine consumption behaviors (Lee et.al., 2011:89). Every products has some benefits and values that consumers mostly prefer one product based on these benefits or values. According to Woodruff (1997), perceived value has some basic concepts such as: "perceived value is related with product; it is perceived by consumers and influences buying decision" (Broekhuizen, 2006:44). Most of studies explain the importance of values in marketing strategies. In this point, Hsieh (2016) investigated the relationship between perceived value, brand image and purchase intention. He determined how product's values effected consumer decision making and preferences that marketing strategies should be planned based on these values.

Demirgüneş (2015) investigated the effect of perceived value on risk and satisfaction of buying mobile phone and she determined that perceived value had significant effect on customer satisfaction.

Chi et.al. (2011) found out when consumers perceived higher value, they felt higher purchase intention. Ondang (2015) found out both of attitude and perceived value had an effect on purchase intention. Kim and Hwang (2012) investigated internet users' value perception of mobile internet technology and they found out hedonic value had an effect on internet service perception and higher perception of hedonic value provided higher perception of internet service quality. Sun et.al. (2015) explained mobile game addiction through consumer value (hedonic value and social value) and flow and ease of use and they proposed hedonic value and social value influenced mobile game addiction.

Some studies show that perceived value can be also investigated based on consumption values theory. Sheth, Newman and Gross (1991) provided "consumption values theory" to explain benefits and values of products. Recent studies about consumer buying behavior has shown that today's complicated buying behavior of various products(goods, services, brands, industrial products, political party etc.) can be explained by consumption values model (Surisutto,2010; Hur ad Hur,2014; Mishra,2015; Lee et.al., 2015; Suki and Suki,2015; Yıldırım and Candan,2015). According to Sheth et.al. (1991)'s consumption values model, there are five basic value dimensions as "functional, social, emotional, conditional and epistemic". Functional value/benefit represents the benefits of physical performance and attributes; social value/benefit represents the social meaning of the product that symbolizes social class; emotional value/benefit represents the feelings that product provides; epistemic value/benefit represents product's benefits that satisfying novelty-seeking need; conditional value/benefit represents the benefits that providing specific periods' or conditions' need (Hsieh;2016:3). Some current studies which including the relationship between products and consumption values are presented in Table 2.

There is a gap that researches have ignored *Consumption Values Theory* for a long time in the study field of game industry. Investigating gamers purchase behavior is an important issue as much as consumer behavior. For example, gamers will buy items in gaming market when they perceive items or games more valuable. In this point, consumption values theory can be adopted for games and gamers buying behavior can be explained through this approach (Park and Lee, 2011:2179).

METHOD AND MATERIALS

Some human habits and some behaviors can change into addiction that many people have some addiction such as game addiction, shopping addiction, internet addiction etc. in the fast-techno life. Mobile games have been a part of mobile life that almost every people played a mobile game at once in his/her life. Accordingly, mobile games are thought as a specific product that consumers use and buy them to meet their own needs and wants that it is purposed to find out whether there is a significant relationship between perceived values of mobile games and game addiction. So, the study will test the below hypothesis:

H_1: There is a significant relationship between consumption values and game addiction.

The study reached the primary data through survey method. The survey included two basic measures as consumption values scale and mobile game addiction scale. This study adapted Sheth, Newman and Gross (1991)'s approach of consumption values and game addiction scale of Lemmens, Valkenburg and Peter (2009) for mobile games. Both of two scales was reliable that Cronbach's Alpha value for consumption values was found as 0,88 and Cronbach's Alpha value for mobile game addiction was found as 0,75. (see Table 3).

Table 2. Some Sample Studies Investigating Perceived Value through Consumption Value Theory

Researchers	Product/Behavior type	Sample Case	Findings
Bodker, Gimpel and Hedman(2009)	Smart Phone	Qualitative study:16 participants in Denmark	The paper explained consumption values theory could be used for smart phone.
Park and Lee (2011)	Game items	Survey was collected from 327 participants in South Korea	The paper determined that consumption values theory could be adapted for game items and gaming marketing. Especially, functional value is so valid for buying game items.
Jarenfors and Sturesson (2012)	Smartphones	Ethnographic study: 10 participants	The study explained that respondents gave different response for consumption values of smartphones through different day time.
Candan, Ünal and Erciş (2013)	Personal care products	426 university students from Turkey	The paper indicated that there were significant relationships between consumption values and brand loyalty.
Wang, Liao and Yang (2013)	Mobile Application	282 mobile apps. Users	The paper found out conditional value had a significant effect on mobile App users' behavioral intention.
Denys and Mendes (2014)	Destination	329 people from European union nationalities.	The paper determined that consumption values can explain destination choices of tourists.
Lee, Levy and Yap (2015)	Sustainable consumption	561 residents, Auckland, New Zealand	The paper determined that sustainable consumption behavior is related with consumption values.
Yıldırım and Candan (2015)	Green products	420 residents, Turkey	The paper showed that green products buyers can be segmented through consumption values and personal values. Also, it was seen that consumption values influences buying green product behavior.
Lai, Chou, Wang and Yang (2015)	Tablet personal computer	131 respondents	The paper explains the effect of values (pragmatic and symbolic) on tablet PC preference.
Mishra (2015)	Facebook advertisements	1208 respondents	He explained the importance of social value in digital devices.
Awuni and Du (2016)	Green purchasing intention	309 young adults from Chinese city	The paper explained the relationship between green purchasing intentions and consumption values.
Jamrozy and Lawonk (2017)	Eco-tourism	314 respondents	The paper found emotional value, functional value, epistemic value and boredom alleviation value had an effect on ecotourism purchase behavior

Source: compiled by author

This study preferred to use consumption values scale to determine values of mobile games. So, this study developed an alternative consumption values scale for mobile games that included five basic value dimensions as functional value, social value, emotional value, conditional value and epistemic value. The consumption values scale had five factors with 28 statements (items). Every statements were evalu-

Table 3. The Results of Cronbach's Alpha Test

Scales	Cronbach's Alpha	N of items
Consumption Values	0,883	28
- Functional values	0,784	8
- Social Values	0,852	6
- Emotional values	0,791	4
- Conditional values	0,854	5
- Epistemic values	0,772	5
Mobile Game Addiction	0,750	21
- Salience	0,875	3
- Tolerance	0,671	3
- Mood modification	0,890	3
- Relapse	0,785	3
- Conflict	0,540	3
- Problems	0,765	3

ated via five likert scale ranging from strongly disagree (1) to strongly agree (5) by participants. The development of consumption values scale is showed in Table 4.

Lemmens, Valkenburg, and Peter (2009)'s game addiction scale with 21-item was preferred to measure mobile game addiction level in this study. Seven dimensions (Salience, tolerance, mood modification,

Table 4. The Scale of Consumption Values/Benefits for Mobile Games

Values/Benefits	In a scale
Functional value/benefit (FV):	To measure functional value of mobile games, 8 statements were used in the last version of the survey. Cost, quality and product content were investigated in this value dimension.
Social value/benefit (SV):	The study tried to measure positive social value of mobile games with 4 statements In addition, the study developed 2 negative statements to measure negative perception of playing mobile games.
Emotional value/benefit (EV):	With 4 statements, the study measured the perceived emotional value of mobile games that the study investigated what kinds of emotions influenced mobile game playing behavior.
Conditional value/benefit CV):	The study developed 5 statements to measure conditional value of mobile games. These statements expressed some conditions about playing mobile games such as time and place.
Epistemic value/benefit (EPV):	The study measured epistemic value of mobile games via 5 statements that investigating the perception degree of mobile game as innovative, new, popular and trendy.

relapse, withdrawal, conflict and problems) with each dimensions were adapted for mobile game addiction and participants evaluated every items via five likert scale(1:never to 5:very often). In this study, salience expressed the degree of desire of playing mobile game; tolerance factor determined how much time participants spend for mobile games; mood modification expressed positive feelings about playing mobile games; relapse factor determined the degree of deterioration; withdrawl factor determined feelings about being unable to play mobile games; conflict factor expressed participants' discrepancy situation because of playing mobile games and problems expressed participants' problems because of playing mobile games.

RESULTS

Young adults are more defenseless toward technology addiction because they are interested in technological products much more than elders in general (Park and Lee, 2012). Based on the assumption that young adults are mostly interested in online, video or mobile games, the study included young people as a research mass in this paper. From 500 e-survey forms, 386 survey forms were accepted for analysis. So, the study analyzed survey forms that collected from 276 male and 110 female. All of the participants said that they always bought free mobile games for their smartphones or tablets. Male participants (n= 142; 51%) preferred to pay for mobile games much more than female participants. Most of participants were male (71%) and they were mostly aged 21 years old (Mean=21,22; SD=0,91). Females (n=110) were mostly aged 19 years old and older (Mean=19,45; SD=1,35).

Almost half of participants had income between $ 180 (1000 Turkish Liras) and $360 (2000 Turkish Liras) (n=192; 50%) and most of participants preferred to stay in student house (n=210; 54%). Male participants spent much more time in playing mobile games (n=185; 67%). Male participants mostly preferred to play mobile games during course (n=187; 48%) and female participants mostly preferred to play mobile games when they were alone. Most of male participants (%68) changed mobile games continually. Most of female participants (%46) preferred to play same mobile games for a long time. In addition, almost all of male participants (n=262; 95%) played video and online games in their causal life but most of female participants (n=102; 93%) didn't play video or online games in their causal life.

Factor analysis was used to determine the coherence of variables for consumption values model and mobile game addiction model. Five factors were determined for consumption values model as expected and this result was coherent with prior studies. 24 items with factor loadings were found as valid variables for consumption values model for mobile games and 4 items were eliminated from this model. Total variance was found as 69,369 and KMO-Barlett test result had a enough reliability (Kaiser-Meyer-Olkin Measure of Sampling Adequacy: 0,879;Approx. Chi-Square: 13015,128; df. 391; $p \leq 0,001$). Five factors with 14 items were found as valid factors for mobile game addiction model and KMO-Barlett test's result supported this model for its reliability(Kaiser-Meyer-Olkin Measure of Sampling Adequacy: 0,709; Approx. Chi-Square: 11005,034; df. 345; $p \leq 0,001$).Total variance of mobile game addiction model was found as 64,039.This result was different from prior studies about game addiction. Tolerance factor and conflict factor were eliminated from the model as a result of factor analysis.

To test H_1, canonical correlation analysis was carried out and multiple relationships between factors was tested. Although five canonical function was found, only one function was found as a significant ($p<0,05$). As seen in Table 6, canonical correlation coefficient value was 0,502 and function 1 explained 25 percent of total variance. As a result of canonical correlation, one significant function was determined that it was found out that there were significant relationships and this function could express this relationship (R_c= 0,502 ; Canonical Root (r^2)=0,252 ; Wilk's Lambda= 0,514, Chi-Square= 218,866 ; df= 25;;$p<0,05$).

There were significant correlations between factors of consumption values and factors of mobile game addiction. The highest correlation was found between emotional value and mood modification and the lowest

Table 5. Means, Factor Loadings and Variances

Consumption Values Model	Mean	Factor Loadings	Variance
Factor 1= Social Value(SV)			21,361
SV2.Playing mobile game provides me social acceptable	4,62	,955	
SV3.I began to buy and play mobile games after I saw people that playing mobile game who were close to me.	4,54	,832	
SV4.I get rid of playing mobile game, If my friends are opposite to it.	4,32	,726	
SV5.I don't prefer to play mobile game that my social environment doesn't approve it.	3,25	,783	
SV6.I prefer to play the most popular mobile game to keep social trend	4,01	,835	
Factor 2= Emotional Value(EV)			17,214
EV1Playing mobile game makes me feel good	4,50	,870	
EV2.Playing mobile game makes me relax	4,32	,574	
EV3.I always enjoy playing mobile game	4,40	,897	
EV4.I feel bad, If I can't play mobile game	4,28	,674	
Factor 3= Conditional Value(CV)			13,251
CV1.I play mobile game whenever I get bored during the course at the university	3,80	,785	
CV2.I play mobile game whenever I travel by bus, train, plane etc.	3,53	,560	
CV3.I play mobile game in my leisure time	3,50	,598	
CV4.I play mobile game whenever I am alone	3,78	,765	
CV5.I get rid of playing mobile game, If it is harmful	3,62	,742	
Factor 4=Functional Value(FV)			10,033
FV1.The mobile game has standard quality as same as other digital games	3,86	,751	
FV2.The mobile game is well-designed as same as other digital games	3,50	,569	
FV3.I always trust the security of mobile games.	4,58	,652	
FV6.The mobile game is always economic	3,21	,560	
FV7.The mobile game is always cheaper than other digital games.	3,02	,451	
FV8.I usually prefer to buy and play cheap mobile games.	3,52	,640	
Factor 5=Epistemic Value(EPV)			7,213
EPV1.I think mobile games are so innovative	2,89	,532	
EPV2.I prefer to buy and play new and different mobile games	3,12	,670	
EPV3.I always look for the most popular mobile games	3,51	,549	
EPV4.I prefer to buy and play the trendy mobile games	3,88	,353	
Mobile Game Addiction Model			
Factor 1= Salience(S)			18,910
S1.Did you think about playing a game all day long?	4,12	,784	
S2.Did you spend much free time on games?	4,18	,710	
S3.Have you felt addicted to a game?	3,48	,652	
T1.Did you play longer than intended?(tolerance factor)	3,85		

continued on following page

Table 5. Continued

Consumption Values Model	Mean	Factor Loadings	Variance
Factor 2= Mood Modification(MM)			15,320
MM1.Did you play games to forget about real life?	4,50	,725	
MM2.Have you played games to release stress?	4,32	,655	
MM3.Have you played games to feel better?	4,40	,630	
Factor 3= Relapse(R)			12,455
R1.Were you unable to reduce your game time?	3,45	,680	
R3.Have you failed when trying to reduce game time?	3,60	,575	
Factor 4=Withdrawal(W)			10,368
W1.Have you felt bad when you were unable to play?	4,80	,632	
W3.Have you become stressed when unable to play?	3,50	,560	
Factor 5=Problems(P)			6,985
P1.Has your time on games caused sleep deprivation?	3,80	,544	
P2.Have you neglected other important activities (e.g., school, work, sports) to play games?	4,11	,463	
P3.Did you feel bad after playing for a long time?	4,20	,470	

Table 6. Canonical Correlation

Canonical Function	Canonical Correlation Coefficient(Rc)	Canonical Root	Wilk's Lambda	Chi-Square	df	P(Sig.)
1	0,502	0,252	0,514	218,866	25	$p \leq 0{,}001$

correlation was found between epistemic value and relapse. Withdrawal and problems didn't have significant canonical loadings that the study didn't evaluate these factors in mobile game addiction model. According to canonical loadings, it was found out that the highest canonical loading was belonged to emotional value in consumption values model (CL=0,784). In mobile addiction model, the highest canonical loading was belonged to mood modification (CL=0,881). In addition, social value (CL= -0,762) and conditional value (CL=0,621) had higher canonical loading that these factors were dominant in consumption values model. Functional value (CL=0,615) had also higher effect on mobile game addiction.

Epistemic value (CL=0,423) has lower value in consumption values model that the impact of these factors would be less on mobile game addiction. In mobile game addiction model, salience (CL=0,549) and relapse (CL=0,346) had higher value and it can be said that consumption values would have higher impact on mood modification, salience and relapse. These results indicated that university students who bought and played mobile games with higher perception of emotional and conditional value, had higher mobile addiction. Especially, emotional values of mobile games supported playing mobile games for its positive emotions and feelings as an addiction. Social value had a negative correlation with mobile game addiction. Functional value and epistemic value of mobile games had a positive correlation with mobile game addiction. The redundancy index of consumption values set was found as 0,657 that this value was enough to say that the canonical correlations were significant and set of consumption values cluster could explain almost 66%(total variance) of the set of mobile game addiction cluster. In summary, according to canonical correlation relationships, it can be said that young people who perceive high consumption values, also have higher addiction for mobile games (see Table 7).

Table 7. Canonical Loadings of Consumption Values (Set-1) and Mobile Game Addiction (Set-2)

Set 1-Consumption Values		Set 2- Mobile Game Addiction	
Variables	**Canonical Loadings(CL)**	**Variables**	**Canonical Loadings(CL)**
X1:Functional value	0,615	Y1: Salience	0,549
X2:Social Value	- 0,762	Y2:Mood modification	0,881
X3:Emotional Value	0,784	Y3: Relapse	0,346
X4:Conditional Value	0,621	Y4: Withdrawal	0,218
X5:Epistemic Value	0,423	Y5: Problems	0,207
Redundancy Index: CV1-1: 0,657 (Proportion of Variance of Set-1)			

SOLUTIONS AND RECOMMENDATIONS

The literature provides alternative measures for perceived values and addiction that preferred scales and measures can change the results for further studies. Another limitation was all of the participants were university students from Turkey that other countries' young adults or university students can response differently. Although there are limitations for this study, empirical findings can guide further studies and it is thought to contribute the related literature. The study provides some evidences that consumption values model can be used for mobile games. As a result, this study shows that there is a strong relationship between perceived emotional, functional and conditional values and tendency to be an addicted. Participants weren't so addicted people but they were excessive players and had a tendency to be an addicted. This study is the first one that indicating the relationship between perceived value and game addiction in the related literature.

FUTURE RESEARCH DIRECTIONS

The study focused on how game players perceive mobile games and whether there was a significant relationship between mobile game addiction and perceived value. According to empirical findings, this study showed that there was a significant relationship between perceived value and game addiction. This study has some limitations such as sample, methods, time etc. Future studies can find different results through different sample case and methodologies. In this context, we can suggest the below list for further studies:

- Future studies can use different sample case to investigate the relationship between perceived value and game addiction.

- Future studies can prefer alternative perceived value approach to determine game value and also they can analyze perceived value of computer games, video games or another specific digital game.
- When there is different statistical test, the empirical findings can prove strong relationship between perceived value and game addiction.

CONCLUSION

Innovative mobile devices with larger screens and better performance provided great development and growth in mobile game industry. The first step for mobile gaming was achieved by N-Gage platform of Nokia in 2003. Then Nokia left its place in gaming industry to new technologies as smartphones and i-phone (Feijoo et.al., 2012).Today gives many opportunities for mobile game industry that assumptions show that mobile game industry can be a leader industry in gaming market in the future (Kontio, 2011). The arrival of smartphones has increased playing mobile games and game consumption behavior. Accordingly game market became an attractive market for new enterprises and game designers and providers. Understanding how consumers buy online / mobile game or why consumers pay for /mobile game is an important issue both for academician and businesses (De Souza and De Freitas, 2017).

This study explained the relationship between perceived value and game addiction. The results indicated that participants perceived emotional value/benefit of mobile games higher than other benefits/ values. Firstly, as consistent with perceived emotional benefit, participants were mostly addicted to mobile games because of mood modification. So, it can be said that young people mostly play and buy mobile games to feel relax and good and enjoy. When young people need more enjoyment or need to feel relax, they can be more addicted to mobile games. Secondly, conditional values of mobile games can influence mobile game addiction. Because mobile/cell phones make games more accessible and players are free to play mobile games in every time and everywhere. Accordingly, conditional benefits can increase the tendency of being mobile game addicted. Functional values also motives players to play mobile game much more.

Being mobile and cheap or almost free, mobile games attracts players and may cause excessive playing behavior much more. Epistemic value of mobile games didn't have a dominant influence on mobile game addiction. So, it can be said that young people mostly don't give weight to epistemic benefits or values for mobile games. On the other side, social values/benefits can decrease the tendency of being mobile game addicted. As it is consistent with the literature, people generally beware of social reaction and they want to be approved by their social environment. For example, girls mostly use cell phone to be more social (Geser, 2006; De-Sola Gutierrez, 2016) but they don't play online games. Young males prefer to play online or mobile games and they are mostly less social than young females.

However, literature indicates that young females are more addicted to cellphone/mobile phone/smartphone (Oksman, 2007; Ozkan and Solmaz, 2015; De-Sola Gutierrez et.al., 2016), the study determined young males were excessive players and they were closer to be addicted. Young males played and bought mobile games much more than young females. In addition, young males spent much more time for playing mobile games and they were playing video or online games in their causal life, too. Like as online game addiction (Wang et.al, 2014) and computer game addiction (Vollmer et.al.,2014), males are more closer to be addicted to mobile games.

ACKNOWLEDGMENT

The study was presented in *The Second International Conference On Current Trends In The Middle East – 2018, Turkey.*

REFERENCES

Ahn, J., & Randall, G. (2007). *Computer Game Addiction.* Retrieved January 13, 2018, from http://andrewd.ces.clemson.edu/courses/cpsc414/spring07/chp/team3.pdf

Anderson, J. C., & Gerbing, D. W. (1984). The effect of sampling error on convergece, improper solutions and goodness-of-fit indices for maximum likelihood confirmatory factor analysis. *Psychometrika, 49*(2), 155–173. doi:10.1007/BF02294170

Awuni, J. A., & Du, J. (2016). Sustainable Consumption in Chinese Cities: Green Purchasing Intentions of Young Adults Based on the Theory of Consumption Values. *Sustainable Development, 24*(2), 124–135. doi:10.1002d.1613

Baysak, E., Kaya, F. D., Dalgar, I., & Candansayar, S. (2016). Online Game Addiction in a Sample from Turkey: Development and Validation of the Turkish Version of Game Addiction Scale. *Klinik Psikofarmakoloji Bülteni, 26*(1), 21–31. doi:10.5455/bcp.20150502073016

Beranuy, M., Carbonell, X., & Griffiths, M. D. (2013). A Qualitative Analysis of Online Gaming Addicts in Treatment. *International Journal of Mental Health and Addiction, 11*(2), 149–161. doi:10.100711469-012-9405-2

Bødker, M., Gimpel, G., & Hedman, J. (2009). *The user experience of smart phones: a consumption values approach.* Retrieved January 13, 2018, from http://citeseerx.ist.psu.edu/viewdoc/download?doi=10.1.1.472.30&rep=rep1&type=pdf

Brian, D. N. G., & Wiemer-Hastings, P. (2005). Addiction to the Internet and Online Gaming. *Cyberpsychology & Behavior, 8*(2), 110–113. doi:10.1089/cpb.2005.8.110 PMID:15938649

Broekhuizen, T. L. J. (2006). *Understanding channel purchase intentions: Measuring online and offline shopping value perceptions.* Retrieved January 13, 2018, from https://www.van-haaften.nl/images/documents/pdf/Measuring%20Online%20and%20Offline%20Shopping%20value%20perception.pdf

Candan, B., Ünal, S., & Erciş, A. (2013). Analysing the relationship between consumption values and brand loyalty of young people: A study on personal care products. European Journal Research on Education. Special ıssue. *Human Resource Management*, 29–46. doi:10.11648/j.jhrm.20130102.11

CGA (Causal Games Association). (2016). *The Mobile Games Market, How to Compete in the Crowded Marketplace, Causal Games Sector Report 2016.* Retrieved November 1, 2019 from http://progamedev.net/wp-content/uploads/2016/07/Newzoo_CGA_How_to_Compete_in_Mobile_Games.pdf

Chang, L. D. M., Ling Tam, A. Y., & Suki, N. M. (2016). Moderating effect of races towards consumers' feeling of TCM usage. Handbook of Research on Leveraging Consumer Psychology for Effective Customer Engagement, 306-323.

Charlton, J. P., & Danforth, I. D. W. (2007). Distinguishing addiction and high engagement in the context of online game playing. *Computers in Human Behavior*, *23*(3), 1531–1548. doi:10.1016/j.chb.2005.07.002

Chen, H., Rong, W. M. X., Qu, Y., & Zhang, X. (2017). *An Extended Technology Acceptance Model for Mobile Social Gaming Service Popularity Analysis* (Vol. 2017). Hindawi Mobile Information Systems.

Chi, H., Yeh, H., & Tsai, Y. (2011). The influences of perceived value on consumer purchase intention: The moderating effect of advertising endorser. *Journal of International Management Studies*, *6*(1), 1–6.

Chiu, S. I., Lee, J. Z., & Huang, D. H. (2004). Video Game Addiction in Children and Teenagers in Taiwan. *Cyberpsychology & Behavior*, *7*(5), 571–581. doi:10.1089/cpb.2004.7.571 PMID:15667052

Claudio Feijoo, C., Gómez-Barroso, J. L., Aguado, J. M., & Ramos, S. (2012). Mobile gaming: Industry challenges and policy implications. *Telecommunications Policy*, *36*(3), 212–221. doi:10.1016/j.telpol.2011.12.004

Davis, F. D. (1989). Perceived Usefulness, Perceived Ease of Use, and User Acceptance of Information Technology. *Management Information Systems Quarterly*, *13*(3), 319–340. doi:10.2307/249008

Davis, R. A. (2001). A cognitive-behavioral model of pathological Internet use. *Computers in Human Behavior*, *17*(2), 1, 187–195. doi:10.1016/S0747-5632(00)00041-8

De la Puente, M. P., & Balmori, A. (2007). Addiction to cell phones: Are there neurophysiological mechanisms involved? *Proyecto*, *61*, 8–12.

De-Sola Gutierrez, J., Rodriguez de Fonseca, F., & Rubio, G. (2016). Cell-Phone Addiction: A Review. *Frontiers in Psychiatry*, *7*(175), 1–15. PMID:27822187

De Souza, L. L. F., & De Freitas, A. A. F. (2017). Consumer behavior of electronic games' players: A study on the intentions to play and to pay. *Revista ADM*, *52*, 419–430.

Demirgüneş, B. K. (2015). Relative Importance of Perceived Value, Satisfaction and Perceived Risk on Willingness to Pay More. *International Review of Management and Marketing*, *5*(4), 211–220.

Denys, V., & Mendes, J. (2014). Consumption values and destination evaluation in destination decision making. *Journal of Spatial and Organizational Dynamics*, *2*(1), 4–22.

Dieckmann, T. (1999). The evolution of conventions with mobile players. *Journal of Economic Behavior & Organization*, *38*(1), 93–111. doi:10.1016/S0167-2681(98)00125-5

Fisher, S. (1994). Identifying video game addiction in children and adolescents. *Addictive Behaviors*, *19*(5), 545–553. doi:10.1016/0306-4603(94)90010-8 PMID:7832013

Geser, H. (2006). *Are girls (even) more addicted? Some gender patterns of cell phone usage*. Zürich: Universität Zürich, Philosophische Fakultät, Soziologisches Institut.

Griffiths, M. D. (2000). Video game violence and aggression: Comments on 'Video game playing and its relations with aggressive and prosocial behaviour' by O. Weigman and E.G.M. van Schie. *British Journal of Social Psychology*, *39*(Pt 1), 147–149. doi:10.1348/014466600164381 PMID:10774533

Griffiths, M. D. (2015). Online Games, Addiction And Overuse Of. In R. Mansell & P. H. Ang (Eds.), *The International Encyclopedia of Digital Communication and Society* (pp. 1–8). John Wiley & Sons, Inc.

Griffiths, M. D., & Hunt, N. (1995). Computer Game Playing in Adolescence: Prevalence and Demographic Indicators. *Journal of Community & Applied Social Psychology*, *5*(3), 189–193. doi:10.1002/casp.2450050307

Handjam. (n.d.). *The History of Mobile Gaming*. Retrieved November 1, 2019 from http://handjam.co.uk/the-history-of-mobile-gaming/

Hsieh, H. Y. (2016). The Relationship among Consumer Value, Brand Image, Perceived Value and Purchase Intention- A Case of Tea Chain Store in Tainan City. *Proceedings of the Eighth Asia-Pacific Conference on Global Business, Economics, Finance and Banking*.

Hsu, C. L., & Lu, H. P. (2007). Consumer behavior in online game communities: A motivational factor perspective. *Computers in Human Behavior*, *23*(3), 1642–1659. doi:10.1016/j.chb.2005.09.001

Hur, W. H., & Hur, J. J. Y. (2015). Exploring the Relationship Between Green Consumption Value, Satisfaction, and Loyalty to Hybrid Car in Elderly Consumers. *Human Factors and Ergonomics in Manufacturing & Service Industries*, *25*(4), 398–408. doi:10.1002/hfm.20556

Jamrozy, U., & Lawonk, K. (2017). The multiple dimensions of consumption values in ecotourism. *International Journal of Culture, Tourism and Hospitality Research*, *11*(1), 18–34. doi:10.1108/IJCTHR-09-2015-0114

Jarenfors, O., & Sturesson, S. (2012). *Value Creation through smartphones: An ethnographic study about consumer value and social interaction through smartphones. University of Gothenburg*. School of Business, Economics and Law.

Jiang, G., Peng, L., & Liu, R. (2015). Mobile Game Adoption in China: The Role of TAM and Perceived Entertainment, Cost, Similarity and Brand Trust. *International Journal of Hybrid Information Technology*, *8*(4), 213–232. doi:10.14257/ijhit.2015.8.4.24

Karapetsas, A. V., Karapetsas, V. A., Zygouris, N. X., & Fotis, A. I. (2014). Internet Gaming Addiction. Reasons, Diagnosis, Prevention and Treatment. *ENCEPHALOS*, *51*, 10–14.

Kayabaşı, A., Mucan, B., & Tanyeri, M. (2012). Analysis on young consumer' consumer values and their attitudes toward foreign firms. *Procedia: Social and Behavioral Sciences*, *58*, 1326–1335. doi:10.1016/j.sbspro.2012.09.1116

Kaye, J. (2014). *Always On the Movie, A History of Mobile Games*. Retrieved November 1, 2019 from http://www.proelios.com/wp-content/uploads/2013/12/A-History-of-Mobile-Gaming.pdf

Kim, D. J., & Hwang, Y. (2012). A study of mobile internet user's service quality perceptions from a user's utilitarian and hedonic value tendency perspectives. *Information Systems Frontiers*, *14*(2), 409–421. doi:10.100710796-010-9267-8

Kim, H. M. (2013). Mobile Media Technology And Popular Mobile Games In Contemporary Society. *International Journal of Mobile Marketing*, *8*(2), 42–54.

Kontio, P. (2011). *Mobile Gaming Business.* Retrieved October 13, 2018, from https://pdfs.semanticscholar.org/b5e8/6e8db601a9918470ce0df345b9847872577b.pdf

Koo, D. M. (2009). The moderating role of locus of control on the links between experiential motives and intention to play online games. *Computers in Human Behavior, 25*(2), 466–474. doi:10.1016/j.chb.2008.10.010

Ku, C. H., Kwak, M., Yurov, K. M., & Yurova, Y. V. (2014). A Study of the Influence of Gaming Behavior on Academic Performance of IT College Students. *Gaming Behavior and Academic Performance. Twentieth Americas Conference on Information Systems,* Savannah, GA.

Kuss, D. J. (2013). Internet gaming addiction: Current perspectives. *Psychology Research and Behavior Management, 6,* 125–137. doi:10.2147/PRBM.S39476 PMID:24255603

Lai, M. C., Chou, F. S., Wang, C. C., & Yang, Y. J. (2015). Users' perception of mobile devices: The pragmatic and symbolic consumption values of tablet personal computers. *Asian Journal of Information and Communications, 7*(2), 1–13.

Lee, C. K. C., Levy, D. S., & Yap, C. S. F. (2015). How does the theory of consumption values contribute to place identity and sustainable consumption? *International Journal of Consumer Studies, 39*(6), 597–607. doi:10.1111/ijcs.12231

Lee, D., Trail, G. T., Kwon, H. H., & Anderson, D. F. (2011). Consumer values versus perceived product attributes: Relationships among items from the MVS, PRS, and PERVAL scales. *Sport Management Review, 14*(1), 89–101. doi:10.1016/j.smr.2010.05.001

Lemmens, J. S. (2010). *Causes and consequences of pathological gaming.* Amsterdam: Amsterdam School of Communication Research. Retrieved October 13, 2018, from https://pure.uva.nl/ws/files/1018758/84048_thesis.pdf

Lemmens, J. S., Valkenburg, P. M., & Peter, J. (2009). Development and Validation of a Game Addiction Scale for Adolescents. *Media Psychology, 12*(1), 77–95. doi:10.1080/15213260802669458

Liang, T. P., & Yeh, Y. H. (2009). Situational Effects on the Usage Intention of Mobile Games. In C. Weinhardt, S. Luckner, & J. Stößer (Eds.), *Designing E-Business Systems. Markets, Services, and Networks WEB 2008, LNBIP 22* (pp. 51–59). doi:10.1007/978-3-642-01256-3_5

Lim, W. M., Ting, D. H., Khoo, P. T., & Wong, W. Y. (2012). Understanding Consumer Values And Socialization –A Case Of Luxury Products. *Management & Marketing Challenges for the Knowledge Society, 7*(2), 209–220.

Liu, Y., & Li, H. (2011). Exploring the impact of use context on mobile hedonic services adoption: An empirical study on mobile gaming in China. *Computers in Human Behavior, 27*(2), 890–898. doi:10.1016/j.chb.2010.11.014

Mayra, F. (2015). Mobile Games. In The International Encyclopedia of Digital Communication and Society. John Wiley & Sons, Inc.

Mishra, A. (2015). Consumption Value of Digital Devices: An Investigation through Facebook Advertisement. *Social Networking, 4*(03), 51–61. doi:10.4236n.2015.43007

Nalwa, K., & Anand, A. P. (2004). Internet Addiction in Students: A Cause of Concern. *Cyberpsychology & Behavior*, *6*(6), 653–656. doi:10.1089/109493103322725441 PMID:14756932

Nathan, R. J., Fook Chiun, D. C., & Suki, N. M. (2016). An online marketing strategies assessment for companies in airlines and entertainment industries in Malaysia. Handbook of Research on Leveraging Consumer Psychology for Effective Customer Engagement, 1-15.

Newzoo. (2018). *2018 Global Games Market Report. Free verison.* Retrieved November 1, 2019 from https://cdn2.hubspot.net/hubfs/700740/Reports/Newzoo_2018_Global_Games_Market_Report_Light.pdf

Ng, B. D., & Wiemer-Hastings, P. (2005). Addiction to the Internet and Online Gaming. *Cyberpsychology & Behavior*, *8*(2), 110–113. doi:10.1089/cpb.2005.8.110 PMID:15938649

Nguyen, D. (2015). *Understanding Perceived Enjoyment and Continuance Intention in Mobile Games. Information Systems Science. Department of Information and Service Economy*. Aalto University School of Business.

Oksman, V. (2007). Young people and seniors in Finnish 'mobile information society. *Journal of Interactive Media in Education*, *02*, 1–21.

Ondang, J. P. (2015). Influence of Perceived Value And Attitude Toward Consumer Purchase Intention To Billy Coffee House Customer At Mega Smart Area Manado. *Jurnal Berkala Ilmiah Efisiensi*, *15*(05), 800–807.

Ozkan, M., & Solmaz, B. (2015). Mobile Addiction Of Generation Z And Its Effects On Their Social Lifes. (An application among university students in the 18-23 age group). *Procedia: Social and Behavioral Sciences*, *205*, 92–98. doi:10.1016/j.sbspro.2015.09.027

Park, B. W., & Lee, K. C. (2011). Exploring the value of purchasing online game items. *Computers in Human Behavior*, *27*(6), 2178–2185. doi:10.1016/j.chb.2011.06.013

Park, N., & Lee, H. (2012). Social Implications of Smartphone Use: Korean College Students' Smartphone Use and Psychological Well-Being. *Cyberpsychology, Behavior, and Social Networking*, *15*(9), 491–497. doi:10.1089/cyber.2011.0580 PMID:22817650

Schwartz, R. H. (2013). Excessive participation in on-line internet action games by two American teenagers: Case report, description of extent of overuse, and adverse consequences. *Open Journal of Pediatrics*, *3*(03), 201–203. doi:10.4236/ojped.2013.33035

Sepehr, S., & Head, M. (2013). *Online Video Game Addiction: A Review and an Information Systems Research Agenda*. Retrieved October 13, 2018, from https://pdfs.semanticscholar.org/2438/f642dc7be774a226d66eabac87256d450989.pdf

Sheth, J. N., Newman, B. I., & Gross, B. L. (1991). *Consumption Values and Market Choices-Theory and Applications*. Cincinnati, OH: South-Western Publishing Co.

Skoric, M. M., Teo, L. L. C., & Neo, R. L. (2009). Children and Video Games: Addiction, Engagement, and Scholastic Achievement. *Cyberpsychology & Behavior*, *12*(5), 567–572. doi:10.1089/cpb.2009.0079 PMID:19624263

Srisutto, S. (2010). *Country Branding, Consumption Values, and Purchase Decision Confidence: A Case Study of Tourists to Thailand* (PhD thesis). Lincoln University.

Suki, N. M. (2016). *Handbook of Research on Leveraging Consumer Psychology for Effective Customer Engagement.* https://www.igi-global.com/book/handbook-research-leveraging-consumer-psychology/149284

Suki, N. M., & Suki, N. M. (2015). Consumption values and consumer environmental concern regarding green products. *International Journal of Sustainable Development and World Ecology*, *22*(3), 269–278. doi:10.1080/13504509.2015.1013074

Sun, Y., Zhao, Y., Jia, S. Q., & Zheng, D. Y. (2015). *Understanding the Antecedents of Mobile Game Addiction: The Roles of Perceived Visibility, Perceived Enjoyment and Flow*. Retrieved October 13, 2018, from https://pdfs.semanticscholar.org/419c/b97897f014d2d932afbf8c35b0b1e45fe424.pdf

Tavormina, M. G. M., & Tavormina, R. (2017). Playıng Wıth Vıdeo Games: Goıng To A New Addıctıon? *Psychiatria Danubina*, *29*(3), 422–426. PMID:28953802

Vollmer, C., Randler, C., Horzum, M. B., & Ayas, T. (2014, January-March). Computer Game Addiction in Adolescents and Its Relationship to Chronotype and Personality. *SAGE Open*, *4*(1), 1–9. doi:10.1177/2158244013518054

Wan, C. S., & Chiou, W. B. (2006). Why Are Adolescents Addicted to Online Gaming? An Interview Study in Taiwan. *Cyberpsychology & Behavior*, *9*(6), 762–766. doi:10.1089/cpb.2006.9.762 PMID:17201603

Wang, C. W., Chan, C. I. W., Mak, K. K., Ho, S. Y., Wong, P. W. C., & Ho, R. T. H. (2014). Prevalence and Correlates of Video and Internet Gaming Addiction among Hong Kong Adolescents: A Pilot Study. *TheScientificWorldJournal*, *2014*, 1–9. doi:10.1155/2014/874648 PMID:25032242

Wang, H. Y., Liao, C., & Yang, L. H. (2013). What Affects Mobile Application Use? The Roles of Consumption Values. *International Journal of Marketing Studies*, *5*(2), 11–22. doi:10.5539/ijms.v5n2p11

Wood, R. T. A. (2008). Problems with the Concept of Video Game "Addiction": Some Case Study Examples. *International Journal of Mental Health and Addiction*, *6*(2), 169–178. doi:10.100711469-007-9118-0

Woodruff, R. B. (1997). Customer value: The next source for competitive advantage. *Journal of the Academy of Marketing Science*, *25*(2), 139–153. doi:10.1007/BF02894350

Woog, K. (2016). Proposed Gaming Addiction Behavioral Treatment Method. Addicta: The Turkish. *Journal of Addiction*, *3*(2), 271–279.

Wu, J.H., Wang, S.C., & Tsai, H.H. (2010). Falling in love with online games: The uses and gratifications perspective. *Computers in Human Behavior, 26*(6), 1862–1871.

Yıldırım, S., & Candan, B. (2015). Segmentation of Green Product Buyers Based On Their Personal Values and Consumption Values. *Environmental Values*, *24*(5), 641–661. doi:10.3197/09632711 5X14384223590212

Young, K. (1996). Psychology Of Computer Use: XL. Addictive Use Of The Internet: A Case That Breaks The Stereotype. *Psychological Reports*, *79*(3 Pt 1), 899–902. doi:10.2466/pr0.1996.79.3.899 PMID:8969098

Young, K. (2004). Internet Addiction: A New Clinical Phenomenon and Its Consequences. *The American Behavioral Scientist*, *48*(4), 402–415. doi:10.1177/0002764204270278

Young, K. (2009). Understanding Online Gaming Addiction and Teatment Issues for Adolescents. *The American Journal of Family Therapy*, *37*(5), 355–372. doi:10.1080/01926180902942191

Zorbaz, S. D., Ulas, O., & Kızıldag, S. (2015). Relation between Video Game Addiction and Interfamily Relationships on Primary School Students. *Educational Sciences: Theory and Practice*, *15*(2), 489–497.

Chapter 9
Antecedents of Global Brands Preference Among Generation Y in Malaysia

Asmat Nizam Abdul-Talib
https://orcid.org/0000-0001-6820-2918
Universiti Utara Malaysia, Malaysia

Mahjabin Yusof
MARA Professional College, Seri Iskandar, Malaysia

ABSTRACT

Consumers in Asia are known for preferring global brands as opposed to the locally manufactured ones. The emergence of global brands in the marketplace has brought many benefits as well as many obstacles, especially for local marketers. This study explored the antecedents of global brands preference among Gen-Y in Malaysia, notably country-of-origin, quality, design, and advertising. Three hundred students of higher learning institutions in Malaysia were selected to take part in the study. Multiple regression analysis was used to analyze the data. It was found that the country-of-origin, quality, and design positively influence global brands preference among Gen-Y. However, advertising was found to influence preferences negatively. The findings could help local marketers develop and execute their marketing plan better and global marketers to improve their strategies and be more competitive. Marketers should focus on the above aspects in their marketing plan to capture the markets of Gen-Y in Malaysia and thus addressing their needs and wants better.

INTRODUCTION

Globalization has changed the landscape of business and marketing, taking the world by storm. The world is fast becoming a borderless market, and globalization is introducing the concept of the whole world as one gigantic marketplace. Globalization not only helps businesses in offering their products to a larger and more profitable market, but it also helps integrate people across cultures and close geographical gaps

DOI: 10.4018/978-1-7998-3042-9.ch009

within countries (Govil & Rashmi, 2013), making the world even smaller than before. With the help of globalization, global brands began making their appearances (Winit et al., 2014).

Brands are considered as the lifeblood of companies because they help generate market share, increase customer loyalty, amplify channel power, offer the potential for higher profit margins, and guard against aggressive attacks (Kim, 2019; Armstrong & Kotler, 2013; Steenkamp, 2014). A brand is considered the image used to identify a specific product and what anchors the product to a customer's minds. Consumers in Asia Pacific, including Malaysia, are showing preference for global brands. Even if local brands are increasingly becoming premium, most consumers are influenced by the perception that global brands possess more quality than local ones (McCaskill, 2016). A research done by Nielsen for the annual Nielsen Global Brand-Origin Report in 2017 showed that Malaysian consumers are showing preference for global manufacturers' brands across the majority of the 34 categories. Several categories that highlight consumer preference of global brands are baby wipes and/or diapers (90%), baby food and/or formula (87%), pet foods (14%), feminine care products (15%), vitamins and/or supplements (16%), and skincare products (18%) (Hew, 2017). One the main reasons many firms are in favor of marketing global brands and projecting the image of global brands as compared to local brands because of the preferences of many consumers (Zakaria, Wan-ismail, Abdul-Talib, 2015; Steenkamp, Batra, & Alden, 2003).

Global brands have been in the local market for a long time that they have managed to capture the hearts of Malaysians and somehow anchor their image and value in Malaysian customers' minds. Consumers prefer global brands because they are perceived to deliver high quality, expertise, authority, and credibility (Batra et al., 2000). Moreover, global brands enjoy high prestige and status in the minds of most consumers (Zhao, Zhao & Deng, 2018; Batra et al., 2000; Steenkamp et al., 2002). Thus, it has become quite a challenge and problem for Malaysian businesses to compete with global brands since Malaysian customers have long trusted the global brands and prefer them to the local brands.

Researches have suggested that, in general, Malaysians spend their time and money shopping for products, and that their preference would be the global brands. This means that the local brands seem to fall into disfavor (Mandler, 2019; Anuar & Shah, 2014; Boon, Teo, Sidin, Izzudin, & Nor, 2013; Gin, Chin, & Suan, 2012; Sze et al., 2000). Consumers have shown preferences to global brands even when the quality and value offered are not necessarily superior to their local counterparts (Bedi, 2009; Schuiling & Kapferer, 2004; Shocker, Srivastava, & Ruekert, 1994). From the brand perspective, Generation Y considers well-known and famous brands as a measure of their social standing and status. Therefore, they are willing to spend lavishly on a favored brand (O'Cass & Choy, 2008). Sankar (2006) asserted that Generation Y consumers, specifically, show preference to the brands that are marketed by developed countries, especially the western countries because the brands are perceived to be of superior quality and have better attributes, not to mention contributing to a better social status in the society. As a result, Malaysian marketers to have a major disadvantage in competing against international brands to attract Generation Y.

More research that delve into aspect of consumer behavior and psychology in the digital economy is deemed necessary (Ling Chang, Ling Tam, & Suki, 2016; Nathan, Fook Chiun, & Suki, 2016; Suki, 2016). Accordingly, the principal goal of this research was to examine whether country-of-origin, design, quality, and advertising are factors Generation Y in Malaysia consider when purchasing global brands. Design is positively influential to consumers when purchasing global brands (Foroudi, 2018; Anuar & Shah, 2014; Landwehr, Wentzel, & Herrmann, 2012; Motameni & Shahrokhi, 1998; Steenkamp, 2014). Quality or value is also considered one of the main motives of consumers when they make a purchasing decision because the perceived value is associated with prestige perception (Özsomer, 2012). Country-of-origin also plays an imperative role for consumers when choosing global brands (Sze et al., 2012). One of the most important marketing mix strategies to persuade consumers to purchase a brand is advertising (Armstrong & Kotler, 2013). Most global brands are supported by advertisements to promote and communicate the superior quality of the brands (Tafsir, Shaari, Muchtar and Firmansya, 2018 Batra et al., 2000; Steenkamp et al., 2002).

The present research contributes to the existing literature on consumer behavior and purchasing decision-making, especially among Generation Y. Furthermore, the value of a brand is measured by the standard of the country it was produced, and if the brand is from any developed western countries, then it will be perceived as having good quality or value. Marketers need to know whether or not country-of-origin, design, quality, and advertising are important determinants for consumers when purchasing a brand because they can strategize properly to meet consumer expectations and needs.

The subsequent section will review the relevant literature for the development of a theoretical framework and testing of the hypotheses. Next, the method of the study, including sampling selection and data collection procedure, and analysis will be discussed. Then, the result will be discussed. Next, the theoretical and practical implications of this study will be highlighted, followed by the limitations and suggestions for future research. Subsequently, the conclusion of this research will be presented.

LITERATURE REVIEW

A brand is more than simply a name; it is an identity. It is an embodiment of what a product could offer. A company's identity is communicated to the external world through branding. Branding usually functions as the central manifestation of a company's identity. Moreover, branding involves the key identity attributes of the company in a "condensed" form. Hence, brands act as an ambassador for a company, and they provide key information about how consumers will judge the company and evaluate the products it produces (Ning, 2019; Karjalainen, 2003).

Global Brands

Steenkamp et al. (2003); Özsomer (2012); Tafsir, Shaari, Muchtar and Firmansya (2018) found that customers perceive and believe that global brands connote better quality, status, and prestige. According to Özsomer, if consumers believe that if the brands are selling in other world markets, then the company must be committed to the brand and will not risk its brand names by producing low-quality products. Szze et al. (2000) also revealed that consumers seeking high-status in society tended to favor global brands because of the linkage with high prestige and status.

In their research, Steenkamp (2014) observed that consumers preferred global brands because of their associations with higher prestige, and some of these brands can draw upon the myths associated with a foreign cultural origin. Being global and foreign is considered mysterious and enchanting than local brands (Abd-Razak & Abdul Talib, 2009). Besides, global brands benefit from economies of scope in marketing – pooling the best ideas of marketing campaigns and media spillover, especially those related to world travel.

Generation Y of Malaysian Muslim Consumers

Generation Y is known as the generation born entirely in the 20th-century era (Reed, 2007). They are also called the Echo Boomers, the Net Generation (Tyler, 2008), and the Millennium Generation born between 1982 and 2003 (Durkin, 2008; Howe & Strauss, 2000; Nikodemska-Wołowik, Bednarz, & Foreman). The Millennials are invulnerable to brand loyalty unlike the former generations, and they will shift their loyalty instantly to marketers who can provide new and stylish brands ahead of time. Since Generation Y has been exposed to various brands, local or global (Evelyn, Eva, & Robin, 2011), they have a wide selection of brands to choose from, and, hence, less loyal (Lazarevic, 2012).

The Malaysian National 2013 Census documented 13 million individuals in Malaysia aged between 10 and 34 years old, which constitute 44 of 32 million people in Malaysia (Department of Statistics Malaysia, 2014). On spending, Generation Y in Malaysia spent almost 60% of their monthly income on daily necessities, 64.6% on transportation, 55.2% on entertainment and leisure, and 44.2% car loan installment (Ganesan, 2012). All generations were found to be influenced by various factors, such as their lifestyles, values, and life experiences when purchasing a brand (Williams & Page, 2011). However, Generation Y tended to favor brands with good quality and price (Tjandra et al., 2015). They are also known to be innovators or early adopters of new brands (Ladhari, Gonthier, & Lajante, 2019; Lingelbach et al., 2012). As a result, they are a lucrative market segment for numerous global firms because of their preferences to global brands (Lu and Xu, 2015).

Islam is the official religion in Malaysia. Muslim consumers in Malaysia make up almost 50% of the 32 million Malaysian people. Because they are a lucrative market for halal products, marketers should not disregard the Muslim consumer market because it is a growing market. Even multinational corporations are beginning to notice the expanding size of Muslim consumers (Ali, 2016). The growing Muslim population indicates increasing purchasing power. Muslim consumers tend to evaluate the attributes of various brands to determine the quality, safety and health values before purchasing them. Thus, manufacturers must continuously improve the add-on value of the brands (Mohezar, 2016). Furthermore, marketers need to be market-oriented to understand the needs and wants of Muslim consumers better and know the Islamic principles, practices, and values to compete better (Zakaria & Abdul Talib, 2010).

Country-of-Origin

Country-of-origin shapes consumers' positive or negative assumptions of a brand marketed in the global marketplace (Cateora, Gilly, & Graham, 2010). Consumers may acknowledge or disregard a particular product based on the country from which the brands are manufactured. Yassin et al. (2007) revealed that the country-of-origin influenced brand equity via brand distinctiveness, brand loyalty, and brand awareness. The information on country-of-origin plays a deciding factor in a purchase decision (Khan, Ashraf, & Malik, 2019). Consumer perceptions of the quality of the product change within product groups. However, if a particular product category has a positive country-of-origin image, consumers will prefer the products from that particular country (Ahmed, Johnson, Ling, Fang, & Hui, 2002). In short, country-of-origin influences consumers' preferences toward a brand (Kinra, 2006). We hypothesized the following:

H1. There is a positive relationship between country-of-origin and preference of Generation Y in Malaysia toward global brands

Quality

Product quality affects consumer preference in purchasing a product. Consumers judge and evaluate brands based on the superiority or excellent attributes of a product (Tafsir, Shaari, Muchtar and Firmansya 2018; Abdul-Talib & Abd-Latif, 2015; Aaker, 1997), both external and internal (Holbrook, 1999; Molina-Castillo & Munuera-Aleman, 2009; Sanchez-Fernandez & Iniesta-Bonillo, 2007), as well as the appearance and performance of the brands (Swinker & Hines, 2006). For many consumers, although global brands may also communicate a higher prestige and status, quality seems to be the determining factor when purchasing a product (Steenkamp et al., 2003). This is because the quality is linked with product reliability and thus offers greater customer satisfaction (Kiong, Gharleghi, Yin-Fah, & & Lim, 2014). Sze et al. (2000) observed that global brands are often equated with good quality; consumers tend to prefer global brands to local ones.

High-quality products have a big impact on consumer preference and loyalty (Ning, 2019; Zakaria & Abdul Talib 2011; Hsu, 2011). Hasan, Javad, and Ali (2013); Ladhari, Gonthier, & Lajante (2019) emphasized that quality is one of the important determinants of consumer preference, which leads to consumers purchasing the brands offered in the global marketplace. This leads to the second hypothesis:

H2. There is a positive relationship between quality and preference of Generation Y in Malaysia toward global brands

Design

Previous research demonstrated that consumers felt more emotionally inclined toward particular brands that are more superior in terms of aesthetical charm and visual delight (Hsu, Chen, Yang, Lin, & Liu, 2018; Patwardhan & Balasubramanian, 2011). Aesthetic appeal and design are becoming one of the critical elements in a firm's marketing strategy as they create a positive impact on consumers' brand evaluation. The importance of design as a vital element of a brand, including the elements of colours (Garber, Burke, & Jones, 2000), shapes (Folkes & Matta, 2004; Wansink & van Ittersum, 2003) as well as pictures (Underwood, 2003), has triggered many researchers into studying its impact on consumer behavior. A symbiotic association between several types of visual design and consumer brand's evaluation was found (Foroudi, 2018; Orth & Malkewitz, 2008). Consumers' responses toward a brand vary from the perception of design (Hekkert, 2006; Zamani, Abdul-Talib and Ashari, 2016), as well as the whole package of a particular brand (Chrysochou, & Festila, 2019; Orth & Malkewitz, 2008).

The design and aesthetics aspect of a brand is the main competitive advantage, and thus play a major role in shaping consumers' preference in purchasing a brand (Hsu, Chen, Yang, Lin, & Liu, 2018; Zolli, 2004) . It was revealed that the purchase intention towards a foreign brand was shaped and influenced by the brand design (Anuar & Shah, 2014). Thus, we hypothesized the following hypothesis:

H3. There is a positive relationship between design and the preference of Generation Y in Malaysia toward global brands

Advertising

A number of elements affect consumers when they make their purchase, and one of them is advertisement (Raza, Abu Bakar, & Mohamad, 2019). It was found that Vietnamese people accepted advertising because of the collectivistic culture (Khanh & Hau, 2007). Through advertising, consumers could be informed and persuaded to purchase the brands advertised globally (Raza, Abu Bakar, & Mohamad, 2019; Abdul-Talib & Mohd Adnan, 2017; Kent & Allen, 1994). Advertised brands will be remembered and favored by consumers regardless of the messages and strategies of the advertisements (Mandler, 2019; Shapiro, 1999). Advertising is known for building awareness and securing consumers' memory and attention (Chu & Keh, 2006; Keller, Tellis, & Ambler, 2007). Because of advertising, consumers could be influenced to believe that global brands offer more benefits than the local brands (Adapa, 2008). In short, advertising affects the purchase decision-making process of consumers (Armstrong & Kotler, 2013; Belch & Belch, 2003; Khan, Ashraf, & Malik, 2019). This leads to the fourth hypothesis:

H4. There is a positive relationship between advertising and the preference of Generation Y in Malaysia toward global brands

The conceptualization of the research hypotheses is shown in Figure 1.

Figure 1. Research model

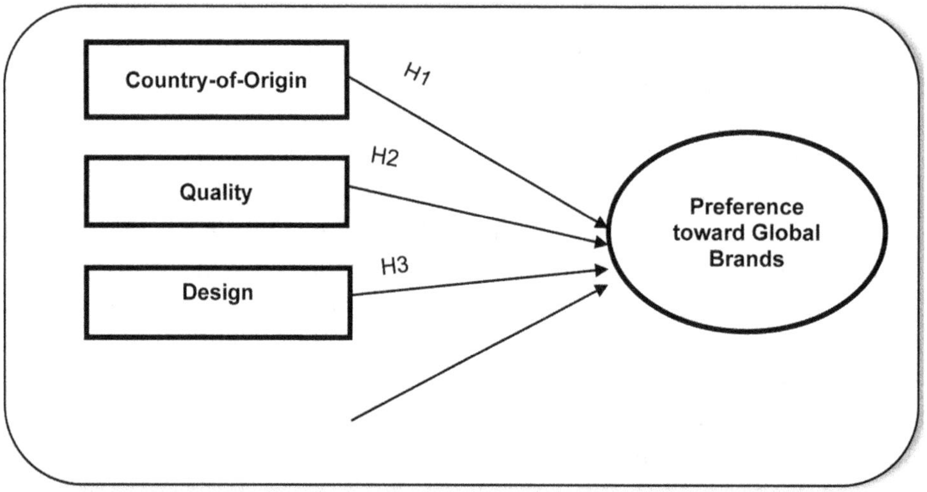

METHODOLOGY

Participants and Procedures

Generation Y consumers are those between 14 and 31 years old, and are often referred to as the "youth market" (Kueh & Voon, 2007; Abu Bakar & Abdul-Talib, 2013; Nikodemska-Wołowik, Bednarz, & Foreman, 2019). While adult consumers have been explored in depth, much less attention has been given to young emergent consumers on their spending behaviour Shukla, 2008). Generation Y was the focal point of this research largely because they possess higher purchasing power for daily expenditure (Nikodemska-Wołowik, Bednarz, & Foreman, 2019; Nowak, Thach, & Olsen, 2006). Also, Generation Y in Malaysia makes up the largest consumer pool, making them the largest purchasers of goods and services in the market; hence, the perfect target as participants of research on consumer behavior (Abdul-Talib, Abdul-Latif & Abd-Razak, 2016; Wong 2015).

In order to teste these hypotheses, data was collected using a convenience sample technique from 300 students in three higher education institutions in Malaysia and the questionnaires were distributed equally among these institutions. Despite its limitations, various researchers have used the convenience sampling method in consumer research on the assumption that everyone is a consumer of different products every day (Ha, John, Janda, & Muthaly, 2011; Pappu, Quester, & Cooksey, 2005; Thakor & Lavack, 2003).

Instruments

We adopted measures used in previous research, and all items used in this study are listed in Table 1. A questionnaire was used to collect the data, and it consisted of six sections: a demographic section and five sections that asked questions related to the dependent and independent variables of brand preference, country-of-origin, quality, design, and advertising. The questions on the key variables were measured on a five-point Likert scale.

Table 1. Measurement Sources

Variables	Authors
Preference for global brands	Shu et al. (2013)
Country-of-origin	Lascu and Babb (1995)
Quality	Pappu et al. (2005)
Design	Esmaeilpour (2015)
Advertising	Liu (2002)

RESULTS

Table 2 shows a list of fifteen brand preferences of Gen-Y consumers in Malaysia. The list include For individual brands, the most preferred brand was the sports brand Adidas (13.4%) while only 9% preferred the technology powerhouse's brand Apple. Another sports giant, Nike, was preferred by 7.4% of the participants, followed by the Japanese automotive company, Honda, Swedish food giant, Nestle, and Korean electronics company, Samsung (6.4%, 6.3%, and 6.1%, respectively). The Swedish clothing retailer H&M was preferred by 5.8% while the Japanese electronics company, Sony, was preferred by 4.2%. Overall, global brands were preferred by the majority of the participants (87.7%). Meanwhile, only 12.3% preferred local brands.

Next, we ran a factor analysis to reduce a large amount of data or items into similar groupings so that they could be understood further. The principal components used were univariate initial with maximum likelihood of promax rotation cross-loaded at 0.30 level of confidence. Any items that scored below

Table 2. Favorite Brands of Generation Y in Malaysia

Brands	Frequency	Percentage
Adidas	121	13.4
Local brands	111	12.3
Apple	81	9.0
Nike	67	7.4
Honda	58	6.4
Nestle	57	6.3
Samsung	55	6.1
H&M	52	5.8
Sony	38	4.2
Other global brands	260	28.9
Total	900	100.0

0.30 were eliminated because they were considered unacceptable (Hair et al., 2014). Thus, the original 45 items were reduced to 26 items to form five factors based on the strength of the relationship between the variables. The pattern matrix in Table 3 shows the number of loading strongly related to each other in the form of five factors. All item loadings significantly relied on one component, except one item that was loaded on two factors, which were subsequently removed. The factor loading supported the research model composed of five variables (global brands preference, country-of-origin, quality, design, and advertising). All five factors were deemed reliable (see Table 3) with the score of 0.774 (global brand preference), 0.788 (country-of-origin), 0.819 (quality), 0.791 (design), and 0.932 (advertising). Nineteen items that did not load adequately into the five loading factors were eliminated from the final scale. The final item loadings are presented in Table 3 where all five factors were found to be reliable and possessed a strong relationship with the items under the same factor.

A reliability analysis is conducted to test the measures of the scale items to check that the items are free from random errors, hence, generating consistent results that are reliable enough to be included as part of the research (Zikmund, 2012). Based on the reliability analysis, all the variables scored 0.7 and above, suggesting that the measures were reliable.

Pearson correlation was utilized next to measure of the strength of two variables (Hair et al., 2014). Based on the r coefficient, only three independent variables were significantly associated with global brands preference. They were country-of-origin ($r = 0.422$), quality ($r = 0.5660$, and design ($r = 0.595$ (see Table 5). Of the three r values, design had the highest value, which indicates that design has the highest correlation with Generation Y's preference of global brands, followed by quality and country-of-origin. Advertising has a negative link with global brands preference, but the relationship was not significant.

We then ran a regression analysis to examine the effect of the independent variables on a dependent variable (Abdul-Latif & Abdul-Talib, 2017; Zikmund, 2012). The relationship between the dependent and independent variables was analyzed at the 95% confidence interval.

Table 6 indicates that the t-value for Country-of-Origin was 2.363, higher than the minimum value of 2 at a p-value of 0.019, which was less than 0.05. These two indicators suggest a significant positive relationship between Country-of-Origin and global brands preference. Thus, H1 was accepted. The t-value

Table 3. The Pattern Matrix

Variable	Factor 1	Factor 2	Factor 3	Factor 4	Factor 5
Preference1	.858				
Preference2	.747				
Preference3	.738				
Preference4	.618				
Country-of-origin1		.776			
Country-of-origin2		.767			
Country-of-origin3		.691			
Country-of-origin4		.522			
Country-of-origin5		.433			
Country-of-origin6		.461			
Quality1			.942		
Quality2			.588		
Quality3			.576		
Quality4			.449		
Quality5			.446		
Design1				.808	
Design2				.788	
Design3				.462	
Design4				.457	
Design5				.415	
Advertising1					.947
Advertising2					.883
Advertising3					.858
Advertising4					.837
Advertising5					.754
Advertising6					.751
KMO = 0.919; Bartlett's Test =1452.037; 5-Factors extracted; n = 300					

Table 4. Overall Cronbach's Alpha for Variables

Variables	Number of Items	Cronbach's Alpha (n=300)
Preference for global brands	4	**0.774**
COO	6	**0.788**
Quality	5	**0.819**
Design	5	**0.791**
Advertising	6	**0.932**

Table 5. Correlation Matrix

Variables	GBP	COO	Q	A	D
Preference for global brands	1.00				
COO	.422**	1.00			
Quality	.566**	.497**	1.00		
Advertising	-.032	.077	.070	1.00	
Design	.595**	.463**	.663**	.043	1.00
****. Significant at 0.01 level**					

Figure 2. The Correlation Model

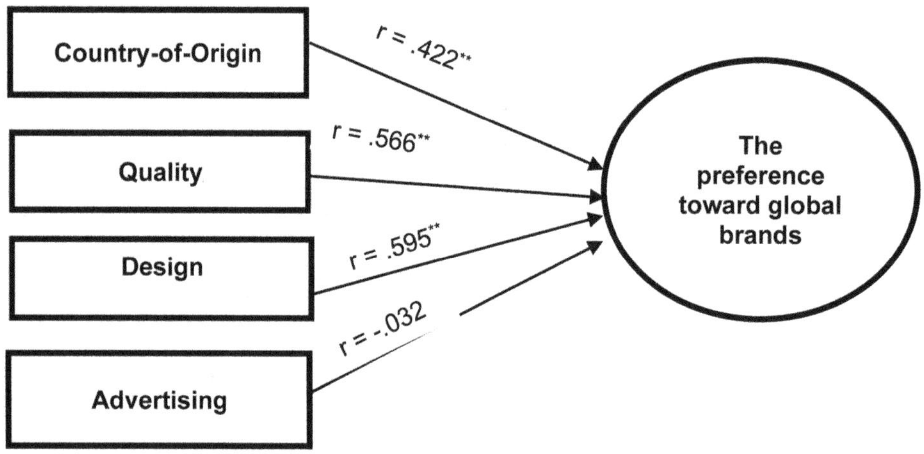

for Quality was 4.269 for Quality, higher than the minimum value of 2 at a p-value of 0.00. These two indicators suggest a significant positive relationship between Quality and global brands preference. Thus, H2 was accepted. The t-value for Design was 5.976, higher than the minimum value of 2 at a p-value of 0.00. Based on this analysis, Design was the most significant factor of all the factors in this study. Hence,

Table 6. Summary of the Regression Analysis

Model	Unstandardized Coefficient		Standardized Coefficient	t	sig
	B	Std. Error	Beta		
Constant	.467	.238		1.965	.050
COO	.143	.061	.123	2.363	.019*
Quality	.292	.069	.264	4.269	.000*
Design	.420	.070	.362	5.976	.000*
Advertising	.424	.225	-.076	-1.710	.088

*Significant at 0.05

H3 was accepted. Finally, the t-value for Advertising was -1.710, lower than the minimum value of 2 at a p-value of 0.088, which was higher than 0.05. These two indicators suggest an insignificant negative relationship between Advertising and global brands preference. Hence, H4 was rejected.

DISCUSSION

The present study found that the majority of the sampled Generation Y in Malaysia preferred global brands, such as Nike, Adidas, Apple, and others. Therefore, it can be concluded that Generation Y in Malaysia prefers global brands to local brands. The finding is consistent with past studies that reported a similar observation (Sze et al., 2012; Teo et al., 2013; Kiong et al., 2013; Tan & Chin, 2012; Mohammad Shah & Ibrahim, 2014).

The study also observed that country-of-origin, quality, and design played a significant role in influencing Generation Y to prefer global brands. Only advertising did not any significant influence on global brands preference. Despite various literatures' affirmation of advertising as an important factor in purchase decision, the empirical evidence repudiate this hypothesis. This is consistent with the findings of Versraten (2015), where advertising credibility does not positively affect consumers' attitude towards brands. As advertising (H4) shows to be insignificant, only three research hypotheses were supported (i.e., H1, H2, and H3). Despite various literatures' affirmation of advertising as an important factor in purchase decision, the empirical evidence repudiate this hypothesis. This is consistent with the findings of (Verstraten, 2015), where advertising credibility do not positively affecting consumers' attitude towards brands. As advertising (H4) proven to be insignificant, only three research hypotheses were supported (i.e., H1, H2, and H3). This finding contributes to the literature by filling the gap identified earlier, specifically by considering advertising as another potential determinant of global brands preference. However, no empirical support was found for the influence of advertising.

The finding has practical implications. Firstly, local marketers understand their target market with better clarity. They can learn from global marketers about why their products are being sought after, especially Generation Y. Particularly, they need to improve the design of their products, as it was found to be the most significant factor in influencing brand preference. Consumers prefer brands that have aesthetical and practical functions. Even though many creative design and packaging techniques have been developed, unfortunately, many local marketers, especially small/medium entrepreneurs, tend to neglect this aspect of a brand. If the products are of good quality, but the design is perceived to be unattractive, then they are not likely to be the preferred choice by consumers.

In addition to the design, local marketers must also ensure that the quality of the local brands to be on par with global brands or even exceeds them. If the quality is perceived to be similar, consumers may prefer the global brands to the local brands for the fact that the global brands are produced outside the country. In this regard, the country-of-origin matters to the consumers. Sometimes, the 'Made in Malaysia' label is not sought after by Generation Y in Malaysia as they prefer the brands to be manufactured by other countries, preferably the developed ones. So, the quality aspects need to be considered and strengthened when developing new brands in the future. This study also can be utilized by global marketers on how to innovate and offer consumers better brands and choices.

LIMITATIONS AND FUTURE RESEARCH

The findings should be interpreted by considering the limitations of this study. Firstly, the study did not specify any product category when examining global brands preference. By doing so, we could generalize the findings to various product categories, which could be beneficial for marketers. Secondly, Generation Y has been observed to have a lavish spending habit (Aquino, 2012). This research could help local and global marketers to understand the preference of Generation Y and serve them better. Because the focus of this study was Generation Y, the finding could not be generalizable to other consumers in other age groups. Thirdly, even though the sample size of 300 was deemed acceptable, a bigger sample size of up to 1000 participants could help reduce the sampling error size and increase the accuracy of the research (Zikmund et al., 2011). To compensate for this limitation, future researchers may use an interview to get in-depth data on the motives and other factors that influence consumers to prefer global brands to local brands. Future researchers may wish to focus on the tween market because they could influence their parents in purchase decisions. They are also a lucrative untapped market that marketers could capitalize on.

REFERENCES

Aaker, J. L. (1997). Dimensions of Brand Personality. *JMR, Journal of Marketing Research, 34*(3), 347–356. doi:10.1177/002224379703400304

Abd-Razak, I. S., & Abdul-Talib, A. N. (2009). *Explorative study of proactive and responsive export market orientation: an in-depth interview.* In Australian and New Zealand Marketing Academy (ANZMAC) Conference, Melbourne, Australia. Available at: www. duplication. net. au/ANZMAC09/papers/ANZMAC2009-288.pdf

Abdul-Latif, S. A., & Abdul-Talib, A. N. (2017). Consumer racism: A scale modification. *Asia Pacific Journal of Marketing and Logistics, 29*(3), 616–633. doi:10.1108/APJML-02-2016-0026

Abdul-Talib, A. N., Abd-Latif, S. A., & Abd-Razak, I. S. (2016). A study on the boycott motivations of Malaysian non-Muslims. *Journal of Islamic Marketing, 7*(3), 264–287. doi:10.1108/JIMA-11-2014-0071

Abdul-Talib, A. N., & Abdul-Latif, S. A. (2015). Antecedents to willingness to Boycotts among Malaysian muslims. In *Emerging Research on Islamic Marketing and Tourism in the Global Economy* (pp. 70–106). IGI Global. doi:10.4018/978-1-4666-6272-8.ch004

Abdul-Talib, A. N., & Mohd Adnan, M. M. (2017). Determinants of consumer's willingness to boycott surrogate products. *Journal of Islamic Marketing, 8*(3), 345–360. doi:10.1108/JIMA-08-2015-0065

Abu Bakar, A. R., & Abdul-Talib, A. N. (2013). A case study of an internationalization process of a private higher education institution in Malaysia. *Gadjah Mada International Journal of Business, 15*(3).

Adapa, S. (2008). Adoption of internet shopping: Cultural considerations in India and Australia. *Journal of Internet Banking and Commerce, 13*(2), 1–17. doi:10.1007/978-3-531-92534-9_12

Ahmed, Z. U., Johnson, J. P., Ling, C. P., Fang, T. W., & Hui, A. K. (2002). Country-of-origin and brand effects on consumers' evaluations of cruise lines. *International Marketing Review* (Vol. 19). doi:10.1108/02651330210430703

Anuar, K., & Shah, M. (2014). *Determinants of International Brand Recognition among Malaysian Consumers*. Academic Press.

Armstrong, G., & Kotler, P. (2013). Marketing; An Introduction. *Marketing Teacher, 170*. doi:10.1016/0166-4972(92)90011-6

Batra, R., Ramaswamy, V., Alden, D., Steenkamp, J., & Ramachander, S. (2000). Effects of Brand Local and Nonlocal Origin on Consumer Attitudes in Developing Countries. *Journal of Consumer Psychology, 9*(2), 83–95. doi:10.1207/S15327663JCP0902_3

Belch, G. A., & Belch, M. A. (2003). Organizing for Advertising and Promotion. In Advertising and Promotion, Sixth Edition (p. 819). Academic Press.

Boon, C., Teo, C., Sidin, S., Izzudin, M., & Nor, M. (2013). *Social Sciences & Humanities Exploring Influences of Consumer Socialization Agents on Branded Apparel Purchase among Urban Malaysian Tweens*. Academic Press.

Bryman, A., & Cramer, D. (2001). Quantitative Data Analysis with SPSS Release 10 for Windows. *Analysis* (Vol. 1). doi:10.4324/9780203471548

Chang, L. D. M., Ling Tam, A. Y., & Suki, N. M. (2016). Moderating effect of races towards consumers' feeling of TCM usage. Handbook of Research on Leveraging Consumer Psychology for Effective Customer Engagement, 306-323.

Chrysochou, P., & Festila, A. (2019). A content analysis of organic product package designs. *Journal of Consumer Marketing, 36*(4), 441–448. doi:10.1108/JCM-06-2018-2720

Chu, S., & Keh, H. T. (2006). Brand value creation: Analysis of the Interbrand-Business Week brand value rankings. *Marketing Letters, 17*(4), 323–331. doi:10.100711002-006-9407-6

DeVellis, R. F. (2003). Applied Social Research Methods Series: Vol. 26. Scale Development: Theory and Applications. Academic Press.

Folkes, V., & Matta, S. (2004). The Effect of Package Shape on Consumers' Judgments of Product Volume: Attention as a Mental Contaminant. *The Journal of Consumer Research, 31*(2), 390–401. doi:10.1086/422117

Foroudi, P. (2018). Influence of brand signature, brand awareness, brand attitude, brand reputation on hotel industry's brand performance. *International Journal of Hospitality Management, 76*(A), 271-285.

Ganesan, A. (2012). *Consumption, Spending and Investment Behaviour of Malaysia Generation Y*. Faculty of Accountancy and Management, Universiti Tunku Abdul Rahman.

Gin, T. S., Chin, S., & Suan, T. (2012). Consumer Purchase Preferences Towards Foreign and Domestic Branded Electrical Appliances. *International Journal of Undergraduate Studies, 1*(1), 15–20.

Ha, H., John, J., Janda, S., & Muthaly, S. (2011). The effects of advertising spending on brand loyalty in services. *European Journal of Marketing*, *45*(4), 673–691. doi:10.1108/03090561111111389

Hair, J., Celsi, M., Money, A., Samouel, P., & Page, M. (2014). *Essentials of business research methods*. Academic Press.

Hasan, S., Javad, M., & Ali, M. (2013). Iranian Consumers ' Purchase Intention Toward Global Brands. *Interdisciplinary Journal of Contemporary Research in Business*, *5*(8), 361–372.

Hekkert, P. (2006). Design aesthetics : principles of pleasure in design Design aesthetics : principles of pleasure in design. *Psychological Science*, *48*(2), 157–172. doi:10.1016/j.chb.2014.06.004

HewV. (2017, November 23). Retrieved from http://www.marketing-interactive.com: https://www.marketing-interactive.com/global-or-local-what-do-malaysian-consumers-prefer/

Holbrook, M. (1999). Probing Explorations, Deep Displays, Virtual Reality, And Profound Insights: The Four Faces Of Stereographic Three-Dimensional Images In Marketing And Consumer Research. *Advances in Consumer Research*. Retrieved from https://www.acrwebsite.org/volumes/display.asp?id=8251

Hsu, C.-L., Chen, Y.-C., Yang, T.-N., Lin, W.-K., & Liu, Y.-H. (2018). Does product design matter? Exploring its influences in consumers' psychological responses and brand loyalty. *Information Technology & People*, *31*(3), 886–907. doi:10.1108/ITP-07-2017-0206

Hsu, K.-T. (2011). The Advertising Effects of Corporate Social Responsibility on Corporate Reputation and Brand Equity: Evidence from the Life Insurance Industry in Taiwan. *Journal of Business Ethics*, *109*(2), 189–201. doi:10.100710551-011-1118-0

Karjalainen, T. (2003). Strategic brand identity and symbolic design cues. *6th Asian Design Conference*. Retrieved from http://www.idemployee.id.tue.nl/g.w.m.rauterberg/conferences/cd_donotopen/ADC/final_paper/197.pdf

Kent, R. J., & Allen, C. T. (1994). Competitive Interference Effects in Consumer Memory for Advertising : The Role of Brand Familiarity. *Journal of Marketing*, *58*(July), 97–105. doi:10.1177/002224299405800307

Khan, M. A., Ashraf, R., & Malik, A. (2019). Do identity-based perceptions lead to brand avoidance? A cross-national investigation. *Asia Pacific Journal of Marketing and Logistics*, *31*(4), 1095–1117. doi:10.1108/APJML-12-2017-0332

Khanh, N. T. T., & Hau, L. N. (2007). Preferred Appeals as a Reflection of Culture: Mobile Phones Advertising in Vietnam. *Asia Pacific Business Review*, *13*(1), 21–39. doi:10.1080/13602380600652987

Kim, J. (2019). Imperative challenge for luxury brands. *International Journal of Retail & Distribution Management*, *47*(2), 220–244. doi:10.1108/IJRDM-06-2017-0128

Kinra, N. (2006). The effect of country-of-origin on foreign brand names in the Indian market. *Marketing Intelligence & Planning*, *24*(1), 15–30. doi:10.1108/02634500610641534

Ladhari, R., Gonthier, J., & Lajante, M. (2019). Generation Y and online fashion shopping: Orientations and profiles. *Journal of Retailing and Consumer Services*, *48*, 113–121. doi:10.1016/j.jretconser.2019.02.003

Lazarevic, V. (2012). Encouraging brand loyalty in fickle generation Y consumers. Young Consumers. *Insight and Ideas for Responsible Marketers, 13*(1), 45–61. doi:10.1108/17473611211203939

Malhotra, N. K., Birks, D. F., & Wills, P. (2012). *Marketing Research : An Applied Approach.* Marketing Research.

Mandler, T. (2019). Beyond reach: An extended model of global brand effects. *International Marketing Review, 36*(5), 647–674. doi:10.1108/IMR-01-2018-0032

McCaskill, A. (2016, April 26). *Nearly 75% of Global Consumers List Brand Origin as Key Purchase Driver.* Academic Press.

Mohezar, S. S. (2016). *Halal Cosmetics Adoption Among Young Muslim Consumers in Malaysia: Religiosity Concern. Global Journal Al-Thaqafah.*

Molina-Castillo, F. J., & Munuera-Aleman, J. L. (2009). The joint impact of quality and innovativeness on short-term new product performance. *Industrial Marketing Management, 38*(8), 984–993. doi:10.1016/j.indmarman.2008.06.001

Nathan, R. J., Fook Chiun, D. C., & Suki, N. M. (2016). An online marketing strategies assessment for companies in airlines and entertainment industries in Malaysia. Handbook of Research on Leveraging Consumer Psychology for Effective Customer Engagement, 1-15.

Nikodemska-Wołowik, A. M., Bednarz, J., & Foreman, J. R. (2019). Trends in young consumers' behaviour - implications for family enterprises. *Economia e Sociologia, 12*(3), 11–24. doi:10.14254/2071-789X.2019/12-3/1

Ning, L. (2019). Research on the Influence of Negative Information of Brand Spokesmen on Brand Attitude. *European Journal of Business and Management, 11*(21), 143–147.

Nowak, L., Thach, L., & Olsen, J. E. (2006). Wowing the millennials: Creating brand equity in the wine industry. *Journal of Product and Brand Management, 15*(5), 316–323. doi:10.1108/10610420610685712

O'Cass, A., & Choy, E. (2008). Studying Chinese generation Y consumers' involvement in fashion clothing and perceived brand status. *Journal of Product and Brand Management, 17*(5), 341–352. doi:10.1108/10610420810896095

Özsomer, A. (2012). The Interplay Between Global and Local Brands: A Closer Look at Perceived Brand Globalness and Local Iconness. *Journal of International Marketing, 20*(2), 72–95. doi:10.1509/jim.11.0105

Pallant, J. (2013). *SPSS survival manual: a step by step guide to data analysis using SPSS.* Academic Press.

Pappu, R., Quester, P. G., & Cooksey, R. W. (2005). Consumer-based brand equity: Improving the measurement – empirical evidence. *Journal of Product and Brand Management, 14*(3), 143–154. doi:10.1108/10610420510601012

Patwardhan, H., & Balasubramanian, S. K. (2011). Brand romance: A complementary approach to explain emotional attachment toward brands. *Journal of Product and Brand Management, 20*(4), 297–308. doi:10.1108/10610421111148315

Raza, S. H., Abu Bakar, H., & Mohamad, B. (2019). *The effects of advertising appeals on consumers' behavioural intention towards global brands. Journal of Islamic Marketing*. doi:10.1108/jima-11-2017-0134

Reed, C. (2007). Generation Y Research: What Makes 'Y' Tick. *Brand Strategy, 38.*

Sanchez-Fernandez, R., & Iniesta-Bonillo, M. (2007). The concept of perceived value: A systematic review of the research. *Marketing Theory*, *7*(4), 427–451. doi:10.1177/1470593107083165

Shapiro, S. (1999). When an Ad's Influence Is Beyond Our Conscious Control: Perceptual and Conceptual Fluency Effects Caused By Incidental Ad Exposure. *The Journal of Consumer Research*, *26*(1), 16–36. doi:10.1086/209548

Shu, S., Strombeck, S., & Hsieh, C. (2013). *Consumer Ethnocentrism, Self-Image Congruence and Local Brand Preference : A Cross-National Examination*. doi:10.6126/APMR.2013.18.1.03

Steenkamp, E. M. (2002). How perceived brand globalness creates brand value. *Journal of International Business Studies*, *34*(1), 53–65. doi:10.1057/palgrave.jibs.8400002

Steenkamp, E. M. (2003). How perceived brand globalness creates brand value. *Journal of International Business Studies*, *34*(1), 53–65. doi:10.1057/palgrave.jibs.8400002

Steenkamp, J.-B. (2014). How global brands create firm value: The 4V model. *International Marketing Review*, *31*(1), 5–29. doi:10.1108/IMR-10-2013-0233

Suki, N. M. (2016). *Handbook of Research on Leveraging Consumer Psychology for Effective Customer Engagement*. https://www.igi-global.com/book/handbook-research-leveraging-consumer-psychology/149284

Sze, J., Ho, Y., Ong, D., Teik, L., Ing, W. P., Tay, G., ... Peng, N. C. (2000). *Global Versus Local Brand : Perceived Quality And Status-Seeking Motivation In The Automobile Industry*. Academic Press.

Tabachnick, B. G., & Fidell, L. S. (2007). Using Multivariate Statistics (5th ed.). doi:10.1037/022267

Tafsir, M., Shaari, R., Muchtar, H., & Firmansya, F. (2018). The Effects of Product Quality and Interpersonal Communication on Customer Loyalty. *International Journal on Advanced Science, Education, and Religion*, *1*(1), 1–8. doi:10.33648/ijoaser.v1i1.1

Thakor, M. V., & Lavack, A. M. (2003). Effect of perceived brand origin associations on consumer perceptions of quality. *Journal of Product and Brand Management*, *12*(6), 394–407. doi:10.1108/10610420310498821

Tyler, K. (2008). Generation Gaps. *HRMagazine*, *53*, 69–73.

Underwood, R. L. (2003). the Communicative Power of Product Packaging: Creating Brand Identity Via Lived and Mediated Experience. *Journal of Marketing Theory and Practice*, *11*(1), 62–76. doi:10.1080/10696679.2003.11501933

Verstraten, R. (2015). *The Effect of Advertising Credibility: Could it Change Consumers' Attitude and Purchase Intentions?* (Unpublished dissertation). Erasmus University Rotterdam.

Wansink, B., & van Ittersum, K. (2003). Bottoms Up! The Influence of Elongation on Pouring and Consumption Volume. *The Journal of Consumer Research*, *30*(3), 455–463. doi:10.1086/378621

Winit, W., Gregory, G., Cleveland, M., & Verlegh, P. (2014). Global vs local brands: How home country bias and price differences impact brand evaluations. *International Marketing Review*, *31*(2), 102–128. doi:10.1108/IMR-01-2012-0001

Zakaria, N., & Abdul Talib, A. (2010). Applying Islamic market-oriented cultural model to sensitize strategies towards global. *Journal of Islamic Marketing*, *1*(1), 51–62. doi:10.1108/17590831011026222

Zakaria, N., & Talib, A. N. A. (2011). What did you say? A cross-cultural analysis of the distributive communicative behaviors of global virtual teams. In *2011 International Conference on Computational Aspects of Social Networks (CASoN)* (pp. 7-12). IEEE. 10.1109/CASON.2011.6085910

Zakaria, N., Wan-Ismail, W. N. A., & Abdul-Talib, A. N. (2015). Superfluous or Moderation?: The Effect of Religious Value on Conspicuous Consumption Behavior for Luxury Products. In Emerging Research on Islamic Marketing and Tourism in the Global Economy (pp. 1-18). IGI Global.

Zamani, S. N. M., Abdul-Talib, A. N., & Ashari, H. (2016). Strategic orientations and new product success: The mediating impact of innovation speed. International Information Institute (Tokyo). Information, 19(7B), 2785.

Zhao, X., Zhao, K., & Deng, J. (2018). Geography Still Matters: Examine the Role of Location in Online Markets for Foreign Branded Products. *Decision Sciences*, *50*(2), 285–310. doi:10.1111/deci.12337

APPENDIX

Global Brand Preference (Adopted from Shu et al., 2013).

[1] I like global brands better than local brands.
[2] I would use global brands more as compared to local brands.
[3] Global brands are my preferred brands.
[4] I would be inclined to buy global brands as opposed to local brands.

Country-of-Origin (Adopted from Lascu and Babb, 1995).

[5] When buying an expensive item, such as a car, TV or refrigerator, I always seek to find out what country the brands were made in.
[6] I look for the "Made in …" labels in clothing.
[7] A person should always look for country-of-origin information when buying a brand that has a high risk of malfunctioning, e.g. when buying a watch.
[8] When I am buying a new brand, the country of origin is the first piece of information that I consider.
[9] To buy a brand that is acceptable to my friends and my family, I look for the product's country of origin.
[10] If I have little experience with a brand, I search for country-of-origin information about the brand to help me make a more informed decision.

Quality (Adopted from Pappu et al., 2005)

[11] Global brands normally are of good quality materials.
[12] Global brands normally offer products of consistent quality.
[13] Global brands are reliable products.
[14] I am proud to buy global brands as they are associated with good quality.
[15] The quality of most global brands is flawless.

Design (Adopted from Esmaeilpour, 2015)

[16] The design of global brands is normally very elegant.
[17] I particularly find the design of most global brands as attractive.
[18] Global brands normally have distinctive features.
[19] Good global brands design help to foster awareness.
[20] Global brands are normally very pleasant.

Advertising (Adopted from Liu, 2002)

[21] Advertised global brands are related to my daily life.
[22] Global brand advertisements are useful to me to make important purchase decisions.
[23] Global brand advertisements employ famous personalities to encourage my purchase.
[24] Global brands advertisements provide information for me to make buying decisions.
[25] Global brands advertising results in better products for me.
[26] In general, global brands advertising results in lower price for consumers.

Chapter 10
Understanding Cultural Hybridization and Globalization Through the Benefits and Risks on Economic Growth

Dzulfikar Mahtar
Universiti Utara Malaysia, Malaysia

Norbayah Mohd Suki
https://orcid.org/0000-0002-8422-2449
Universiti Utara Malaysia, Malaysia

ABSTRACT

The purpose of this writing is to critically examine various issues and understand the main talking point in globalization, which is the impact it brings to the economic growth and the benefits and risks associated with it. In a fast-paced world, where information and communication is power, globalization in a nutshell is a worldwide agenda that is primarily targeted to bring the best out of each and every member of the economic cycle. Globalization in the world's business is undeniably known as a catalyst that paved the way for aspiring entrepreneurs and business entities to acquire new wealth elsewhere by venturing into a new territory. The development of an ascending trend of integrated and holistic global economy has made globalization a worldwide agenda that implies the opening of a border for foreign business to come in and vice versa.

INTRODUCTION

Cultural hybridization and globalization could be closely call as an item that involved the process or activities of blending of local culture with foreign one through economic generating effort and make adjustments to fit cultural norms of adopted destination. There a various activity that predetermined the condition. More research that delve into aspect of consumer behavior and psychology in the digital

DOI: 10.4018/978-1-7998-3042-9.ch010

economy is deemed necessary (Ling Chang, Ling Tam, & Suki, 2016; Nathan, Fook Chiun, & Suki, 2016; Suki, 2016). Accordingly, this study examines the best elements and key aspects by categorically eight main key points which resembles main component in this economic term.

Key Aspects

As the primary source of determining the healthy economic accomplishments of a certain nation, trade to GDP (Gross Domestic Product) ratios are increasing for most countries. Gone are the days that neighboring nation will go as far as the member next door to do trade. The evolution of economic transaction has evolved from the Barter trade in which everybody are finding each other needs and substitute it with the party that holds their wants vice versa. This has created an imbalance effects in domestic market and the introduction of money has diminished the Barter's effectiveness back in the day. In present day, economic superpower and the G8 members especially has spread their wings and venturing into a new untapped market of developing nation and creating business opportunity for the 'invaded' nation and flourishing their economic practices. With exception of maybe North Korea, Cuba and other communist aligned nation, the international trade business has never ceased to amaze us with its volume and value of trade. Regardless the size of the country, if the men/women who hold power played their trading card rights, all layers in local economy could be highly and lucratively beneficial on all fronts.

Second in the list are the rate of expansion of financial capital flows between countries. Small and sophisticated countries in the Scandinavian region has giving us the point to ponder over this one particular point. Iceland to be precise, has been steadily progress as a nation with a healthy GDP back in the 80's and 90's. Iceland in a nutshell is a small Scandinavian country that become independence from Denmark in 1944. Economic wise, Iceland has been thriving on fishing industry and relied heavily on aluminum smelting and related businesses for their income. The booming of its fisheries activities and geo mineral exploration of aluminum components, Iceland has sustainably maintained steady progress in the economic endeavor. With a recorded GDP of USD 13 Billion as at 2007, this is a classic tale of how the mighty have fallen. The act of globalization proposed and showcased by their top three banks, Kaupthing, Glitnir and Landbanski preceding the financial crisis is alarmingly a tale of legend. From one of the promising nation in the European region, Iceland gone from boom to bust in no time. The expansion of financial capital flows mainly with the Netherland and United Kingdom was driven by ready access to credit in international financial markets. The aftermath of these condition has hurt the nation bad and the recovery session took longer than expected and show us that globalization in particular the capital flows of money could go wrong.

Foreign Direct Investment (FDI) and cross border merger and acquisition also has been rapidly happening all across the international markets' scene. Multinational Corporations (MNC's) and establish international firms has been frequently visiting the shore of potential market. With money is not an object plus the wide capability of its workforce multiple that with smart partnerships with local establishments, most Fortune 500 companies has been championing these cause for decades. There are several factors that attract them to conduct business in the foreign shores and the most potent point is the relative low cost or running the business in the countries of choice. South East Asia nation such as Vietnam, Indonesia and Laos PDR has been the destinations of choice for sports apparels and shoe manufacturing giants such as Nike and Adidas. Lower price of the cost materials needed to produce certain items comparing form the astronomically cost as of its place of origin has driven the exercise much farther than expected. It also helped created the job opportunities to the adopted nation while stabilizing the labour force markets in the local scene while uplifting the domestic environment scenarios.

There is also an emerging trend of rising number of global brands and these includes from emerging countries. Closer to home, Malaysia's has been regarded ad\s the biggest of latex based products producers. The rubber glove giant Top Glove has been flying the country flag high in the international trade scene. In financial sector, the tiger of Maybank has been roaming freely in the 'financial jungle' of ASEAN member's countries and continuously flexing it claws further in the new and exciting financial markets. Plantation giants such as Sime Darby has also been tapping the land bank across the region by setting up plantation sites that cause the envy of many in the industry. Petronas and Proton are the giants in their own right and the invigorating factor of latest takeover by China conglomerate Geely Auto Group in particular has driven Proton into a new height. With resounding brands including Volvo, Lotus and Proton Holdings under its stewardship, Geely has introduced the Toyota's Prius, Honda's Insight, Nissan's Leaf and Tesla smart electric vehicles direct competition, the all-round smart car brand Lynk & Co. These has proved that traditional giant in the industries are facing new and exciting brands in the international markets and in order to not be left behind in the pursuit of perfection, all of the players must up the ante or facing the consequences of getting left way back in the race.

Next components of the key aspects of cultural hybridization through globalization economic practice is deeper specialization of labour components hailed from many countries. Fast Moving Consumer Good's (FMCG) across the globe are now mainly hailed from China and the vast number of businesses that produced the everyday products worth relatively lower costs are straightforwardly associated with the 'Dragon of Asia'. India's has supplied the highest number of personnel helming the Customer Service Representative's position in most Call Centers worldwide regardless the industries and with total over a billion inhabitants, no wonder the citizens of 'Gandhi Ji' nation are roaming across the world. In more highly technological advancement of certain industry, the people of Deutschland or Germany for the mass has established themselves in the automotive and precision engineering industry.

The future of automobile, Mercedes Benz has a cutting-edge innovation namely associated with their flagship model the S class. It was marketed in the luxury segment in the United Sate of America and renowned actor from the Avenger's trilogy African American actor Mr. Samuel L. Jackson has been the proud unofficial spokesperson for the brand. Stuttgart ultra-high-performance car maker, The Porsche, has find its fan in the most recognized faced of American sitcom Jerry Seinfeld. It has been said that after the Royal Highness of Brunei, he owns the largest fleet of high-performance Porsche currently in the market. Bavarian Motor Werks or popularly known as the BMW which, headquartered in Munich, has been closely associated with the James Bond brand at the height of its prowess. With the suave and dashing Wales actor Mr. Pierce Brosnan in the starring roles, who can forget the coolness of the Model 7 Series and Z4 when there are put on tarmac for high octane dramatic chasing scenes?

The six points is the new trend of Global Supply Chains and new inception of fresh trade of investment routes, China's silk and India's spice route all been in the past now. In world of today, the three international economic organizations are namely the World's Bank, International Monetary Fund (IMF) and the World Trade Organization (WTO). Apart of this, North American Free Trade Agreement (NAFTA) is a treaty between Mexico, the United States of America and Canada. The introduction of the body like Asia Pacific Economic Council (APEC) and the now defunct proposal of Trans Pacific Partnership Agreement (TPPA) has given us proof that not all initiatives is viable enough to put into practices. The complication of the Global Supply Chain set up and the perseverance of certain participating economic countries seldom put a hindrance in the once bright fully widely accepted ideas. The vast size of the treaty also played the major roles in the unsuccessfully adaptation new trading route and with giants such as the United States of America, Canada, Japan, Mexico, Australian and New Zealand and the rest form ASEAN region that made up the total numbers of participants to 12 (twelve) has put a strained in the already flourishing business trade with the nation. Existing Global Supply Chain mechanism will be affected by this decision and the harmonious circumstances establish before has been compromised.

The later points that I want to touch here is the increasing levels of international labor migration and migration within countries that closely related in the business venture. It does sound familiarly with the previous point stated but I would like to shift the perspective upon these element in a new economic purveyance. Professional across the world or to be exact the participating country of origin in the globalization initiative usually has a steady and comprehensive set up ready before hand. To minimize cost, giants like Johnsons & Johnson's, General Electric Company (GEC), Nestlé's, AVON, Boeing to name a few has been importing the tech wiz from all over the place in the global labor market. Engineers, Information and Communication Experts, Finance Heads and Human Resources chief candidates has been source out in the market using Management Information Systems programs. The Hardware and software prove to be smart and crucial in determining the best and right candidates are interviewed and chosen for specific oost that are available in the market. The cost are cheaper, and sometimes, albeit most of the times the interview sesiion are conducted using Skype and other relating Google applications. Simple. Savvy. And smart. These factors been helping the corporations tremendously and the importance of these part of business cycle is second to none.

As agreed widely in the world, the increase connectivity factor of people and business through mobile and Wifi's cultural hybridization and globalization practice has shaped the economic condition entirely different form the previous era. There is no more log book of orders, and online ledgers has simplify thing and increase the efficiency aspect of trade. Ease of usage, small cost involved and accessibility advantage is a welcome sight for all members in the economic activities, Electronical procurement can be done without hassle while shipping and logistical setting via different methods of transportation can be strategically formulated, implemented and evaluated and highest level with minimal costs involved.

Benefits and Risks Associated with Globalization and its Impact on Economic Growth.

On the green side of equation, the benefits, first and foremost the is the technological innovation. Competition brings unmeasurable drive and with it's' it has built the spirit of striving to be the best and the rapid growth of technological innovation in the international trading world without borders are endless. Nations who has the best infrastructural setup in this aspect often has a upper hand and the international transaction and without the ever increasing Information and Communication Technology experts, hails from the United States of America, Japan, South Korea, Finland and Singapore proved that who hold the advantage in this elements will prosper. Research and Development Division/Department (R&D) is a breeding place of what's new in the market. Bosch's India Chief Information Officer popularly admitted that's there is not a day without a innovation and it R&D Center and the importance of generating new and fresh ideas has also specifically position the technological giants of the World's top Technological Advanced corporations such as Apple, Sony, and Samsung has place a Billion Dollars sum n this respective division/department.

The large economies of scale that comes with the globalization exercises can never be view slightly. The set-up of vast and comprehensive Manufacturing Plant in the country of choice has sophisticatedly trigger a wide change in the local social and economic climate. Real estate industry will be booming, while the demographical aspects of one inactive area of a certain areas has been upgraded by the mushrooming of satellites town that includes the residential area, commercial are, and business area of choice. Emerging developing countries particularly in the East, will benefit hugely and the supporting local business entities will also thrive with the new business. Locals are now supplied with a jobs that paid handsomely well, and with it comes other perks and benefits offered by the Multinational Corporation's (MNC's) that one never experienced before. The value of surrounding land also will gradually increase and resulting in healthy local financial industries and financial markets. The purchasing power parity (PPP) of the subsequent market will elevated to the comfortable rate and local peoples who has the money are feat with a variety of choice that increase the value of their money substantially.

The risks involved in the other hands, are interdependence, threat to sovereignty and inequitable distribution of wealth across the hierarchy. Interdependence can be loosely translated as the dependence of two or more things on each other and in business economic perspective the context are much larger. It often occurs when the fulfillment of the trading partners are specifically tailored to some requirements that the trade must also be happening with other unmet requirements. Strong and big corporations always exploited this condition and the interdependence effect of normally developing country is often marginalized by irresponsible party. Cultural hybridization practices in the globalization has also open up an unwanted element that could tarnished the local setting and norms with the influx of new establishments, with different upbringing and rational view on patriotism. The classic tale 'sell soul to the devil' could be best describe this scenario and with the pride of a nation at stake, corrective action should be taken seriously to perfectly control the alarming situation domestically.

Categorically, another importance risk associated with the economic growth impacts of globalization act is the inequitable distribution of wealth. The bigger shark in the ocean often has the biggest catch and with the disparagingly advantage held upon their hands, larger corporations has been shamely acted irresponsibly in coping the rewards of their business endeavor. Profit maximization and monetary actualization is described as the Holy Grail of business and with its come the unspoken urge to acquire unsurmountable wealth. These situations often occurs when the participating nation in the trade with smaller statue are hastily making decision that may look profitable in the immediate time. With closer inspection, the dreams has been tarnished by the act of greed and to quote Mr. Gordon Gekko played by the charismatic actor Mr. Michael Douglas, 'Greed ...is good'. This is as classic as it gets when it comes to this issues. Corporations, main from America has been portray as the mightier one and this big nation in the business equation need to stabilizes their moral compass right and starts trade with a clear and noble conscience.

Negative Impacts of Globalization

After thorough consideration, there are mainly 5 (five) issues that highlight the negative impacts impose by the act of globalization. Corporations often go for short term gains. Here, the opportunity and chances were there for grab and therefore every opportunist that can smells 'money' will surely jump on the occasion that will definitely benefit them. Each and every action taken in the trading exercises are solely targeted to acquire as much as monetary gains in the shortest time possible. 'Grab and go' as they said and to achieve that firms are usually used gung-ho approach in order to fully maximize their gain and in the same time doesn't give any attention on what happening on the surrounding area.

Job has also be outsourced to the max. This condition occurs when the demand for professionals and high skilled labor are at all-time high. These are mainly due to the lower cost involved and the same quality level of deliverance showcased by the specific workers in the market. Traditional Human Resource Management function has also slowly diminish and the introduction of smart recruitment program that took p[lace recently has changing the trends and again low cost are the main contributing factor to these condition. Ease of implementation plus less time needed to accomplish various Human Resource functions has made the outsourcing jobs effort simple and achievable. Gone are the days of hard recruitment and interviewing session and all related task in the area are made sufficiently user friendly also help firms big time.

The most pertinent matters regarding the destruction of the environment. Large corporations who shifted their production facility at a new shore often put a little emphasize on the well-being of the new surrounding environment of their adopted place. Large manufacturing plant and new commercial areas has been erected and these actions pretty much has messed up with the ecosystem and the self-sufficient habitat. These condition also isn't help by the practiced of red tape all over the documentation and paper work involved in getting approval from the local government. Certain authorities seemingly close one eyes of them and with the right price, everything should proceed without much hassle. There are many Non-Governmental Organizations (NGO's) and non-profit establishments who are championing the cause and as responsible citizens of the world, the support for them is crucial.

Deplorable working condition, crowded factory with unhealthy working environment are also possessed a constant issue of neglecting human rights. These are happening mainly to the third world country which mass production are taking place. Manual labor often take place and in extreme cases, under age children also force to work as only paltry fees involved in remuneration process. Basic needs and other entitlement haven't been met due to extreme cost cutting measure. As long as there's a demand for goods, the product should materialize no matter what and the irresponsible act shown by firms are simply heart wrenching and disgusting at the same time.

Cultural hybridization act happening through globalization effort also deemed a nuisance in the social environment, particularly at the adopted business nation. Social environment disturbance as it formally known, the myriad of contrasting culture often resulting in conflict. The social establishment and accepted culture here maybe is not accepted elsewhere and the action of assimilation process seldom goes as planned. Different view towards specific issues and the facts that things that seems ok here and may not be ok there could create tension and end up in social environment disturbance at a large scale. Mediocrity and tolerance in action specifically linked to the trading act and process should be practice in order to please everybody in the business cycle. Respect and high level of acceptance should go hand in hand in order to ensure the proposed economic transaction doesn't pose any harm to the social environment in the future. Should there be any changes in the social environment ecosystem, both participating agents should study and made an effort to examine the social background thoroughly before taking any further decision. Good and best management practices undergo by businesses will definitely help them in a large scale and for that to become reality, open mind, heart and humility is a must.

Outcomes

The biggest outcome for me is the integration of economics. The mightier and wealthier counterparts are bringing the business to the new market and these act has open up various opportunities and the possibilities are limitless. However, there is an issue of equality and inequality here and the great balancing act upon these facts should be practiced prudently. Capitalism and monopoly power also should be cope in order to ensure that each and every parts of the economic cycle enjoying the fruit of their labor at best rate. With big corporations comes greater responsibilities and the facts that they have money in mind, the act of responsible trading should be conducted. Recognition in respected areas should also give the upper hand for firms and the weight it carries should also be aimed as the catalyst for change for them. Worldwide recognition also has increased the marketability factor for them and enhancing their image even further.

Companies should counted accountability for their action and responsible act of trading should take place in each and every action imposed by them and the accountability factor will determine their responsibility even further. Great firms with even greater social compass seem a rarity these days and the inception of this rare treat in the business world today spells success in the long run for the firms and adopted nation alike. Free trade are happening across the world. New business ventures are mushrooming in every corner of the industries that targeted to exploit the facts that the adopted nation are willing to give. Cultural hybridization also has also made the world shrinking at an alarming pace. Undoubted speed in communication, access to information have never been easier and the ease of doing business these days has pretty much elevate the decision making much easier than before. Information is power and the outcome from these facts proved crucial enough for those who inspire to became the captain of the industry.

The ever-changing landscape of the environment due to rampant business activities also post a constant threat to the well-being of mother nature. Deforestation, unauthorized land clearing and other illegal activities involved has been treating the natural condition of the environment in a wrong tune. Big corporations and Multinational Corporations (MNC's) alike are keen to emphasize utmost attention to this intricate issue. Known facts that starting from end of the 90's, environment Non-Governmental Organization (NGO's) such as Greenpeace, World Business Council for Sustainable Development and Society for the Environment (SocEnv) UK to name a few. All of these entities has put a stronghold in every effort regarding with the care of the environment.

Additionally, cultural hybridization and globalization in economic pursuit has enable participating nations to project growth. In the same period of time, the contributing factors like the new job opportunities and the inception of new source of making a living among local residents have also help the nation to eradicate poverty. The supporting business components of the main business activities have also provide new sources of income that ultimately lead to new income generating process. It could also help them t o make a better living and upgrade their social lifestyles and ultimately this would help them to find a best education to their loved ones.

CONCLUSION

Cultural Hybridization, globalization and other term coined as same meaning as those are mainly discussed on the surface by the main stream media due to certain unspoken agreement. With major media outlet being from the superpower nation, the dissemination of information are seldom one sided and the global audiences are normally ended to take on whatever things that has been reported to us without having to critically discuss the content of a certain issues. Globalization as a whole has carry a huge burden of responsibility upon themselves and the act has been wholeheartedly complicated when conflict arises among the members of the trading activities. Cultural and social infringement seldom taken into account seriously and as with any other imbalances, the bigger party will also hold the ace card. Greed has been the driving factor of us human in making inconsiderate and irresponsible decisions regarding future business venture.

People must be taken accountable for their action and the sustainable business model must be adhered to ensure that the consequences of the decisions would not going to haunt the next generation in years to come. With clear emphasization on the green issues, it is without a doubt that business entities and subsequent members of the set up should place a priority on this prime subject and the ability of us in making responsible and calculated decision now would prove monumental in size. As far as any business venture go, the culmination of calculated thinking now is crucial in ensuring that there is a chance for future generation enjoying whatever nature has to offer.

REFERENCES

Chang, L. D. M., Ling Tam, A. Y., & Suki, N. M. (2016). Moderating effect of races towards consumers' feeling of TCM usage. Handbook of Research on Leveraging Consumer Psychology for Effective Customer Engagement, 306-323.

Nathan, R. J., Fook Chiun, D. C., & Suki, N. M. (2016). An online marketing strategies assessment for companies in airlines and entertainment industries in Malaysia. Handbook of Research on Leveraging Consumer Psychology for Effective Customer Engagement, 1-15.

Suki, N. M. (2016). *Handbook of Research on Leveraging Consumer Psychology for Effective Customer Engagement*. https://www.igi-global.com/book/handbook-research-leveraging-consumer-psychology/149284

Chapter 11
A Decent Work and Economic Growth:
The Potential of Asnaf Entrepreneur in Achieving Sustainable Development Goals (SDGs)

Siti Khalilah Binti Basarud-Din
Zakat Kedah Board, Malaysia

Hafizah Binti Zainal
Kedah Zakat Board, Malaysia

ABSTRACT

Asnaf entrepreneur is a micro SME entrepreneur who plays a significant role in the contribution of the economic sectors. In 2018, Malaysia registered a total of 907,065 SMEs, with micro-enterprises accounting for 2.3% (20,612) of the total. The poor and needy entrepreneur is also part of the successful key to support Malaysian to achieve Sustainable Development Goals (SDGs). The objective of this study is to identify the potential of poor and needy entrepreneur in Kedah Zakat Board (LZNK) to achieve SDGs. This paper uses a conceptual study method and explore the literature as a guide for enhancing knowledge on this area. This paper suggests a potential sustainable development model with four variables of poor and needy entrepreneurs in achieving SDGs goals. The contributions and implications of the study are discussed at the end of this paper.

INTRODUCTION

Poverty is part of the global issues that have affected society, particularly in the Muslim community. In Malaysia, the poverty rate decreased from 0.6% to 0.4% between 2014 and 2016. (Malaysian Statistics Department, 2016). However, the income inequality gap has not matched the real income of the poor (Khazanah Research Institute, 2018). According to the Pew Research Centre (2014), 77% of Malaysians

DOI: 10.4018/978-1-7998-3042-9.ch011

believe that the gap between rich and poor is a major problem. Impact of the situation, zakat plays a key role in the growth of the Muslim economic system in all aspects of the economy, education, regulation and so on. Zakat's aim is to achieve socio-economic justice (Adnan & Bakar 2009). Zakat is the fourth pillar in Islam that all affordable Muslims must fulfill to underprivileged people. Zakat's word linguistically refers to the act of cleansing or purifying something that is dirty. In legal terms, zakat pays a certain amount of surplus wealth to the specified beneficiaries each year. There are 8 beneficiaries in Glorious al-Quran, such as the destitute, the poor, the zakat workers (Amil), the new Muslim (Muaallaf), free slaves, the indebted, on the path of Allah and the stranded traveller. Abu Bakar and Abdul Rashid (2010) stated that zakat can be productive and sustainable if poverty alleviation can be managed efficiently and effectively.

A good platform for zakat to become productive and sustainable, which gives the poor and needy an opportunity to engage in business until they can earn their own living independently and be self-sufficient (Mohamed, Mastuki, Yusuf, & Zakaria, 2018). Poor and needy entrepreneur is a micro SME entrepreneur who plays a significant role in the contribution of the economic sectors. In 2018, Malaysia registered a total of 907,065 SMEs, with micro-enterprises accounting for 2.3% (20,612) of the total (SME Annual Report, 2018). Despite having such a large role, micro-entrepreneurship conditions still pose many challenges in accessing capital. The role of zakat is therefore essential to the welfare of the needy by providing capital to generate circulation income for recipients to pay zakat through business opportunities. The different programmes for entrepreneurship have been developed by the zakat institution. The zakat institution seeks to create an effective way for the poor and needy to become an entrepreneur and to improve their social and economic life through the Asnaf Entrepreneurship Programme (AEP). The difference between the entrepreneurship programmes of the zakat institutions and other entrepreneurship programmes is that the source of capital given to the poor to start a business is the use of zakat money.

The purpose of the programs is specifically to help poor and needy people get involved in business so that they can get away from their current predicament and possibly become zakat payers. However, the rate of success is still low. Mostly, their business faces some challenges in a market competitor. According to Khalique, Isa, Shaari, Abdul and Ageel (2011) indicated that their business is challenging to survive in competitive advantage such as business capital, human capital (Haron, Said, Jayaraman, & Ismail, 2013), lack of business knowledge (Kazimoto, 2014; Muhammad, Char, Yasoa, & Hassan, 2010), networking (Khalique et al., 2010) and social relations (Alam, Jani, Senik, & Domil, 2011). All of these factors would make it impossible for poor and needy entrepreneurs to be sustainable in the marketplace. It is because zakat Kedah would only provide the capital without providing proper guidance and monitoring to sustain the business in the market. Therefore, the zakat institution needs a programme to help the poor and needy to become successful business entrepreneurs.

More research that delve into aspect of consumer behavior and psychology in the digital economy is deemed necessary (Ling Chang, Ling Tam, & Suki, 2016; Nathan, Fook Chiun, & Suki, 2016; Suki, 2016). Accordingly, the objective of this study is to identify the potential Kedah Zakat Board (LZNK) entrepreneur to receive SDGs. Nowadays, the issues of zakat are becoming a popular debate among researchers. Mostly, the researcher focuses on poor and needy businesses in a number of areas such as behaviour (Mahmood, Al Mamun, Ahmad, & Ibrahim, 2019), successful entrepreneurs (Halim, Said, & Yusuf, 2012; Afif Muhamat, Jaafar, Emrie Rosly, & Abdul Manan, 2013), entrepreneur development (Hassan, & Rom, 2016; Nadzri, Omar, & Rahman, 2018), business productive (Ismail, & Hussain, 2017) and business capital (Harun, Hassan, Jasni, & Rahman, 2010). However, the study on the implementation of SDGs in zakat management for poor and needy entrepreneurs is still limited. Therefore, this paper is a preliminary attempt to identify the extent to which the zakat institution can adapt to zakat management among asnaf entrepreneurs on the basis of SDG methods. This study contributes significantly to zakat management's knowledge on implementing the SDGs model for improving asnaf business.

LITERATURE REVIEW

Maqasid Shariah of Zakat

Maqasid means the purpose, the intent, the objective, the principle, the goal or the end. Al-Raysuni (2005) defined that maqasid as the higher objectives of the law-giver. Maqasid Shariah is an Islamic knowledge and institutional framework with five basic goal. These include the protection of faith, life, progeny, intellect and wealth. The aims of the Maqasid Shariah are interpreted in a comprehensive manner that goes beyond the narrow interests of individuals or entities to the broader and predominant interests that take into account the broadest sphere of Islamic society. In other words, maqasid involves seeking benefits and preventing harm to the wider community's best interests. Accordingly, maqasid is aimed at protecting society and ensuring its well-being and social development.

Al-Ghazali (2008) summarises the maqasid shariah in 5 (five) aspects. These aspects are religion, the soul, the intellect, the lineage and the property. The maqasid shariah is concerned with the fulfillment of the five aspects according to the level of priority. The fact that the maqasid shariah is divided into three levels of necessity which are necessities (daruriyyat), needs (hajiyyat) and luxuries (tahsiniyyat) (Al-Ghazali, 2008). Requirements were considered to be essential to human life itself, including food, shelter, clothing, education and health care. Needs are a distinct category of human needs that encompasses all things and activities that are not key to the preservation of faith (religion), life, intellect, offspring and property (wealth), but are necessary for the alleviation of life's hardships and difficulties. Luxuries that refer to things and activities that refine and embellish people's lives. It is not primarily a way of alleviating or relieving hardships and basic needs, but rather of adding elegance to life.

Zakat is a medium of purification and sharing of wealth to strengthen the economy of Muslims. Each of the distribution schemes provided to the zakat community plays an important role in ensuring that all needs of the Asnaf are met and in accordance with the Shariah approach. In order to ensure that each zakat distribution scheme is provided for the achievement of the zakat obligation objective, the zakat distribution should be carried out in accordance with maqasid shariah on the basis of five priorities, namely religion, life, intellect, lineage and property, as indicated by Al-Ghazali (2008). Best practices in gathering and distributing zakat will generate the best results. Sustainable Development Goal (SDGs) is one of the popular methods will be used to achieve part of zakat maqasid. Nevertheless, there are some fundamental differences between zakat and SDGs. The maqasid principle originates from the Islamic religion stated in al-Quran, while the SDGs are formed of united nations that are not religiously based (Zainal, Othman and Mustaffa, 2019). Meanwhile, Suprayitno, Aslam, & Harun (2017) stated that there are many goals of the SDGs to address the Islamic values of poverty and hunger. The SDGs have been established to protect human rights, including social, economic and environmental aspects. In accordance with the SDGs goals, the zakat distribution scheme will support the zakat recipient and will also improve the efficiency and effectiveness of the zakat institution in Malaysia.

Sustainable Development Goals (SDGs)

The Sustainable Development Goals (SDGs), also known as the Global Goals, were adopted by all United Nations Member States in 2015 as a universal call for action to end poverty, protect the planet and ensure that all people enjoy peace and prosperity by 2030 (United Nations Development Programme, 2019). They proposed 17 high level Sustainable Development Goals (SDGs) (refer to Figure 1) and 169 specific targets, encompassing the social, economic and environmental dimensions of development. The SDGs replace the Millennium Development Goals (MDGs), which launched a global effort to overcome poverty in 2000. Among other development priorities, the MDGs recognised measurable, universally agreed goals to address extreme poverty and hunger, prevent fatal diseases, and intensify primary education for all children.

Figure 1. 17 high level Sustainable Development Goals (SDGs)
Source: Sustainable Development Goals (2019).

Initially, the MDGs ended in 2015 are not fully achieving 100% of the suggested goals, then the SDGs model is formed. This programme is based on the "No One Left Behind" principle with a goal of ensuring that all benefit from sustainable development. However, SDGs are also focused on ending the poverty issue is a problem for developing countries. Furthermore, the SDG programme seeks to ensure that future generations are able to meet all the basic requirements. This programme encompasses people, planets, prosperity, peace and partnership, which is expected to put an end to the current issue in developing countries (Zainal, Othman & Mustaffa, 2019).

Asnaf Enterprenuer in Kedah Zakat Board (LZNK)

Asnaf is a predicament person who is eligible to receive zakat or sadaqah. Asnaf who has physical and mental strength would be classified as productive person that can be received zakat fund (Rosbi & Sanep, 2011) as business funds. he potential asnaf as an entrepreneur in business would have been granted by the zakat institution in terms of capital aid and business facilities. According to Isma Addi Jumri (2007), asnaf entrepreneurs are individuals who need a process of business creation, in order to carry out their

Table 1. Goals, Objectives and Indicators of Sustainable Development Goals

No	Goals	Targets	Indicators
1	No Poverty	7	12
2	Zero Hunger	8	14
3	Good Health and Well-Being	13	26
4	Quality Education	10	11
5	Gender Equality	9	14
6	Clean Water and Sanitation	8	11
7	Affordable and Clean Energy	5	6
8	Decent Work and Economic Growth	12	17
9	Industry, Innovation and Infrastructure	8	12
10	Reduced Inequalities	10	11
11	Sustainable Cities and Communities	10	15
12	Responsible Consumption and Production	11	13
13	Climate Action	5	7
14	Life Below Water	10	10
15	Life on Land	12	14
16	Peace, Justice and Strong Institutions	12	23
17	Partnerships for the Goals	19	25

Source: Sustainable Development Goals (2019); Zainal, Othman and Mustaffa (2019).

duties, responsibilities and efforts as a business person stimulated by the encouragement and assistance of the zakat institutions. Asnaf entrepreneur is defined as a micro-entrepreneur. Small and Medium Enterprises Corporation (2017) defines micro entrepreneurs as entrepreneurs with annual sales of less than RM300,000 or less than 5 full-time employees.

Asnaf does not have the quality required to be a successful entrepreneur in terms of the weaknesses and barriers they face. Capital shortages are an important factor that should be emphasised for asnaf entrepreneur's growth and development (Nkonge, 2013). This financial crisis is one of the main causes of the inability of asnaf entrepreneurs to maintain their businesses (Haron, Said, Jayaraman, & Ismail 2013). This situation is also explained by Muhammad, Char, Yasoa and Hassan (2010) who identified that the main problems faced by entrepreneurs are lack of knowledge of marketing techniques, branding, loyalty and customer satisfaction as well as lack of networking with others locally or internationally. On the other hand, Alam, Jani, Senik and Domil (2011) found that asnaf entrepreneurs in Malaysia have social relations problems that are key to achieving competitive advantage and that many micro-entrepreneurs in Malaysia are losing out on opportunities. Zakat institution is therefore a key role in helping asnaf become a successful entrepreneur.

The role of LZNK to help the poor and needy by implementing entrepreneurship programmes such as the Asnaf Entrepreneur Programme (AEP) as an alternative to poverty alleviation. The zakat programmes would transform asnaf as self-actualisation from recipient to zakat payer. The difference between the entrepreneurship programmes of the zakat institutions and the other entrepreneurship programmes is that the source of capital given to the poor and needy to start up their business is the use of zakat money.

Asnaf entrepreneur played a significant role in the Malaysian economy. Despite the level of economic growth, almost all enterprises are the basis of the economic and social order in terms of numerical and job creation capabilities. Asnaf entrepreneur's ability and elasticity to keep up with social and economic changes and to recognise that they could be a great tool for achieving the Sustainable Development Goals (SDGs).

The Potentials Asnaf Entrepreneur in Sustainable Development Goals.

Small enterprises account for over 90% of all businesses and provide more than 60% of total employment globally (SEED, 2019). The asnaf enterprises tend to employ a larger share of women, youth and people from poorer populations and are sometimes the only source of employment in rural communities. In other words, asnaf has always played important roles in the Malaysian economy. Asnaf entrepreneur is the foundation of the economic and social order in terms of numerical, innovation and job creation capability. Malaysia is now more aware of the capability and elasticity of small business to keep up with social and economic changes by achieving the globalization of world goals. Part of that, asnaf entrepreneur as a vital role to play in Malaysia's economy, based on their capability in their business area. Therefore, the zakat institution also recognises that asnaf entrepreneur can be a great tool for achieving the Sustainable Development Goals (SDGs) (Figure 1).

Agricultural Sector

The agricultural sector plays a role in the economy of Malaysia. Mostly, asnaf is employed by the agricultural sector as a farmer. The agricultural sector plays a key role in creating and maintaining a sustainable supply of food in the economy (Beck, T., Demiruc-Kunt, A. and Livine, 2005). Agriculture remains an important sector of Malaysia's economy, contributing 12% to the national GDP and providing employment for 16% of the population. According to the Department of Statistics Malaysia (2018) showed that the agriculture sector contributed 8.2% or RM96.0 billion to the Gross Domestic Product (GDP) in 2017. The Oil palm was a major contributor to the GDP of agriculture sector at 46.6 per cent followed by other agriculture (18.6%), livestock (11.4%), fisheries (10.5%), rubber (7.3%) and forestry & logging (5.6%). Furthermore, rice is the basic diet of the people of Malaysia and symbolises the traditional Malay culture. The production of rice in 1998 reached 1.94 million tonnes, it plays an important part in agriculture in the country (Department of Statistics Malaysia, 2018).

Other than that, asnaf farmers also produce a number of fruits and vegetables for the domestic market, including bananas, coconut, durian, pineapple and others. This situation has shown that asnaf entrepreneurs also continue to play a role in Malaysia's economy activities. At the same time, they contribute to the SDGs supportive goals of zero hunger in the production of the needs of Malaysian society, such as food and drink. In order to ensure that Malaysia is free from hunger, governments and the zakat institution need to encourage an asnaf entrepreneur to have a competitive market opportunity.

Rural Products

Some of the LZNK asnaf entrepreneur from the village that produces natural and herbal sources. Today, consumer trends in the demand for natural products, especially rural-urban products, are increasing. Their business supports the government's initiative to keep the people of Malaysia healthy. One of the most recent initiatives taken by the Malaysian Government to boost rural incomes is to facilitate the growth of small enterprises under the One-District-One Industry programme (briefly ODOI). The programme was launched in 2003 and was inspired by the success story of the One-Tambon-One-Product Programme (OTOP) in Thailand.

Both ODOI and OTOP are based on the Japanese One-Village-One-Product (OVOP) concept which that in the Oita prefectural in 1979. The aim is to encourages rural entrepreneurs to produce at least one product of commercial value per village using available natural resources (Kader, Mohamad, M & Ibrahim 2009). According to the United Nations Environment Programme in 2015, showed that 9% of the sampled SMEs were found to be actively involved in the healthcare sector, showing a large number of SMEs in this area (OECD, 2017).

Job Opportunity

Small and Medium Enterprises (SMEs) contributed more than a third of RM1.2 trillion of national gross domestic product (GDP) and also created employment opportunities for 5.7 million employees, which account for almost half of total employment and represent 98.5% of establishments in Malaysia (New Strait Times, 2017). According to OECD (2017), formal SMEs contribute up to 60% of total employment and up to 40% of GDP to emerging economies. This implies, therefore, enabling this asnaf entrepreneur to thrive in a critical area in order to achieve this global goal. This means that asnaf entrepreneurs have the most important role to play in contributing to Malaysia's GDP by creating jobs in other asnaf and local areas. This goal, known as 'shared prosperity,' also reduces poverty by creating local area jobs and changing asnaf communities for a better life. On the other hand, a potential asnaf entrepreneur with self-transcendence motivation would change their status from a predicament person to a zakat payer. The recycle life is good for Malaysia's economics activities.

Innovation

An innovative asnaf entrepreneur is considered to be a driving force for innovation and competitiveness, achieving sustainable development. They can solve the social and environmental problems (Kardosa, 2012). Applying innovation to SME has competitive advantages that have a positive impact on the economical facet of sustainable development (Tonis, 2015). The Government of Malaysia has worked diligently to encourage SME to be part of the national innovation system through various programmes and platforms. Asnaf or a rural entrepreneur are also key to the production of innovations for substitute products using natural sources such as virgin oil (beauty care), spinach (healthy snack), plant extract or herbs (substitute drug medicine) and recycled products as craftsmanship. They would be the driving force behind innovation, and most of the breakthrough innovations in recent decades have come from new and small firms because, unlike large enterprises, they can operate outside dominant paradigms and without strong ties to existing products and technologies. (Beck et al. 2005). Then, going to look at the critical situation of an asnaf entrepreneur's ability to maintain their business skills. It is therefore crucial for small businesses to invest in R&D and innovation programmes as it always ensures that they move forward.

Figure 2. The Potential Model of Poor and Needy Entrepreneur in Achieving of SDGs

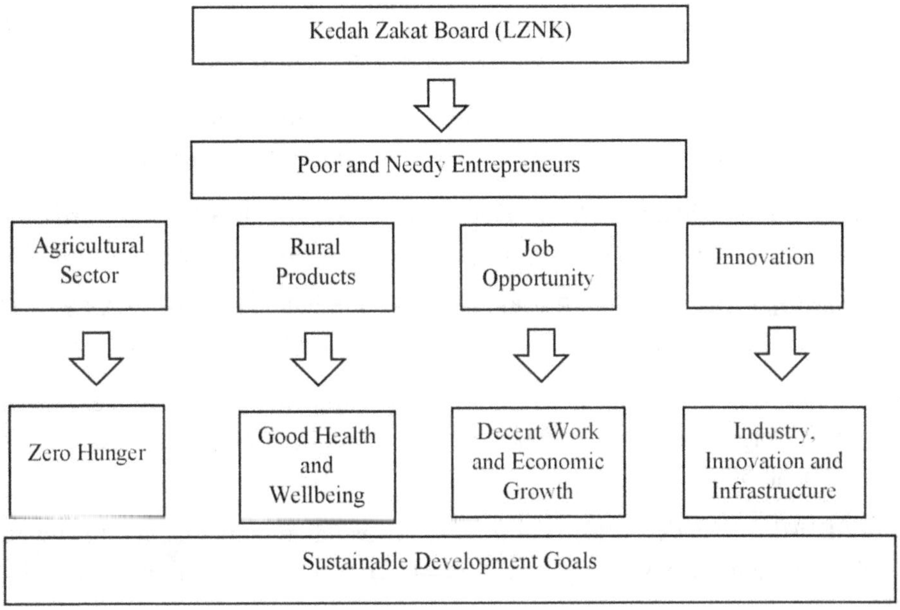

CONCLUSION

Malaysian one of the countries implementing the global objectives of achieving the SDGs in 2030. The Sustainable Development Goals (SDGs) are human rights-based programmes that cover three dimensions, including social, environmental and economic. SMEs are part of the economy of Malaysia's backbone. In this case, the role of the SME continues to be played by Malaysia in achieving the SDGs. SME has evolved over the last decade to become the greatest force not to be reckoned with in the global development equation. Therefore, one of the potential institutions that contribute to the SDGs is the zakat institution. LZNK is a zakat institution that adopts SDGs in its zakat distributions to achieve decent work and economic growth. Therefore, the zakat institution, especially the LZNK and the policy makers, need to support and encourage them to make their business environment and policies more productive. As with all businesses, asnaf entrepreneurs need support to enable their innovations to materialise in a successful venture. This means that LZNK should increase asnaf entrepreneur's access to financial services, facilities, business knowledge and markets competitive. This will boost asnaf entrepreneur's ability to access markets and grow their businesses.

REFERENCES

Afif Muhamat, A., Jaafar, N., Emrie Rosly, H., & Abdul Manan, H. (2013). An appraisal on the business success of entrepreneurial asnaf: An empirical study on the state zakat organization (the Selangor Zakat Board or Lembaga Zakat Selangor) in Malaysia. *Journal of Financial Reporting and Accounting*, *11*(1), 51–63. doi:10.1108/JFRA-03-2013-0012

Al-Ghazali. (2008). al-Mustasfa min 'Ilm al-Usul. Beirut: Dar al-Kutub al-'Ilmiyyah.

Al-Raysuni, A. (2005). *Imam al-Shatibi's Theory of the Higher Objectives and Intents of Islamic Law*. London: International Institute of Islamic Thought. doi:10.2307/j.ctvkjb1w9

Alam, S. S., Jani, M. F. M., Senik, Z. C., & Domil, A. K. A. (2011). Assessing barriers of growth of food processing SMIs in Malaysia: A factor analysis. *International Business Research*, *4*(1), 252–259.

Alam, S. S., Jani, M. F. M., Senik, Z. C., & Domil, A. K. A. (2011). Assessing barriers of growth of food processing SMIs in Malaysia: A factor analysis. *International Business Research*, *4*(1), 252–259.

Beck, T., Demiruc-Kunt, A., & Livine, R. (2005). SMEs, Growth and Poverty: A Cross-Country Evidence. *Journal of Economic Growth*, *10*(3), 199–229. doi:10.100710887-005-3533-5

Chang, L. D. M., Ling Tam, A. Y., & Suki, N. M. (2016). Moderating effect of races towards consumers' feeling of TCM usage. Handbook of Research on Leveraging Consumer Psychology for Effective Customer Engagement, 306-323.

Department of Statistics Malaysia. (2018). *Agriculture.* Available online from https://www.dosm.gov.my/v1/index.php?r=column/ctwoByCat&parent_id=45&menu_id=Z0VTZGU1UHBUT1VJMFlpaXRRR0xpdz09

Halim, H. A., Said, J., & Yusuf, S. N. S. (2012). Individual characteristics of the successful asnaf entrepreneurs: Opportunities and solutions for zakat organization in Malaysia. *International Business and Management*, *4*(2), 41–49.

Haron, H., Said, S. B., Jayaraman, K., & Ismail, I. (2013). Factors Influencing Small Medium Enterprises (SMES) in Obtaining Loan. *International Journal of Business and Social Science*, *4*(15), 182–195.

Harun, N. H., Hassan, H., Jasni, N. S., & Rahman, R. A. (2010). Zakat for asnafs' business by Lembaga Zakat Selangor. *Management Accounting Research*, *9*(2), 123–138.

Hassan, N. M., & Rom, N. A. M. (2016). Mobile Entrepreneur Program by Zakat Institution: An Exploratory Study. *Social Science*, *11*(7), 7494–7497.

Ismail, I. A., & Hussain, M. N. (2017). Productive Zakat Distribution by Zakat Institutions in Malaysia. *International Journal of Academic Research in Business and Social Sciences*, *7*(3), 2222–6990.

Kader, R. A., Mohamad, M. R. B., & Ibrahim, A. A. H. C. (2009). Success factors for small rural entrepreneurs under the one-district-one-industry programme in Malaysia. *Contemporary Management Research*, *5*(2). doi:10.7903/cmr.1173

Kardos, M.Research on European Union Countries. (2012). The Relationship between entrepreneurship, innovation and sustainable development. Research on European Union Countries. *Procedia Economics and Finance*, *3*, 1030–1035. doi:10.1016/S2212-5671(12)00269-9

Kazimoto, P. (2014). Assessment of Challenges facing Small and Medium Enterprises towards International Marketing Standards: A Case Study of Arusha Region Tanzania. International Journal of Academic Research in Accounting. *Finance and Management Sciences*, *4*(2), 303–311.

Khalique, M., Isa, A. H. B. M., Shaari, N., Abdul, J., & Ageel, A. (2011). Challenges faced by the small and medium enterprises (SMEs) in Malaysia: An intellectual capital perspective. *International Journal of Current Research, 3*(6), 398–401.

Mahmood, T. M. A. T., Al Mamun, A., Ahmad, G. B., & Ibrahim, M. D. (2019). Predicting Entrepreneurial Intentions and Pre-Start-Up Behaviour among Asnaf Millennials. *Sustainability, 11*(18), 4939. doi:10.3390u11184939

Muhammad, M. Z., & Char, A. K., bin Yasoa, M. R., & Hassan, Z. (2010). Small and medium enterprises (SMEs) competing in the global business environment: A case of Malaysia. *International Business Research, 3*(1), 66–75.

Muhammad, M. Z., Char, A. K., Yasoa, M. R., & Hassan, Z. (2010). Small and medium enterprises (SMEs) competing in the global business environment: A case of Malaysia. *International Business Research, 3*(1), 66–75.

Nadzri, F. A. A., Omar, N., & Rahman, R. A. (2018). Enterprise Governance of Micro Entrepreneurs in Malaysia: Comparison between the Amanah Ikhtiar Malaysia and Asnaf's Economic Development Program. *Global Journal Al-Thaqafah*, 25-40.

Nathan, R. J., Fook Chiun, D. C., & Suki, N. M. (2016). An online marketing strategies assessment for companies in airlines and entertainment industries in Malaysia. Handbook of Research on Leveraging Consumer Psychology for Effective Customer Engagement, 1-15.

New Straits Time. (2017). *SMEs doing well despite slower national economic growth: Rahman Dahlan.* Available online from https://www.nst.com.my/news/nation/2017/10/287258/smes-doing-well-despite-slower-national-economic-growth-rahman-dahlan

Nkonge, B. K. (2013). Challenges faced by Small and Medium Enterprise Suppliers when bidding for tenders. A case of Thika District. *International Journal of Academic Research in Business and Social Sciences, 3*(12), 194–220. doi:10.6007/IJARBSS/v3-i12/426

OECD. (2017). *Financing SMEs and Entrepreneurs 2016: An OECD Scoreboard.* OECD Publishing.

Rosbi, A. R., & Sanep, A. (2011). Strategi Pembangunan Keusahawan Asnaf dan Miskin melalui Agihan Bantuan Modal Zakat. *Jurnal Pengurusan, 33*, 37–44. doi:10.17576/pengurusan-2011-33-03

SEED. (2019). *Sustainable Development Goals.* Available online from https://seed.uno/topics/sdgs

Small and Medium Enterprises Corporation. (2017). *Definisi Baharu PKS.* Dicapai daripada http://www.smecorp.gov.my/images/pdf/GarisPanduan_Definisi_Baharu_PKS_updated.pdf

SME Annual Report. (2018). *Small and Medium Enterprise Annual Report 2018.* Available online from http://www.smecorp.gov.my/index.php/en/laporan-tahunan/3342-laporan-tahunan-pks-2017-18

Suki, N. M. (2016). *Handbook of Research on Leveraging Consumer Psychology for Effective Customer Engagement.* https://www.igi-global.com/book/handbook-research-leveraging-consumer-psychology/149284

Suprayitno, E., Aslam, M., & Harun, A. (2017). Zakat and SDGs: Impact zakat on human development in the five states of Malaysia. *International Journal of Zakat*, *2*(1), 61–69.

Sustainable Development Goals. (2019). Available online from https://sustainabledevelopment.un.org/sdgs

Tonis, R. (2015). SMEs role in achieving sustainable development. Journal of Economic Development. *Environment and People*, *4*(1), 41–50. doi:10.26458/jedep.v4i1.102

United Nations Development Programme (UNDP). (2019). *Sustainable Developments Goals*. Available online from https://www.undp.org/content/undp/en/home/sustainable-development-goals.html

Zainal, H., Othman, Z., & Mustaffa, F. (2019). The Implementation of Sustainable Development Goals Model Through Initiative of Zakat Management in Kedah. *International Journal of Zakat and Islamic Philanthropy*, *1*(1), 1–6.

Chapter 12

Proactive and Responsive Export Market Orientation Behaviours, Antecedents, and Firm Performance:

A Qualitative Study on Exporting SMEs

Asmat Nizam Abdul-Talib
https://orcid.org/0000-0001-6820-2918
Universiti Utara Malaysia, Malaysia

Ili-Salsabila Abd-Razak
Universiti Utara Malaysia, Malaysia

ABSTRACT

This paper details about the qualitative study of proactive and responsive export market orientation. An interview series was conducted to assess whether the issue of proactive and responsive export market orientation exist among exporters, identification of the exporters' characteristics (antecedents) and understand the behaviors effect on performance consequences. Findings from the interview were recorded in a qualitative codebook. Discussions and conclusion made on the qualitative findings revealed that the issue of proactive and responsive export market orientation is present, different characteristics lead to different behaviors, and the behaviors affect the exporters' performance consequences differently.

INTRODUCTION

Small- and medium-sized enterprises (SMEs) contribute significantly to inclusive economic development and employment around the globe. According to a report by OECD/ERIA in 2018 (SME Policy Index: ASEAN 2018), SMEs in ASEAN, including micro-enterprises, form around 97% to 99% of enterprise population in member states, and they are mostly engaged in labour-intensive and low value-added

DOI: 10.4018/978-1-7998-3042-9.ch012

industries, such as retail, trade and agricultural activities. While the enterprises account for the largest share of employment in the economy at around 66.3%, their contribution to the gross value added is only 42.2%, suggesting that their productivity and growth are trailing behind the larger enterprises.

A similar report by ERIA-OECD in 2014 (ASEAN SME Policy Index 2014) indicated that SMEs are underrepresented as exporters, with only 10% to 30% of them are engaged in export activities. However, Gonzalez (2017) found that the SMEs engaged in export activities appeared to be exporters instead of buyers of foreign inputs, suggesting that the exporting SMEs have more export market orientation to push their products and services to the international market than larger enterprises. It is therefore interesting to investigate exporting SME behaviors of export market orientation, the antecedents of the behaviors, and the impact on their performance.

There is a growing scholarly interest in proactive and responsive market orientation behaviors. The literature informs about the generic activities of market orientation that focus on the intelligence of latent or new needs (proactive market orientation) and current or expressed needs (responsive market orientation). Since the seminal works of Jaworski, Kohli, and Sahay (2000), and Narver, Slater, and MacLahlan (2004) on the dimensions of market orientation, the number of research studies on the topic is growing. Past studies have examined the relationship between proactive and responsive market orientation behaviors and new product success (e.g., Atuahene-Gima, Slater, & Olsen, 2005; Narver et al., 2004; Tsai, Chou, & Kuo, 2008), entrepreneurship and innovation (e.g., Li, Lin, & Chu, 2008; Nasution, Mavondo, Matanda, & Ndubisi, 2011; Zhang & Duan, 2010), competitive strategies (e.g., Voola & O'Cass, 2010), the ambidextrous and dynamic effects (e.g., Alpkan, Sanal, & Ayden, 2012; Herhausen, 2016; Wei, Zhao, & Zhang, 2014), and export performance (e.g., Munawar, Rahayu, Disman, & Wibowo, 2019), among others.

According to Jaworski et al. (2000), the early literature on market orientation appeared to focus on responsive behaviors only. However, concentrating on a single dimension of export market orientation does not comprehensively inform how exporting business organisations behave. Hence, the dual dimensions of market orientation behavior (proactive and responsive) were proposed to address the concern (Atuahene-Gima et al., 2005; Jaworski et al., 2000; Narver et al., 2004), resulting in a significant increase in the number of studies examining the issue, thus, contributing to the current body of knowledge.

However, despite the growing literature (Cadogan, Diamantopoulos, & Siguaw, 2002; Knight, & Kim, 2009), little is known about the international market extension of market orientation, also referred to as export or international market orientation. As an extended concept, it is reasonable to theorise that exporting companies to international markets behave differently when their export market orientations are different. Abdul-Talib and Abd-Razak (2013; 2012) were perhaps the earliest researchers that examined the proactive and responsive market orientation behaviors of exporters and international marketers. Since then, several studies have been carried out, such as Munawar et al. (2019), who found that proactive market orientation and management commitment to internal resources MCIR had a positive influence on export performance. Blocker, Flint, Myers, and Slater (2011) explored how proactive customer orientation, a dimension of market orientation, creates customer value in the global market. They showed that proactive customer orientation was the most consistent driver of customer value at the multinational level, with robust effects were shown for the interaction between proactive and responsive customer orientation in creating superior value.

Past studies have also examined various issues related to export market orientation, including its antecedents and impact on performance. Several antecedents of export market orientation and export performance have been considered, such as export experience, export dependence, and coordinating capabilities as antecedents of export market orientation (Cadogan, Diamantopoulos, & Siguaw, 2002; Cadogan et al., 2001). These studies found that export market orientation activities, defined as activities related to generating, disseminating and responding to export intelligence, were positively associated with export performance of the firms. Past researchers also focused on the measurement of market orientation (Cadogan, Diamantopoulos, & de Mortanges, 1999; Zou, Taylor, & Osland, 1998). Zou et al.'s scale is still being by researchers in their work (Cadogan et al., 2001; Cadogan, Cui, & Kwok, 2003).

The focus in recent studies was on the relationship between market orientation export performance. Katsikea, Theodosiou, and Makri (2019) explored how the generation and dissemination of export market intelligence activities help exporters develop effective export sales strategies in serving foreign customers, suggesting that exporters must actively engage in market intelligence activities to bolster their strategic decision-making process. The present study adds to the recent literature by considering the influence of different behaviors of market orientation on performance and the antecedents of such orientation behavior. To achieve this, the present study

Following Abdul-Talib and Abd-Razak (2013), the present study defines proactive export market orientation as activities of generating, disseminating and responding to the intelligence about the export market's latent or new needs and solutions. On the other hand, responsive market orientation refers to the same set of activities administered to the current needs and solutions. Besides, more research that delve into aspect of consumer behavior and psychology in the digital economy is deemed necessary (Ling Chang, Ling Tam, & Suki, 2016; Nathan, Fook Chiun, & Suki, 2016; Suki, 2016). Specifically, the present study explores whether exporting SMEs have proactive and responsive export market orientation, the antecedents of proactive and responsive export market orientation, and the effect of proactive and responsive export market orientation on export performance.

METHODOLOGY

The present study used a qualitative approach because such an approach is more useful for discovering and providing in-depth information about issues, hidden motivations, and values (Hair, Money, Samouel, & Page, 2007). A series of interviews were conducted with Malaysian SME exporters and several agencies involved in assisting the SMEs to export. The interviews were useful to identify the export market orientation (proactive and responsive behavior) of the SMEs, the characteristics (antecedents) of the exporters that influence their export market orientation behavior, and the effect of the behavior on performance. SME exporters were deemed to represent Malaysian exporters because Malaysia is an export-driven economy and in 2012 was ranked 24th place among 144 countries in the Economic Complexity Index (ECI) (Simoes & Hidalgo, 2011; Hausmann et al., 2011).

An interview protocol was distributed to the relevant informants, who were the senior management team of the exporting firms. The team tended to include the owners/president, managing directors, and export/marketing managers. The questions in the protocol focused on the variables of interests, i.e., the firm's current behavior of export market orientation, the antecedents of market orientation, and the effect on performance. The protocol was developed based on the relevant literature. During the interview sessions, the variables of interest were probed. A total of 12 firms were interviewed. Each firm was represented by one informant and treated as one case study. The interviews were recorded and transcribed after each session. The transcriptions were then reviewed, and relevant categories/themes based on the research objectives were later developed. The interviews were concluded when no new themes emerged.

FINDINGS

The interviews were transcribed in a qualitative codebook that had three columns. The first column represented the name of the variables. The second column provided the operational definition of the variables based on the literature. The third column represented the relevant excerpts. The qualitative codebook is shown in Table 1. Following Yin's (1994) recommendation on analysing a case, the present study employed a cross-case analysis for multiple case studies.

Background of Firms Involved

Firm 1 is a shipbuilder operating in Pulau Kambing, Terengganu. Its corporate headquarters is located in Kuala Lumpur. The marketing executive in the commercialisation department was the informant. The company had been in business since 1977. It began as a subsidiary of the government under a government's agency before it was privatised in 1987. The first export activity began in 1988. Currently, it is exporting various ships and separate components to four countries. Its clientele ranges from government agencies to private companies. Its products include components, like hull to complete, sophisticated boats, and vessels.

Firm 2 is located in Kedah. It produces components for a giant international aircraft manufacturer and was established as a result of a joint venture between two foreign companies in the year 2000.

Firm 3 is an HR training and consultancy company situated in the Klang Valley. The business began its operation in 1994 as a result of a joint venture between a French man, who had a training background in the automotive industry, and a Malay man as the local partner. It has international offices including in Shanghai and New Delhi. Most of its clients are contract clients from various industries, especially automotive, airlines, manufacturing, logistics and retail, apart from government agencies.

Firm 4 is a subsidiary of a timber-based manufacturer specialising in the production of solid and engineered wooden doors. The company began operating in 1980. It is located in Selangor. Its export markets include South Korea, Australia, Europe, and the United States. The company has its marketing and distribution channel in the United Kingdom and the United States. It was the first Malaysian door manufacturer that owns significant equity control over its distributors abroad.

Firm 5 is a traditional garment producer (songket and batik) located in Terengganu. It was established in the 1970s. It began exporting to neighbouring markets in the 1990s. Recently, it experienced a high demand from the domestic market; however, it did not manage to meet the demand because of its limited supply. Now, the firm is beginning to export again but at a much smaller scale.

Firm 6 is a traditional shipbuilder in Pulau Duyong, Terengganu. It produces an extensive range of wooden ships, ranging from local traditional fisherman boats named Penambang to cruisers and yachts, all built traditionally with wood. The main export products are cruisers and yachts. The clients are individuals from Singapore, Australia, New Zealand, England, France, and other European and African nations. A client from Singapore, who was the country's president of a yacht club, also acts as its liaison officer in promoting the boats around the globe. Established in 1955, it served its first foreign client in 1965. However, since the economic downturn in 1997, there had been no foreign client up until March 2009). However, there was a request from an Australian movie maker to produce boats in April that year, and the shipbuilder is now aggressively looking for new markets abroad under the management of the owner's son.

Table 1. The Qualitative Codebook

Variable	Operational Definition	Samples of Verbatim Interview Conversation
Export Market Orientation Dimensions		
Proactive Export Market Orientation (PEMO)	Export market orientation behavior that focuses on the latent (unseen/future) potentials in the export market	• It is possible for exporters to cater to new (latent) needs, with less or no competitors (MATRADE RD) • To uncover the future needs, we'll have to have assistance from relevant bodies like the Malaysian Timber Council (MTC) and FRIM to predict the needs (Firm 8) • We spend a lot to produce designs and products that we believe would be a hit in the market based on our research (Firm 12)
Responsive Export Market Orientation (REMO)	Export market orientation behavior that focuses on the expressed potentials in the export market	• Our clients would direct us to produce specific component and we'll cater to that (Firm 2) • Our customers would inform us about their needs, and we develop the product based on their needs (Firm 6) • We depend on our customers to understand their current needs (Firm 8)
Antecedents of Export Market Orientation		
Export External Factors		
Market Dynamism	The rate of change of customer preferences, market segments, and demand patterns within the export market	• At this scale, the demand pattern seldom changes (Firm 1) • We don't experience much change in market dynamism (Firm 2) • Our market expectation remains stable (Firm 9) • Normally, customers' expectation doesn't really change (Firm 10) • Our customers love new products (Firm12)
Competitive Turbulence	The rate of competitive intensity within the export market (originating from export market competitors)	• We experienced competition from neighbouring producers with similar products (Firm 5) • Not very many players in this industry; we have unique skills and resources to produce the product (Firm 6) • Competition is very high in our industry (Firm 11)
Technological Turbulence	The rate of industrial and technological change within the export market	• We don't experience much technological change in this industry (Firm 2) • Technological changes are happening but not very fast (Firm 11) • New technologies are often being introduced in this industry (Firm 12)
Regulatory Turbulence	The rate of changes concerning the regulatory aspects of the industry within the export market	• We don't have specific sets of regulations to obey other than the general customs regulations which are quite fixed (Firm 1) • We are not aware of those things (Firm 6) • We have to adhere to standards that are often revised in the export market to keep the business, such as the environment-related standards (Firm 8) • Pricing regulations do affect our market (Firm 12)

continued on following page

Table 1. Continued

Variable	Operational Definition	Samples of Verbatim Interview Conversation
Export Structures		
Export Formalization	The extent to which rules determine members' roles, authority relations, communication norms, sanctions and procedures within the export organisation	• Certain sets of procedures exist (Firm 1) • SOP is used to execute export operation (Firm 2) • Everyone has their roles to entertain our customer's needs (Firm 3) • We are aware of our roles in export operation in this company (Firm 9)
Export Departmentalization	The number of departments into which export operations are segregated and compartmentalised within the organisation	• We normally set up an ad hoc team to supervise the production to cater to the client's needs, which comprise different functions such as finance, engineering, and HR (Firm 1) • We don't have departments within the export operation (Firm 6) • I myself handle everything in export operation (Firm 8)
Export Centralization	The lack of delegation of export market decision-making and participation of export function members in those decisions	• We don't delegate the role of decision-making to everyone; it is the boss who'll decide whether we'll proceed with any project involving foreign clients (Firm1) • Everything regarding marketing need is to be decided by the top management (Firm 10) • We tend to encourage employees to participate in decision-making (Firm 11) • Basically, everything here needs approval from the top (Firm 12)
Export Specialization	The utilisation of special marketing and managerial talent, skills or time in export activities in the export organisation	• The same employees would handle export and domestic operation, but different management team would supervise that. We have specialised personnel to observe export operation (Firm 2) • This centre is specially formed to serve foreign customers (Firm 10) • Employees are expected to have specialised knowledge related to the export market, such as language and culture (Firm 12)
Export Systems		
Export-Based Reward System	The extent of which reward is allocated to employees based on export market-based criteria, such as export customer satisfaction, export market share, and export customer retention	• Those with knowledge of the export market are regarded as influential around here (Firm 11) • We often survey our export customers to assess our salespeople (Firm 12)
Export-Based Recruit System	The extent of which recruitment for the export organisation is made on export market-based criteria, such as the knowledge of the export market, the interest in the export market, and exporting experience	• Those involved in export operation need to understand the work ethics of the clients (Firm 2) • Foreign language is important to be in this company (Firm 3) • Normally, our clients would come with their own translators, so it is not necessary for us to know their language very well (Firm 6) • We don't necessarily employ workers with an export background (Firm 9)

continued on following page

Table 1. Continued

Variable	Operational Definition	Samples of Verbatim Interview Conversation
Export-Based Training System	The extent of which training is conducted with a focus on export market-based criteria, such as courses for foreign languages and export market cultures to understand the export market better	• We would train employees with specific courses regularly, and we even open it to others from outside the company (Firm 2) • In training, we focus on skills to develop the product and explain the art to the client (Firm 6) • We send people for training and workshops related to our export product and export market (Firm 8)
Leadership Factors		
Management Commitment to Exporting	The formation of attitudes and expectations placed upon export operations by the managers	• The boss is very enthusiastic with the export operation, but we handle it very cautiously (Firm 1) • We are very keen to continue serving our export market (Firm 4) • We are expanding our operation to new markets soon (Firm 7) • With the supply problem resolved, we hope to cater to the export market even more (Firm 8)
Management Emphasis on Export Market Orientation	The signals from the management about the importance of being responsive to export potentials in the export market	• Our management considers information regarding export client as very important (Firm 1) • We don't really understand the foreign market before, but now it is important to us (Firm 6) • We heighten our reputation very much, so it is important to keep informed about the global industry (Firm 12)
Management Consensus on Exporting	The degree of agreement among the managers in running the export operations	• Generally, our managers agree when it comes to conducting an export operation, or at least we'll compromise until an agreement is reached (Firm 2) • Managers don't go about quarrelling when conducting export operation; everything is already put in place (Firm 3) • We assess the risks together and decide together (Firm 7)
Business-Specific Factors		
Export Experience	The degree exporters understand the export market through knowledge and experience gained by conducting an export operation in the market	• We have a lot of experience dealing with various kinds of clients (Firm 1) • We've served clients from about 10 markets and are able to detect the range of favourable products we offer (Firm 6) • We are among the most experienced players in the industry with more than 30 years involvement in the export market (Firm 12)
Export Resource	The availability of human, financial, information and other resources to operate and innovate in the export market	• We even forked out our own expenses to enable R&D process to take place (Firm 7) • Specific resources are available for the use of this centre (Firm 10) • We've allocated a lot of resources for R&D, investing in new machines and technology to maintain our cutting-edge advantage (Firm 12)

continued on following page

Firm 12 is a plastic products manufacturer operating in Penang and Kuala Lumpur. Its head office is situated in Kuala Lumpur. It also has a plant in China and a sales office in the United States. It began its operation in 1972. The export market was served since 1977. Therefore, it has a wide export exposure. Its major export markets are Singapore, the United States, European nations, and China. During the interview session, only the Singaporean market was discussed.

DISCUSSION

SMEs' Export Market Orientation Behaviors

The interviewed firms in the present study exhibited the generic activities of export market-oriented organisations by generating, disseminating, and responding to their export market intelligence. Apart from focusing on export customers and competitors in generating the required intelligence, other export market elements, such as export market standards and regulations and participants within the export supply chain like suppliers and retailers were also given attention. The finding thus supports the study by among others, Jaworski et al. (2000), and Zamani, Abdul-Talib, & Ashari (2016). Steps were taken by the exporters to ensure that the generated intelligence was distributed across the organisation and responded well.

In focusing on the needs and wants (potentials) of their export market, these firms realised the existence of the different potentials (latent and expressed). They also realised the different methods involved in generating, disseminating, and responding to these potentials' intelligence. In other words, different approaches were needed to deal with different potentials (latent and expressed). For example, in catering to expressed potentials, intelligence was usually generated through direct communication with the customer. In generating the intelligence of latent potentials, the exporters tended to search for information from other sources, such as industry-related bodies like FRIM and MTC for timber-based product exporters.

Antecedents of Export Market Orientation

The antecedents of export market orientation among the interviewed exporters seemed to be varied. Different antecedents appeared to influence the export market orientation of the exporters differently. The differences could be attributed to the diverse industries and sizes of exporting organisations. However, the present study was not concerned about the different antecedents; instead, it was interested in understanding how these exporters react to the different antecedents as far as the export market orientation behavior is concerned. Hence, the different antecedents signify an important indicator of how the exporters are likely to behave either proactively or responsively in their export market orientation.

Performance Consequences

Performance consequences were operationalised as long-term and short-term performance consequences. Different exporters seemed to indicate the different performance outcomes over the years. While some had enjoyed good performance in the past, others began to experience better performance in recent years. One of the reasons could be due to the different export market orientation behaviors exhibited by the firms.

These findings lead to three key assumptions: (a) exporters behave differently in their export market orientation, (b) different behaviors of export market orientation are influenced by different antecedents, and (c) different behaviors result in different performance outcomes, be they long term or short term.

THEORETICAL AND PRACTICAL IMPLICATIONS

The present study demonstrated that SMEs in Malaysia exhibit proactive and responsive behaviors of export market orientation in offering latent and expressed solutions to foreign markets. It was also found that different antecedents appeared to affect different export market orientation behaviors, which affected different performance outcomes. These empirical observations contribute to the theoretical development of export market orientation, especially with respect to proactive and responsive export market orientation behaviors, the antecedents that influence the behaviors, and the effect of the behaviors on long-term and short-term performance. Researchers may now opt to use export-specific proactive and responsive behaviors of export market orientation to understand the impact of the different behaviors on export market export performance and the antecedents of such behaviors.

Managers may benefit from the observations by assessing the firm's export market orientation behaviors (i.e., proactive or responsive behaviors) and understand how the different behaviors affect the performance of the firm. As different behaviors are affected by different antecedents, managers should consider committing their resources to influence the antecedents so that the firm could behave appropriately to serve the latent or expressed solutions to the export market to achieve the intended performance outcomes.

CONCLUSION

The findings from the interviews revealed that SME exporters behaved proactively and responsively to cater to latent or new needs and solutions in the export market. It was also found that different antecedents influenced different export market orientation behaviors. For example, some SMEs had vast export resources compared to the others, and some had a departmentalised structure in export operation, affecting their behavior of whether to be proactive or responsive in catering to the export market needs. As a result, the different behavior also appeared to make a difference in the firm's performance.

While the link between the antecedents, the market orientation behavior, and performance outcomes remains speculative as a result of the methodological approach used, further investigation is necessary to verify and validate the link. If the link is supported, SME exporters could benefit as they will be able to decide the preferred behavior in dealing with export market needs as a result of the export market environment (i.e., antecedents) to achieve the desired performance.

REFERENCES

Abdul-Talib, A. N., & Abd-Razak, I. S. (2012). Export market oriented behaviors within the medical tourism industry: A case study. *International Journal of Tourism Policy*, *4*(4), 289–301. doi:10.1504/IJTP.2012.052546

Wei, Z., Zhao, J., & Zhang, C. (2014). Organizational ambidexterity, market orientation, and firm performance. *Journal of Engineering and Technology Management, 33*, 134–153. doi:10.1016/j.jengtecman.2014.06.001

Yin, R. K. (1994). *Case study research: Design and methods* (2nd ed.). Sage.

Zamani, S. N. M., Abdul-Talib, A. N., & Ashari, H. (2016). Strategic orientations and new product success: The mediating impact of innovation speed. International Information Institute (Tokyo). Information, 19(7B), 2785.

Zhang, J., & Duan, Y. (2010). The impact of different types of market orientation on product innovation performance: Evidence from Chinese manufacturers. *Management Decision, 48*(6), 849–867. doi:10.1108/00251741011053433

Zou, S., Taylor, C. R., & Osland, G. E. (1998). The EXPERF Scale: A cross-national generalized export performance measure. *Journal of International Marketing, 6*(3), 37–58. doi:10.1177/1069031X9800600307

Chapter 13
Managing Innovation:
Technology, Consumer and Sustainability Perspective, and the Challenges

Siao Fong Tan
Universiti Utara Malysia, Malaysia

ABSTRACT

This study emphasizes the overview of technology innovation that comprises the definition and the technological innovation categories distinction; the overview of consumer attitude towards product innovation focused on the consumer demand on innovative products, the stimulus purchasing factor, and the consumer satisfactory factors over product innovation; overview of sustainability innovation; innovation management as part of the strategic management; and challenges on innovative strategy formulation and implementation. Innovation strategy formulation requires detailed assessments on potential technological advancement, consumers' attitudes on innovative products, and sustainability impact on innovative initiatives. Innovation strategy is perceived as part of the strategic management, and the implementation depends on intra-organizational factors. The employee innovation adoptions as the connection between technological innovation, consumer behavior towards product innovation, and innovative sustainability for innovation strategy formulation can be further studied.

INTRODUCTION

Innovation can be heard everywhere. Innovation touches every aspect of people daily life. It is not only technological in how people perceived but it covers all areas which includes humanities, sociology, economics, businesses, educations and even arts and history. It emerged beyond to sustainability in modern society. There will be no ending for innovation. Innovation is defined in many ways from different perspective. By dictionary innovation is defined as "the action or process of innovating" and innovate is defined as "make changes in something established, especially by introducing new methods, ideas, or products".

DOI: 10.4018/978-1-7998-3042-9.ch013

The discontinuous technology innovation can lead to either a radical innovation or to an incremental innovation. A technological discontinuous does not impact the existing market infrastructure. Incremental innovation is most common where the product features and usage are evolved and expanded to provide consumer satisfaction.

The incremental innovation does not change the macro market and technological perspective, it only reflects in micro perspective. Imitative innovation is adopting the others innovation in the own products, or it is called innovation followers. Organization adopted imitative innovation to increase its competencies while research and development is not the strength of the organization.

Overview of Consumer Attitude towards Product Innovation

The rising customer expectation has become the market pull factor that pressures organization in putting efforts for product innovation. Customer expectation does not stay, in fact the speed of customer changing expectation has keep increasing. There are multiple models that demonstrate the consumer behavior in purchasing stimulus. The famous one is Marlow's Hierarchy of Needs ranging the purchasing motivation from bottom to up: (1) psychological needs, (2) safety needs, (3) social needs, (4) esteem needs and (5) self-actualization needs (Marlow. 1970). Kotler et all (2018) further expand the self-actualization needs to affiliation, admiration and status that enhance the purchasers image and position. Here we can relate the product innovation with consumer esteem needs and self-actualization needs where product innovation satisfies these needs.

Organization in modern economy takes new product development seriously to gain better position in growth and survival (Bhuiyan,2013). The new product development is embedding with innovation strategies to create value to customers and consumers. In strategic marketing, market orientation and product innovation are highly interrelated if it is properly executed. Market orientation emphasizes two component, customer focus in market intelligence and coordination related to market intelligence to create superior buyer value.(Kohli & Jaworski, I990). The components of customer focus are not just limit to customer research, but also include taking action after the evaluation of customer current and future needs and market factors. Product innovation comes along with market intelligence in new product development. Organizations are slowly shifting from product orientation to market orientation in view of higher success rates. Lukas and Ferrell (2000) study also associates market or customer orientation with product innovation where the introduction of new-to-the-world products has increased why me-too products were reduced.

Consumer nowadays is no longer satisfied in status quo but looking forward for something new and exciting. For a simple example, people cook to satisfy hunger needs. Cooking on gas on stove no longer satisfying, more and more electric cooking appliances launches in market and now these appliances are further evolves to equip with intelligence capabilities. The evolvement and innovations are the results of never satisfied consumer behavior. Innovation has also to a certain extent been recognized as a key characteristic of the individual in psychology. In Martin Heidegger's philosophy of human nature, there are three elements of human nature identified: (1) it is human nature to be practically involved in a complex world rather than rationally involved with a conceptually simplified world; (2) it is human nature to be authentic (i.e., unconventional, uncommitted to one's paradigm) at least some of the time; and (3) it is human nature to be cooperative. From Heidegger's theory, Carol J. Steiner presents a philosophy of innovation. Suggesting that rather conventional science, technology or engineering, innovation success is mostly credited to unauthenticity of individuals (i.e. unconventional and unscientific). From

Chapter 13
Managing Innovation:
Technology, Consumer and Sustainability Perspective, and the Challenges

Siao Fong Tan
Universiti Utara Malysia, Malaysia

ABSTRACT

This study emphasizes the overview of technology innovation that comprises the definition and the technological innovation categories distinction; the overview of consumer attitude towards product innovation focused on the consumer demand on innovative products, the stimulus purchasing factor, and the consumer satisfactory factors over product innovation; overview of sustainability innovation; innovation management as part of the strategic management; and challenges on innovative strategy formulation and implementation. Innovation strategy formulation requires detailed assessments on potential technological advancement, consumers' attitudes on innovative products, and sustainability impact on innovative initiatives. Innovation strategy is perceived as part of the strategic management, and the implementation depends on intra-organizational factors. The employee innovation adoptions as the connection between technological innovation, consumer behavior towards product innovation, and innovative sustainability for innovation strategy formulation can be further studied.

INTRODUCTION

Innovation can be heard everywhere. Innovation touches every aspect of people daily life. It is not only technological in how people perceived but it covers all areas which includes humanities, sociology, economics, businesses, educations and even arts and history. It emerged beyond to sustainability in modern society. There will be no ending for innovation. Innovation is defined in many ways from different perspective. By dictionary innovation is defined as "the action or process of innovating" and innovate is defined as "make changes in something established, especially by introducing new methods, ideas, or products".

DOI: 10.4018/978-1-7998-3042-9.ch013

The discontinuous technology innovation can lead to either a radical innovation or to an incremental innovation. A technological discontinuous does not impact the existing market infrastructure. Incremental innovation is most common where the product features and usage are evolved and expanded to provide consumer satisfaction.

The incremental innovation does not change the macro market and technological perspective, it only reflects in micro perspective. Imitative innovation is adopting the others innovation in the own products, or it is called innovation followers. Organization adopted imitative innovation to increase its competencies while research and development is not the strength of the organization.

Overview of Consumer Attitude towards Product Innovation

The rising customer expectation has become the market pull factor that pressures organization in putting efforts for product innovation. Customer expectation does not stay, in fact the speed of customer changing expectation has keep increasing. There are multiple models that demonstrate the consumer behavior in purchasing stimulus. The famous one is Marlow's Hierarchy of Needs ranging the purchasing motivation from bottom to up: (1) psychological needs, (2) safety needs, (3) social needs, (4) esteem needs and (5) self-actualization needs (Marlow. 1970). Kotler et all (2018) further expand the self-actualization needs to affiliation, admiration and status that enhance the purchasers image and position. Here we can relate the product innovation with consumer esteem needs and self-actualization needs where product innovation satisfies these needs.

Organization in modern economy takes new product development seriously to gain better position in growth and survival (Bhuiyan,2013). The new product development is embedding with innovation strategies to create value to customers and consumers. In strategic marketing, market orientation and product innovation are highly interrelated if it is properly executed. Market orientation emphasizes two component, customer focus in market intelligence and coordination related to market intelligence to create superior buyer value.(Kohli & Jaworski, I990). The components of customer focus are not just limit to customer research, but also include taking action after the evaluation of customer current and future needs and market factors. Product innovation comes along with market intelligence in new product development. Organizations are slowly shifting from product orientation to market orientation in view of higher success rates. Lukas and Ferrell (2000) study also associates market or customer orientation with product innovation where the introduction of new-to-the-world products has increased why me-too products were reduced.

Consumer nowadays is no longer satisfied in status quo but looking forward for something new and exciting. For a simple example, people cook to satisfy hunger needs. Cooking on gas on stove no longer satisfying, more and more electric cooking appliances launches in market and now these appliances are further evolves to equip with intelligence capabilities. The evolvement and innovations are the results of never satisfied consumer behavior. Innovation has also to a certain extent been recognized as a key characteristic of the individual in psychology. In Martin Heidegger's philosophy of human nature, there are three elements of human nature identified: (1) it is human nature to be practically involved in a complex world rather than rationally involved with a conceptually simplified world; (2) it is human nature to be authentic (i.e., unconventional, uncommitted to one's paradigm) at least some of the time; and (3) it is human nature to be cooperative. From Heidegger's theory, Carol J. Steiner presents a philosophy of innovation. Suggesting that rather conventional science, technology or engineering, innovation success is mostly credited to unauthenticity of individuals (i.e. unconventional and unscientific). From the consumer behavior perspective, it's the inner innovation in human nature that urges the needs of product innovation. It's the psychological desires of individual to be extraordinary. Product innovation can enhance relationship with consumers; consumers feel they are special, being valued and product innovation solves their getting complex daily life.

Overview of Sustainability Innovation

"Sustainability", is a big world in modern society. It's been talked and discussed in every aspect of life. Sustainability meant for continuous resources for future generations. Various environmental research and reports show that with the speed of current production and consumption, the sustainability is going to be a global issue. For larger picture, sustainability encompasses three major aspects: social, economic and environment and these three aspects are intersecting and further detail the view of sustainability development to social-economic, social-environment and economic-environment aspects (Barbier, 1987). Industrialization has huge impact on environment. Ironically, innovation and technology form parts of the industrialization process and contributed to industrialization spurt. However the current and coming sustainability issues had forced organizations to think and act innovatively, along with the stricter government policies.

"Innovation is the act that endows resources with a new capacity to create wealth. Innovation indeed creates a resource. There is no such thing as a resource until man finds a use for something in nature and thus endows it with economic value" (Drucker, 1985). Innovation has been expanding in view of sustainability, to reduce the use of scares resources, venture into scares resources substitution, to put to end the action of damaging the earth. Innovation is just not only satisfying customers need or creates competitive advantage for the organization. Sustainability is not only treated as the process to fix the environmental issue for example pollution and scares resources issues which very happening in between 1990s to 2000s. Indeed, from 2000s, sustainability innovation idea has been brought up and defined as combine all the aspect in a systems thinking approach that drives entrepreneurial innovation.

From organization's perspective, sustainability is seeing as in very different opinion. Some believe that sustainability is some opportunity to create competitive advantage and stand out from competitors. Conversely, sustainability is seeing as constrain to organization especially from costing perspective. For the organization that believes in sustainability development, the sustainability innovation becomes the key aspect or even core of the business model. A year 2012 MIT-Sloan global survey shows that although only 37% of the respondents stated that they have profited from sustainability activities, however 63% of the respondents agreed that their changed their business model in response to sustainability (David, et all, 2013). It is obvious that the organizations are in the mode of sustainability transition. The sustainability development is highly intertwined by technology in the social structure (Rip & Kemp, 1998) where the socio-technologies are evolving in incremental manner due to complexity of social structures (Dosi, 1982; Frantzeskaki & Loorbach, 2010; Markard & Truffer, 2006). Hence, sustainability can consider as one of the factor that drive innovation.

Relationship of Technology, Consumer Attitude and Sustainability towards Innovation

Technology is always associated with Innovation. It is said to be the results of innovation. Technology has become the core development of modern economies in an organization; otherwise the organization

Table 1. Innovation Landscape Map

Business model	Type of innovation strategy	
Require new business model	*Disruptive*	*Architectural*
Leverage existing business model	*Routine*	*Radical*
	Leverage technical competency	Required new technical competency
	Technical competency	

Table 2. Chuck's innovative strategy

Market	**Disruptive**	Market Innovation	Disruptive Innovation
	Incremental	Incremental Innovation	Product Innovation
		Incremental	**Disruptive**
		Product	

"Creativity" always been heard in organization mission or tag line. Indeed many of the organization faces tremendous challenges when trying the catch up with the latest trend for being innovative. One of the biggest problems is the organization failed to identify the need for innovativeness change. This is particularly common in traditional and conservative organization where the leaders are comfort in current performance and fail to mitigate the possible future risk.

Many organizations also recognize they are unsure how to position themselves to adopt innovative strategies. They cannot identify the cause of innovative initiative whether to create something really new in market, supplement the existing products with some innovation or be innovate in sustainability. Strategic management is long term planning for goal achievement. Innovation management is much shorter due to technological change that progresses too fast. An effective strategy formulation and implementation needs to be driven by strong leadership (Hrebiniak, 2005). The leaders under-estimate the importance or failed to recognize the importance of innovation in core competency and competitive advantage identification. A failure innovation strategy implementation also causes by unclear direction and low commitment from top management.

Many times the brilliant innovative ideas just do not meet the economies of scales that allow the organization to continue the development. The organization had to consider carefully before the investment of capital and resources to realized innovative initiatives. In other word, not all innovative initiatives have economic values. Many organizations fall into this trap for trying to become the market leaders. The organization faces challenge in the innovation strategy formulation especially when they wrongly selected the innovative strategy that does not meet the economies of scales which represent the organization financial success.

The innovation strategy implementation and execution required realignment of strategy, organization structures, human capital, staff skillset, systems, policies and leadership styles. The innovative idea from a brilliant leader required intra-organizational cooperation to achieve his/her vision. Often the innovation strategy faces barriers from intra-organizational issue. The common failure is cause by miss-match of structure with innovation strategy. An organization that decided to on product differentiation strategy from innovative perspective requires a sophisticated research and development department that provides technical knowledge on product development. Hence this research and development department gained the superiority in the organization structure while marketing play the roles for product positioning. Miss-matched of human resource skillsets can be another barrier to achieve the organizational goal. To run innovative projects required talents with specific skillsets which can source from intra-organization or acquire from inter-organization. If an innovative strategy over-look this aspects, the whole strategy is unlike to even start. Same concept applies to organization systems and policies where an organization faces challenge during innovation strategy implementation. Employees' resistance also causes strategy implementation issue where the innovative internal process for efficiencies may cause job loss to operational staff especially those who shows skillsets gap.

Sustainability issues may become the show stopper to innovative strategy implementation. The limited earth resources and environmental issues awareness had keep increasing among people and nations. In modern economies, any of the organizations are expose to the strict regulations and watch of activist. A small component that might cause environmental issue would be called-off forcedly by regulator or pressure from activists. If the innovation strategy is potentially exposed to sustainability issues during development, the organization faces stiffer condition for innovative products launching.

Influence of Consumer Innovation Adoption to Innovation Strategy

Consumer innovation adoption plays an important role to encourage the organizations to venture into innovative product and market their new product more effectively. Rogers (1995, 21) defines the adoption process as ''the process through which an individual or other decision-making unit passes from first knowledge of an innovation, to forming an attitude toward the innovation, to a decision to adopt or reject, to implementation of the new idea, and to confirmation of this decision." Organization innovation strategy is highly dependent on consumer's innovation acceptance. Roger (2003, 177) describes the innovation adoption as a decision to fully utilization of innovation products by consumer. Innovation adoption by consumer is influenced by consumer's perception on innovative products, judging from innovative product characteristics which include "relative advantage", "complexity", "compatibility", "trialability", and "observability" (Roger, 2013, 277). In Arts et al. (2011) research, they suggested that the marketing strategy of innovation products should relate to consumer intention and behavior as consumer innovation adoption in order to precisely predict the consumer demand on innovative products.

Innovation adoption is further influenced by eco-innovation adoption. Eco-innovation is highly emphasized in recent years by nations and NGOs. Many researches on level of consumer adoption on eco-innovative products had been conducted to study the consumer's behavior and adoption on eco-innovative products. Jansson's (2011) survey shows that consumer's eco-innovation adoption also highly influenced by the five innovative characteristic as proposed by Roger (2003).

FUTURE RESEARCH DIRECTIONS

Strategic management had been perceived as solution for all organization problems and it was treated as essence of organization management. All the leaders are well aware of its importance for organization sustainability but still many organizations could not avoid the fallen to be happened. Although innovation management is perceived as part of the strategic management but many firms proved that the excellence innovation management is the fate turning point for those organizations that struggled for survival. It is

Mowery, D., & Rosenberg, N. (1979). The influence of market demand upon innovation: A critical review of some recent empirical studies. *Research Policy*, *8*(2), 102–153. doi:10.1016/0048-7333(79)90019-2

Nathan, R. J., Fook Chiun, D. C., & Suki, N. M. (2016). An online marketing strategies assessment for companies in airlines and entertainment industries in Malaysia. Handbook of Research on Leveraging Consumer Psychology for Effective Customer Engagement, 1-15.

Pisano. (2015). *You need an Innovation Strategy*. Retrieved from https://hbr.org/2015/06/you-need-an-innovation-strategy

Rip, A., & Kemp, R. (1998). Technological change. In S. Rayner & E. L. Malone (Eds.), *Human Choice and Climate Change – Resources and Technology* (pp. 327–399). Columbus: Battelle Press.

Rogers, E. M. (1995). *Diffusion of innovations* (4th ed.). New York: The Free Press.

Rogers, E. M. (2003). *Diffusion of innovations* (5th ed.). New York: The Free Press.

Skillicorn, N. (2016). *What is innovation? 15 experts share their innovation definition*. Retrieved from https://www.ideatovalue.com/inno/nickskillicorn/2016/03/innovation-15-experts-share-innovation-definition

Song, X. M., & Montoya-Weiss, M. M. (1998). Critical Development Activities for Really New versus Incremental Products. *Journal of Product Innovation Management*, *15*(2), 124–135. doi:10.1111/1540-5885.1520124

Steiner, C. (1995). A Philosophy for Innovation: The Role of Unconventional Individuals in Innovation Success. *Journal of Product Innovation Management*, *12*(5), 431–440. doi:10.1111/1540-5885.1250431

Stern, P. C. (1999). A Value-Belief-Norm Theory of Support for Social Movements: The Case of Environmentalism. *Research in Human Ecology.*, *6*(2), 81–97.

Suki, N. M. (2016). *Handbook of Research on Leveraging Consumer Psychology for Effective Customer Engagement*. https://www.igi-global.com/book/handbook-research-leveraging-consumer-psychology/149284

Tidd, J., & Bessant, J. (2014). *Strategic innovation management*. New York: John Wiley & Sons.

Chapter 14
The Implication of Sustainability Innovation:
Blue Ocean Strategy

Izwan Shukor
Universiti Utara Malaysia, Malaysia

ABSTRACT

In the past, the economy was solely dependent on natural resources, but it moved to manufacturing and is now focusing on service delivery. Government roles in implementing policies are needed in order to ensure natural resources are transformed. The production of business delivery is getting more innovative; therefore, research and development are aligned with the goals for sustainability.

INTRODUCTION

In the modern day the entrepreneurship has become closely related to innovation. It became one of the challenges of modern entrepreneurships that need to be overcome by most enterprise. Innovation is critically significant not only to enterprise but also to the people and its nation. The pace of technological advancement and innovation will be accelerated much more in the future. The revolution of the economic phase moves from one to another as it aligns with the objective of the country's economy moving forwards. At first, most of the world economies are fully dependent natural resources economies. As according to Organization Economic Corporations for Development (n.d.), some study shows that there is negative relationship between the lavishness of natural resources to the sustainable of economic growth. It was also found that between the growths of Gross Domestic Product (GDP) with the ratio of natural resources exports to GDP in 97 developing countries has negative relationship (Sachs& Warner, 1995). According to OECD (2008), it is been assumed in such transition country's economy will expose to risk as if they are not taking explicit measure when there is such negative relationship to the resource's endowments (Kronenberg, 2004). Extant research noted that most countries start to move forwards on taking steps to improve and start to plan and implemented policies to ensure natural resources to be transformed to be more sustain and positively contribute to social wellbeing of the people. Indeed, more research that

DOI: 10.4018/978-1-7998-3042-9.ch014

delve into aspect of consumer behavior and psychology in the digital economy is deemed necessary (Ling Chang, Ling Tam, & Suki, 2016; Nathan, Fook Chiun, & Suki, 2016; Suki, 2016).

World economic make a transition moving forwards from natural resources dependency to manufacturing economy driven as most of the third world are doing now. With the advancement of technology progressively it changes the human life to better place as it not only for automated tools but also to become highly advance for new technology (West, 2015). The technological advancement can neither be stop nor be slow down. As according to West (2015), people can keep on criticized about the dehumanizing impact as it is significant for us to regulate what best for the employment in the country that could affect the economy of the countries. The manufacturing industries has been put the environmental aspect at risk and vulnerable. To improve such issue from spreading the industry has been fast moving shifting it nature to innovation driven economy. For instance, as according Tan & Phang (2005), in order to be continuously competitive in the market, the development have led the economist in Singapore to be more innovative by developing its own brand to be more marketable of their product and services. It is also mentioned that efficiency in doing business are not enough to ensure the survival and the growth of the organization (Tan & Phang, 2005). It can be said that, innovation economy driven can be considered to be familiarizing in the concept of economy in achieving it uppermost level of economy. These are the reasons why most country starting to shift the level of innovation economy driven.

As well all can be seen most big companies are really on how they can really be more innovative effort and focusing on how they are trying to survive in such competitive and modern world. The worlds of business have becoming more dynamic and complex. For example, Nokia, Kodak, Blackberry such multi-billionaire company that have loss its influence and power in this vast flea market. The company is well anticipating the vision of their company to be expected to be surviving for very long term. Around the world things have change in this modern era, which predominantly every element in around the world in various aspects needs to be more innovative. Nowadays global industries are getting more highlights on the Industrial Revolution 4.0. As mentioned by Rojko (2017), the idea of Industrial 4.0 basically is more emphasizing on the viability and the usage of Internet of Things, adaption and integration between technical processes and business process in the companies and digital mapping and virtualizing the real world into a whole new level. As according to Manda (2019), the concept in the new industrial revolution 4.0 required more innovative products and services, business model that adapt to innovation that are led by the technological advancement. As things in the business are getting more innovate, research and development (R&D) has become a crucial driver to ensure the sustainability of the company as much as it significant to business to Industrial Revolution 4.0 (Manda, 2019).

As they moving forward to that achievement, the nation needs to be more innovation and be less independent of the natural resources. Resources also should be secure for the next generation as this issue brings to the concept of sustainability. Focuses been given to the strategies in ensuring the digitalization as it should be able to bring positivity towards the issue of society and development challenges by intensification emphasis on sustainability growth of the country (Buhr, 2015). These challenges need to be address not only to enterprise but also the government in dealing with the issues in such innovative ways.

SUSTAINABILITY INNOVATION

The activities in doing entrepreneurship in this modern era and digitalization are become harder. It is becoming more complex. Societal and environmental issues are now at the forefront shall be face by most enterprises globally. All of the organization currently in the way to the journey towards sustainability. Organization needs to start to engage the entirely internal, external customer and all relevant stakeholders' to stimulated collective energy in order to address this issue. Therefore, it is must for all organizations; firms or enterprises start on transforming by designing programs that help the people to learn about obstacles that arise in facing sustainability. Such issue can be resolve through people on way by engaging through innovation. As according to Kanter (2006), it is been reported that there are growing interest on products and services in offering new structures and functionality in meeting with sustainability with innovation that already been mostly include to all aspect such as global information, digital technology and etc.

As according to Blowfield, et. al. (2008), sustainability innovation can be defined in so many ways. At first the past principle in defining sustainability innovation is clearly innovation directly towards sustainability goals. For example, innovation that is done by generating electricity with less emission as compared production from current power station. The next usage of this term is the innovation of process producing product in which it excludes the sustainability issues as a main subject but still in the direction of the development production and the usage of the products in such sustainability manner. Lastly, the term for sustainable innovation in which the concept are sustainable within the company. The definition not only to achieve the sustainability goals but to improve the process to be more sustain with innovative driven in order to ensure the key survival of the organization in these competitive markets.

Business sustainability is placing such value and its significance towards the stakeholders, the environment and also the society. It is the ability or capability to maintain or sustain without endangering the potential of the next generation in carrying out businesses. It is important to ensure the survival of the business bring lower impact on the global or local environment or the public itself. The challenges that need to be face by current business it essential to be transform into opportunity or bigger prospect that could enlarge nature of the business itself. In entrepreneurship, innovation can help the business or the organization to keep on thinking and came out with new products. When limitation of the revolution on the products rises due to limited of resources and these limitations has create boundary to the organization in moving forwards. The conditions stimulate the way of thinking to seek for new alternative to solve such problem with limited resources.

As they strive to achieve new options in searching or getting out from the vast competitive market it is crucial for the organization to look such condition as an advantage to help them being enable to see the struggle of their current position from a different point of views. By looking upon new ways of solving the issues, it could be possibly helping the business to create new goals with new competitive advantages factors. It would be a catastrophic for the business if the company only perceive the sustainable innovation approaches as one tool that to get bigger profit. They should use the concept of sustainability and innovation to be embedded in the culture of the company for longer survival in the market and prosperity. The concept of sustainable innovation not only able to grow profit for longer term but also de-risk the business from any harm in the future.

IMPLICATION ON SUSTAINABLE INNOVATION

Reduce Resource and Energy Consumption

The usage of innovation sustainability in business will help not only for the company to last long in the market but also to preserve our planet. The consumption that we consume not only to fulfil our needs but also to protect the place that we are living in. With the innovation sustainability it helps not only business but also the community to reduce resources consumption as it is the one of the highest priority issues in sustainability. The change in climate whether, the pollution that happen to our surrounding can be threat to our long-term prosperity. In this context, for business it the responsibility of the corporate to ensure the way of doing the business, operatively and management are accountable to the environment and reduce negative impact as lows as possible. As according to Scott (2017), eradicating or eliminate no product or could be said as waste and others in such forms becoming more innovative in the process. Waste minimization it has been taken to be seen as a first effort on moving forwards to sustainability. The effort on waste minimization has enabled to assist in promoting innovation by reducing the disposal cost and diminish its pollutant and outlays of pollution.

Maximize Societal and Environmental Benefits

The effort of sustainable innovation would help the company to benefit environment as well as society. As according to Bocken et al. (2014), instead of emphasizing or prioritizing on economic growth a system designed for sustainable innovation should be benefiting the societal and environmental. For example, as mentioned by Bocken et. al (2014) the focuses should be advantages that is provided to the society and the environment respectively. In such way, the model of the sustainable business model could be not concentrating on the economically such a hybrid car when it first was introduced but, in the future, it will somehow change the market view that based in the change in the regulatory system. The approaches of innovation in sustainability well provide advantages the society as well as the ecosystem. Sustainability innovation brings high value of the waste into something valuable. As according to Kurdve et. al (2015), as it mentioned that from the environmental and businesses perspective by decreasing the usage if material is way better than reuse the waste tool which can be considered that is way better than recycling the material far way better than treatment recovery over energy usage or removal the waste in the landfill to be spread to our ecosystem and environment. As much can be said preventive approaches are better than cure. By converting the waste into high value resources this will helps the ecosystem to reduce the issues on wastage of natural resources. The issue of wastage of resources can be counterpart through recycling which could be considered as traditional method in preserving the natural resources.

Promote a Closed Loop System Where Nothing is Wasted

The concept of sustainability is interconnected between ecological societal and economical. With such determination by company to promote sustainability, as they highly valued the resources and raw material in such a way of recycling reuse it still helps the environment from being exposed to the externalities produce by the company. The externalities that are less produce could help the company to reduce to pay on the expenses and eventually somehow will lower the cost of the production. With innovation element consider in creating better product, in the way they recycling it can transform the product to their other new products. This will not only benefit to lower the cost of production but also brings value to the societal as it affordable to the users and therefore increase the profitability of the company which will cultivate the development economy of the countries.

As according to European Parliament (2016), the concept of circular economy suggests that such concept can reduce the waste to a minimum level. It is been said that the product can be kept in the economy even though the lifetime period of the products reaches it end. In other words, the material will be used again and again by ensuring the consistencies of the value are well preserved. The concept where wastes are to be considered as valuable resources has been used to many companies in different kind of sectors and industries.

Promote Delivery of Functionality / Experience Over Ownership

Apart from that, the sustainability innovation could help the company or enterprises to promote delivery of functionality or experiences over possession. The usage of the concept helps the company to have better understanding on the knowledge on what is being developed from the products. The suggestion of such values is to shift the consumer to a user. As according to EY (2014), there is a change need to be made by rediscovering for the role of technology and the consumers. It is been expected to make a transition from industrial product to creation of intangibles in which this transition known as service dominant logical behavioural economic that interpreting the value creation. From such value it creates the product that are emphasizing on functionality in which it can reuse or to be repaired. As according to White et. al (2019), there will be lot of potential for aggressive expansion and greater long-term profit for the firm not only be able to considered sustainable operations but getting into the model of business and use for strategic approaches. For example, growing in "sharing economy" illustrates the extensive environmental and economic achievements are promising through shifting users sustainably in this perspective, converting from have possession of the products to gain access to current products and services.

Encourage as System Built on Collaboration and Sharing

Engagement with the stakeholder in promoting sustainable innovation in the company or organization is very crucial in order to ensure such concept become a success longevity of the product and the organization in the world of business. To succeed the effort of sustainability innovation in the company, it is a must for the stakeholder to have collaboration and share the knowledge skills and ability among the stakeholders themselves. Different innovative business strategy could help to find all the strength and weaknesses but it requires the internal stakeholders of the organization to be innovative who typically don't have in their job descriptions. The collaboration among the stakeholder helps the management to seek the solutions for enhancement of the product. The stakeholders of the company or firm have better understanding on the products or services that are being developed. The faults or flaws of the product only can be seen from the perspective of the stakeholders. The management need to pay attention on what the stakeholder could probably decide what best for the whole products. The inclusion among all stakeholders is the key to a success product.

IMPACT FOR NOT APPLYING TO SUSTAINABILITY INNOVATION

Company Profitability Will Start to Slow Down the Pace

Company will face a serious implication on the performance as they are unable to understand on the application and the success of sustainability innovation could lead them into. The company may face a fall down on the profitability if they not apply the sustainability innovations. Unable to comply with the demands, profit will start to move slow as consumers start to find alternative that is more affordable and has its own features. Such unhappy stakeholder and investors could be the obstacles to company profitability. Companies can improve the way of their strategy by having better understanding the interconnection on the companies' environment, the capability on being innovative and emphasizing on brand quality with highly level of committed workforce and providing such effective and efficient communication approaches. Most of the companies have been able to see in way of improving the process of the operations, the brands itself and profitability can be done through social responsiveness and sustainability initiatives (Nastanski, et.al, 2014). For instances, the sports brand Nike is one of the examples. The company were once being viewed as a company that provide slave wages, workforce is forced to do overtime, and haphazard abuse, yet the company has led the way for the use of social approachability and as a "reagent for innovation and use of sustainability values to produce ongoing value of creation" (Paine, 2014).

Performance are Low and Less Productivity

When the company unable to be more innovative on its products creation it considered being less variation on the products. To sustain for longer term, management of the company should look back in the early process, without the control over resources consumption it will harm the productions along with the deterioration of the environment. Therefore, as a producer as well as consumers they need to ensure such consumption over natural resources need to be well manage so that the resources are able to meet the currents need without compromising the next or future generations. For instance, as mentioned by Interagency Report (2012), the application science and technology to increase the yield, Green Revolution improved the quality and increasing the productivity with supplemented input have benefited large numbers of shareholders in agricultural industries. The applications of technological have increase the productivity as well as it preserves the environment. They mentioned that they need to move forwards on converting from supply-driven innovation to demand-driven innovation. Such practices have been taken initiative by several other countries in ensuring inclusivity.

As according to National Economic Advisory Council (n.d.) the concept of the New Economic Model is one of the approaches use by the government in ensuring sustainability to both economic and environment. Malaysia dependencies on natural consumption are not sustainable in as the exploitation on natural resources that have the key survival to the national productions. The government has taken the issue into consideration in ensuring the environments are well preserve by promoting innovation through entrepreneurship.

Market Share Will Drop and Loyalty Towards the Product are Deteriorating

As productivity goes down with profit, investors are not interested to invest in the company as it loses the investor's profit shares. The falls down are due to the company unable to comply with the demands of the peoples. People's needs are dynamic as it rapidly changes and businesses need to stay alert on the current market. In order to stay alert with the trend, this is where element of innovation needs to be applied. In some industries, customer expect new product and new services whether there is more stability on the product but if the company be more innovative with their own product or services they can really stand out to the customer will take second look or to those customers that has lose trust on their products could give the company chances to take look back on the new product that they have to offers. Innovation in that area it is the best way to show growth in the business.

The innovation on the products could make the uniqueness and exclusivity of the product which gives competitive advantages as compared the other that have in the current markets. The company will lose its attractiveness if the products that they produce are the same as others, in which here customer prescription towards the product will look upon the differences on the quality the price and others. The level of ambition of business model innovations needs to be high and focused on maximizing societal and environmental benefits, rather than economic gain only. Business model innovations for sustain-ability may not be economically viable at the start (e.g. as in the time when the first hybrid car was introduced) but may become so in the future due to regulatory or other changes

CHALLENGES IN IMPLEMENTING SUSTAINABILITY INNOVATION

The reluctant in some organization to implemented the innovation appears it encounter several problems in the journey towards sustainability. It requires from the top management to the lower level of the organization need to encounter and belief in such concept can help the organization to sustain well and remain significant in the market. Some organization may have lack of method for systematic sustainable product innovation. In the early action need to take to understand on what way the company should do. Proper training and reliable information for sustainability innovation should be given to the entire internal stakeholder inside the organization. For example, as according to United Nation System Task Team (2015), with the way of a company providing knowledge based with technological along with the capability for innovation it is highly significant to allow the essential facilitation to all is foundation in ensuring overall sustainable development.

It will become the limitation of the existing technologies if the countries are unable to develops the capability to innovate in which it includes all sectors that could affect the society, environment and also the economy. It is also need for reliable information as it requires the organization to study on what's would be the best to creation of the product that could sustain and compete with other's product in the current market. They need to identify what are the strength and the weaknesses of the product; throughout this process it will help the company to find systematic approaches that consistently help the stakeholders to create more innovative products.

Another counterpart is the lack of data on impacts of current initiatives. Absences to the key performance of indicators in sustainability innovation are the loop holes for such efforts. Innovation is about a trial and error it could provide a high risk in ensuring for a high profit. Innovative is a brand-new thing that brings extra value to our products. There is default to be measured as the sustainability if innovations are more subjective as it can be. As according to Callander and Matouschek (2019), there is a risk to innovation as there is a relationship between the willingness to experiment and engaging to risk. It establishes the concept of trial approach and it is the process of learning to improve our current performance. The main point of risk for innovation has a string relationship with the willingness of agents to experiment and willingness to deal with the risk. To discover this association, cultivate a model of trial and error learning process with risk adverse agents. We show how risk abhorrence drives equally the pronouncement whether to experiment and the boldness of experimentation of individual agents. In such way learning trial and error are sufficient in order to help the business to get a collective data in assist the way for sustainable innovations. Most of top management would be more likely to do so rather than not to hold onto and grow and fall behind from their competitors. As far as being concern of the issue is that, problems does not solve over time, by meaning it take time to improve to understand the real issue before it can have better shape and longer in the world of businesses (Callander, & Matouschek (2019).

Another common problem that may face by most of the company in getting the sustainability innovation to be done is the perception of the stakeholders. Some may reluctant to see such effort as the key to a success business model. Some may perceive it incurred cost with low opportunity of success. As according to Mosher and Smith (2015), in order to ensure the successfulness of sustainability innovations, it is the organization responsibilities taking it at high level of priority to confront with the pressure of business manager and to make a clear understand of the vision towards sustainability. For example, as according to Whelan and Fink (2016), in the industries for constructions and property for operates rate on slim edge found that ten largest contractors are having an average before tax on profit margin of negative 0.5% in the year of 2017. Thus, priority is been given to ensuring cost saving to al kind if business, in such sustainable business cannot be seen as separable entities for the origination as it need to move along with excursion of the company in applying sustainability innovation approaches. The support of from top to bottom and all over the hierarchy of the organization should be taken seriously and understand the effort for the survival of the organization.

Blue Ocean Strategy with Sustainable Innovation

The blue ocean strategy helps the business to make a strategic marketing plan for entrepreneurs to explore the vast and variety marketing options. The model allows the businesses to pursuit innovation that applicable to both new emergence firms or the well establishes firms. As according to Alhadddi (2014), the initiative that have in the Blue Ocean Strategy for sustainability initiatives steered by the same way of the Blue Ocean Strategy used to create value and determination for innovations. Based on this strategy also as cited by Alhaddi (2014), the implementation of Blue Ocean Strategy offers the creation of potential growth that brings profit by means of retreating from the competition of the current market and building uncontested of new market space by way of enhancing and the value of innovations. In order for the company to create benefits towards the environment society and the economy by finding its solution, application techniques, sustainability would be the key driver for the companies to achieve its goals. Alhaddi (2014), also cited that the Blue Ocean Strategy is where competition in the market are becoming irrelevant to the businesses and it allows to grow with unlimited profits.

As noted by Wirtenberg, Russels, & Lipsky, (2009), the significant and the relevancy of the innovation are to be practice for sustainable growth for organizations. Generally, it can be said that the basically innovation are considered as the organization capability as it is not limited only to products or technologies. The innovation allows new prospect for the business and its stakeholder to grow and sustain. It can be said that those two values are inseparable value as it looks as the foundation for Blue Ocean Strategy. For Blue Ocean Strategy in term of innovations it is being use where as it focuses on concealing the market competition to be irrelevant as a result to be nature in uncontested market. From this strategy of marketing the innovation would be a successful as it aligned with the cost of the production of the company, the price of the product and its utility. In those sense, the Blue Ocean Strategy also pursuit for take full advantage of the buyer value and lessen the cost of production through the establishments of the Value Innovations (Alhaddi, 2014). It deals with value to the company (by minimizing the cost of the company, maximizing the profitability) and as for the buyer (putting more value of the product with low prices) (Alhaddi,2014).

For example, as according to Han Kim and Mauborgne (2006), as they mentioned that innovation value will be unrealistic if it based on the conventional orthodox strategic way of thinking. Such as when CNN was make known to for instances, the channel of NBC, CBS, and ABC scoff at the idea of news that are broadcasted for 24/7, on 7 days a week without well-known broadcasters. It does shows here that, ridicule does not enthuse rapid imitation. From the view of Blue Ocean Strategy that can be implied, as the company used the functionality and the emotional pleas to the customer in order to break from the competition. As according to Kim and Mauborgne (2005), mentioned that the well-known beauty products business, The Body Shops as they change the emotional pleas convert to functionality appeal by introducing the product that are practically benefit as compare to the artificial beauty products in the markets. By bringing the uniqueness and individuality of each customer as they use to create emotional appeal, targeting on the self -esteem of the customers. The implementation of the Blue Ocean Strategy brings into the sustainability of the societal, where the Body Shop Company has been able to generated profit and been increase the revenue, as well as growth and expansion of the business.

FUTURE RESEARCH DIRECTIONS

The emergence of new company in the industries, innovation has become a crucial part for the business to survive. In this current economic system, there will be a huge gap between the new emergence of business and well-established company or firms. As according to Tu et. al (2014), the execution on the system of free market economic, it creates a huge gap between the rich and poor in which the number are gradually increase from time to time, in which this could result to the gap those who poor become more poorer and those who are richer are getting more reacher. The applications of Blue Ocean Strategy to implemented sustainability in the businesses are based on the value creation and innovation effort between the concept of sustainability and the Blue Ocean Strategy. As according to Alhaddi (2014), it is been recommended that creating profitability and its growth in the way of diminishing or shrinking the relevancy competition and create new canvas of market space where on it owns flourish to expand in the market. The main goal of Blue Ocean Strategy is to create value for the buyer and reduction for the cost for the companies. The Blue Ocean strategy also can be as realm to growth for innovation that to be created in the new market space and sources to grow the business profitability. As can be such strategy of marketing helps the business to manage not only for the company but also for its stakeholder.

CONCLUSION

As for the conclusion, innovation and sustainability are the factors that could never be separable. It is crucial relevant and impotence for not only to enterprise but also to people and nation. Innovative people will increase the level of economy of their particular countries. Other than that, as current technology is so dynamic and its kept to change, this goes as well for innovation which it will be accelerated much more in the future. The effect of practice sustainability innovation company will be able reduce resources and energy consumption. Products that is produce should be use at as efficient as possible without compromising the resources and energy usage. Apart from that, it can benefit the society and environment as well. When suitability as the key in managing the business, it is no brainer without realizing that it has already helps the society a healthy as well as it also be able preserve the environment from adversity disruption.

With sustainable innovation also, it helps to promote a closed loop system where nothing is wasted. As according to European Parliament, product that is produce by company shall not only be taken in traditional linear model of economy in the way of take-make-consume and throw away after the product has reach it limit of lifetime. Instead the product needs to can be lease recycle reuse or repair in the sense that the product can be use and still relevant and encompass of high value. Another benefit through managing sustainability innovation in business, it also promotes delivery of functionality rather than ownership. From this concept in steering the business it also encourages as system built on collaboration and sharing. Internally in the organization, encouragement and engagement among the stakeholder in the organization to be innovative in suitability would be important such way can be crucial part to know the weaknesses and strengths of the products.

However, the company will be affected of they not implement such concept to their business. First, company might face slowly pace of income and profitability. With new product and much more sustainable that can last long without compromising the consumer wellbeing, people would be rather to seek other options. Performance will slowly be getting to a low level and less product is being produce. When there is less productivity as it unable to meet the requirement of consumers and environment demands. Once the performance starting to get and they loosen they profit might as well investors would be out from the deal. With investors loss it trusts to the company' future, the same things go to our customer, when there is lack to innovation on the product, people get bored as its loss it competitive advantages or it uniqueness, consumer will start to seeks other option that could benefit and able to meet their demands.

It is important taking care of the loyalty of customer as they bring positive mother of words to our targeted consumers. Neither of the effort would be a success if the company unable to overcome its obstacle. Company need systematic method to sustain product innovation. Collective data from research and development would be useful investment for the future of the company through innovation. Management from the company or firm need be able to change the way of thinking towards the perception on sustainable innovations among the stakeholders. It requires the support from all level of hierarchy from top level to bottom level. Eventually, the blue ocean strategy with sustainable innovation helps the business explore other marketing in a way using the tools have help the business to be innovative. The business able to seeks option that have beyond the existing market with such strategy in create potential growth of the business as it enters the blue ocean as there is no competitive among other that create same business. The tool allows business to be pioneer to the result of sustainable innovation.

REFERENCES

Alhaddi, H. (2014). Blue Ocean Strategy and Sustainability for Strategic Management. *International Proceedings of Economics Development and Research*, *82*, 125.

Blowfield, M., Visser, W., & Livesey, F. (2008, September). Sustainability innovation: mapping the territory. In *Corporate Responsibility Research Conference*. Cambridge University Press.

Bocken, N. M., Short, S. W., Rana, P., & Evans, S. (2014). A Literature and Practice Review to Develop Sustainable Business Model Archetypes. *Journal of Cleaner Production*, *65*, 42–56. doi:10.1016/j.jclepro.2013.11.039

Buhr, D. (2015). *Industry 4.0 – New Tasks for Innovation Policy*. Retrived on 9 Dec 2019 from http://library.fes.de/pdf-files/wiso/11480.pdf

Callander, S., & Matouschek, N. (2019). The Risk of Failure: Trial and Error Learning and Long-Run Performance. *American Economic Journal. Microeconomics*, *11*(1), 44–78. doi:10.1257/mic.20160359

Chang, L. D. M., Ling Tam, A. Y., & Suki, N. M. (2016). Moderating effect of races towards consumers' feeling of TCM usage. Handbook of Research on Leveraging Consumer Psychology for Effective Customer Engagement, 306-323.

European Parliament. (2016). *Closing the loop New circular economy package*. Retrieved on 9 Dec 2019 from http://www.europarl.europa.eu/RegData/etudes/BRIE/2016/573899/EPRS_BRI%282016%29573899_EN.pdf

EY. (2014). *Shifting from Consumption to Experience*. Retrieved on 9 Dec 2019 from https://www.ey.com/Publication/vwLUAssets/EY-Shifting-from-consumer-to-experience/$FILE/EY-Shifting-from-consumer-to-experience.pdf

Fontaine, M. (2013). Corporate Social Responsibility And Sustainability: The New Bottom Line? *International Journal of Business and Social Science*, *4*(4).

Han Kim, W., & Mauborgne, R. (2006). *Blue Ocean Strategy*. Academic Press.

Kanter, R. M. (2006). Innovation: The Classic Traps. *Harvard Business Review*, *84*(11), 72–83, 154. PMID:17131564

Kronenberg, T. (2004). The Curse of Natural Resources In The Transition Economies. *Economics of Transition*, *12*(3), 399–426. doi:10.1111/j.0967-0750.2004.00187.x

Kurdve, M., Shahbazi, S., Wendin, M., Bengtsson, C., & Wiktorsson, M. (2015). Waste Flow Mapping To Improve Sustainability Of Waste Management: A Case Study Approach. *Journal of Cleaner Production*, *98*, 304–315. doi:10.1016/j.jclepro.2014.06.076

Manda, M. I., & Ben Dhaou, S. (2019, April). Responding to the challenges and opportunities in the 4th Industrial revolution in developing countries. In *Proceedings of the 12th International Conference on Theory and Practice of Electronic Governance* (pp. 244-253). ACM. 10.1145/3326365.3326398

Mosher & Smith. (2015). *Sustainability Incorporated Integrating Sustainability into Business*. Retrieved on 9 Dec 2019 from https://sustainability.com/wp-content/uploads /2016/07/sustainability_incorporated.pdf

Nastanski, M., & Baglione, S. L. (2014). Sustainability: Benefits of Social Responsibility to Brand Value & Profit. *Journal of International Management Studies*, *9*(2), 164–173.

Nathan, R. J., Fook Chiun, D. C., & Suki, N. M. (2016). An online marketing strategies assessment for companies in airlines and entertainment industries in Malaysia. Handbook of Research on Leveraging Consumer Psychology for Effective Customer Engagement, 1-15.

Organization Economic Corporation Development. (n.d.). The Economic Significance of Natural Resources: Key Points for Reformers. In *Eastern Europe. Caucasus And Central Asia*. Author.

Paine, L. (2014, July). Sustainability in the boardroom. *Harvard Business Review*, 87–95.

Interagency Report. (2012). *Sustainable Agricultural Productivity Growth and Bridging The Gap For Small-Family Farms*. Author.

Rojko, A. (2017). Industry 4.0 Concept: Background and Overview. *International Journal of Interactive Mobile Technologies*, *11*(5), 77–90. doi:10.3991/ijim.v11i5.7072

Sachs, J. D., & Warner, A. M. (1995). *Natural resource abundance and economic growth*. NBER Working Paper No. 5398. Cambridge, MA: National Bureau of Economic Research.

Scott, J. T. (2017). *The Sustainable Business: A Practitioner's Guide to Achieving Long-Term Profitability and Competitiveness*. Routledge.

Suki, N. M. (2016). *Handbook of Research on Leveraging Consumer Psychology for Effective Customer Engagement*. https://www.igi-global.com/book/handbook-research-leveraging-consumer-psychology/149284

Tan, K. S., & Phang, S. Y. (2005). *From Efficiency-Driven to Innovation-Driven Economic Growth: Perspectives from Singapore*. The World Bank. doi:10.1596/1813-9450-3569

Tu, J. C., Shih, M. C., Hsu, C. Y., & Lin, J. H. (2014). Developing Blue Ocean Strategy Of Sustainable Product Design And Development For Business Opportunities Of BOP Groups In Taiwan. *Mathematical Problems in Engineering*, *2014*, 2014. doi:10.1155/2014/297524

United Nation System Task Team. (2015). *Post 2015 Development Agenda*. Science Technology and Innovation for Sustainable Development in The Global Partnership For Development Beyond 2015. Retrieved on 9 Dec 2019 from https://www.un.org/en/development/desa/policy/untaskteam_undf/thinkpieces/28_thinkpiece_science.pdf

Whelan, T., & Fink, C. (2016). The Comprehensive Business Guide for Sustainability. *Harvard Business Review*. Retrieved on 9 Dec 2019 from https://hbr. org/2016/10/the-comprehensive-businesscase-for-sustainability

White, K., Habib, R., & Hardisty, D. J. (2019). How to SHIFT Consumer Behaviors to be More Sustainable: A Literature Review and Guiding Framework. *Journal of Marketing*, *83*(3), 22–49. doi:10.1177/0022242919825649

Wirtenberg, J., Russell, W., & Lipsky, D. (2009). *The Sustainable Enterprise Field Book*. Greenleaf Publishing Limited.

Chapter 15
Inverted Grammar Classroom:
Detecting Grammar Errors in Student Video Presentations

Chelster Sherralyn Jeoffrey Pudin
Universiti Malaysia Sabah, Malaysia

Eugenia Ida Edward
Universiti Malaysia Sabah, Malaysia

ABSTRACT

Flipped learning is basically a pedagogical model that reverses classroom activities. Materials or contents are provided online (in learning management systems or other learning platforms) and students will study the material prior to the lesson. Therefore, classroom time can be used to engage in activities such as problem-solving, discussion, and analysis. This study is an extended study of a previous research which explored the effects of the flipped learning approach in a grammar classroom. For this study, the focus is shifted to the grammatical errors made by students in their video presentation during the flipped learning session. The analysis of the findings showed that students' grammar errors are mainly on missed formation errors, addition error, omission error, and lastly, improper ordering. The findings of this study give ESL practitioners a better insight into student errors and should lead to improved grammar usage in the classroom through blended learning.

INTRODUCTION

For decades, the higher education system in Malaysia has seen its courses delivered on a standard fourteen weeks of face-to-face lectures and tutorials. This is despite the fact that technology has seen an advancement in providing free flexible access to materials and information. As tradition dictates, a number of hours should be put aside for formal lecture and tutorials. However, as more studies have been conducted on the ineffectiveness of traditional lecture to students' learning, recently in 2012, MOOC (Massive Open Online Courses) has been introduced to the world of academia as a way to engage active

DOI: 10.4018/978-1-7998-3042-9.ch015

learning for students. It serves as an interactive user forums to support community interactions among students, professors, and teaching assistants and it is free.

Education today in the globalised world is about adapting to changing world. How and what we teach has to change as well. Learners learn anywhere and anytime without confinement of classroom (Abdul Karim Alias, 2010). Hence, students learn more effectively when the delivery of lectures is blended with the use of technology and can be learned at flexible hours. Blended learning an approach that combines face to face instruction with technology, emphasizing customised learning (Abdul Karim Alias, 2014) while flexible learning opportunity to improve students learning experience through flexibility in time, pace, mode of study, teaching approach, forms of assessment and staffing. Therefore, blended learning and flexible learning can enrich learning experience, optimise student engagement, to achieve deep meaningful learning (Abdul Karim Alias, 2014).

One approach to achieve deep and meaningful learning is through a 'flipped classroom'. Flipped classroom was first introduced by Baker (2000) and Lage et al.(2000), and popularized through online videos and activities by many others. Studies have shown that the average concentration span of adult is less than twenty minutes. In order to make a one hour lesson interesting, is to create a video that lasts for ten to fifteen minutes which can cover a forty minutes lesson. The video is then uploaded to any learning platforms for students to view. By doing this, a flipped classroom has just been created. In essence, the flipped classroom basically reverses classroom activities. Materials or contents are provided online (in learning management system or other learning platforms) and students will study the material prior coming to class. Therefore, classroom time can be used to engage in activities such as problem solving, discussion and analysis.

More research that delve into aspect of consumer behavior and psychology in the digital economy is deemed necessary (Ling Chang, Ling Tam, & Suki, 2016; Nathan, Fook Chiun, & Suki, 2016; Suki, 2016). This study is an extended study of a previous research by Pudin (2016) which explored the effects of the flipped learning approach in a grammar classroom through students' perceptions on its effectiveness and feasibility. The study has garnered strong positive responses from students' as most of them favoured flipped classroom in learning grammar. Even though most of the students would prefer flipped learning in grammar lessons, they were some negative setbacks experienced by them especially on grammatical errors done by their peers in the videos. Hence, for this study, the focus is shifted to the grammatical errors made by students in their video presentation during the flipped learning session.

There are two research questions that were formulated as a focus to this study. They are:

1. What are the most common grammatical errors in students' video presentation?
2. What are the possible sources for these errors?

LITERATURE REVIEW

Many kinds of errors arise for students learning English because they do not master English well. They commit errors by not using the rules of the components and elements of the second language (Ramelan, 1992). Brown said, "Second language learning is a process that is clearly not unlike first language learning in its trial and errors nature." It means that the students learning English cannot avoid errors in learning a second language (Gass and Slinker, 1994). Grammar is one of the basic components of any language, which must be learnt by students (Praninskas, 1980). According to Raja T. Nasr (1988), grammar is a very useful and important part of any language. There are many rules in grammar, including articles, parts of speech, sentence pattern, and tense, etc (Cook and Richard, 1980). Learners make errors in both comprehension and production. According to Pudin et al. (2015), grammar errors that may frequently occur in students' oral and written production involve the use of articles, verb tense, prepositions, subject-verb agreement; and syntactic, involving word order.

Errors made by their students need to be analysed correctly in order to be able to arrange an effective learning strategy. As stated by Corder (1981), Error Analysis (EA) is a procedure used by both researchers and teachers, which involves collecting samples of the learner's language, identifying the errors in the sample, describing these errors, classifying them according to their nature and causes, and evaluating their seriousness. The study of errors is carried out by means of EA. An error occurs when the deviation arises as a result of knowledge. A mistake occurs when learners fail to perform their competence (Muhsin, 2016). According to Ellis (2008), errors reflect gaps in a learners' knowledge. They occur because the learner does not know what is correct. While, mistakes reflect occasional lapses in performance, they occur because the learner is unable to perform what he or she knows. The definition above shows that mistake is a fault that is made by the learner, and they can make a correction. Meanwhile, error is a fault that is made by the learner, and he or she is unable to make a correction. However, when the student commits an error, they can correct it.

There are two sources of errors namely, inter-lingual errors and intra-lingual errors. Richards (1974) states that inter-lingual errors are errors caused by the interference of the learner's mother tongue. Errors of this nature are frequent, regardless of the learner's language background. Therefore, inter-lingual errors are caused by interference from native language to the target language that they learn. Before someone masters the concept of the target language they will always use the concept of their native language. The other kind of error is intra-lingual errors. Intra-lingual errors can be classified into four categories: overgeneralisation, ignorance of rule restriction, incomplete application of rules, and false concept hypothesized. This intra-lingual error is sometimes called a semantic error.

Soetikno (1996) weights the ways surface structure is altered. Learners may omit necessary items or add unnecessary ones, they may misfire an item or miss order them. Thus, the errors may be in the form of omission, addition, misinformation, and improper ordering. Omission errors are characterized by the absence of an item that must appear in a well-formed utterance. Addition errors are characterized by the presence of an item, which must not appear in a well-formed utterance. Additional errors include double marking, regularization and simple addition. Missed formation errors are characterized by the use of the wrong form of morpheme or structure. While in omission errors the items is not supplied at all, in missed formation errors the learners supplied something, but it is incorrect. Improper ordering errors are characterized by the incorrect placement of a morpheme or group morphemes in an utterance.

METHODOLOGY

For the purpose of this research, case study method was used. Four steps were employed, namely, identifying the errors, classifying the errors, quantifying the errors, and analysing the source of the error (Gay, 1987). The description of the data dealt with the students' grammatical errors in their video presentation.

Subjects

A total of 31 students with higher Malaysian University Entrance Test (MUET) were selected as the subjects for the study. The subjects were first year students from the Faculty of Psychology and Education (TESL). These subjects have obtained a higher Malaysian University Entrance Test (MUET) results that range from Bands 3, 4 and 5. As a requirement from the university, students with higher band of MUET (Band 3, 4, and 5) will take advanced English courses at the Centre for the Promotion of Knowledge and Language. Since the subjects were in their first year, they were to take UB00602 Grammar in Context. This course is the crucial course related to the study.

Instrument

In order to achieve the study purpose, the researchers collected samples of students' video presentation to ascertain and analyse the most grammatical errors made by these students.

Data Collection Procedure

The data collection procedure began with briefing students on how flipped learning concept is implemented in the classroom. The first step of flipped learning was preparing materials for the grammar presentation and deciding which learning portal to be used as the flipped learning platform. Secondly, students were to group themselves and shoot a video for grammar presentation. Thirdly, they decide which video service they will use to publish their video. The fourth step was to make the other students accountable for watching the video. This was done by providing exercises or online discussion related to the video. And finally the last step was to reinforce information and knowledge gained from the video by having discussion and group activities in the classroom. After all groups have completed their grammar presentation videos, the researchers then compile the videos for error analysis.

Data Analysis

The data gathered from the videos were entered and analysed in SPSS version 24. Descriptive statistics was selected to ascertain the frequency of grammar errors made by the students in their video presentation.

RESULTS AND DISCUSSION

The analysis of the data, was done in two steps, which are identifying and classifying the errors. In identifying the errors, students' grammar errors were identified from their videos and description of errors were made to determine the frequency of occurrence of the errors. The next step was classifying the errors into four kinds of errors, which include omission, addition, missed information, and improper ordering (Soetikno, 1996). The description of errors is presented in Table 1.

The types of errors in general were acknowledged according to their frequency of occurrence and relative significance are shown in Table 2. In total, fifty-four errors were found in the students' presentation. These errors are relatively small in number perhaps due to the reason that the students are TESL (Teaching of English as Second Language) students with higher proficiency in the English language.

Table 1. Description of Errors

Types of errors	Description
Missed Formation	Use of the wrong form of morpheme or structure
Addition	Presence of an item, which must not appear in a well-formed utterance.
Omission	Absence of an item that must appear in a well-formed utterance
Improper Ordering	Incorrect placement of a morpheme or group morphemes in an utterance.

Table 2. Types of Errors

Errors	Frequency
Missed Formation	22
Addition	16
Omission	12
Improper Ordering	4
Total	54

Based on the frequency, missed formation error is the highest with 22, followed by addition error with 16, then omission error with 12 and lastly improper ordering with 4.

The examples of the errors made by the students are as follows:

a) Missed formation errors

These errors are indicated by the use of the wrong morpheme or structure. In this error, students supplied items to their sentences which are incorrect.

Concorde

In a sentence, the subject and the verb must agree in number. This means, singular subject takes singular verb and plural subject takes plural verb. For example,

The mystery go on - The mystery goes on (correct)
Jason is a student who study smart - Jason is a student who studies smart (correct)

In the following sentence, a concord error occurred because non-count nouns were taken as being plural nouns when they are supposed to be singular nouns. In this situation, the plural helping verb should not be employed.

Example:

Rice are uncountable nouns - Rice is uncountable nouns (correct)
Water are important for mankind - Water is important for mankind (correct)

In addition, plural helping verb was also added with sentences beginning with one of + plural noun. As per rule, one of is followed by plural noun/pronoun and singular helping verb. This error occurs when learners try to apply rules used to produce plural sentences. They generalise the sentence as being a plural sentence because of the plural noun that followed the earlier phrase one of.

Example:

One of the boys are from China - One of the boys is from China (correct)

One of the brothers work with their father - One of the brothers works with their father (correct)

Articles

When learners do not fully understand the rules of using articles, these problems occurred. The above utterance has employed 'the' before the proper nouns. We do not normally use definite article 'the' with proper nouns although in English 'the' is used to refer to names of geographical areas (the North Pole), names composed of common nouns and proper nouns (the Maldives), and so on. However, this definite article 'the' cannot be used with proper nouns, such as names of people, names of countries etc.

Example:

At first, The Katrina was only a category 1 hurricane - At first, Ø (zero article) Katrina was only a category 1 hurricane (correct)

The German magazine Geo published a report - A German magazine Geo published a report (correct)

In the summer, the place gets very hot- In Ø (zero article) summer, the place gets very hot (correct)

Tense Markers/Double Marking

In English, tense is marked on verbs but errors occurred when infinitive marker "to" appeared with a tensed verb which is wrong for an infinitive always begins with "to" followed by a base form with some exceptions for the phrase look forward to which is followed by a gerund and not a base form. The word to in this phrase is a preposition and not an infinitive.

Example:

I look forward to meet you - I look forward to meeting you (correct)

She seems to knew about the man who she met yesterday - She seems to know about the man who she met yesterday (correct)

She always shows reluctance to finished a job - She always shows reluctance to finish a job (correct)

Apart from tense markers, double marking can also occur in tenses. For example:

I definitely didn't knew you so well.

You normally didn't asked me.

You didn't asked me a questions* (2 errors identified- double marking and addition plural marking morpheme-s to a singular noun).

In these examples, "pasteness" is marked at two levels i.e at the auxiliary verb (didn't) and at the main verb (knew and asked). As per grammar rule, however, allows marking 'pasteness' only on the auxiliary verb when a sentence contains both an auxiliary and a main verb as in the above erroneous utterance (Tizazu, 2014).

Wrong choice of parts of speech

This error occurred when students selected an incorrect part of speech to their sentences which had caused erroneous utterance. Table 3 is a summary of wrong choice of parts of speech supplied by the students.

Table 3. A Summary of Wrong Choice of Parts of Speech

Wrong parts of speech	Examples
Pronoun	Let we proceed to our lesson She's name is Aveny Let we discuss the answers together
Preposition	Later you can ask me in the end of the class We all finish assignment in the last minute
Noun (Quantifiers)	I have much problems Nazrin only have a little friend

b) Addition error

These errors are indicated by the presence of an item, which must not appear in a well-formed utterance.

Plural Markers

Plural marking morpheme-s used for singular nouns as the following examples. The nouns must be in their singular form but students' changed into the plural form, hence, the utterance becomes erroneous in terms of number.

Example:

Amount of somethings – Amount of something (correct)
A lots of weight- A lot of weight (correct)
This clauses contains subjects and verbs - This clauses contain subjects and verbs (correct)
You didn't asked me a questions - You didn't ask me a question (correct)

Auxiliary Verbs

Compound verbs are used to mark grammatical information, such as passive, progressive, perfective, future, interrogation, negation (in statements), etc. In the sentences given below, however, the auxiliary verbs are used, but they convey none of the above functions. This error occurred possibly due to students' sheer ignorance of the functions of these auxiliary verbs especially when they appear in comjugation with main verbs.

Example:

He is look refreshed- He looks refreshed (correct)

I was enjoyed he holiday in Greece when we had a great time- I enjoyed the holiday in Greece where we had a great time (correct)

Negation

Double negatives are used to express a positive meaning as the two negatives cancel out with each other. If they are used correctly, double negatives are effective in creating variety in sentence construction. Learners of L2, however, use double negation unintentionally so that they end up expressing the opposite of what they meant. In this example, we have two negatives in the one sentence – I didn't do nothing – whereas the speaker's intention was to indicate just one negative, which was to deny any hand, act or part in whatever had occurred.

Example:

I didn't do nothing today – I didn't do anything today (correct)

They aren't many people, aren't they?- They aren't many people, are they?

Addition of Parts of Speech

Some addition of parts of speech were also observed in the students' errors. Table 4 shows examples of the utterances of entail words which are deemed surplus for the requirement of a well-formed sentence.

Table 4. The Utterances of Entail Words

Part of speech addition	Examples
Preposition	Please submit all your reports in next week Can you introduce about yourself please?
Nouns (quantifiers)	I had a good enough sleep

Example:

c) Omission error

These errors are indicated by an absence of an item that must appear in a well-formed utterance. Omission in grammatical morphemes (articles, preposition, auxiliary verbs etc) is observed. The discussion below follows how grammatical morphemes are omitted in students' utterances and their impact on the grammaticality of sentences. Based on a study done by Pudin and Saru (2014), the obvious negative transfer seen in the writings of Malaysian ESL grammar students is the wrong usage of the -be verb. The reason is because Ellis (2008) has said that learners will avoid using linguistic structures which they find difficult because of the differences between their native. In Malay, it does not have the equivalent auxiliaries of the be verb. Unlike the English language, the main verbs in the Malay language are not inflected and not marked for tense. The tense is instead denoted by time adverbs (yesterday) and other tense indicators, for instance "already" and "not yet". Thus, this dissimilar usage of the verb system has led to omission. In this

Table 5. Inappropriate Usage Of Be As A Result Of Negative Transfer From Malay

Omission of auxiliary verb	Examples
Be	The friend who ^very tall – The friend who is very tall (correct) I ^ burning the midnight oil – I am burning the midnight oil (correct) He ^looking very tired – He is looking very tired (correct) He^ walking here right now – He is walking here right now

study, the auxiliary verb be is not employed in the context where be should take place. Some of the inappropriate usage of be as a result of negative transfer from Malay are listed in Table 5.

Apart from the omission of the be-verb, perhaps due to L1 negative transfer, another omission error is observed in the missing of the plural morpheme –s. The students' left off the –s from the plural nouns. As a result, the concord (SVA) is violated in the given sentence.

Example:

I have a few pimple than I used to - I have a few pimples than I used to (correct)

They left the house a few minute ago - They left the house a few minutes ago (correct)

...from those page, you need to answer all questions - ...from those pages, you need to answer all questions (correct)

d) Improper ordering

These errors are indicated by the incorrect placement of a morpheme or incorrect sequence. For example:

It's mean that – It means that (correct)
Why this is happen – Why is this happening (correct)
Why you didn't stand up- Why didn't you stand up (correct)
What's happen next? What happens next? (correct)
What's really happened? What really happened? (correct)

CONCLUSION

As a conclusion, the main purpose of this study was to investigate students' frequency of errors in their grammar presentation videos. Based on the findings, 53 errors were detected from students' presentation and were classified into four categories according to the frequency of errors. In general, these errors done by the students were contributed mostly from overgeneralization of grammar rules and negative transfer from mother tongue (L1). This happens when a second language leaner applies a grammatical rule across all members of a grammatical class without making the appropriate exception because they face difficulties in learning the target language.

Based on the results of this study, some recommendations can be proposed to minimise the students' errors in dealing with grammar rules. Firstly, inverted classroom can be considered by language teachers in teaching grammar to do away with the traditional grammar classroom where drilling is always emphasised. To ensure the effectiveness of a flipped classroom, record a video of presentation/lecture for 10-20 minutes. The video should be available on demand and viewed prior to face to face lecture. It should also integrate with learning activities in social media (e.g padlet, smart2ums, Schoology etc.) and the learning activities in classroom. Secondly, language teachers should develop interactive materials to appeal to students' needs. The materials should be interactive with clear and simple examples for students to learn and understand in class as well as on social media platforms. Thirdly, learning grammar should not be in isolation but integrated with other skills so that students' will be able to apply the rules in and use them correctly in language learning.

It is therefore recommended that based on the results of this study, the teaching of grammar can be more fun and interactive by adopting the flipped or inverted classroom. The flipped classroom can indeed create rich and meaningful learning activities despite the errors students make in learning grammar rules.

REFERENCES

Abdul Karim Alias. (2010). *Flipped classroom: Total classroom makeover*. Retrieved from: https://www.openlearning.com/courses/flippedlearning

Abdul Karim Alias. (2014). *Flipped classroom, mobile learning, whatsapp, and learning nuggets*. Retrieved from: http://onestoplearning.blogspot.my/search?q=flipped+classroom

Baker, J. W. (2000). *The 'classroom flip: Using web course management tools to become the guide by the side. 11th International Conference on College Teaching and Learning*, Jacksonville, FL.

Brown, H. D. (1980). *Principles of Language and Teaching*. Prentice Hall, Inc.

Chang, L. D. M., Ling Tam, A. Y., & Suki, N. M. (2016). Moderating effect of races towards consumers' feeling of TCM usage. Handbook of Research on Leveraging Consumer Psychology for Effective Customer Engagement, 306-323.

Cook, S., Richard, S.W., (1980). *The Scope of Grammar: the Study of Modern Grammar*. Academic Press.

Corder, S. P. (1981). *Error Analysis and Interlanguage*. Oxford: Oxford University Press.

Ellis, R. (2008). *The study of second language acquisition* (2nd ed.). Oxford: Oxford University Press.

Gass, S., & Slinker, L. (1994). *Second Language Acquisition: an Introductory Course*. Mahwah, NJ: LEA.

Gay, L. R. (1987). *Educational Research.* Competencies for Analysis and Application.

Lage, M. J., Platt, G. J., & Treglia, M. (2000). Inverting the classroom: A gateway to creating an inclusive learning environment. *The Journal of Economic Education*, *31*(1), 30–43. doi:10.1080/00220480009596759

Muhsin, M. A. (2016). Analysing the students errors in using simple present (A case study at Junior High School in Makassar). *Pacific Science Review B: Humanities and Social Sciences*, 81-87.

Nathan, R. J., Fook Chiun, D. C., & Suki, N. M. (2016). An online marketing strategies assessment for companies in airlines and entertainment industries in Malaysia. Handbook of Research on Leveraging Consumer Psychology for Effective Customer Engagement, 1-15.

Praninskas, J. (1980). *Rapid Review of English Grammar*. Prentice Hall, Inc.

Pudin, C. S. J. (2016). *Exploring a flipped learning approach in teaching Grammar for ESL Students*. Paper presented at International Conference on Education and Psychology, Universiti Malaysia Sabah.

Pudin, C.S.J., & Saru, E. H. (2014). The Reality of Teaching English without L1 reference in an ESL Classroom. *MANU Jurnal Pusat Penataran Ilmu dan Bahasa, 21*, 149.

Pudin, C. S. J., Storey, J. M., Loh, Y. L., Swanto, S., & Din, W. A. (2015). Exploring L1 interference in the writings of Kadazandusun ESL students. *Indonesian Journal of Applied Linguistics*, *5*(1), 54–62. doi:10.17509/ijal.v5i1.831

Raja, T. N. (1988). *Grammar Practice Activities*. London: Cambridge University.

Ramelan. (1992). *Introduction to Linguistic Analysis*. IKIP Semarang Press.

Richards, J. C. (1974). *Error Analysis*. Longman Group Ltd.

Soetikno, I. (1996). *Analysis Wacana*. Jakarta: Gramedia Pustaka Utama.

Suki, N. M. (2016). *Handbook of Research on Leveraging Consumer Psychology for Effective Customer Engagement*. https://www.igi-global.com/book/handbook-research-leveraging-consumer-psychology/149284

Tizazu, Y. (2014). A linguistic analysis of errors in learners' compositions: The case of arba minch university students. *International Journal of English Language and Linguistics*, *2*(2), 69–101.

Chapter 16
Green Consumer Behaviour:
Integration of Theory of Planned Behaviour and Technology Acceptance Model

Muhammad Farooq Akhtar
Universiti Utara Malaysia, Malaysia

Norazah Mohd Suki
https://orcid.org/0000-0002-8422-2449
Universiti Utara Malaysia, Malaysia

ABSTRACT

Environment preservation is a global concern. Textile industry disposes of chemicals which effects environment and human life (water borne diseases). United Nations develops 17 Sustainable Development Goals (UNSDG's) to protect environment. Five SDG's addressing textile industry namely good health and well-being, clean water and sanitation, responsible production and consumption, climate action and life below water. Role of textile industry to achieve SDG's is inevitable. Textile policy of Pakistan 2014-19 confirms that international buyer is concerned about the environment which evidently shows potential of green marketing in textile sector of Pakistan. Green marketing encourages environment friendly marketing practices (product, price, place, promotion). The objective of this study is to integrate the theory of planned behavior and technology acceptance model. Green consumer behavior of textile sector of Pakistan is conceptualized with this extended lens. This study enhances the body of knowledge by conceptualizing green consumer behavior of textile sector through extended model. Practically, this study remains beneficial for marketing professionals and researchers to understand green consumer behavior of textile sector. Success of green marketing is the success of society to curb environmental problems.

INTRODUCTION

Environmental preservation is a global concern. Competition among companies across the globe affects natural environment which causes global warming, waterborne diseases, depletion of ozone layer and air pollution etc. Industrialists not safely dispose of their chemicals which contaminate underground water. Unfortunately, pure water is not available to over 844 million people and cause death of 6000 children

DOI: 10.4018/978-1-7998-3042-9.ch016

each day (Organization, 2017). Waterborne diseases affect human lives in world especially in developing countries (Anwar, Lateef, & Siddiqi, 2010).

Environment transformed form fringe to established issue due to media, national and international legislation, pressure groups and radical changes in public opinion about environment (Wagner, 2002). Consumers of this century are more concerned about quality of life on the earth and considered environmentally friendly products than ancestors (Khan & Mohsin, 2017; Krause, 1993). Scholars also reported that consumers having high concerns for environment spend more on environmentally friendly products (Antil, 1984; Shabecoff, 1993). Green marketing develops ecological awareness among consumers which will shift their attention towards environmentally friendly products (Suki & Suki, 2019).

Sustainable Textile Sector

United Nations enforce 17 Sustainable Development Goal's out of which 5 directly demands attention of textile industry. This industry shall take care of third, sixth, tweveth, thirteenth and fourteenth SDG which embark on good health and well-being, clean water and sanitation, responsible production and consumption, climate action and life below water respectively. The role of textile industry to enforce UNSDG's is inevitable.

Textile industry contributes 20 percent in overall large-scale manufacturing sector of Pakistan. This sector holds 59 percent pie of exports and provides bread and butter to 40 percent industrial workforce due to its long supply chain (Economic Advisor's Wing Finance Division, 2019). Textile policy 2014-19 of Pakistan confirms that international buyer is concerned about the environment (Ministry of Textile Industry, February 2015), which evidently shows potential of green marketing in Pakistan.

Theory of planned behavior is mostly cited theory in pro-environmental context and technology acceptance model in technology adoption and use. The variables given in technology acceptance model fulfil the basic criteria of inclusion of theory of planned behavior (Ajzen, 2010) and may improve predictive power of the theory. Groening and colleagues (Groening, Sarkis, & Zhu, 2018) provide green marketing consumer level theory review. The review holds frequently used theories in pro-environmental consumer behavior. Scant literature is available on combine use of TPB and TAM to investigate green consumer behavior of textile sector.

More research that delve into aspect of consumer behavior and psychology in the digital economy is deemed necessary (Ling Chang, Ling Tam, & Suki, 2016; Nathan, Fook Chiun, & Suki, 2016; Suki, 2016). Accordingly, the objective of this study is to integrate the theory of planned behavior and technology acceptance model. This study sought to answer the following research questions;

1. Does green attitude towards behavior has significant effect on green consumer intentions?
2. Do green subjective norms have significant effect on green consumer intentions?
3. Do perceive ease of use to purchase green products has significant effect on green attitude towards the behavior?
4. Does perceived usefulness of green products has significant effect on green attitude towards behavior?
5. Do perceive usefulness of green products has significant effect on green consumer intentions?
6. Does perceived ease of use significantly moderate the relationship between green attitude towards the behavior and green consumer intentions?
7. Does perceived ease of use significantly moderate the relationship between green subjective norms and green consumer intentions?

THEORY OF PLANNED BEHAVIOR

Theory of planned behavior is one of the most powerful models to identify consumer behavior (Riebl et al., 2015; Timm & Deal, 2016). Scholars using TPB to predict pro-environmental behaviors since 1995 (Yuriev, Dahmen, Paillé, Boiral, & Guillaumie, 2020). The increasing use of theory of planned behavior shows its significance to predict individual consumer behaviors (Yuriev et al., 2020). Researchers continuously use this theory to identify the determinants of green consumer behavior i.e. to utilize alternative transportation (Muñoz, Monzon, & López, 2016), recycling of waste (Echegaray & Hansstein, 2017), water saving (Lam, 2006), conservation of energy (Allen & Marquart-Pyatt, 2018), other settings (Gkargkavouzi, Halkos, & Matsiori, 2019). Predictive power of TPB changes in different settings due to contextual factors (Andersson, Shivarajan, & Blau, 2005).

Green Attitude Towards the Green Behavior

Green attitude towards the behavior is referred to "the degree to which a person has a favourable or unfavourable evaluation or appraisal of the behavior" (Ajzen, 1991). Green attitude towards the behavior is an important antecedent to determine behavioral intentions (Ajzen, 1991; Kim & Chung, 2011). Theory of planned behavior disclosed that more an individual has favourable attitude towards behavior more behavioral intentions holds. Numerous scholars empirically prove this argument in different settings

Figure 1. Theory of Planned Behavior
Source: Ajzen, 1991

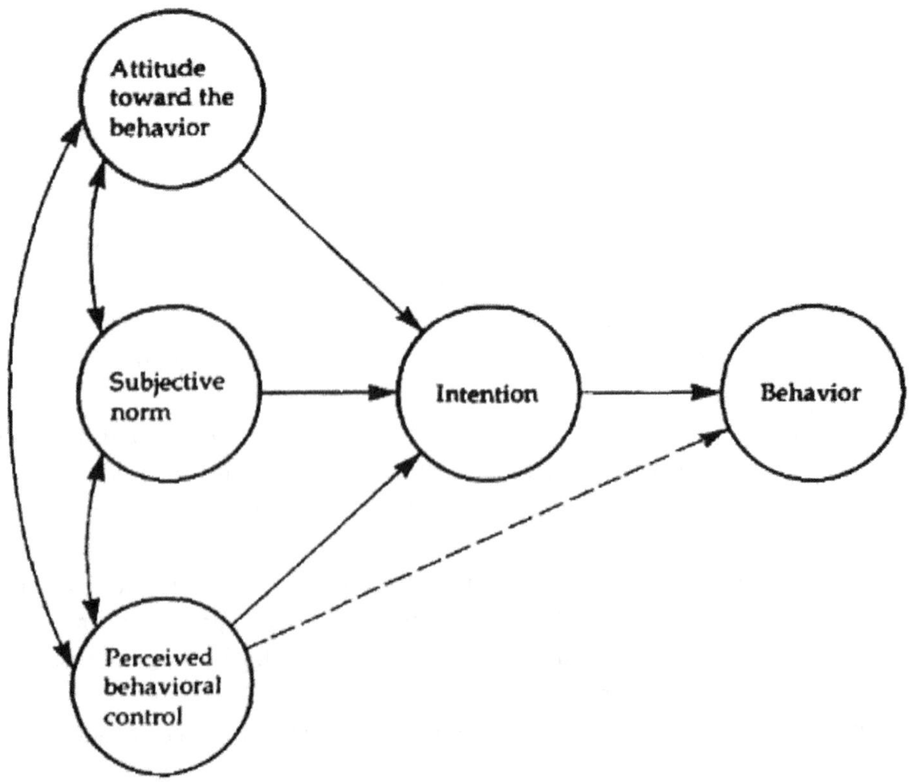

(Bautista, 2019; Maichum, Parichatnon, & Peng, 2016; Mancha & Yoder, 2015; Norazah & Norbayah, 2015; Paul, Modi, & Patel, 2016). Thus, based on the above rationale, the authors propose;

P1: Green attitude towards the behavior has significant effect on green consumer intentions.

Green Subjective Norms

Theory of planned behavior (Ajzen, 1991) refers green subjective norms as "the perceived social pressure to perform or not to perform the behavior". Numerous researchers investigated linkages between subjective norms and behavioral intentions (Mancha & Yoder, 2015) while on the other hand some scholars claim that subjective norms have no impact on behavioral intentions (Chang & Chou, 2018; Norazah & Norbayah, 2015; Paul et al., 2016; Taufique & Vaithianathan, 2018). The discussion on subjective norms stimulates the researchers to propose;

P2: Green subjective norms have significant effect on green consumer intentions.

Green Perceived Behavioral Control

"The degree of perceived behavioral control refers to the perceived ease or difficulty of performing the behavior and it is assumed to reflect past experience as well as anticipated impediments and obstacles" (Ajzen, 1991). Theory of planned behavior is extended version of theory of reasoned action (Fishbein & Ajzen, 1977), which assumed that intention is the only predictor of behavior. Perceived behavioral control was added in the model of Theory of Reasoned action because people have difficulty to perform certain behavior. Some scholars claim that perceived behavioral control has direct impact on green consumer behavior (Kautish, Paul, & Sharma, 2019) on the contrary, other researchers investigated positive impact of perceived behavioral control on behavioral intentions (Mancha & Yoder, 2015; Norazah & Norbayah, 2015). The existing findings lead the authors to propose;

P3: Perceived ease of use of green products has significant effect on green attitude towards the behavior.

Green Intentions

Intention is an indication that how much a consumer is ready to perform a behavior (Rezai, Teng, Mohamed, & Shamsudin, 2012). Scholars explained green consumer intentions as that consumer is willing to purchase environment friendly products (Fishbein & Ajzen, 2005; Mostafa, 2007). Green consumers are now interested in green products as well as environment (Sreen, Purbey, & Sadarangani, 2018). Green consumer intentions are considered important construct to achieve green consumer behavior (Mancha & Yoder, 2015). Thus, to understand the green consumer intentions of textile sector, we added this construct to the study.

TECHNOLOGY ACCEPTANCE MODEL

Technology acceptance model developed by (Davis, 1985). This model contains user motivation (perceived usefulness, perceived ease of use and attitude towards the technology) and resultant variables (behavioral intentions and use of technology). Perceived usefulness and perceived ease are the key variables of this model which directly or indirectly explains behavioral intentions and technology use (Marangunić & Granić, 2015).

This model talks about "why do people use technology". In green marketing same question may be asked "why do people purchase green products". This model explains that if consumer perceived green products useful and easy to buy then comes up with favourable attitude.

Figure 2. Technology Acceptance Model
Source: Davis, 1985

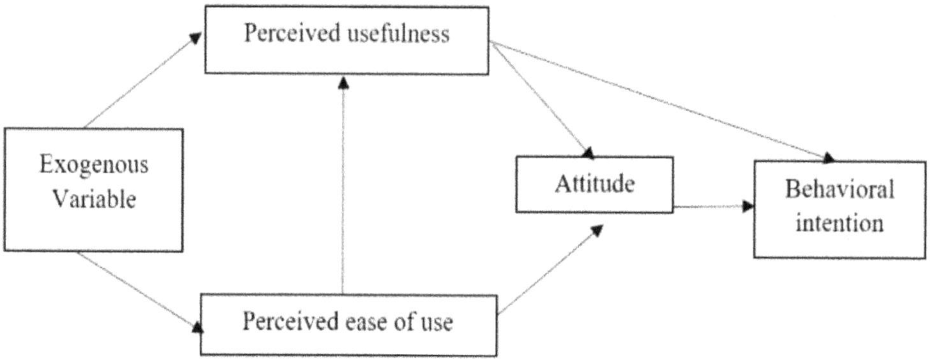

Perceived Usefulness of Green Products

Consumer purchase products which they feel are useful. Marketing is all about creating and capturing value. When consumer considers the product useful then green purchase is possible. So, the authors propose the following relationships:

P4: Perceived usefulness of green products has significant effect on green attitude towards behavior.
P5: Perceived usefulness of green products has significant effect on green consumer intentions.

Perceived Ease of Use on the Use of Green

Perceived ease of use comes from theory of planned behavior as well as from the technology acceptance model while perceived usefulness can be considered as an important variable to consider. Consumers are not considering until the marketers must follow the new ways to address the problem. Green perceived behavioral control is about person's perceived ability to perform certain behavior. Expectancy-value model of attitude assumed that perceived behavioral control is the final product set of control beliefs and perceived easiness or hindrance to perform specific behavior. So, the authors propose the following relationships:

P6: Perceived ease of use of green products has significantly moderates the relationship between green attitude towards behavior and green consumer intentions.

Figure 3. Proposed Model
Source: Proposed Model

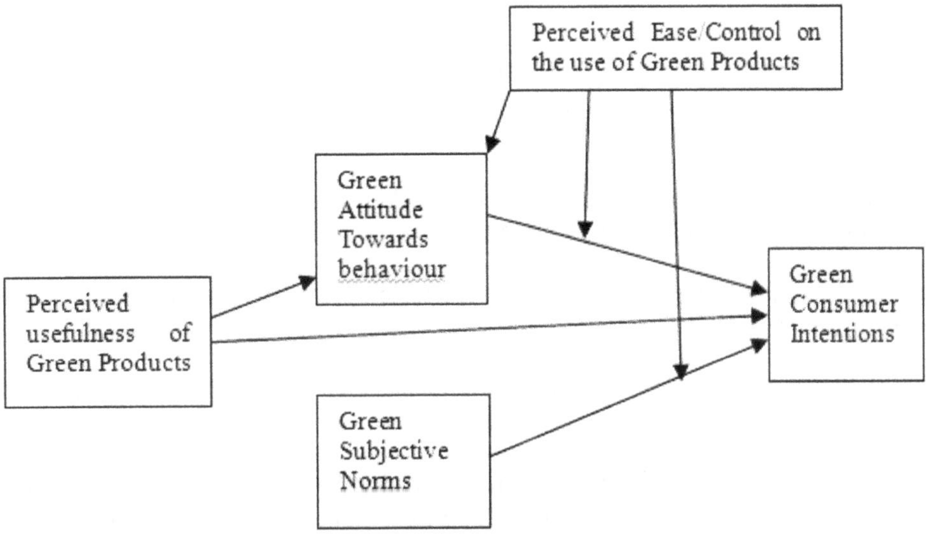

P7: Perceived ease of use of green products has significantly moderates the relationship between green subjective norms and green consumer intentions.

CONCLUSION

This study extended the literature of green marketing by merging theory of planned behavior and technology acceptance model by conceptualizing green consumer behavior of textile industry (branded clothes) in Pakistan. Marketing can be defined as "creating and capturing value". When any organization wants to create value, they need to know exactly which type of value their customers demand. This problem will be solved through consumer behavior research. This is the era of green marketing but unfortunately untapped. Green marketing harness lot of benefits for businessman but it requires identification of significant determinants of green consumer behavior of textile industry (branded clothes) of Pakistan. Marketers can get insight from this study to understand consumer's behavior of textile products of Pakistan. Green consumer intentions identification will also be beneficial for the society. This study will be helpful to reduce water base pollution which will ultimately reduce water borne diseases.

REFERENCES

Ajzen, I. (1991). The theory of planned behavior. *Organizational Behavior and Human Decision Processes, 50*(2), 179–211. doi:10.1016/0749-5978(91)90020-T

Ajzen, I. (2010). *Predicting and changing behavior.* Psychology Press.

Rezai, G., Teng, P. K., Mohamed, Z., & Shamsudin, M. N. (2012). Consumers' awareness and consumption intention towards green foods. *African Journal of Business Management*, *6*(12), 4496.

Riebl, S. K., Estabrooks, P. A., Dunsmore, J. C., Savla, J., Frisard, M. I., Dietrich, A. M., ... Davy, B. M. (2015). A systematic literature review and meta-analysis: The Theory of Planned Behavior's application to understand and predict nutrition-related behaviors in youth. *Eating Behaviors*, *18*, 160–178. doi:10.1016/j.eatbeh.2015.05.016 PMID:26112228

Shabecoff, P. (1993). *A fierce green fire; the American environment movement*. Academic Press.

Sreen, N., Purbey, S., & Sadarangani, P. (2018). Impact of culture, behavior and gender on green purchase intention. *Journal of Retailing and Consumer Services*, *41*, 177–189. doi:10.1016/j.jretconser.2017.12.002

Suki, N. M. (2016). *Handbook of Research on Leveraging Consumer Psychology for Effective Customer Engagement*. IGI Global. https://www.igi-global.com/book/handbook-research-leveraging-consumer-psychology/149284

Suki, N. M., & Suki, N. M. (2015). Consumers' environmental behavior towards staying at a green hotel: Moderation of green hotel knowledge. *Management of Environmental Quality*, *26*(1), 103–117. doi:10.1108/MEQ-02-2014-0023

Suki, N. M., & Suki, N. M. (2019). *Correlations between awareness of green marketing, corporate social responsibility, product image, corporate reputation, and consumer purchase intention. In Corporate Social Responsibility: Concepts, Methodologies, Tools, and Applications* (pp. 143–154). IGI Global. doi:10.4018/978-1-5225-6192-7.ch008

Taufique, K. M. R., & Vaithianathan, S. (2018). A fresh look at understanding Green consumer behavior among young urban Indian consumers through the lens of Theory of Planned Behavior. *Journal of Cleaner Production*, *183*, 46–55. doi:10.1016/j.jclepro.2018.02.097

Timm, S. N., & Deal, B. M. (2016). Effective or ephemeral? The role of energy information dashboards in changing occupant energy behaviors. *Energy Research & Social Science*, *19*, 11–20. doi:10.1016/j.erss.2016.04.020

Wagner, S. A. (2002). *Understanding green consumer behavior: A qualitative cognitive approach*. Routledge. doi:10.4324/9780203444030

Yuriev, A., Dahmen, M., Paillé, P., Boiral, O., & Guillaumie, L. (2020). Pro-environmental behaviors through the lens of the theory of planned behavior: A scoping review. *Resources, Conservation and Recycling*, *155*, 104660. doi:10.1016/j.resconrec.2019.104660

Compilation of References

Aaker, J. L. (1997). Dimensions of Brand Personality. *JMR, Journal of Marketing Research, 34*(3), 347–356. doi:10.1177/002224379703400304

Aaker, J., & Akutsu, S. (2009). Why do people give? The role of identity in giving. *Journal of Consumer Psychology, 19*(3), 267–270. doi:10.1016/j.jcps.2009.05.010

Abd Razak, I. S., & Abdul-Talib, A. N. (2009). *Explorative study of proactive and responsive export market orientation: an in-depth interview.* In Australian and New Zealand Marketing Academy (ANZMAC) Conference, Melbourne, Australia. Available at: www. duplication. net. au/ANZMAC09/papers/ANZMAC2009-288.pdf

Abdul Karim Alias. (2010). *Flipped classroom: Total classroom makeover.* Retrieved from: https://www.openlearning.com/courses/flippedlearning

Abdul Karim Alias. (2014). *Flipped classroom, mobile learning, whatsapp, and learning nuggets.* Retrieved from: http://onestoplearning.blogspot.my/search?q=flipped+classroom

Abdul-Latif, S. A., & Abdul-Talib, A. N. (2017). Consumer racism: A scale modification. *Asia Pacific Journal of Marketing and Logistics, 29*(3), 616–633. doi:10.1108/APJML-02-2016-0026

Abdul-Talib, A. N., Abd-Latif, S. A., & Abd-Razak, I. S. (2016). A study on the boycott motivations of Malaysian non-Muslims. *Journal of Islamic Marketing, 7*(3), 264–287. doi:10.1108/JIMA-11-2014-0071

Abdul-Talib, A. N., & Abd-Razak, I. S. (2012). Export market oriented behaviors within the medical tourism industry: A case study. *International Journal of Tourism Policy, 4*(4), 289–301. doi:10.1504/IJTP.2012.052546

Abdul-Talib, A. N., & Abd-Razak, I. S. (2013). Cultivating export market oriented behavior in halal marketing: Addressing the issues and challenges in going global. *Journal of Islamic Marketing, 4*(2), 187–197. doi:10.1108/17590831311329304

Abdul-Talib, A. N., & Abdul-Latif, S. A. (2015). Antecedents to willingness to Boycotts among Malaysian muslims. In *Emerging Research on Islamic Marketing and Tourism in the Global Economy* (pp. 70–106). IGI Global. doi:10.4018/978-1-4666-6272-8.ch004

Abdul-Talib, A. N., & Mohd Adnan, M. M. (2017). Determinants of consumer's willingness to boycott surrogate products. *Journal of Islamic Marketing, 8*(3), 345–360. doi:10.1108/JIMA-08-2015-0065

Abrams, D., & Hogg, M. (1988). Comments on the motivational status of self-esteem in social identity and intergroup discrimination. *European Journal of Social Psychology, 18*(4), 317–334. doi:10.1002/ejsp.2420180403

Abu Bakar, A. R., & Abdul-Talib, A. N. (2013). A case study of an internationalization process of a private higher education institution in Malaysia. *Gadjah Mada International Journal of Business, 15*(3).

Atsmon, Y., Dixit, V., & Wu, C. (2011). *Dimensions of brand personality.* Insights & Publications, McKinsey & Company. Retrieved from www.mckinsey.com/insights/marketing_sales/tapping_chinas_luxury-goods_market

Atuahene-Gima, K., Slater, S. F., & Olson, E. M. (2005). The contingent value of responsive and proactive market orientations for new product program performance. *Journal of Product Innovation Management, 22*(6), 464–482. doi:10.1111/j.1540-5885.2005.00144.x

Audrin, C., Brosch, T., Sander, D., & Chanal, J. (2018). More than meets the eye: The impact of materialism on information selection during luxury choices. *Frontiers in Behavioral Neuroscience, 12,* 12. doi:10.3389/fnbeh.2018.00172 PMID:30197590

Auriol, E., & Schilizzi, S. G. M. (2003). Quality Signaling through Certification. *Theory and an Application to Agricultural Seed Market.* IDEI Working Papers 165.

Awuni, J. A., & Du, J. (2016). Sustainable Consumption in Chinese Cities: Green Purchasing Intentions of Young Adults Based on the Theory of Consumption Values. *Sustainable Development, 24*(2), 124–135. doi:10.1002d.1613

Bagheri, M. (2014). Luxury consumer behavior in Malaysia: Loud brands vs. quiet brands. *Procedia: Social and Behavioral Sciences, 130,* 316–324. doi:10.1016/j.sbspro.2014.04.037

Bagozzi, R. P., Gopinath, M., & Nyer, P. U. (1999). The role of emotions in marketing. *Journal of the Academy of Marketing Science, 27*(2), 184–206. doi:10.1177/0092070399272005

Bain & Company, Inc. (2019). *Luxury Goods Worldwide Market Study, Fall–Winter 2018.* Retrieved from https://www.bain.com/contentassets/8df501b9f8d6442eba00040246c6b4f9/bain_digest__luxury_goods_worldwide_market_study_fall_winter_2018.pdf

Baker, J. W. (2000). *The 'classroom flip: Using web course management tools to become the guide by the side. 11th International Conference on College Teaching and Learning*, Jacksonville, FL.

Bakos, Y., & Katsamakas, E. (2008). Design and Ownership of Two-Sided Networks: Implications for Internet Platforms. *Journal of Management Information Systems, 25*(2), 171–202. doi:10.2753/MIS0742-1222250208

Barbier, E. C. (1987). The Concept of Sustainable Economic Development. *Environmental Conservation, 14*(2), 101–110. doi:10.1017/S0376892900011449

Basel Committee on Banking Supervision (BCBS) (2018). *Sound Practices: implications of fintech developments for banks and bank supervisors.* Author.

Basili, M., & Rossi, M. A. (2019). (in press). Platform-mediated reputation systems in the sharing economy and incentives to provide service quality: The case of ridesharing services. *Electronic Commerce Research and Applications.*

Batra, R., Ramaswamy, V., Alden, D., Steenkamp, J., & Ramachander, S. (2000). Effects of Brand Local and Nonlocal Origin on Consumer Attitudes in Developing Countries. *Journal of Consumer Psychology, 9*(2), 83–95. doi:10.1207/S15327663JCP0902_3

Baumeister, R. F. (1982). Self-esteem, self-presentation, and future interaction: A dilemma of reputation. *Journal of Personality, 50*(1), 29–45. doi:10.1111/j.1467-6494.1982.tb00743.x

Bautista, R. (2019). Green behavior and generation: A multi-group analysis using structural equation modeling. *Asia-Pacific Social Science Review, 19*(1), 1–16.

Baym, N. K., & Burnett, R. (2009). Amateur experts: International fan labour in Swedish independent music. *International Journal of Cultural Studies, 12*(5), 433–449. doi:10.1177/1367877909337857

Baysak, E., Kaya, F. D., Dalgar, I., & Candansayar, S. (2016). Online Game Addiction in a Sample from Turkey: Development and Validation of the Turkish Version of Game Addiction Scale. *Klinik Psikofarmakoloji Bülteni, 26*(1), 21–31. doi:10.5455/bcp.20150502073016

Becker, G. S., Murphy, K. M., & Werning, I. (2005). The equilibrium distribution of income and the market for status. *Journal of Political Economy, 113*(2), 282–310. doi:10.1086/427463

Beck, T., Demiruc-Kunt, A., & Livine, R. (2005). SMEs, Growth and Poverty: A Cross-Country Evidence. *Journal of Economic Growth, 10*(3), 199–229. doi:10.100710887-005-3533-5

Belch, G. A., & Belch, M. A. (2003). Organizing for Advertising and Promotion. In Advertising and Promotion, Sixth Edition (p. 819). Academic Press.

Belk, R. W. (1984). Three scales to measure constructs related to materialism: Reliability, validity, and relationships to measures of happiness. In T. Kinnear (Ed.), *Advances in Consumer Research* (Vol. 11, pp. 291–297). Provo, UT: Association for Consumer Research.

Belk, R. W. (1985). Materialism: Trait aspects of living in the material world. *The Journal of Consumer Research, 12*(3), 265–280. doi:10.1086/208515

Belk, R. W. (1996). Hyperreality and globalization: Culture in the age of Ronald McDonald. *Journal of International Consumer Marketing, 8*(3-4), 23–37. doi:10.1300/J046v08n03_03

Benedicktus, R. L., Brady, M. K., Darke, P. R., & Voorhees, C. M. (2010). Conveying trustworthiness to online consumers: Reactions to consensus, physical store presence, brand familiarity, and generalized suspicion. *Journal of Retailing, 86*(4), 322–335. doi:10.1016/j.jretai.2010.04.002

Benson, R., & Powers, M. (2011). *Public media and political independence. Lessons for the Future of Journalism from Around the World.* http://newstv.mediasapiens.ua/sites/mediaosvita.com.ua/files/mariastv/public– media–and–political–independence_4.pdf

Beranuy, M., Carbonell, X., & Griffiths, M. D. (2013). A Qualitative Analysis of Online Gaming Addicts in Treatment. *International Journal of Mental Health and Addiction, 11*(2), 149–161. doi:10.100711469-012-9405-2

Berger, J., & Schwartz, E. M. (2011). What drives immediate and ongoing word of mouth? *JMR, Journal of Marketing Research, 48*(5), 869–880. doi:10.1509/jmkr.48.5.869

Bhatnagar, A., Misra, S., & Rao, H. R. (2000). On risk, convenience, and internet shopping behavior. *Communications of the ACM, 43*(11), 98–114. doi:10.1145/353360.353371

Bhattacharya, C. B., & Sen, S. (2003). Consumer-Company Identification: A Framework for Understanding Consumers' Relationships with Companies. *Journal of Marketing, 67*(2), 76–88. doi:10.1509/jmkg.67.2.76.18609

Bhattacherjee, A. (2002). Individual trust in online firms: Scale development and initial test. *Journal of Management Information Systems, 19*(1), 211–242. doi:10.1080/07421222.2002.11045715

Bhuiyan, N. (2013). A Framework for successful new product development. *Journal of Industrial Engineering and Management, §§§*, 4.

Bigné, E., Caplliure, E. M., & Miquel, M. J. (2016). eWOM on travel agency selection: Specialized versus private label. *Psychology and Marketing, 33*(12), 1046–1053. doi:10.1002/mar.20938

Biswas, D. (2004). Economics of information in he web economy, towards a new theory? *Journal of Business Research, 57*, 724–733. doi:10.1016/S0148-2963(02)00355-7

Blocker, C. P., Flint, D. J., Myers, M. B., & Slater, S. F. (2011). Proactive customer orientation and its role for creating customer value in global markets. *Journal of the Academy of Marketing Science, 39*(2), 216–233. doi:10.100711747-010-0202-9

Blowfield, M., Visser, W., & Livesey, F. (2008, September). Sustainability innovation: mapping the territory. In *Corporate Responsibility Research Conference*. Cambridge University Press.

Blumer, H. (1969). Fashion: From class differentiation to collective selection. *The Sociological Quarterly, 10*(3), 275–291. doi:10.1111/j.1533-8525.1969.tb01292.x

Bocken, N. M., Short, S. W., Rana, P., & Evans, S. (2014). A Literature and Practice Review to Develop Sustainable Business Model Archetypes. *Journal of Cleaner Production, 65*, 42–56. doi:10.1016/j.jclepro.2013.11.039

Bødker, M., Gimpel, G., & Hedman, J. (2009). *The user experience of smart phones: a consumption values approach*. Retrieved January 13, 2018, from http://citeseerx.ist.psu.edu/viewdoc/download?doi=10.1.1.472.30&rep=rep1&type=pdf

Boon, C., Teo, C., Sidin, S., Izzudin, M., & Nor, M. (2013). *Social Sciences & Humanities Exploring Influences of Consumer Socialization Agents on Branded Apparel Purchase among Urban Malaysian Tweens*. Academic Press.

Boo, S., & Kim, J. (2013). Comparison of negative eWOM intention: An exploratory study. *Journal of Quality Assurance in Hospitality & Tourism, 14*(1), 24–48. doi:10.1080/1528008X.2013.749381

Booth, J. R., & Smith, R. L. II. (1986). Capital raising, underwriting and the certification hypothesis. *Journal of Financial Economics, 15*(1), 261–281. doi:10.1016/0304-405X(86)90057-7

Bourdieu, P. (1986). The Forms of Capital. In J. Richardson (Ed.), *Handbook of Theory: Research for the Sociology of Education* (pp. 241–258). New York: Greenwood.

Boyd, D. M., & Ellison, N. B. (2008). Social Network Sites: Definition History, and Scholarship. *Journal of Computer-Mediated Communication, 13*(1), 210–230. doi:10.1111/j.1083-6101.2007.00393.x

Brewer, M. B., & Kramer, R. M. (1986). Choice behavior in social dilemmas: Effects of social identity, group size, and decision framing. *Journal of Personality and Social Psychology, 50*(3), 543–549. doi:10.1037/0022-3514.50.3.543

Brian, D. N. G., & Wiemer-Hastings, P. (2005). Addiction to the Internet and Online Gaming. *Cyberpsychology & Behavior, 8*(2), 110–113. doi:10.1089/cpb.2005.8.110 PMID:15938649

Broekhuizen, T. L. J. (2006). *Understanding channel purchase intentions: Measuring online and offline shopping value perceptions*. Retrieved January 13, 2018, from https://www.van-haaften.nl/images/documents/pdf/Measuring%20Online%20and%20Offline%20Shopping%20value%20perception.pdf

Bronner, F., & de Hoog, R. (2011). Vacationers and eWOM: Who posts, and why, where, and what? *Journal of Travel Research, 50*(1), 15–26. doi:10.1177/0047287509355324

Brown, H. D. (1980). *Principles of Language and Teaching*. Prentice Hall, Inc.

Brown, J. S., & Duguid, P. (1991). Organizational learning and communities-of-practice: Toward a unified view of working, learning, and innovation. *Organization Science, 2*(1), 40–57. doi:10.1287/orsc.2.1.40

Brown, J., Broderick, A. J., & Lee, N. (2007). Word of mouth communication within online communities: Conceptualizing the online social network. *Journal of Interactive Marketing, 21*(3), 2–20. doi:10.1002/dir.20082

Brüggemann, M., Humprecht, E., Nielsen, R. K., Karppinen, K., Cornia, A., & Esser, F. (2015). Framing the Newspaper Crisis. *Journalism Studies, 17*(5), 533–551. doi:10.1080/1461670X.2015.1006871

Bruno, N., & Nielsen, R. K. (2012). *Oxford: Reuters Institute for the Study of Journalism*. http://reutersinstitute.politics.ox.ac.uk/sites/default/files/Survival%20is%20Success%20Journalistic%20Online%20Start-Ups%20in%20Western%20Europe_0.pdf

Bryman, A., & Cramer, D. (2001). Quantitative Data Analysis with SPSS Release 10 for Windows. *Analysis* (Vol. 1). doi:10.4324/9780203471548

Brynjolfsson, E., Eggers, F., & Gannamaneni, A. (2017). Using Massive Online Choice Experiments to Measure Changes in Wellbeing. *5th IMF Statistical Forum.*

Buchanan, T., & Whitty, M. T. (2014). The online dating romance scam: Causes and consequences of victimhood. *Psychology, Crime & Law*, *20*(3), 261–283. doi:10.1080/1068316X.2013.772180

Buhr, D. (2015). *Industry 4.0 – New Tasks for Innovation Policy*. Retrived on 9 Dec 2019 from http://library.fes.de/pdf-files/wiso/11480.pdf

Bureau of Economic Analysis (BEA). (2019). *Digital Economy Accounted for 6.9 Percent of GDP in 2017*. Author.

Burton, J., & Khammash, M. (2010). Why do people read reviews posted on consumer-opinion portals? *Journal of Marketing Management*, *26*(3–4), 230–255. doi:10.1080/02672570903566268

Byrne, D., Corrado, C., & Sichel, D. (2017). The Rise of Cloud Computing: Minding Your P's, Q's and K's. *5th IMF Statistical Forum.*

Cadogan, J. W., Cui, C., & Kwok, Y. L. E. (2003). Export market-oriented behavior and export performance. *International Marketing Review*, *20*(5), 493–513. doi:10.1108/02651330310498753

Cadogan, J. W., Diamantopoulos, A., & de Mortanges, C. P. (1999). A measure of export market orientation: Scale development and cross-cultural validation. *Journal of International Business Studies*, *30*(4), 689–707. doi:10.1057/palgrave.jibs.8490834

Cadogan, J. W., Diamantopoulos, A., & Siguaw, J. A. (2002). Export market-oriented activities: Their antecedents and performance consequences. *Journal of International Business Studies*, *33*(3), 615–626. doi:10.1057/palgrave.jibs.8491036

Cadogan, J. W., Paul, N. J., Salminen, R. T., Puumalainen, K., & Sundqvist, S. (2001). Key antecedents to "export" market-oriented behaviors: A cross-national empirical examination. *International Journal of Research in Marketing*, *18*(3), 261–282. doi:10.1016/S0167-8116(01)00038-6

Caillaud, B., & Jullien, B. (2003). Chicken & egg: Competition among intermediation service providers. *The RAND Journal of Economics*, *34*(2), 309–328. doi:10.2307/1593720

Callander, S., & Matouschek, N. (2019). The Risk of Failure: Trial and Error Learning and Long-Run Performance. *American Economic Journal. Microeconomics*, *11*(1), 44–78. doi:10.1257/mic.20160359

Campbell, C., Ferraro, C., & Sands, S. (2014). Segmenting consumer reactions to social network marketing. *European Journal of Marketing*, *48*(3/4), 432–452. doi:10.1108/EJM-03-2012-0165

Candan, B., Ünal, S., & Erciş, A. (2013). Analysing the relationship between consumption values and brand loyalty of young people: A study on personal care products. European Journal Research on Education. Special ıssue. *Human Resource Management*, 29–46. doi:10.11648/j.jhrm.20130102.11

Casaló, L. V., Flavián, C., Guinalíu, M., & Ekinci, Y. (2015). Avoiding the dark side of positive online consumer reviews: Enhancing reviews' usefulness for high risk-averse travelers. *Journal of Business Research*, *68*(9), 1829–1835. doi:10.1016/j.jbusres.2015.01.010

Castaneda, M., Martinez, C., Marte, R., & Roxas, B. (2015). Explaining the environmentally-sustainable consumer behavior: A social capital perspective. *Social Responsibility Journal, 11*(4), 658–676. doi:10.1108/SRJ-02-2014-0019

Caswell, J. A., & Mojduszka, E. M. (1996). Using informational labeling to influence the market for quality in food products. *American Journal of Agricultural Economics, 78*(5), 1248–1253. doi:10.2307/1243501

Celani, A., & Singh, P. (2011). Signaling theory and applicant attraction outcomes. *Personnel Review, 40*(2), 222–238. doi:10.1108/00483481111106093

CGA (Causal Games Association). (2016). *The Mobile Games Market, How to Compete in the Crowded Marketplace, Causal Games Sector Report 2016.* Retrieved November 1, 2019 from http://progamedev.net/wp-content/uploads/2016/07/Newzoo_CGA_How_to_Compete_in_Mobile_Games.pdf

Chakravarty, A., Liu, Y., & Mazumdar, T. (2010). The differential effects of online word-of-mouth and critics' reviews on pre-release movie evaluation. *Journal of Interactive Marketing, 24*(3), 185–197. doi:10.1016/j.intmar.2010.04.001

Chang, L. D. M., Ling Tam, A. Y., & Suki, N. M. (2016). Moderating effect of races towards consumers' feeling of TCM usage. Handbook of Research on Leveraging Consumer Psychology for Effective Customer Engagement, 306-323.

Chang, J. J. S. (2008). An analysis of advance fee fraud on the internet. *Journal of Financial Crime, 15*(1), 71–81. doi:10.1108/13590790810841716

Chang, J. J. S., & Chong, M. D. (2010). Psychological influences in e-mail fraud. *Journal of Financial Crime, 17*(3), 337–350. doi:10.1108/13590791011056309

Chang, L., & Arkin, R. M. (2002). Materialism as an attempt to cope with uncertainty. *Psychology and Marketing, 19*(5), 389–406. doi:10.1002/mar.10016

Chang, S.-H., & Chou, C.-H. (2018). Consumer Intention toward bringing your own shopping bags in Taiwan: An application of ethics perspective and theory of planned behavior. *Sustainability (Switzerland), 10*(6), 1815. doi:10.3390u10061815

Charlton, J. P., & Danforth, I. D. W. (2007). Distinguishing addiction and high engagement in the context of online game playing. *Computers in Human Behavior, 23*(3), 1531–1548. doi:10.1016/j.chb.2005.07.002

Chatterjee, P. (2001). Online reviews: Do consumers use them? *Advances in Consumer Research. Association for Consumer Research (U. S.), 28*, 129–133.

Chaudhuri, H. R., & Majumdar, S. (2006). Of diamonds and desires: Understanding conspicuous consumption from a contemporary marketing perspective. *Academy of Marketing Science Review, 2006*(11).

Chaudhuri, H. R., Mazumdar, S., & Ghoshal, A. (2011). Conspicuous consumption orientation: Conceptualisation, scale development and validation. *Journal of Consumer Behaviour, 10*(4), 216–224. doi:10.1002/cb.364

Chen, E. Y. I., Yeh, N.-C., & Wang, C. P. (2008). Conspicuous consumption: A preliminary report of scale development and validation. *Advances in Consumer Research. Association for Consumer Research (U. S.), 35*, 686–687.

Cheng, Y. H., & Ho, H. Y. (2015). Social influence's impact on reader perceptions of online reviews. *Journal of Business Research, 68*(4), 883–887. doi:10.1016/j.jbusres.2014.11.046

Chen, H., Rong, W. M. X., Qu, Y., & Zhang, X. (2017). *An Extended Technology Acceptance Model for Mobile Social Gaming Service Popularity Analysis* (Vol. 2017). Hindawi Mobile Information Systems.

Chen, J., Teng, L., Yu, Y., & Yu, X. (2016). The effect of online information sources on purchase intentions between consumers with high and low susceptibility to informational influence. *Journal of Business Research, 69*(2), 467–475. doi:10.1016/j.jbusres.2015.05.003

Chen, Q., Zhang, M., & Zhao, X. (2017). Analysing customer behaviour in mobile app usage. *Industrial Management & Data Systems, 117*(2), 425–438. doi:10.1108/IMDS-04-2016-0141

Chen, X., Zhou, L., & Wan, D. (2016). Group social capital and lending outcomes in the financial credit market: An empirical study of online peer-to-peer lending. *Electronic Commerce Research and Applications, 15*, 1–13. doi:10.1016/j.elerap.2015.11.003

Chen, Z., & Lurie, N. H. (2013). Temporal contiguity and negativity bias in the impact of online word of mouth. *JMR, Journal of Marketing Research, 50*(4), 463–476. doi:10.1509/jmr.12.0063

Chesbrough, H. W. (2003). *Open innovation the new imperative for creating and profiting from technology*. Boston: Harvard Business School Press.

Cheung, C. M. K., & Lee, M. K. O. (2012). What drives consumers to spread electronic word of mouth in online consumer-opinion platforms. *Decision Support Systems, 53*(1), 218–225. doi:10.1016/j.dss.2012.01.015

Chevalier, J. A., & Mayzlin, D. (2006). The effect of word of mouth on sales: Online book reviews. *JMR, Journal of Marketing Research, 43*(3), 345–354. doi:10.1509/jmkr.43.3.345

Chi, H., Yeh, H., & Tsai, Y. (2011). The influences of perceived value on consumer purchase intention: The moderating effect of advertising endorser. *Journal of International Management Studies, 6*(1), 1–6.

Chin, B., & Morimoto, L. (2013). Towards a theory of transcultural fandom. *Participations, 10*(1), 92–108.

Chintagunta, P. K., Gopinath, S., & Venkataraman, S. (2010). The effects of online user reviews on movie box office performance: Accounting for sequential rollout and aggregation across local markets. *Marketing Science, 29*(5), 944–957. doi:10.1287/mksc.1100.0572

Chiou, J. S., Hsiao, C. C., & Chiu, T. Y. (2018). The credibility and attribution of online reviews: Differences between high and low product knowledge consumers. *Online Information Review, 42*(5), 630–646. doi:10.1108/OIR-06-2017-0197

Chiu, C. M., Hsu, M. H., & Wang, E. T. (2006). Understanding knowledge sharing in virtual communities: An integration of social capital and social cognitive theories. *Decision Support Systems, 42*(3), 1872–1888. doi:10.1016/j.dss.2006.04.001

Chiu, H. C., Pant, A., Hsieh, Y. C., Lee, M., Hsioa, Y. T., & Roan, J. (2014). Snowball to avalanche: Understanding the different predictors of the intention to propagate online marketing messages. *European Journal of Marketing, 48*(7/8), 1255–1273. doi:10.1108/EJM-05-2012-0329

Chiu, S. I., Lee, J. Z., & Huang, D. H. (2004). Video Game Addiction in Children and Teenagers in Taiwan. *Cyberpsychology & Behavior, 7*(5), 571–581. doi:10.1089/cpb.2004.7.571 PMID:15667052

Chrysochou, P., & Festila, A. (2019). A content analysis of organic product package designs. *Journal of Consumer Marketing, 36*(4), 441–448. doi:10.1108/JCM-06-2018-2720

Chu, S., & Keh, H. T. (2006). Brand value creation: Analysis of the Interbrand-Business Week brand value rankings. *Marketing Letters, 17*(4), 323–331. doi:10.100711002-006-9407-6

Churchill, G. A. Jr, & Moschis, G. P. (1979). Television and interpersonal influences on adolescent consumer learning. *The Journal of Consumer Research, 6*(1), 23–35. doi:10.1086/208745

Chu, S. C., Windels, K., & Kamal, S. (2016). The influence of self-construal and materialism on social media intensity: A study of China and the United States. *International Journal of Advertising, 35*(3), 569–588. doi:10.1080/02650487.2015.1068425

Claudio Feijoo, C., Gómez-Barroso, J. L., Aguado, J. M., & Ramos, S. (2012). Mobile gaming: Industry challenges and policy implications. *Telecommunications Policy*, *36*(3), 212–221. doi:10.1016/j.telpol.2011.12.004

Clow, K., & Donald, B. (2012). *Integrated Advertising, Promotion and Marketing Communications*. Essex: Pearson.

Cohen, D., Prusak, L., & Prusak, L. (2001). *In good company: How social capital makes organizations work* (Vol. 15). Harvard Business School Press Boston.

Coleman, J. (1988). Social capital in the creation of human capital. *American Journal of Sociology*, *94*, 95–120. doi:10.1086/228943

Colombo, M. G., Franzoni, C., & Rossi-Lamastra, C. (2015). Internal social capital and the attraction of early contributions in crowdfunding. *Entrepreneurship Theory and Practice*, *39*(1), 75–100. doi:10.1111/etap.12118

Connelly, B. L., Certo, S. T., Ireland, R. D., & Reutzel, C. R. (2011). Signaling theory: A review and Assessment. *Journal of Management*, *37*(1), 39–67. doi:10.1177/0149206310388419

Cook, S., Richard, S.W., (1980). *The Scope of Grammar: the Study of Modern Grammar*. Academic Press.

Corder, S. P. (1981). *Error Analysis and Interlanguage*. Oxford: Oxford University Press.

Cornia, A., Sehl, A., & Nielsen, R. K. (2016). *Private Sector Media and Digital News*. http://reutersinstitute.politics.ox.ac.uk/sites/default/files/Cornia%20- %20Private%20Sector%20Media%20and%20Digital%20News%20FINAL.pdf

Coté, M., & Pybus, J. (2007). Learning to immaterial labour 2.0: MySpace and social networks. *Ephemera, 7*(1), 88-106.

Coulter, K., & Roggeveen, A. (2012). Like it or not. *Management Research Review*, *35*(9), 878–899. doi:10.1108/01409171211256587

Cramer, J., & Krueger, A. B. (2016). Disruptive change in the taxi business: The case of Uber. *The American Economic Review*, *106*(5), 177–182. doi:10.1257/aer.p20161002

Daley, B., & Green, B. (2014). Market signaling with grades. *Journal of Economic Theory*, *151*, 114–145. doi:10.1016/j.jet.2013.10.009

Darling-Wolf, F. (2004). Virtually multicultural: trans-Asian identity and gender in an international fan community of a Japanese star. *New Media & Society*, *6*(4), 507–528. doi:10.1177/146144804044332

Davis, M. (1992). Codes of ethics, professions, and conflict of interest: A case study of an emerging profession, clinical engineering. *Professional Ethics, A Multidisciplinary Journal, 1*(1/2), 179-195.

Davis, F. D. (1985). *A technology acceptance model for empirically testing new end-user information systems: Theory and results*. Massachusetts Institute of Technology.

Davis, F. D. (1989). Perceived Usefulness, Perceived Ease of Use, and User Acceptance of Information Technology. *Management Information Systems Quarterly*, *13*(3), 319–340. doi:10.2307/249008

Davis, R. A. (2001). A cognitive-behavioral model of pathological Internet use. *Computers in Human Behavior*, *17*(2), 1, 187–195. doi:10.1016/S0747-5632(00)00041-8

De la Puente, M. P., & Balmori, A. (2007). Addiction to cell phones: Are there neurophysiological mechanisms involved? *Proyecto*, *61*, 8–12.

de Run, E. C., Butt, M., & Nee, C. Y. (2010). The influence of role models on young adults purchase. *Jurnal Kemanusiaan*, *15*, 70–81.

De Silva, M., Howells, J., & Meyer, M. (2018). Innovation intermediaries and collaboration: Knowledge–based practices and internal value creation. *Research Policy*, *47*(1), 70–87. doi:10.1016/j.respol.2017.09.011

De Souza, L. L. F., & De Freitas, A. A. F. (2017). Consumer behavior of electronic games' players: A study on the intentions to play and to pay. *Revista ADM*, *52*, 419–430.

Deci, E. L., & Ryan, R. M. (1995). Human autonomy: The basis for true self-esteem. In M. Kemis (Ed.), *Efficacy, agency, and self-esteem* (pp. 31–49). New York: Plenum.

Dellarocas, C. (2003). The digitization of word of mouth: Promise and challenges of online feedback mechanisms. *Management Science*, *49*(10), 1407–1424. doi:10.1287/mnsc.49.10.1407.17308

Deloitte. (2017). *The new luxury consumers. Global Powers of Luxury Goods 2017*. Retrieved from: https://www2.deloitte.com/content/dam/Deloitte/global/Documents/consumer-industrial-products/gx-cip-global-powers-luxury-2017.pdf

Demirgüneş, B. K. (2015). Relative Importance of Perceived Value, Satisfaction and Perceived Risk on Willingness to Pay More. *International Review of Management and Marketing*, *5*(4), 211–220.

Denning, S. (2014). An economy of access is opening for business: Five strategies for success. *Strategy and Leadership*, *42*(4), 14–21. doi:10.1108/SL-05-2014-0037

Denys, V., & Mendes, J. (2014). Consumption values and destination evaluation in destination decision making. *Journal of Spatial and Organizational Dynamics*, *2*(1), 4–22.

Department of Statistics Malaysia. (2018). *Agriculture*. Available online from https://www.dosm.gov.my/v1/index.php?r=column/ctwoByCat&parent_id=45&menu_id=Z0VTZGU1UHBUT1VJMFlpaXRRR0xpdz09

De-Sola Gutierrez, J., Rodriguez de Fonseca, F., & Rubio, G. (2016). Cell-Phone Addiction: A Review. *Frontiers in Psychiatry*, *7*(175), 1–15. PMID:27822187

DeVellis, R. F. (2003). Applied Social Research Methods Series: Vol. 26. Scale Development: Theory and Applications. Academic Press.

Dhar, R., & Nowlis, S. M. (1999). Consumer preference for the no-choice option. *The Journal of Consumer Research*, *24*(2), 215–231. doi:10.1086/209506

Dholakia, U. M., Bagozzi, R. P., & Pearo, L. K. (2004). A social influence model of consumer participation in network- and small-group-based virtual communities. *International Journal of Research in Marketing*, *21*(3), 241–263. doi:10.1016/j.ijresmar.2003.12.004

Diana, S., Tobi, S. N., & Masrom, M. (2015). *Cybercrime over Internet Love Scams in Malaysia : A Discussion on the Theoretical Perspectives, Connecting Factors and Keys to the Problem*. doi:10.5296/jmr.v7i2.6938

Dieckmann, T. (1999). The evolution of conventions with mobile players. *Journal of Economic Behavior & Organization*, *38*(1), 93–111. doi:10.1016/S0167-2681(98)00125-5

Dimara, E., & Skuras, D. (2003). Consumer evaluations of product certification, geographic association and traceability in Greece. *European Journal of Marketing*, *37*(5/6), 690–705. doi:10.1108/03090560310465099

Dimoka, A., Hong, Y., & Pavlou, P. A. (2012). On product uncertainty in online markets: Theory and evidence. *Management Information Systems Quarterly*, *36*(2), 395–426. doi:10.2307/41703461

Dinsmore, J. B., Swani, K., & Dugan, R. G. (2017). To "Free" or Not to "Free": Trait Predictors of Mobile App Purchasing Tendencies. *Psychology and Marketing*, *34*(2), 227–244. doi:10.1002/mar.20985

Dogan, E. (2017). A strategic approach to innovation. *Journal of Management Marketing and Logistics*, *4*(3), 290–300.

Donath, J. (2007). Signals in social supernets. *Journal of Computer-Mediated Communication*, *13*(1), 231–251. doi:10.1111/j.1083-6101.2007.00394.x

Dosi, G. (1982). Technological paradigms and technological trajectories. *Research Policy*, *11*(3), 147–162. doi:10.1016/0048-7333(82)90016-6

Dou, G., He, P., & Xu, X. (2016). One-side value-added service investment and pricing strategies for a two-sided platform. *International Journal of Production Research*, *54*(13), 3808–3821. doi:10.1080/00207543.2016.1148275

Drucker, P. (1985). *Innovation and entrepreneurship: Practices and principles*. New York: Harper & Row.

Duan, W., Gu, B., & Whinston, A. B. (2008). The dynamics of online word-of-mouth and product sales-An empirical investigation of the movie industry. *Journal of Retailing*, *84*(2), 233–242. doi:10.1016/j.jretai.2008.04.005

Durvasula, S., Lysonski, S., & Watson, J. (Eds.). (2015). *Proceedings of the 1997 World Marketing Congress. A Cross-Cultural Examination of a Scale to Measure Trait Aspects of Vanity*. Springer.

EAO. (2010-2014). Yearbook 2010-2014: Television, Cinema, Video and On-Demand Audiovisual Services – the Pan-European Picture. Strasbourg: European Audiovisual Observatory.

EAO. (2016). *Yearbook 2015: Television, VOD, Cinema and Video in 39 European States: Markets and Players, Services and Usage*. Strasbourg: European Audiovisual Observatory.

EBU (European Broadcasting Union). (2013). *Viewpoint: Media Freedom and Pluralism*. http://www3.ebu.ch/files/live/sites/ebu/files/Publications/ebuviewpoint-MediaFreedom_eN.pdf

Echegaray, F., & Hansstein, F. V. (2017). Assessing the intention-behavior gap in electronic waste recycling: The case of Brazil. *Journal of Cleaner Production*, *142*, 180–190. doi:10.1016/j.jclepro.2016.05.064

Economic Advisor's Wing Finance Division. G. o. P. (2019). *Pakistan Economic Survey 2018-2019*. Retrieved from Islamabad: http://www.finance.gov.pk/survey/chapters_19/Economic_Survey_2018_19.pdf

Eisenmann, T., Parker, G., & Van Alstyne, M. W. (2006). Strategies for Two-Sided Markets. *Harvard Business Review*, *84*(10), 92–102.

Eisingerich, A. B., Helen, H., Liu, Y., Michael, H., & Bell, S. J. (2015). Why recommend a brand face-to-face but not on Facebook? How word-of-mouth on online social sites differs from traditional word-of-mouth. *Journal of Consumer Psychology*, *25*(1), 120–128. doi:10.1016/j.jcps.2014.05.004

Ekşi, O., & Candan, F. B. (2018). The effect of lifestyle on conspicuous consumption. *Current Debates in Business Studies*, (15), 109-125.

Ellis, R. (2008). *The study of second language acquisition* (2nd ed.). Oxford: Oxford University Press.

Engel, J. F., Kollat, D. T., & Blackwell, R. D. (1968). *Consumer Behavior*. New York: Holt, Rinehart &Winston.

ERIA-OECD. (2014). *ASEAN SME Policy Index 2014: Towards Competitive and Innovative ASEAN SMEs, Economic Research Institute for ASEAN and East Asia, Jakarta*. https://www.oecd.org/southeast-asia/ASEAN%20SME%20Policy%20Index%2014.pdf

Escobar, A. (2016). The impact of the digital revolution in the development of market and communication strategies for the luxury sector (fashion luxury). *Central European Business Review*, *5*(2), 17–36. doi:10.18267/j.cebr.149

Esmark Jones, C. L., Stevens, J. L., Breazeale, M., & Spaid, B. I. (2018). Tell it like it is: The effects of differing responses to negative online reviews. *Psychology and Marketing, 35*(12), 891–901. doi:10.1002/mar.21142

European Parliament. (2016). *Closing the loop New circular economy package.* Retrieved on 9 Dec 2019 from http://www.europarl.europa.eu/RegData/etudes/BRIE/2016/573899/ EPRS_BRI%282016%29573899_EN.pdf

Evans, D. S. (2003). Some Empirical Aspects of Multi-Sided Platform Industries. *Review of Network Economics, 2*(3), 191–209. doi:10.2202/1446-9022.1026

EY. (2014). *Shifting from Consumption to Experience.* Retrieved on 9 Dec 2019 from https://www.ey.com/Publication/vwLUAssets/EY-Shifting-from-consumer-to-experience/$FILE/EY-Shifting-from-consumer-to-experience.pdf

Felbermayr, A., & Nanopoulos, A. (2016). The role of emotions for the perceived usefulness in online customer reviews. *Journal of Interactive Marketing, 36*, 60–76. doi:10.1016/j.intmar.2016.05.004

Filieri, R. (2015). What makes online reviews helpful? A diagnosticity-adoption framework to explain informational and normative influences in e-WOM. *Journal of Business Research, 68*(6), 1261–1270. doi:10.1016/j.jbusres.2014.11.006

Filieri, R., Hofacker, C. F., & Alguezaui, S. (2018). What makes information in online consumer reviews diagnostic over time? The role of review relevancy, factuality, currency, source credibility and ranking score. *Computers in Human Behavior, 80*, 122–131. doi:10.1016/j.chb.2017.10.039

Filieri, R., McLeay, F., Tsui, B., & Lin, Z. (2018). Consumer perceptions of information helpfulness and determinants of purchase intention in online consumer reviews of services. *Information & Management, 55*(8), 956–970. doi:10.1016/j.im.2018.04.010

Fischer, E., & Reuber, R. (2007). The good, the bad, and the unfamiliar: The challenges of reputation formation facing new firms. *Entrepreneurship Theory and Practice, 31*(1), 53–75. doi:10.1111/j.1540-6520.2007.00163.x

Fishbein, M., & Ajzen, I. (1977). *Belief, attitude, intention, and behavior: An introduction to theory and research.* Academic Press.

Fishbein, M., & Ajzen, I. (2005). Theory-based behavior change interventions: Comments on Hobbis and Sutton. *Journal of Health Psychology, 10*(1), 27–31. doi:10.1177/1359105305048552 PMID:15576497

Fisher, S. (1994). Identifying video game addiction in children and adolescents. *Addictive Behaviors, 19*(5), 545–553. doi:10.1016/0306-4603(94)90010-8 PMID:7832013

Fitzmaurice, J., & Comegys, C. (2006). Materialism and social consumption. *Journal of Marketing Theory and Practice, 14*(4), 287–299. doi:10.2753/MTP1069-6679140403

Fitzsimons, G. J., & Lehmann, D. R. (2004). Reactance to recommendations: When unsolicited advice yields contrary responses. *Marketing Science, 23*(1), 82–94. doi:10.1287/mksc.1030.0033

Flood, R., & Jackson, M. (1991). *Creative Problem Solving: Total Systems Intervention.* Wiley.

Floyd, K., Freling, R., Alhoqail, S., Cho, H. Y., & Freling, T. (2014). How online product reviews affect retail sales: A meta-analysis. *Journal of Retailing, 90*(2), 217–232. doi:10.1016/j.jretai.2014.04.004

Folkes, V., & Matta, S. (2004). The Effect of Package Shape on Consumers' Judgments of Product Volume: Attention as a Mental Contaminant. *The Journal of Consumer Research, 31*(2), 390–401. doi:10.1086/422117

Folse, J. A. G., Porter, M. III, Godbole, M. B., & Reynolds, K. E. (2016). The effects of negatively valenced emotional expressions in online reviews on the reviewer, the review, and the product. *Psychology and Marketing, 33*(9), 747–760. doi:10.1002/mar.20914

Fontaine, M. (2013). Corporate Social Responsibility And Sustainability: The New Bottom Line? *International Journal of Business and Social Science*, *4*(4).

Forehand, M. R., Deshpande´, R., & Reed, A. (2002). Identity Salience and the Influence of Differential Activation of the Social Self-Schema on Advertising Response. *The Journal of Applied Psychology*, *87*(6), 1086–1099. doi:10.1037/0021-9010.87.6.1086 PMID:12558216

Foroudi, P. (2018). Influence of brand signature, brand awareness, brand attitude, brand reputation on hotel industry's brand performance. *International Journal of Hospitality Management, 76*(A), 271-285.

Forsythe, S. M., & Shi, B. (2003). Consumer patronage and risk perception in internet shopping. *The Journal of Consumer Research*, *56*, 863–875.

Frank, R. H. (1985). *Choosing the right pond: Human behavior and the quest for status*. Oxford University Press.

Frantzeskaki, N., & Loorbach, D. (2010). Towards governing infrasystem transitions: Reinforcing lock-in or facilitating change? *Technological Forecasting and Social Change*, *77*(8), 1292–1301. doi:10.1016/j.techfore.2010.05.004

Fred, R., & Forest, R. (2017). *Strategic Management: A Competitive Advantage Approach, Concepts and Cases* (6th ed.). Pearson Global Edition.

Frenzen, J., & Nakamoto, K. (1993). Structure, cooperation, and the flow of market information. *The Journal of Consumer Research*, *20*(3), 360–375. doi:10.1086/209355

Freud, S. (1926). Psycho-analysis. *To Theories Of*, 11.

Galbraith, P. W., & Karlin, J. G. (2012). *Idols and celebrity in Japanese media culture*. Hampshire: Palgrave Macmillan. doi:10.1057/9781137283788

Ganesan, A. (2012). *Consumption, Spending and Investment Behaviour of Malaysia Generation Y*. Faculty of Accountancy and Management, Universiti Tunku Abdul Rahman.

Garcia, R., & Calantone, R. (2002). A critical look at technological innovation typology and innovativeness terminology: A literature review. *Journal of Product Innovation Management*, *19*(2), 110–132. doi:10.1111/1540-5885.1920110

Gass, S., & Slinker, L. (1994). *Second Language Acquisition: an Introductory Course*. Mahwah, NJ: LEA.

Gay, L. R. (1987). *Educational Research*. Competencies for Analysis and Application.

Gebauer, J., Füller, J., & Pezzei, R. (2013). The dark and the bright side of co-creation : Triggers of member behavior in online innovation communities. *Journal of Business Research*, *66*(9), 1516–1527. doi:10.1016/j.jbusres.2012.09.013

Gefen, D. (2002). Reflections on the dimensions of trust and trustworthiness among online consumers. *ACM SIGMIS Database*, *33*(3), 38–53. doi:10.1145/569905.569910

Ger, G., & Belk, R. W. (1996). Cross-cultural differences in materialism. *Journal of Economic Psychology*, *17*(1), 55–77. doi:10.1016/0167-4870(95)00035-6

Ger, G., & Belk, R. W. (1999). Accounting for materialism in four cultures. *Journal of Material Culture*, *4*(2), 183–204. doi:10.1177/135918359900400204

Geser, H. (2006). *Are girls (even) more addicted? Some gender patterns of cell phone usage*. Zürich: Universität Zürich, Philosophische Fakultät, Soziologisches Institut.

Ghose, A. (2009). Internet exchanges for used goods: An empirical analysis of trade patterns and adverse selection. *Management Information Systems Quarterly*, *33*(2), 263–291. doi:10.2307/20650292

Gin, T. S., Chin, S., & Suan, T. (2012). Consumer Purchase Preferences Towards Foreign and Domestic Branded Electrical Appliances. *International Journal of Undergraduate Studies*, *1*(1), 15–20.

Giovannini, S., Xu, Y., & Thomas, J. (2015). Luxury fashion consumption and Generation Y consumers: Self, brand consciousness, and consumption motivations. *Journal of Fashion Marketing and Management*, *19*(1), 22–40. doi:10.1108/JFMM-08-2013-0096

Gkargkavouzi, A., Halkos, G., & Matsiori, S. (2019). Environmental behavior in a private-sphere context: Integrating theories of planned behavior and value belief norm, self-identity and habit. *Resources, Conservation and Recycling*, *148*, 145–156. doi:10.1016/j.resconrec.2019.01.039

Glasspool, L. (2012). From boys next door to boys' love: Gender performance in Japanese male idol media. In *Idols and celebrity in Japanese media culture* (pp. 113–130). Hampshire: Palgrave Macmillan. doi:10.1057/9781137283788_6

Godin, B. (2008). *Innovation: The History of a Category, Project on the Intellectual History of Innovation. Paper No. 1.* Paper presented at: Polish Academy of Sciences, Committee for the Science, Warsaw, Poland.

Gohary, A., Hamzelu, B., & Alizadeh, H. (2016). Please explain why it happened! How perceived justice and customer involvement affect post co-recovery evaluations: A study of Iranian online shoppers. *Journal of Retailing and Consumer Services*, *31*, 127–142. doi:10.1016/j.jretconser.2016.03.013

Goh, K. Y., Heng, C. S., & Lin, Z. (2013). Social media brand community and consumer behavior: Quantifying the relative impact of user-and marketer-generated content. *Information Systems Research*, *24*(1), 88–107. doi:10.1287/isre.1120.0469

Goldberg, M. E., & Gorn, G. J. (1978). Some unintended consequences of TV advertising to children. *The Journal of Consumer Research*, *5*(1), 22–29. doi:10.1086/208710

Goldsmith, R. E., & Horowitz, D. (2006). Measuring motivations for online opinion seeking. *Journal of Interactive Advertising*, *6*(2), 2–14. doi:10.1080/15252019.2006.10722114

Gonçalves, H. M., Silva, G. M., & Martins, T. G. (2018). Motivations for posting online reviews in the hotel industry. *Psychology and Marketing*, *35*(11), 807–817. doi:10.1002/mar.21136

Gonzalez, J. L. (2016). *Using foreign factors to enhance domestic export performance: A focus on Southeast Asia. OECD Trade Policy Papers, No. 191.* Paris: OECD Publishing; doi:10.1787/5jlpq82v1jxw-

González, J. L. (2017). *Mapping the participation of ASEAN small- and medium- sized enterprises in global value chains. OECD Trade Policy Papers, No. 203.* Paris: OECD Publishing; doi:10.1787/2dc1751e-

Gottschalk, S. A., & Mafael, A. (2017). Cutting through the online review jungle— Investigating selective eWOM processing. *Journal of Interactive Marketing*, *37*, 89–104. doi:10.1016/j.intmar.2016.06.001

Gounaris, S., Dimitriadis, S., & Stathakopoulos, V. (2010). An examination of the effects of service quality and satisfaction on customers' behavioral intentions in e-shopping, 24(2), 142-156. *Journal of Services Marketing*. doi:10.1108/08876041011031118

Gray, J. (2003). New audiences, new textualities: Anti-fans and non-fans. *International Journal of Cultural Studies*, *6*(1), 64–81. doi:10.1177/1367877903006001004

Greenstein, S., & Nagle, F. (2014). Digital Dark Matter and the Economic Contribution of Apache. *Research Policy*, *43*(4), 623–631. doi:10.1016/j.respol.2014.01.003

Gregg, A. P., Hepper, E. G., & Sedikides, C. (2011). Quantifying self-motives: Functional links between dispositional desires. *European Journal of Social Psychology*, *41*(7), 840–852. doi:10.1002/ejsp.827

Griffiths, M. D. (2000). Video game violence and aggression: Comments on 'Video game playing and its relations with aggressive and prosocial behaviour' by O. Weigman and E.G.M. van Schie. *British Journal of Social Psychology, 39*(Pt 1), 147–149. doi:10.1348/014466600164381 PMID:10774533

Griffiths, M. D. (2015). Online Games, Addiction And Overuse Of. In R. Mansell & P. H. Ang (Eds.), *The International Encyclopedia of Digital Communication and Society* (pp. 1–8). John Wiley & Sons, Inc.

Griffiths, M. D., & Hunt, N. (1995). Computer Game Playing in Adolescence: Prevalence and Demographic Indicators. *Journal of Community & Applied Social Psychology, 5*(3), 189–193. doi:10.1002/casp.2450050307

Groeger, L., & Buttle, F. (2014). Word-of-mouth marketing: Towards an improved understanding of multi-generational campaign reach. *European Journal of Marketing, 48*(7–8), 1186–1208. doi:10.1108/EJM-02-2012-0086

Groening, C., Sarkis, J., & Zhu, Q. (2018). Green marketing consumer-level theory review: A compendium of applied theories and further research directions. *Journal of Cleaner Production, 172*, 1848–1866. doi:10.1016/j.jclepro.2017.12.002

Gupta, A., Su, B., & Walter, Z. (2004). An empirical study of consumer switching from traditional to electronic channels: A purchase-decision process perspective. *International Journal of Electronic Commerce, 8*(3), 131–161. doi:10.1080/10864415.2004.11044302

Gupta, P., & Harris, J. (2010). How e-WOM recommendations influence product consideration and quality of choice: A motivation to process information perspective. *Journal of Business Research, 63*(9–10), 1041–1049. doi:10.1016/j.jbusres.2009.01.015

Guttentag, D. (2015). Airbnb: Disruptive innovation and the rise of an informal tourism accommodation sector. *Journal Current Issues in Tourism, 18*(12), 1192–1217. doi:10.1080/13683500.2013.827159

Guvenen, F., Mataloni, R. J. J., Rassier, D. G., & Ruhl, K. J. (2017). *Offshore Profit Shifting and Domestic Productivity Measurement.* NBER Working Paper 23324.

Hagel, J. I. (1997). Net gain, expanding markets through virtual communities. *The McKinsey Quarterly, 1*, 141–153.

Hagiu, A., & Wright, J. (2011). *Multi-Sided Platforms.* Harvard Business School.

Ha, H., John, J., Janda, S., & Muthaly, S. (2011). The effects of advertising spending on brand loyalty in services. *European Journal of Marketing, 45*(4), 673–691. doi:10.1108/03090561111111389

Hair, J., Celsi, M., Money, A., Samouel, P., & Page, M. (2014). *Essentials of business research methods*. Academic Press.

Hair, J. F. Jr, Money, A. H., Samouel, P., & Page, M. (2007). *Research methods for business.* West Sussex: John Wiley and Sons Ltd.

Hajli, M. N. (2014). A study of the impact of social media on consumers. *International Journal of Market Research, 56*(3), 387–404. doi:10.2501/IJMR-2014-025

Halim, H. A., Said, J., & Yusuf, S. N. S. (2012). Individual characteristics of the successful asnaf entrepreneurs: Opportunities and solutions for zakat organization in Malaysia. *International Business and Management, 4*(2), 41–49.

Hamby, A., Daniloski, K., & Brinberg, D. (2015). How consumer reviews persuade through narratives. *Journal of Business Research, 68*(6), 1242–1250. doi:10.1016/j.jbusres.2014.11.004

Hamilton, K. L., & Catterall, M. (2005). Towards a better understanding of the low income consumer. *Advances in Consumer Research. Association for Consumer Research (U. S.), 32*(1), 627–632.

Hamilton, K., & Hewer, P. (2010). Tribal mattering spaces: Social-networking sites, celebrity affiliations, and tribal innovations. *Journal of Marketing Management*, *26*(3-4), 271–289. doi:10.1080/02672571003679894

Hamin, Z., Rosalili, W., & Rosli, W. (2018). Cloaked By Cyber Space : A Legal Response to the Risks of Cyber Stalking in Malaysia. doi:10.5281/zenodo.1467931

Han Kim, W., & Mauborgne, R. (2006). *Blue Ocean Strategy*. Academic Press.

Handjam. (n.d.). *The History of Mobile Gaming*. Retrieved November 1, 2019 from http://handjam.co.uk/the-history-of-mobile-gaming/

Hani, A. (2019, August 8). Credit cards, personal loans landing Malaysians in debt trap. *The Malaysian Reserve*. Retrieved from https://themalaysianreserve.com/2019/08/08/credit-cards-personal-loans-landing-malaysians-in-debt-trap/

Hanna, R., Rohm, A., & Crittenden, V. L. (2011). We're all connected: The power of the social media eco system. *Business Horizons*, *54*(3), 785–807. doi:10.1016/j.bushor.2011.01.007

Hardt, M. (1999). Affective labor. *Boundary 2*, *26*(2), 89-100.

Hargittai, E. (2007). Whose space? Differences among users and non-users of social network sites. *Journal of Computer-Mediated Communication*, *13*(1), 276–297. doi:10.1111/j.1083-6101.2007.00396.x

Haron, H., Said, S. B., Jayaraman, K., & Ismail, I. (2013). Factors Influencing Small Medium Enterprises (SMES) in Obtaining Loan. *International Journal of Business and Social Science*, *4*(15), 182–195.

Harris, S. R., & Ferris, K. O. (2011). *Stargazing: Celebrity, fame, and social interaction*. Routledge.

Harun, N. H., Hassan, H., Jasni, N. S., & Rahman, R. A. (2010). Zakat for asnafs' business by Lembaga Zakat Selangor. *Management Accounting Research*, *9*(2), 123–138.

Hasan, S., Javad, M., & Ali, M. (2013). Iranian Consumers ' Purchase Intention Toward Global Brands. *Interdisciplinary Journal of Contemporary Research in Business*, *5*(8), 361–372.

Hassan, N. M., & Rom, N. A. M. (2016). Mobile Entrepreneur Program by Zakat Institution: An Exploratory Study. *Social Science*, *11*(7), 7494–7497.

Hausmann, R., Hidalgo, C. A., Bustos. S., Coscia, M., Chung, S., Jimenez, J., Simoes, A., & Yildirim, M. (2011). The atlas of economic complexity. Cambridge, MA: Puritan Press.

Hautz, J., Füller, J., Hutter, K., & Thürridl, C. (2014). Let users generate your video ads? The impact of video source and quality on consumers' perceptions and intended behaviors. *Journal of Interactive Marketing*, *28*(1), 1–15. doi:10.1016/j.intmar.2013.06.003

Hazleton, V., & Kennan, W. (2000). Social capital: Reconceptualizing the bottom line. *Corporate Communications*, *5*(2), 81–87. doi:10.1108/13563280010372513

Heinonen, K. (2011). Consumer activity in social media: Managerial approaches to consumers' social media behavior. *Journal of Consumer Behaviour*, *10*(6), 356–364. doi:10.1002/cb.376

Hekkert, P. (2006). Design aesthetics : principles of pleasure in design Design aesthetics : principles of pleasure in design. *Psychological Science*, *48*(2), 157–172. doi:10.1016/j.chb.2014.06.004

Hennig-Thurau, T., Gwinner, K. P., Walsh, G., & Gremler, D. D. (2004). Electronic word-of-mouth via consumer-opinion platforms: What motivates consumers to articulate themselves on the Internet? *Journal of Interactive Marketing*, *18*(1), 38–52. doi:10.1002/dir.10073

Hennig-Thurau, T., Walsh, G., & Walsh, G. (2003). Electronic word-of-mouth: Motives for and consequences of reading customer articulations on the internet. *International Journal of Electronic Commerce*, *8*(2), 51–74. doi:10.1080/10864415.2003.11044293

Herhausen, D. (2016). Unfolding the ambidextrous effects of proactive and responsive market orientation. *Journal of Business Research*, *69*(7), 2585–2593. doi:10.1016/j.jbusres.2015.10.139

Hermida, A., Fletcher, F., Korell, D., & Logan, D. (2012). Share, like, recommend. Decoding the social media news consumer. *Journalism Studies*, *13*(5-6), 815–824. doi:10.1080/1461670X.2012.664430

Herzog, C., & Kari, K. (2014). Policy Streams and Public Service Media Funding Reforms in Germany and Finland. *European Journal of Communication*, *29*(4), 416–432. doi:10.1177/0267323114530581

He, S. X., & Bond, S. D. (2013). Word-of-mouth and the forecasting of consumption enjoyment. *Journal of Consumer Psychology*, *23*(4), 464–482. doi:10.1016/j.jcps.2013.04.001

HewV. (2017, November 23). Retrieved from http://www.marketing-interactive.com: https://www.marketing-interactive.com/global-or-local-what-do-malaysian-consumers-prefer/

Himitsu no Arashi-chan. (2012b). Tokyo: Tokyo Broadcasting System.

Ho-dac, N. N., Carson, S. J., & Moore, W. L. (2013). The effects of positive and negative online customer reviews : Do brand matter? *Journal of Marketing*, *77*(6), 37–53. doi:10.1509/jm.11.0011

Hoffman, D. L., Novak, T. P., & Peralta, M. (1999). Building consumer trust online, in (coord.). *Communications of the ACM*, *42*(4), 80–85. doi:10.1145/299157.299175

Ho, J. Y. C., & Dempsey, M. (2010). Viral marketing : Motivations to forward online content ☆. *Journal of Business Research*, *63*(9–10), 1000–1006. doi:10.1016/j.jbusres.2008.08.010

Holbrook, M. (1999). Probing Explorations, Deep Displays, Virtual Reality, And Profound Insights: The Four Faces Of Stereographic Three-Dimensional Images In Marketing And Consumer Research. *Advances in Consumer Research.* Retrieved from https://www.acrwebsite.org/volumes/display.asp?id=8251

Holt, D. B. (1997). Poststructuralist Lifestyle Analysis: Conceptualizing the Social Patterning of Consumption in Post-modernity. *The Journal of Consumer Research*, *23*(4), 326–350. doi:10.1086/209487

Howard, J. A. (1989). *Consumer behavior in marketing strategy*. Academic Press.

Hrebiniak, L. G. (2005). Obstacles to Effective Strategy Implementation. *Organizational Dynamics*, *35*(1), 12–31. doi:10.1016/j.orgdyn.2005.12.001

Hsieh, H. Y. (2016). The Relationship among Consumer Value, Brand Image, Perceived Value and Purchase Intention- A Case of Tea Chain Store in Tainan City. *Proceedings of the Eighth Asia-Pacific Conference on Global Business, Economics, Finance and Banking.*

Hsu, C. L., & Lu, H. P. (2007). Consumer behavior in online game communities: A motivational factor perspective. *Computers in Human Behavior*, *23*(3), 1642–1659. doi:10.1016/j.chb.2005.09.001

Hsu, C.-L., Chen, Y.-C., Yang, T.-N., Lin, W.-K., & Liu, Y.-H. (2018). Does product design matter? Exploring its influences in consumers' psychological responses and brand loyalty. *Information Technology & People*, *31*(3), 886–907. doi:10.1108/ITP-07-2017-0206

Hsu, K.-T. (2011). The Advertising Effects of Corporate Social Responsibility on Corporate Reputation and Brand Equity: Evidence from the Life Insurance Industry in Taiwan. *Journal of Business Ethics*, *109*(2), 189–201. doi:10.100710551-011-1118-0

Hsu, L., Wang, K., & Chih, W. (2015). Effects of web site characteristics on customer loyalty in B2B e-commerce : Evidence from Taiwan. *Service Industries Journal*, *33*(11), 1026–1050. doi:10.1080/02642069.2011.624595

Hsu, M. H., Ju, T. L., Yen, C. H., & Chang, C. M. (2007). Knowledge sharing behavior in virtual communities: The relationship between trust, self-efficacy, and outcome expectations. *International Journal of Human-Computer Studies*, *65*(2), 153–169. doi:10.1016/j.ijhcs.2006.09.003

Hu, Y., & Kim, H. J. (2018). Positive and negative eWOM motivations and hotel customers' eWOM behavior: Does personality matter? *International Journal of Hospitality Management*, *75*, 27–37. doi:10.1016/j.ijhm.2018.03.004

Huang, J. H., & Chen, Y. F. (2006). Herding in online product choice. *Psychology and Marketing*, *23*(5), 413–428. doi:10.1002/mar.20119

Huang, M., Cai, F., Tsang, A. S. L., & Zhou, N. (2011). Making your online voice loud: The critical role of WOM information. *European Journal of Marketing*, *45*(7), 1277–1297. doi:10.1108/03090561111137714

Huang, Y. K., & Yang, W. I. (2008). Motives for and consequences of reading internet book reviews. *The Electronic Library*, *26*(1), 97–110. doi:10.1108/02640470810851770

Hudders, L., & Pandelaere, M. (2012). The silver lining of materialism: The impact of luxury consumption on subjective well-being. *Journal of Happiness Studies*, *13*(3), 411–437. doi:10.100710902-011-9271-9

Hughes, D., Rowe, M., Batey, M., & Lee, A. (2012). A tale of two sites: Twitter vs. Facebook and the personality predictors of social media usage. *Computers in Human Behavior*, *28*(2), 561–569. doi:10.1016/j.chb.2011.11.001

Hung, K. H., & Li, S. Y. (2007). The influence of eWOM on virtual consumer communities: Social capital, consumer learning, and behavioral outcomes. *Journal of Advertising Research*, *47*(4), 485–495. doi:10.2501/S002184990707050X

Hur, W. H., & Hur, J. J. Y. (2015). Exploring the Relationship Between Green Consumption Value, Satisfaction, and Loyalty to Hybrid Car in Elderly Consumers. *Human Factors and Ergonomics in Manufacturing & Service Industries*, *25*(4), 398–408. doi:10.1002/hfm.20556

Hu, Ye., & Li, X. (2011). Context-dependent product evaluations : An empirical analysis of internet book reviews. *Journal of Interactive Marketing*, *25*(3), 123–133. doi:10.1016/j.intmar.2010.10.001

Ibarra, A., Karen, E. N., & Kuhn, R. (Eds.). (2015). *Public Service Media in Europe: A Comparative Approach*. London: Routledge. doi:10.4324/9781315722290

IFPI. (2014). *IFPI digital music report 2014: lighting up new markets*. Retrieved from https://www.ifpi.org/downloads/Digital-Music-Report-2014.pdf

Inkpen, A. C., & Tsang, E. W. (2005). Social capital, networks, and knowledge transfer. *Academy of Management Review*, *30*(1), 146–165. doi:10.5465/amr.2005.15281445

Interagency Report. (2012). *Sustainable Agricultural Productivity Growth and Bridging The Gap For Small-Family Farms*. Author.

International Monetary Fund (IMF). (2018). *Measuring the Digital Economy*. IMF Policy Papers.

IOSCO (International Organization of Securities Commissions). (2017). *Research Report on Financial Technologies*. Fintech.

Ismagilova, E., Dwivedi, Y. K., Slade, E., & Williams, M. D. (2017). *Electronic Word of Mouth (eWOM) in the Marketing Context A State of the Art Analysis and Future Directions*. Springer.

Ismail, I. A., & Hussain, M. N. (2017). Productive Zakat Distribution by Zakat Institutions in Malaysia. *International Journal of Academic Research in Business and Social Sciences*, *7*(3), 2222–6990.

Iwabuchi, K. (2004). *Feeling Asian modernities: Transnational consumption of Japanese TV dramas* (Vol. 1). Aberdeen: Hong Kong University Press.

Jamrozy, U., & Lawonk, K. (2017). The multiple dimensions of consumption values in ecotourism. *International Journal of Culture, Tourism and Hospitality Research*, *11*(1), 18–34. doi:10.1108/IJCTHR-09-2015-0114

Jang, K., Park, N., & Song, H. (2016). Social comparison on Facebook: Its antecedents and psychological outcomes. *Computers in Human Behavior*, *62*, 147–154. doi:10.1016/j.chb.2016.03.082

Janssen, M. A., & Jager, W. (2006). Simulating Market Dynamics: Interactions between Consumer Psychology and Social Networks. *The MIT Press Journals*, *9*(4), 343–356. PMID:14761255

Jansson, J. (2011). Consumer Eco-Innovation Adoption: Assessing Attitudinal Factors and Perceived Product Characteristics. *Business Strategy and the Environment*, *20*(3), 192–210. doi:10.1002/bse.690

Jarenfors, O., & Sturesson, S. (2012). *Value Creation through smartphones: An ethnographic study about consumer value and social interaction through smartphones. University of Gothenburg*. School of Business, Economics and Law.

Jarrett, K. (2003). Labour of love: An archaeology of affect as power in e-commerce. *Journal of Sociology (Melbourne, Vic.)*, *39*(4), 335–351. doi:10.1177/0004869003394002

Jaworski, B., Kohli, A. K., & Sahay, A. (2000). Market-driven versus driving market. *Journal of the Academy of Marketing Science*, *28*(1), 45–54. doi:10.1177/0092070300281005

Jenkins, H. (2006). *Convergence culture: where old and new media collide*. New York: New York University Press.

Jenkins, H. (2015). "Cultural acupuncture": Fan activism and the Harry Potter alliance. In L. Geraghty (Ed.), *Popular media cultures* (pp. 206–229). Basingstoke: Springer. doi:10.1057/9781137350374_11

Jeong, E. H., & Jang, S. C. S. (2011). Restaurant experiences triggering positive electronic word-of-mouth (eWOM) motivations. *International Journal of Hospitality Management*, *30*(2), 356–366. doi:10.1016/j.ijhm.2010.08.005

Jeppesen, L. B., & Lakhani, K. R. (2010). Marginality and Problem-Solving Effectiveness in Broadcast Search. *Organization Science*, *21*(5), 955–1123. doi:10.1287/orsc.1090.0491

Jiang, G., Peng, L., & Liu, R. (2015). Mobile Game Adoption in China: The Role of TAM and Perceived Entertainment, Cost, Similarity and Brand Trust. *International Journal of Hybrid Information Technology*, *8*(4), 213–232. doi:10.14257/ijhit.2015.8.4.24

Jiang, P., Jones, D. B., & Javie, S. (2008). How third-party certification programs relate to consumer trust in online transactions: An exploratory study. *Psychology and Marketing*, *25*(9), 839–858. doi:10.1002/mar.20243

Jiménez, F. R., & Mendoza, N. A. (2013). Too popular to ignore: The influence of online reviews on purchase intentions of search and experience products. *Journal of Interactive Marketing*, *27*(3), 226–235. doi:10.1016/j.intmar.2013.04.004

Jin, L., Hu, B., & He, Y. (2014). The recent versus the out-dated: An experimental examination of the time-variant effects of online consumer reviews. *Journal of Retailing*, *90*(4), 552–566. doi:10.1016/j.jretai.2014.05.002

Johnnys' World. (2013). *Top of the J-Pops*. Tokyo: NHK World. [Television documentary]

Kader, R. A., Mohamad, M. R. B., & Ibrahim, A. A. H. C. (2009). Success factors for small rural entrepreneurs under the one-district-one-industry programme in Malaysia. *Contemporary Management Research*, *5*(2). doi:10.7903/cmr.1173

Kamal, S., Chu, S. C., & Pedram, M. (2013). Materialism, attitudes, and social media usage and their impact on purchase intention of luxury fashion goods among American and Arab young generations. *Journal of Interactive Advertising*, *13*(1), 27–40. doi:10.1080/15252019.2013.768052

Kamaruddin, A. R., & Mokhlis, S. (2003). Consumer socialization, social structural factors and decision-making styles: A case study of adolescents in Malaysia. *International Journal of Consumer Studies*, *27*(2), 145–156. doi:10.1046/j.1470-6431.2003.00297.x

Kamineni, R. (2005). Influence of materialism, gender and nationality on consumer brand perceptions. Journal of Targeting. *Measurement and Analysis for Marketing*, *14*(1), 25–32. doi:10.1057/palgrave.jt.5740167

Kanter, R. M. (2006). Innovation: The Classic Traps. *Harvard Business Review*, *84*(11), 72–83, 154. PMID:17131564

Kapeller, J., & Schütz, B. (2015). Conspicuous consumption, inequality and debt: The nature of consumption-driven profit-led regimes. *Metroeconomica*, *66*(1), 51–70. doi:10.1111/meca.12061

Kaplan, A.M., and Haenlein, M. (2012). Social Media: Back to the Roots and Back to the Future. *Journal of Systems and Information Technology, 14*(2), 101-104.

Kaplan, A. M. (2012). If you love something, let it go mobile: Mobile marketing and mobile social media 4x4. *Business Horizons*, *55*(2), 129–139. doi:10.1016/j.bushor.2011.10.009

Kaplan, A. M., & Haenlein, M. (2010). Users of the world, unite! The challenges and opportunities of Social Media. *Business Horizons*, *53*(1), 59–68. doi:10.1016/j.bushor.2009.09.003

Karapetsas, A. V., Karapetsas, V. A., Zygouris, N. X., & Fotis, A. I. (2014). Internet Gaming Addiction. Reasons, Diagnosis, Prevention and Treatment. *ENCEPHALOS*, *51*, 10–14.

Kardos, M.Research on European Union Countries. (2012). The Relationship between entrepreneurship, innovation and sustainable development. Research on European Union Countries. *Procedia Economics and Finance*, *3*, 1030–1035. doi:10.1016/S2212-5671(12)00269-9

Karjalainen, T. (2003). Strategic brand identity and symbolic design cues. *6th Asian Design Conference.* Retrieved from http://www.idemployee.id.tue.nl/g.w.m.rauterberg/conferences/cd_donotopen/ADC/final_paper/197.pdf

Karlin, J. G. (2012). Through a looking glass darkly: television advertising, idols, and the making of fan audiences. In *Idols and celebrity in Japanese media culture* (pp. 72–93). Hampshire: Palgrave Macmillan. doi:10.1057/9781137283788_4

Kasser, T., Ryan, R. M., Couchman, C. E., & Sheldon, K. M. (2004). Materialistic values: Their causes and consequences. *Psychology and Consumer Culture: The Struggle for a Good Life in a Materialistic World*, *1*(2), 11–28.

Katsikea, E., Theodosiou, M., & Makri, K. (2019). The interplay between market intelligence activities and sales strategy as drivers of performance in foreign markets. *European Journal of Marketing*, *53*(10), 2080–2108. doi:10.1108/EJM-06-2017-0402

Katz, M. L., & Shapiro, C. (1985). Network Externalities, Competition, and Compatibility. *The American Economic Review*, *75*(3), 424–440.

Kautish, P., Paul, J., & Sharma, R. (2019). The moderating influence of environmental consciousness and recycling intentions on green purchase behavior. *Journal of Cleaner Production*, *228*, 1425–1436. doi:10.1016/j.jclepro.2019.04.389

Kayabaşı, A., Mucan, B., & Tanyeri, M. (2012). Analysis on young consumer' consumer values and their attitudes toward foreign firms. *Procedia: Social and Behavioral Sciences*, *58*, 1326–1335. doi:10.1016/j.sbspro.2012.09.1116

Kaye, J. (2014). *Always On the Movie, A History of Mobile Games*. Retrieved November 1, 2019 from http://www.proelios.com/wp-content/uploads/2013/12/A-History-of-Mobile-Gaming.pdf

Kazimoto, P. (2014). Assessment of Challenges facing Small and Medium Enterprises towards International Marketing Standards: A Case Study of Arusha Region Tanzania. International Journal of Academic Research in Accounting. *Finance and Management Sciences*, *4*(2), 303–311.

Kenney, M., & Zysman, J. (2016). The rise of the platform economy. *Issues in Science and Technology*, *32*(3), 61–69.

Kent, R. J., & Allen, C. T. (1994). Competitive Interference Effects in Consumer Memory for Advertising : The Role of Brand Familiarity. *Journal of Marketing*, *58*(July), 97–105. doi:10.1177/002224299405800307

Keszei, D., Murphy, K., & Loeur, N. (2018). An Evaluation of American Millennials Leading Global Teams: A Multidimensional Framework for Planning and Optimizing Success. *Journal of Management Policy and Practice*, *19*(1), 10–16.

Khalique, M., Isa, A. H. B. M., Shaari, N., Abdul, J., & Ageel, A. (2011). Challenges faced by the small and medium enterprises (SMEs) in Malaysia: An intellectual capital perspective. *International Journal of Current Research*, *3*(6), 398–401.

Khammash, M., & Griffiths, G. H. (2011). "Arrivederci CIAO.com, Buongiorno Bing.com" - Electronic word-of-mouth (eWOM), antecedences and consequences. *International Journal of Information Management*, *31*(1), 82–87. doi:10.1016/j.ijinfomgt.2010.10.005

Khanh, N. T. T., & Hau, L. N. (2007). Preferred Appeals as a Reflection of Culture: Mobile Phones Advertising in Vietnam. *Asia Pacific Business Review*, *13*(1), 21–39. doi:10.1080/13602380600652987

Khan, M. A., Ashraf, R., & Malik, A. (2019). Do identity-based perceptions lead to brand avoidance? A cross-national investigation. *Asia Pacific Journal of Marketing and Logistics*, *31*(4), 1095–1117. doi:10.1108/APJML-12-2017-0332

Khan, S. N., & Mohsin, M. (2017). The power of emotional value: Exploring the effects of values on green product consumer choice behavior. *Journal of Cleaner Production*, *150*, 65–74. doi:10.1016/j.jclepro.2017.02.187

Khare, A., Labrecque, L. I., & Asare, A. K. (2011). The assimilative and contrastive effects of word-of-mouth volume: An experimental examination of online consumer ratings. *Journal of Retailing*, *87*(1), 111–126. doi:10.1016/j.jretai.2011.01.005

Kietzmann, J. H., Hermkens, K., McCarthy, I. P., & Silvestre, B. S. (2011). Social media? Get serious! Understanding the functional building blocks of social media. *Business Horizons*, *54*(3), 241–251. doi:10.1016/j.bushor.2011.01.005

Kim, A. J., & Ko, E. (2012). Do social media marketing activities enhance customer equity? An empirical study of luxury fashion brand. *Journal of Business Research*, *65*(10), 1480–1486. doi:10.1016/j.jbusres.2011.10.014

Kim, D. J., Ferrin, D. L., & Rao, H. R. (2008). A trust-based consumer decision-making model in electronic commerce: The role of trust, perceived risk, and their antecedents. *Decision Support Systems*, *44*(2), 544–564. doi:10.1016/j.dss.2007.07.001

Kim, D. J., & Hwang, Y. (2012). A study of mobile internet user's service quality perceptions from a user's utilitarian and hedonic value tendency perspectives. *Information Systems Frontiers*, *14*(2), 409–421. doi:10.100710796-010-9267-8

Kim, E. E. K., Mattila, A. S., & Baloglu, S. (2011). Effects of gender and expertise on consumers' motivation to read online hotel reviews. *Cornell Hospitality Quarterly*, *52*(4), 399–406. doi:10.1177/1938965510394357

Kim, H. M. (2013). Mobile Media Technology And Popular Mobile Games In Contemporary Society. *International Journal of Mobile Marketing*, *8*(2), 42–54.

Kim, H. Y., & Chung, J. E. (2011). Consumer purchase intention for organic personal care products. *Journal of Consumer Marketing*.

Kim, J. (2019). Imperative challenge for luxury brands. *International Journal of Retail & Distribution Management*, *47*(2), 220–244. doi:10.1108/IJRDM-06-2017-0128

Kim, J., & Gupta, P. (2012). Emotional expressions in online user reviews: How they influence consumers' product evaluations. *Journal of Business Research*, *65*(7), 985–992. doi:10.1016/j.jbusres.2011.04.013

King, A. A., Lenox, M. J., & Terlaak, A. (2005). The strategic use of decentralized institutions: Exploring certification with the ISO 14001 management standard. *Academy of Management Journal*, *48*(6), 1091–1106. doi:10.5465/amj.2005.19573111

King, R. A., Racherla, P., & Bush, V. D. (2014). What we know and don't know about online word-of-mouth: A review and synthesis of the literature. *Journal of Interactive Marketing*, *28*(3), 167–183. doi:10.1016/j.intmar.2014.02.001

Kinra, N. (2006). The effect of country-of-origin on foreign brand names in the Indian market. *Marketing Intelligence & Planning*, *24*(1), 15–30. doi:10.1108/02634500610641534

Kirmani, A., & Rao, A. R. (2000). No pain, no gain: A critical review of the literature on signaling unobservable product quality. *Journal of Marketing*, *64*(2), 66–79. doi:10.1509/jmkg.64.2.66.18000

Kiron, D., & .... (2013). The Benefits of Sustainability-Driven Innovation. *MIT Sloan Management Review*, *54*(2), 69–73.

Knight, G. A., & Kim, D. (2009). International Business competence and the contemporary firm. *Journal of International Business Studies*, *40*(2), 255–273. doi:10.1057/palgrave.jibs.8400397

Koch, O. F., & Benlian, A. (2015). Promotional tactics for online viral marketing campaigns: How scarcity and personalization affect seed stage referrals. *Journal of Interactive Marketing*, *32*, 37–52. doi:10.1016/j.intmar.2015.09.005

Kohli, A. K., & Jaworski, B. J. (1990). Market Orientation: The Construct, Research Propositions, and Managerial Implications. *Journal of Marketing*, *54*(2), 1–18. doi:10.1177/002224299005400201

Kontio, P. (2011). *Mobile Gaming Business*. Retrieved October 13, 2018, from https://pdfs.semanticscholar.org/b5e8/6e8db601a9918470ce0df345b9847872577b.pdf

Koo, D. (2015). The strength of no tie relationship in an online recommendation: Focused on interactional effects of valence, tie strength, and type of service. *European Journal of Marketing*, *49*(7/8), 1163–1183. doi:10.1108/EJM-01-2014-0022

Koo, D. M. (2009). The moderating role of locus of control on the links between experiential motives and intention to play online games. *Computers in Human Behavior*, *25*(2), 466–474. doi:10.1016/j.chb.2008.10.010

Koon, T. H. (2013). *Preying on Lonely Hearts : A Systematic Deconstruction of an Internet Romance Scammer's Online Lover Persona*. Academic Press.

Kosonen, M. (2006). Knowledge sharing in virtual communities-A review of the empirical research. *International Journal of Web Based Communities*, *5*(2), 144–163. doi:10.1504/IJWBC.2009.023962

Kostyra, D. S., Reiner, J., Natter, M., & Klapper, D. (2016). Decomposing the effects of online customer reviews on brand, price, and product attributes. *International Journal of Research in Marketing*, *33*(1), 11–26. doi:10.1016/j.ijresmar.2014.12.004

Kotler, P., & Armstrong, G. (2011). *Principles of Marketing*. Academic Press.

Kotler, P., Keller, K. L., Ang, S. H., Tan, C. T., & Leong, S. M. (2018). *Marketing management: an Asian perspective*. Pearson.

Kozinets, R. V. (1999). E-Tribalized Marketing?: The Strategic Implications of Virtual Communities of Consumption. *European Management Journal*, *17*(3), 252–264. doi:10.1016/S0263-2373(99)00004-3

Kozinets, R. V. (2002). Can Consumers Escape the Market? Emancipatory Illuminations from the Burning Man. *The Journal of Consumer Research*, *29*(1), 20–38. doi:10.1086/339919

Kozinets, R. V., De Valck, K., Wojnicki, A. C., & Wilner, S. J. S. (2010). Networked Narratives: Understanding Word-of-Mouth Marketing in Online Communities. *Journal of Marketing*, *74*(2), 71–89. doi:10.1509/jm.74.2.71

Kozinets, R. V., Hemetsberger, A., & Schau, H. J. (2008). The wisdom of consumer crowds: Collective Innovation in the Age of Networked Marketing. *Journal of Macromarketing*, *28*(4), 339–354. doi:10.1177/0276146708325382

Krause, D. (1993). Environmental consciousness: An empirical study. *Environment and Behavior*, *25*(1), 126–142. doi:10.1177/0013916593251007

Krishnamurthy, S., & Dou, W. (2008). Advertising with User-Generated Content: A Framework and Research Agenda. *Journal of Interactive Advertising*, *8*(2), 1–7. doi:10.1080/15252019.2008.10722137

Kronenberg, T. (2004). The Curse of Natural Resources In The Transition Economies. *Economics of Transition*, *12*(3), 399–426. doi:10.1111/j.0967-0750.2004.00187.x

Ku, C. H., Kwak, M., Yurov, K. M., & Yurova, Y. V. (2014). A Study of the Influence of Gaming Behavior on Academic Performance of IT College Students. *Gaming Behavior and Academic Performance. Twentieth Americas Conference on Information Systems*, Savannah, GA.

Kumar Roy, S., & Lassar, M., W., & Butaney, G. (2014). The mediating impact of stickiness and loyalty on word-of-mouth promotion of retail websites. *European Journal of Marketing*, *48*(9/10), 1828–184. doi:10.1108/EJM-04-2013-0193

Kuo, Y. F., Wu, C. M., & Deng, W. J. (2009). The Relationships among Service Quality, Perceived Value, Customer Satisfaction, and Post-purchase Intention in Mobile Value-added Services. *Computers in Human Behavior*, *25*(4), 887–896. doi:10.1016/j.chb.2009.03.003

Kurdve, M., Shahbazi, S., Wendin, M., Bengtsson, C., & Wiktorsson, M. (2015). Waste Flow Mapping To Improve Sustainability Of Waste Management: A Case Study Approach. *Journal of Cleaner Production*, *98*, 304–315. doi:10.1016/j.jclepro.2014.06.076

Kuss, D. J. (2013). Internet gaming addiction: Current perspectives. *Psychology Research and Behavior Management*, *6*, 125–137. doi:10.2147/PRBM.S39476 PMID:24255603

Kyodo. (2016). 2003 SMAP single tops chart after massive purchases by fans fearing group's breakup. *The Japan Times*. Retrieved from https://www.japantimes.co.jp/culture/2016/01/24/music/2003-smap-single-tops-chart-massive-purchases-fans-fearing-groups-breakup/#.Wy9me1UzZ0w

Ladhari, R., Gonthier, J., & Lajante, M. (2019). Generation Y and online fashion shopping: Orientations and profiles. *Journal of Retailing and Consumer Services*, *48*, 113–121. doi:10.1016/j.jretconser.2019.02.003

Lage, M. J., Platt, G. J., & Treglia, M. (2000). Inverting the classroom: A gateway to creating an inclusive learning environment. *The Journal of Economic Education*, *31*(1), 30–43. doi:10.1080/00220480009596759

Lai, M. C., Chou, F. S., Wang, C. C., & Yang, Y. J. (2015). Users' perception of mobile devices: The pragmatic and symbolic consumption values of tablet personal computers. *Asian Journal of Information and Communications*, *7*(2), 1–13.

Lam, S. P. (2006). Predicting intention to save water: Theory of planned behavior, response efficacy, vulnerability, and perceived efficiency of alternative solutions 1. *Journal of Applied Social Psychology*, *36*(11), 2803–2824. doi:10.1111/j.0021-9029.2006.00129.x

Lange, F. A. (1873-75). *The History of Materialism* (B. Russell, Trans., 3rd ed.). New York: Arno Press.

Larsen, V., Sirgy, J. M., & Wright, N. D. (1999). Materialism: The construct, measures, antecedents, and consequences. *Academy of Marketing Studies Journal*, *3*(2), 78–110.

Lasi, H., Fettke, P., Kemper, H. G., Feld, T., & Hoffmann, M. (2014). Industry 4.0. *Business & Information Systems Engineering*, *6*(4), 261–264. doi:10.100712599-014-0334-4

Lazarevic, V. (2012). Encouraging brand loyalty in fickle generation Y consumers. Young Consumers. *Insight and Ideas for Responsible Marketers*, *13*(1), 45–61. doi:10.1108/17473611211203939

Lee, C. K. C., Levy, D. S., & Yap, C. S. F. (2015). How does the theory of consumption values contribute to place identity and sustainable consumption? *International Journal of Consumer Studies*, *39*(6), 597–607. doi:10.1111/ijcs.12231

Lee, D., Trail, G. T., Kwon, H. H., & Anderson, D. F. (2011). Consumer values versus perceived product attributes: Relationships among items from the MVS, PRS, and PERVAL scales. *Sport Management Review*, *14*(1), 89–101. doi:10.1016/j.smr.2010.05.001

Lee, E. J., & Shin, S. Y. (2014). When do consumers buy online product reviews? Effects of review quality, product type, and reviewer's photo. *Computers in Human Behavior*, *31*(1), 356–366. doi:10.1016/j.chb.2013.10.050

Lee, H., Lee, D., Kim, T., & Lee, J. (2013). The moderating role of socio-semantic networks on online buzz diffusion. *Journal of Business Research*, *66*(9), 1367–1374. doi:10.1016/j.jbusres.2012.02.038

Lee, J., Park, D. H., & Han, I. (2008). The effect of negative online consumer reviews on product attitude: An information processing view. *Electronic Commerce Research and Applications*, *7*(3), 341–352. doi:10.1016/j.elerap.2007.05.004

Lee, K. S., & Tan, S. J. (2003). E-retailing versus physical retailing, a theoretical model and empirical test of consumer choice. *Journal of Business Research*, *56*(11), 877–885. doi:10.1016/S0148-2963(01)00274-0

Lee, M. K. O., & Turban, E. (2014). A Trust Model for Consumer Internet Shopping. *International Journal of Electronic Commerce*, *6*(1), 75–91. doi:10.1080/10864415.2001.11044227

Lee, S. H., & Ro, H. (2016). The impact of online reviews on attitude changes: The differential effects of review attributes and consumer knowledge. *International Journal of Hospitality Management*, *56*, 1–9. doi:10.1016/j.ijhm.2016.04.004

Lee, T., & Bradlow, E. (2011). Automated marketing research using online customer reviews. *JMR, Journal of Marketing Research*, *48*(5), 881–894. doi:10.1509/jmkr.48.5.881

Lemmens, J. S. (2010). *Causes and consequences of pathological gaming*. Amsterdam: Amsterdam School of Communication Research. Retrieved October 13, 2018, from https://pure.uva.nl/ws/files/1018758/84048_thesis.pdf

Lemmens, J. S., Valkenburg, P. M., & Peter, J. (2009). Development and Validation of a Game Addiction Scale for Adolescents. *Media Psychology*, *12*(1), 77–95. doi:10.1080/15213260802669458

Lens, I., Pandelaere, M., & Warlop, L. (2010). Effects of Advertising Exposure on Materialism and Self-Esteem: Advertised Luxuries As a Feel-Good Strategy? *ACR North American Advances.*, *37*(1), 1–5.

Leyden, D. P., Link, A. N., & Siegel, D. S. (2014). A theoretical analysis of the role of social networks in entrepreneurship. *Research Policy, 43*(7), 1157–1163. doi:10.1016/j.respol.2014.04.010

Liang, S. W. J., Ekinci, Y., Occhiocupo, N., & Whyatt, G. (2013). Antecedents of travellers' electronic word-of-mouth communication. *Journal of Marketing Management, 29*(5–6), 584–606. doi:10.1080/0267257X.2013.771204

Liang, T. P., & Yeh, Y. H. (2009). Situational Effects on the Usage Intention of Mobile Games. In C. Weinhardt, S. Luckner, & J. Stößer (Eds.), *Designing E-Business Systems. Markets, Services, and Networks WEB 2008, LNBIP 22* (pp. 51–59). doi:10.1007/978-3-642-01256-3_5

Li, C.-R., Lin, C.-J., & Chu, C.-P. (2008). The nature of market orientation and the ambidexterity of innovations. *Management Decision, 46*(7), 1002–1026. doi:10.1108/00251740810890186

Lii, Y., & Lee, M. (2012). The joint effects of compensation frames and price levels on service recovery of online pricing error. *Managing Service Quality, 22*(1), 4–20. doi:10.1108/09604521211198083

Lim, W. M., Ng, W. K., Chin, J. H., & Boo, A. W. X. (2014). Understanding young consumer perceptions on credit card usage: Implications for responsible consumption. *Contemporary Management Research, 10*(4), 287–302. doi:10.7903/cmr.11657

Lim, W. M., Ting, D. H., Khoo, P. T., & Wong, W. Y. (2012). Understanding Consumer Values And Socialization –A Case Of Luxury Products. *Management & Marketing Challenges for the Knowledge Society, 7*(2), 209–220.

Lin, H. H., Wang, Y. S., & Chang, L. K. (2011). Consumer responses to online retailer's service recovery after a service failure: A perspective of justice theory. *Managing Service Quality, 21*(5), 511–534. doi:10.1108/09604521111159807

Liu, Y., & Li, H. (2011). Exploring the impact of use context on mobile hedonic services adoption: An empirical study on mobile gaming in China. *Computers in Human Behavior, 27*(2), 890–898. doi:10.1016/j.chb.2010.11.014

Long, C. (2002). Patent signals. *The University of Chicago Law Review. University of Chicago. Law School, 69*(2), 625–679. doi:10.2307/1600501

López, M., & Sicilia, M. (2014). Determinants of E-WOM influence: The role of consumers' internet experience. *Journal of Theoretical and Applied Electronic Commerce Research, 9*(1), 28–43. doi:10.4067/S0718-18762014000100004

Ludwig, S., de Ruyter, K., Friedman, M., Brüggen, E. C., Wetzels, M., & Pfann, G. (2012). More than words: The influence of affective content and linguistic style matches in online reviews on conversion rates. *Journal of Marketing, 77*(1), 87–103. doi:10.1509/jm.11.0560

Luo, Q., & Zhong, D. (2015). Using social network analysis to explain communication characteristics of travel-related electronic word-of-mouth on social networking sites. *Tourism Management, 46*, 274–282. doi:10.1016/j.tourman.2014.07.007

Lüthje, C., Herstatt, C., & Von Hippel, E. (2005). User-innovators and "local" information: The case of mountain biking. *Research Policy, 34*(6), 951–965. doi:10.1016/j.respol.2005.05.005

Madrigal, R. (2001). Social Identity Effects in a Belief-Attitude-Intentions Hierarchy: Implications for Corporate Sponsorship. *Psychology and Marketing, 18*(2), 145–162. doi:10.1002/1520-6793(200102)18:2<145::AID-MAR1003>3.0.CO;2-T

Mafael, A., Gottschalk, S. A., & Kreis, H. (2016). Examining biased assimilation of brand-related online reviews. *Journal of Interactive Marketing, 36*, 91–106. doi:10.1016/j.intmar.2016.06.002

Mahmood, T. M. A. T., Al Mamun, A., Ahmad, G. B., & Ibrahim, M. D. (2019). Predicting Entrepreneurial Intentions and Pre-Start-Up Behaviour among Asnaf Millennials. *Sustainability, 11*(18), 4939. doi:10.3390u11184939

Maichum, K., Parichatnon, S., & Peng, K.-C. (2016). Application of the extended theory of planned behavior model to investigate purchase intention of green products among Thai consumers. *Sustainability (Switzerland)*, *8*(10), 1077. doi:10.3390u8101077

Malhotra, N. K., Birks, D. F., & Wills, P. (2012). *Marketing Research : An Applied Approach*. Marketing Research.

Mancha, R. M., & Yoder, C. Y. (2015). Cultural antecedents of green behavioral intent: An environmental theory of planned behavior. *Journal of Environmental Psychology*, *43*, 145–154. doi:10.1016/j.jenvp.2015.06.005

Manda, M. I., & Ben Dhaou, S. (2019, April). Responding to the challenges and opportunities in the 4th Industrial revolution in developing countries. In *Proceedings of the 12th International Conference on Theory and Practice of Electronic Governance* (pp. 244-253). ACM. 10.1145/3326365.3326398

Mandler, T. (2019). Beyond reach: An extended model of global brand effects. *International Marketing Review*, *36*(5), 647–674. doi:10.1108/IMR-01-2018-0032

Mannion, C., & Brannick, T. (1995). Materialism and its measurement. *IBAR*, (16), 1-15.

Marangunić, N., & Granić, A. (2015). Technology acceptance model: A literature review from 1986 to 2013. *Universal Access in the Information Society*, *14*(1), 81–95. doi:10.100710209-014-0348-1

Margherio, L. (1998). *The Emerging Digital Economy*. Washington, DC: U.S. Department of Commerce.

Marin, L., Ruiz, S., & Rubio, A. (2009). The Role of Identity Salience in the Effects of Corporate Social Responsibility on Consumer Behavior. *Journal of Business Ethics*, *84*(1), 65–78. doi:10.100710551-008-9673-8

Markard, J., & Truffer, B. (2006). Innovation processes in large technical systems: Market liberalization as a driver for radical change? *Research Policy*, *35*(5), 609–625. doi:10.1016/j.respol.2006.02.008

Martens, M. (2011). Transmedia teens: Affect, immaterial labor, and user-generated content. *Convergence*, *17*(1), 49–68. doi:10.1177/1354856510383363

Martin, W. C., & Lueg, J. E. (2013). Modeling word-of-mouth usage. *Journal of Business Research*, *66*(7), 801–808. doi:10.1016/j.jbusres.2011.06.004

Marx, D. W. (2012). The Jimusho system: understanding the production logic of the Japanese entertainment industry. In *Idols and celebrity in Japanese media culture* (pp. 35–55). Hampshire: Palgrave Macmillan. doi:10.1057/9781137283788_2

März, A., Schubach, S., & Schumann, J. H. (2017). "Why Would I Read a Mobile Review?" Device compatibility perceptions and effects on perceived helpfulness. *Psychology and Marketing*, *34*(2), 119–137. doi:10.1002/mar.20979

Maslow, A. H. (1970). *Motivation and personality*. Prentice Hall Inc.

Mat, A., Kori, N. L., Rahman, S. A., Munir, Z. A., & Bahry, N. S. (2016). Conspicuous consumption behaviour: A case study of luxury fashion consumers at selected malls in Kuala Lumpur, Malaysia. *Australian Journal of Basic and Applied Sciences*, *10*(11), 193–198.

Mathwick, C. (2002). Understanding the online consumer: A typology of online relational norms and behavior. *Journal of Interactive Marketing*, *16*(1), 40–55. doi:10.1002/dir.10003

Mathwick, C., Wiertz, C., & de Ruyter, K. (2008). Social Capital Production in a Virtual P3 Community. *The Journal of Consumer Research*, *34*(6), 832–849. doi:10.1086/523291

Mavlanova, T., Benbunan-Fich, R., & Koufaris, M. (2012). Signaling theory and information asymmetry in online commerce. *Information & Management*, *49*(5), 240–247. doi:10.1016/j.im.2012.05.004

Mavlanova, T., Benbunan-Fich, R., & Lang, G. (2016). The role of external and internal signals in E-commerce. *Decision Support Systems*, *87*, 59–68. doi:10.1016/j.dss.2016.04.009

Mayra, F. (2015). Mobile Games. In The International Encyclopedia of Digital Communication and Society. John Wiley & Sons, Inc.

McCaskill, A. (2016, April 26). *Nearly 75% of Global Consumers List Brand Origin as Key Purchase Driver.* Academic Press.

McCay-Peet, L., & Quan-Haase, A. (2017). What is social media and what questions can social media research help us answer. The SAGE Handbook of Social Media Research Methods, 13-26.

McLeod, S. (2008). *Social identity theory.* Simply Psychology.

McStay, A. (2013). *Creativity and advertising: Affect, events and process.* London: Routledge. doi:10.4324/9780203492208

Mediatique. (2012). *The provision of news in the UK.* Author.

Meeker, M. (2016). *Internet Trends 2016.* http://www.kpcb.com/internet–trends

Megginson, W. L., & Weiss, K. A. (1991). Venture capitalist certification in initial public offerings. *The Journal of Finance*, *46*(3), 879–903. doi:10.1111/j.1540-6261.1991.tb03770.x

Mesch, G. S., & Dodel, M. (2018). Low Self-Control, Information Disclosure, and the Risk of Online Fraud. *The American Behavioral Scientist*, *62*(10), 1356–1371. doi:10.1177/0002764218787854

Meyer, R. J. (1982). A descriptive model of consumer information search behavior. *Marketing Science*, *1*, 1.

Meyers, P. W., & Tucker, F. G. (1989). Defining Roles for Logistics During Routine and Radical Technological Innovation. *Journal of the Academy of Marketing Science*, *17*(1), 73–82. doi:10.1007/BF02726356

Michaelson, K. L. (1996). Information, Community and Access. *Social Science Computer Review*, *14*(1), 57–59. doi:10.1177/089443939601400118

Miladinovic-Bogavac, Z. (2017). Business scam in saber space. *Ekonomika (Nis)*, *63*(4), 97–104. doi:10.5937/ekonomika1704097M

Miles & Rigby. (2013). *Demand-Led Innovation. Innovation Policy Challenges for the 21st Century.* Academic Press.

Ministry of Textile Industry. G. o. P. (2015). *Textile Policy 2014-19.* Retrieved from http://www.textile.gov.pk/moti/userfiles1/file/Textile%20Policy%202014-19.pdf

Minkoff, D. C. (1997). Producing Social Capital. *The American Behavioral Scientist*, *40*(5), 606–619. doi:10.1177/0002764297040005007

Mishra, A. (2015). Consumption Value of Digital Devices: An Investigation through Facebook Advertisement. *Social Networking*, *4*(03), 51–61. doi:10.4236n.2015.43007

Mishra, D. P. (2006). The role of certification in service relationships: Theory and empirical evidence. *Journal of Retailing and Consumer Services*, *13*(1), 81–96. doi:10.1016/j.jretconser.2005.08.005

Miyazaki, A. D., & Fernandez, A. (2001). Consumer perceptions of privacy and security risks for online shopping. *The Journal of Consumer Affairs*, *35*(1), 27–44.

Moav, O., & Neeman, Z. (2012). Saving rates and poverty: The role of conspicuous consumption and human capital. *Economic Journal (London)*, *122*(563), 933–956. doi:10.1111/j.1468-0297.2012.02516.x

Moeller, M., Stolla, C., & Doujak, A. (2008). *Strategic Innovation: Building New Growth Businesses*. Neuwaldegg.

Moe, W. W., & Schweidel, D. A. (2012). Online product opinions: Incidence, evaluation, and evolution. *Marketing Science, 31*(3), 372–386. doi:10.1287/mksc.1110.0662

Mohezar, S. S. (2016). *Halal Cosmetics Adoption Among Young Muslim Consumers in Malaysia: Religiosity Concern. Global Journal Al-Thaqafah.*

Molina-Castillo, F. J., & Munuera-Aleman, J. L. (2009). The joint impact of quality and innovativeness on short-term new product performance. *Industrial Marketing Management, 38*(8), 984–993. doi:10.1016/j.indmarman.2008.06.001

Moore, S. G. (2015). Attitude predictability and helpfulness in online reviews: The role of explained actions and reactions. *The Journal of Consumer Research, 42*(1), 30–44. doi:10.1093/jcr/ucv003

Morimoto, L. (2013). Trans-cult-ural fandom: Desire, technology and the transformation of fan subjectivities in the Japanese female fandom of Hong Kong stars. *Transformative Works and Cultures,* (14).

Mosher & Smith. (2015). *Sustainability Incorporated Integrating Sustainability into Business*. Retrieved on 9 Dec 2019 from https://sustainability.com/wp-content/uploads /2016/07/sustainability_incorporated.pdf

Mostafa, M. M. (2007). A hierarchical analysis of the green consciousness of the Egyptian consumer. *Psychology and Marketing, 24*(5), 445–473. doi:10.1002/mar.20168

Mowery, D., & Rosenberg, N. (1979). The influence of market demand upon innovation: A critical review of some recent empirical studies. *Research Policy, 8*(2), 102–153. doi:10.1016/0048-7333(79)90019-2

Muhammad, M. Z., & Char, A. K., bin Yasoa, M. R., & Hassan, Z. (2010). Small and medium enterprises (SMEs) competing in the global business environment: A case of Malaysia. *International Business Research, 3*(1), 66–75.

Muhsin, M. A. (2016). Analysing the students errors in using simple present (A case study at Junior High School in Makassar). *Pacific Science Review B: Humanities and Social Sciences*, 81-87.

Munawar, F., Rahayu, A., Disman, D., & Wibowo, L. (2019). The role of proactive market orientation and management commitment to internal resource on export performance of handicraft industry. *Management Science Letters, 9*(11), 1711–1722. doi:10.5267/j.msl.2019.6.019

Muñoz, B., Monzon, A., & López, E. (2016). Transition to a cyclable city: Latent variables affecting bicycle commuting. *Transportation Research Part a: Policy and Practice, 84*, 4–17.

Muntinga, D. G., Moorman, M., & Smit, E. G. (2011). Introducing COBRAs: Exploring motivations for brand-related social media use. *International Journal of Advertising, 30*(1), 13–46. doi:10.2501/IJA-30-1-013-046

Nadzri, F. A. A., Omar, N., & Rahman, R. A. (2018). Enterprise Governance of Micro Entrepreneurs in Malaysia: Comparison between the Amanah Ikhtiar Malaysia and Asnaf's Economic Development Program. *Global Journal Al-Thaqafah*, 25-40.

Nagaike, K. (2012). Johnny's idols as icons: Female desires to fantasize and consume male idol images. In *Idols and celebrity in Japanese media culture* (pp. 97–112). Hampshire: Palgrave Macmillan. doi:10.1057/9781137283788_5

Nahapiet, J., & Ghoshal, S. (1998). Social capital, intellectual capital, and the organizational advantage. *Academy of Management Review, 23*(2), 242–266. doi:10.5465/amr.1998.533225

Nakamura, L., Samuels, J., & Soloveichik, R. (2017). Measuring the 'Free' Digital Economy within the GDP and Productivity Accounts. *5th IMF Statistical Forum.*

Nalwa, K., & Anand, A. P. (2004). Internet Addiction in Students: A Cause of Concern. *Cyberpsychology & Behavior*, *6*(6), 653–656. doi:10.1089/109493103322725441 PMID:14756932

Nambisan, S., & Baron, R. A. (2007). Interactions in virtual customer environments: Implications for product support and customer relationship management. *Journal of Interactive Marketing*, *21*(2), 42–62. doi:10.1002/dir.20077

Napoli, P. (2015). *Assessing the Health of Local Journalism Ecosystems: A Comparative Analysis of Three New Jersey Communities*. Prepared for the Democracy Fund, the Geraldine R. Dodge Foundation, and the John S. and James L. Knight Foundation. http://wp.comminfo.rutgers.edu/mpii-new/wpcontent/uploads/sites/129/2015/06/Assessing-Local-Journalism_Final-Draft6.23.15.pdf

Narver, J. C., Slater, S. F., & MacLahlan, D. L. (2004). Responsive and proactive market orientation and new-product success. *Journal of Product Innovation Management*, *21*(5), 334–347. doi:10.1111/j.0737-6782.2004.00086.x

Nastanski, M., & Baglione, S. L. (2014). Sustainability: Benefits of Social Responsibility to Brand Value & Profit. *Journal of International Management Studies*, *9*(2), 164–173.

Nasution, H. N., Mavondo, F. T., Matanda, M. J., & Ndubisi, N. O. (2011). Entrepreneurship: Its relationship with market orientation and learning orientation and as antecedents to innovation and customer value. *Industrial Marketing Management*, *40*(3), 336–345. doi:10.1016/j.indmarman.2010.08.002

Nathan, R. J., Fook Chiun, D. C., & Suki, N. M. (2016). An online marketing strategies assessment for companies in airlines and entertainment industries in Malaysia. Handbook of Research on Leveraging Consumer Psychology for Effective Customer Engagement, 1-15.

Naylor, R. W., Lamberton, C. P., & Norton, D. A. (2011). Seeing ourselves in others: Reviewer ambiguity, egocentric anchoring, and persuasion. *JMR, Journal of Marketing Research*, *48*(3), 617–631. doi:10.1509/jmkr.48.3.617

Netzer, O., Feldman, R., Goldenberg, J., & Fresko, M. (2012). Mine your own business: Market-structure surveillance through text mining. *Marketing Science*, *31*(3), 521–543. doi:10.1287/mksc.1120.0713

New Straits Time. (2017). *SMEs doing well despite slower national economic growth: Rahman Dahlan*. Available online from https://www.nst.com.my/news/nation/2017/10/287258/smes-doing-well-despite-slower-national-economic-growth-rahman-dahlan

Newman, N. (2016). *Media, Journalism and Technology Predictions 2016*. Oxford: Reuters Institute for the Study of Journalism. http://digitalnewsreport.org/publications/2016/predictions-2016/

Newzoo. (2018). *2018 Global Games Market Report. Free verison*. Retrieved November 1, 2019 from https://cdn2.hubspot.net/hubfs/700740/Reports/Newzoo_2018_Global_Games_Market_Report_Light.pdf

Nguyen, D. (2015). *Understanding Perceived Enjoyment and Continuance Intention in Mobile Games. Information Systems Science. Department of Information and Service Economy*. Aalto University School of Business.

Nikodemska-Wołowik, A. M., Bednarz, J., & Foreman, J. R. (2019). Trends in young consumers' behaviour - implications for family enterprises. *Economia e Sociologia*, *12*(3), 11–24. doi:10.14254/2071-789X.2019/12-3/1

Ning, L. (2019). Research on the Influence of Negative Information of Brand Spokesmen on Brand Attitude. *European Journal of Business and Management*, *11*(21), 143–147.

Nkonge, B. K. (2013). Challenges faced by Small and Medium Enterprise Suppliers when bidding for tenders. A case of Thika District. *International Journal of Academic Research in Business and Social Sciences*, *3*(12), 194–220. doi:10.6007/IJARBSS/v3-i12/426

Novick, L. R. (1988). Analogical transfer, problem similarity, and expertise. *Journal of Experimental Psychology. Learning, Memory, and Cognition, 14*(3), 510–520. doi:10.1037/0278-7393.14.3.510 PMID:2969945

Nowak, L., Thach, L., & Olsen, J. E. (2006). Wowing the millennials: Creating brand equity in the wine industry. *Journal of Product and Brand Management, 15*(5), 316–323. doi:10.1108/10610420610685712

O'Cass, A., & Choy, E. (2008). Studying Chinese generation Y consumers' involvement in fashion clothing and perceived brand status. *Journal of Product and Brand Management, 17*(5), 341–352. doi:10.1108/10610420810896095

OECD. (2013). *The App Economy*. Digital Economy Papers, No. 230.

OECD. (2017). *Digital Economy Outlook 2017*. Paris: OECD Publishing.

OECD. (2017). *Financing SMEs and Entrepreneurs 2016: An OECD Scoreboard*. OECD Publishing.

OECD. (2019). *Measuring the Digital Transformation: A Roadmap for the Future*. Paris: OECD Publishing.

OECD/ERIA. (2018). *SME Policy Index: ASEAN 2018: Boosting Competitiveness and Inclusive Growth*. OECD Publishing; doi:10.1787/9789264305328-

Oksman, V. (2007). Young people and seniors in Finnish 'mobile information society. *Journal of Interactive Media in Education, 02*, 1–21.

Ondang, J. P. (2015). Influence of Perceived Value And Attitude Toward Consumer Purchase Intention To Billy Coffee House Customer At Mega Smart Area Manado. *Jurnal Berkala Ilmiah Efisiensi, 15*(05), 800–807.

Oostrom, L., Walker, A., Staats, B., Slootbeek-Van Laar, M., Ortega Azurduy, S., & Rooijakkers, B. (2016). *Measuring the Internet Economy in The Netherlands: A Big Data Analysis*. CBS Discussion paper 2016-14.

Ordabayeva, N., & Chandon, P. (2010). Getting ahead of the Joneses: When equality increases conspicuous consumption among bottom-tier consumers. *The Journal of Consumer Research, 38*(1), 27–41. doi:10.1086/658165

Organization Economic Corporation Development. (n.d.). The Economic Significance of Natural Resources: Key Points for Reformers. In *Eastern Europe. Caucasus And Central Asia*. Author.

Organization, W. H. (2017). *Progress on drinking water, sanitation and hygiene: 2017 update and SDG baselines*. Academic Press.

Oswald, L. R. (2010). Marketing hedonics: Toward a psychoanalysis of advertising response. *Journal of Marketing Communications, 16*(3), 107–131. doi:10.1080/13527260802503638

Ozimek, P., & Förster, J. (2017). The impact of self-regulatory states and traits on Facebook use: Priming materialism and social comparisons. *Computers in Human Behavior, 71*, 418–427. doi:10.1016/j.chb.2017.01.056

Ozkan, M., & Solmaz, B. (2015). Mobile Addiction Of Generation Z And Its Effects On Their Social Lifes. (An application among university students in the 18-23 age group). *Procedia: Social and Behavioral Sciences, 205*, 92–98. doi:10.1016/j.sbspro.2015.09.027

Özsomer, A. (2012). The Interplay Between Global and Local Brands: A Closer Look at Perceived Brand Globalness and Local Iconness. *Journal of International Marketing, 20*(2), 72–95. doi:10.1509/jim.11.0105

Paasonen, S. (2018). Affect, data, manipulation and price in social media. *Distinktion: Journal of Social Theory*, 1-16.

Paine, L. (2014, July). Sustainability in the boardroom. *Harvard Business Review*, 87–95.

Pallant, J. (2013). *SPSS survival manual: a step by step guide to data analysis using SPSS*. Academic Press.

Pang, J., & Qiu, L. (2016). Effect of online review chunking on product attitude: The moderating role of motivation to think. *International Journal of Electronic Commerce*, *20*(3), 355–383. doi:10.1080/10864415.2016.1121763

Pan, L. Y., & Chiou, J. S. (2011). How much can you trust online information? Cues for perceived trustworthiness of consumer-generated online information. *Journal of Interactive Marketing*, *25*(2), 67–74. doi:10.1016/j.intmar.2011.01.002

Pan, Y., & Zhang, J. Q. (2011). Born unequal: A study of the helpfulness of user-generated product reviews. *Journal of Retailing*, *87*(4), 598–612. doi:10.1016/j.jretai.2011.05.002

Pappu, R., Quester, P. G., & Cooksey, R. W. (2005). Consumer-based brand equity: Improving the measurement – empirical evidence. *Journal of Product and Brand Management*, *14*(3), 143–154. doi:10.1108/10610420510601012

Park, B. W., & Lee, K. C. (2011). Exploring the value of purchasing online game items. *Computers in Human Behavior*, *27*(6), 2178–2185. doi:10.1016/j.chb.2011.06.013

Park, C., & Lee, T. M. (2009a). Antecedents of online reviews' usage and purchase influence: An empirical comparison of U.S. and Korean consumers. *Journal of Interactive Marketing*, *23*(4), 332–340. doi:10.1016/j.intmar.2009.07.001

Park, C., & Lee, T. M. (2009b). Information direction, website reputation and eWOM effect: A moderating role of product type. *Journal of Business Research*, *62*(1), 61–67. doi:10.1016/j.jbusres.2007.11.017

Park, D. H., Lee, J., & Han, I. (2007). The effect of on-line consumer reviews on consumer purchasing intention: The moderating role of involvement. *International Journal of Electronic Commerce*, *11*(4), 125–148. doi:10.2753/JEC1086-4415110405

Parker, G. G., Alstyne, M. W., & Choudary, S. P. (2016). *Platform revolution: How networked markets are transforming the economy and how to make them work for you*. WW Norton.

Park, N., Kee, K. F., & Valenzuela, S. (2009). Being Immersed in Social Networking Environment: Facebook Groups, Uses and Gratifications, and Social Outcomes. *Cyberpsychology & Behavior*, *12*(6), 729–733. doi:10.1089/cpb.2009.0003 PMID:19619037

Park, N., & Lee, H. (2012). Social Implications of Smartphone Use: Korean College Students' Smartphone Use and Psychological Well-Being. *Cyberpsychology, Behavior, and Social Networking*, *15*(9), 491–497. doi:10.1089/cyber.2011.0580 PMID:22817650

Park, S. B., & Park, D. H. (2013). The effect of low- versus high-variance in product reviews on product evaluation. *Psychology and Marketing*, *30*(7), 543–554. doi:10.1002/mar.20626

Parmentier, G., & Gandia, R. (2013). Managing sustainable innovation with a user community toolkit: The case of the video game Trackmania. *Creativity and Innovation Management*, *22*(2), 195–208. doi:10.1111/caim.12021

Parthasarathy, M., & Forlani, D. (2010). Do satisfied customers bad-mouth innovative products? *Psychology and Marketing*, *27*(12), 1134–1153. doi:10.1002/mar.20377

Patwardhan, H., & Balasubramanian, S. K. (2011). Brand romance: A complementary approach to explain emotional attachment toward brands. *Journal of Product and Brand Management*, *20*(4), 297–308. doi:10.1108/10610421111148315

Paul, J., Modi, A., & Patel, J. (2016). Predicting green product consumption using theory of planned behavior and reasoned action. *Journal of Retailing and Consumer Services*, *29*, 123–134. doi:10.1016/j.jretconser.2015.11.006

Pavlou, P. A. (2003). Consumer acceptance of electronic commerce: Integrating trust and risk with the technology acceptance model. *International Journal of Electronic Commerce*, *7*(3), 101–134. doi:10.1080/10864415.2003.11044275

Pavlou, P. A., Liang, H., & Xue, Y. (2007). Understanding and mitigating uncertainty in online exchange relationships: A principal-agent perspective. *Management Information Systems Quarterly*, *31*(1), 105–136. doi:10.2307/25148783

Paxton, P. (1999). Is Social Capital Declining in the United States? A Multiple Indicator Assessment. *American Journal of Sociology*, *105*(1), 88–127. doi:10.1086/210268

Peter, J. P., & Ryan, M. (1976). An investigation of perceived risk at the brand level. *JMR, Journal of Marketing Research*, *13*(2), 184–188. doi:10.1177/002224377601300210

Peter, P. J., & Tarpey, L. X. Sr. (1975). A comparative analysis of three consumer decision strategies. *The Journal of Consumer Research*, *2*(1), 29–37. doi:10.1086/208613

Phan, M., Thomas, R., & Heine, K. (2011). Social media and luxury brand management: The case of Burberry. *Journal of Global Fashion Marketing*, *2*(4), 213–222. doi:10.1080/20932685.2011.10593099

Phelps, J. E., Lewis, R., Mobilio, L., Perry, D., & Raman, N. (2004). Viral marketing or electronic word-of-mouth advertising: Examining consumer responses and motivations to pass along email. *Journal of Advertising Research*, *44*(4), 333–348. doi:10.1017/S0021849904040371

Piliavin, J. A., & Charng, H.-W. (1990). Altruism: A review of recent theory and research. *Annual Review of Sociology*, *16*(1), 27–65. doi:10.1146/annurev.so.16.080190.000331

Pisano. (2015). *You need an Innovation Strategy*. Retrieved from https://hbr.org/2015/06/you-need-an-innovation-strategy

Podoshen, J. S., & Andrzejewski, S. A. (2012). An examination of the relationships between materialism, conspicuous consumption, impulse buying, and brand loyalty. *Journal of Marketing Theory and Practice*, *20*(3), 319–334. doi:10.2753/MTP1069-6679200306

Podoshen, J. S., Li, L., & Zhang, J. (2011). Materialism and conspicuous consumption in China: A cross-cultural examination. *International Journal of Consumer Studies*, *35*(1), 17–25. doi:10.1111/j.1470-6431.2010.00930.x

Pradhan, J. (2010). It's My Passion, That's My Mission to Decide, I'm Going Worldwide: the Cosmopolitanism of Global Fans of Japanese Popular Culture (Master of Arts). University of Massachusetts Amherst.

Praninskas, J. (1980). *Rapid Review of English Grammar*. Prentice Hall, Inc.

Prendergast, G., Paliwal, A., & Chan, K. K. F. (2018). Trust in online recommendations: An evolutionary psychology perspective. *International Journal of Advertising*, *37*(2), 199–216. doi:10.1080/02650487.2016.1239879

Presi, C., Saridakis, C., & Hartmans, S. (2014). User-generated content behaviour of the dissatisfied service customer. *European Journal of Marketing*, *48*(9/10), 1600–1625. doi:10.1108/EJM-07-2012-0400

Price, L. J., & Dawar, N. (2002). The joint effects of brands and warranties in signaling new product quality. *Journal of Economic Psychology*, *23*(2), 165–190. doi:10.1016/S0167-4870(02)00062-4

Pudin, C. S. J. (2016). *Exploring a flipped learning approach in teaching Grammar for ESL Students*. Paper presented at International Conference on Education and Psychology, Universiti Malaysia Sabah.

Pudin, C.S.J., & Saru, E. H. (2014). The Reality of Teaching English without L1 reference in an ESL Classroom. *MANU Jurnal Pusat Penataran Ilmu dan Bahasa*, *21*, 149.

Pudin, C. S. J., Storey, J. M., Loh, Y. L., Swanto, S., & Din, W. A. (2015). Exploring L1 interference in the writings of Kadazandusun ESL students. *Indonesian Journal of Applied Linguistics*, *5*(1), 54–62. doi:10.17509/ijal.v5i1.831

Purnawirawan, N., De Pelsmacker, P., & Dens, N. (2012). Balance and sequence in online reviews: How perceived usefulness affects attitudes and intentions. *Journal of Interactive Marketing*, *26*(4), 244–255. doi:10.1016/j.intmar.2012.04.002

Purnawirawan, N., Eisend, M., De Pelsmacker, P., & Dens, N. (2015). A Meta-analytic investigation of the role of valence in online reviews. *Journal of Interactive Marketing*, *31*, 17–27. doi:10.1016/j.intmar.2015.05.001

Quoquab, F., Pahlevan, S., & Hussin, N. (2016). Counterfeit Product Purchase: What Counts—Materialism or Religiosity? *Advanced Science Letters*, *22*(5-6), 1303–1306. doi:10.1166/asl.2016.6739

Rajagopalan, S. (2011). Shahrukh Khan as media text: Celebrity, identity and emotive engagement in a Russian online community. *Celebrity Studies*, *2*(3), 263–276. doi:10.1080/19392397.2011.609333

Raja, T. N. (1988). *Grammar Practice Activities*. London: Cambridge University.

Ramelan. (1992). *Introduction to Linguistic Analysis*. IKIP Semarang Press.

Ramey, G. (1996). D1 Signaling Equilibria with Multiple Signals and a Continuum of Types. *Journal of Economic Theory*, *69*(2), 508–531. doi:10.1006/jeth.1996.0066

Raza, S. H., Abu Bakar, H., & Mohamad, B. (2019). *The effects of advertising appeals on consumers' behavioural intention towards global brands. Journal of Islamic Marketing*. doi:10.1108/jima-11-2017-0134

Reed, C. (2007). Generation Y Research: What Makes 'Y' Tick. *Brand Strategy, 38*.

Reed, A. II. (2004). Activating the Self-Importance of Consumer Selves: Exploring Identity Salience Effects on Judgements. *The Journal of Consumer Research*, *31*(2), 286–295. doi:10.1086/422108

Rege, A. (2009). What's Love Got to Do with It? Exploring Online Dating Scams and Identity Fraud. *International Journal of Cyber Criminology*.

Reimer, T., & Benkenstein, M. (2016). Altruistic eWOM marketing: More than an alternative to monetary incentives. *Journal of Retailing and Consumer Services*, *31*, 323–333. doi:10.1016/j.jretconser.2016.04.003

Reyns, B. W. (2015). A routine activity perspective on online victimisation. *Journal of Financial Crime*, *22*(4), 396–411. doi:10.1108/JFC-06-2014-0030

Rezai, G., Teng, P. K., Mohamed, Z., & Shamsudin, M. N. (2012). Consumers' awareness and consumption intention towards green foods. *African Journal of Business Management*, *6*(12), 4496.

Richards, J. C. (1974). *Error Analysis*. Longman Group Ltd.

Richardson, P. S., Dick, A. S., & Jain, A. K. (1994). Extrinsic and intrinsic cue effects on perceptions of store brand quality. *Journal of Marketing*, *58*(4), 28–36. doi:10.1177/002224299405800403

Richins, M. L. (1987). Media, materialism, and human happiness. In W. Melanie & A. Paul (Eds.), *Advances in Consumer Research* (Vol. 14, pp. 352–356). Provo, UT: Association for Consumer Research.

Richins, M. L., & Dawson, S. (1992). A consumer values orientation for materialism and its measurement: Scale development and validation. *The Journal of Consumer Research*, *19*(3), 303–316. doi:10.1086/209304

Richter, C., Kraus, S., Brem, A., Durst, S., & Giselbrecht, C. (2017). Digital entrepreneurship: Innovative business models for the sharing economy. *Creativity and Innovation Management*, *26*(3), 300–310. doi:10.1111/caim.12227

Riebl, S. K., Estabrooks, P. A., Dunsmore, J. C., Savla, J., Frisard, M. I., Dietrich, A. M., ... Davy, B. M. (2015). A systematic literature review and meta-analysis: The Theory of Planned Behavior's application to understand and predict nutrition-related behaviors in youth. *Eating Behaviors*, *18*, 160–178. doi:10.1016/j.eatbeh.2015.05.016 PMID:26112228

Rindfleisch, A., Burroughs, J. E., & Denton, F. (1997). Family structure, materialism, and compulsive consumption. *The Journal of Consumer Research*, *23*(4), 312–325. doi:10.1086/209486

Rip, A., & Kemp, R. (1998). Technological change. In S. Rayner & E. L. Malone (Eds.), *Human Choice and Climate Change – Resources and Technology* (pp. 327–399). Columbus: Battelle Press.

Roberts, J. A., Manolis, C., & Tanner, J. F. Jr. (2003). Family structure, materialism, and compulsive buying: A reinquiry and extension. *Journal of the Academy of Marketing Science*, *31*(3), 300–311. doi:10.1177/0092070303031003007

Robitschek, C. (1998). Personal growth initiative: The construct and its measure. *Measurement & Evaluation in Counseling & Development*, *30*(4), 183–198. doi:10.1080/07481756.1998.12068941

Rochet, J. C., & Tirole, J. (2006). Two-Sided Markets: A Progress Report. *The RAND Journal of Economics*, *37*(3), 645–667. doi:10.1111/j.1756-2171.2006.tb00036.x

Rogers, E. M. (1995). *Diffusion of innovations* (4th ed.). New York: The Free Press.

Rojko, A. (2017). Industry 4.0 Concept: Background and Overview. *International Journal of Interactive Mobile Technologies*, *11*(5), 77–90. doi:10.3991/ijim.v11i5.7072

Rokeach, M. (1973). *The nature of human values*. New York: Free press.

Rosbi, A. R., & Sanep, A. (2011). Strategi Pembangunan Keusahawan Asnaf dan Miskin melalui Agihan Bantuan Modal Zakat. *Jurnal Pengurusan*, *33*, 37–44. doi:10.17576/pengurusan-2011-33-03

Rossi, A., & Vismara, S. (2018). What do crowdfunding platforms do? A comparison between investment-based platforms in Europe. *Eurasian Business Review*, *8*(1), 93–118. doi:10.100740821-017-0092-6

Rousseau, D. M., Sitkin, S. B., Burt, R. S., & Camerer, C. (1998). Not so different after all: A cross discipline view of trust. *Academy of Management Review*, *23*(3), 395–404. doi:10.5465/amr.1998.926617

Sachs, J. D., & Warner, A. M. (1995). *Natural resource abundance and economic growth*. NBER Working Paper No. 5398. Cambridge, MA: National Bureau of Economic Research.

Sachs, G. (2015). *The Future of Finance - The Socialization of Finance*. Equity Research.

Safi, H., Azouri, M., & Azouri, A. (2018, May). L'influence des réseaux sociaux sur le comportement du consommateur: Le cas de l'industrie des biens luxueux. *La Revue Gestion et Organisation*, *10*(1), 29–35. doi:10.1016/j.rgo.2018.04.001

Sanchez-Fernandez, R., & Iniesta-Bonillo, M. (2007). The concept of perceived value: A systematic review of the research. *Marketing Theory*, *7*(4), 427–451. doi:10.1177/1470593107083165

Sandhu, S. K., & Paim, L. (2016). Consuming for status among Malaysian working women. *Journal of Emerging Economies & Islamic Research*, *4*(3).

Sassi, S., & Goaied, M. (2013). Financial development, ICT diffusion and economic growth: Lessons from MENA region. *Telecommunications Policy*, *37*(4-5), 252–261. doi:10.1016/j.telpol.2012.12.004

Schiffman, L. G., & Kanuk, L. L. (2004). *Consumer behaviour* (8th ed.). Prentice-Hall Inc.

Schlosser, A. E. (2011). Can including pros and cons increase the helpfulness and persuasiveness of online reviews? The interactive effects of ratings and arguments. *Journal of Consumer Psychology*, *21*(3), 226–239. doi:10.1016/j.jcps.2011.04.002

Schmit, V., & Thierry, B. (2018). The online-word-of-mouth: Research perspectives on multicriteria rating. *Le Travail Humain*, *81*(3), 227–246. doi:10.3917/th.813.0227

Schroeder, J. E., & Dugal, S. S. (1995). Psychological correlates of the materialism construct. *Journal of Social Behavior and Personality, 10*(1), 243.

Schwartz, R. H. (2013). Excessive participation in on-line internet action games by two American teenagers: Case report, description of extent of overuse, and adverse consequences. *Open Journal of Pediatrics, 3*(03), 201–203. doi:10.4236/ojped.2013.33035

Schwedt, G., Chevalier, M., & Gutsatz, M. (2012). *Luxury retail management: How the World's top brands provide quality product and service support.* Hoboken, NJ: Wiley.

Scott, K. (2009). *Terminal materialism vs. instrumental materialism: Can materialism be beneficial?* (Doctoral dissertation). Oklahoma State University.

Scott, J. T. (2017). *The Sustainable Business: A Practitioner's Guide to Achieving Long-Term Profitability and Competitiveness.* Routledge.

SEED. (2019). *Sustainable Development Goals.* Available online from https://seed.uno/topics/sdgs

Segal, B., & Podoshen, J. S. (2013). An examination of materialism, conspicuous consumption and gender differences. *International Journal of Consumer Studies, 37*(2), 189–198. doi:10.1111/j.1470-6431.2012.01099.x

Sepehr, S., & Head, M. (2013). *Online Video Game Addiction: A Review and an Information Systems Research Agenda.* Retrieved October 13, 2018, from https://pdfs.semanticscholar.org/2438/f642dc7be774a226d66eabac87256d450989.pdf

Shabecoff, P. (1993). *A fierce green fire; the American environment movement.* Academic Press.

Shao, G. (2009). Understanding the Appeal of User-Generated Media: A Uses and Gratification Perspective. *Internet Research, 19*(1), 7–25. doi:10.1108/10662240910927795

Shapiro, S. (1999). When an Ad's Influence Is Beyond Our Conscious Control: Perceptual and Conceptual Fluency Effects Caused By Incidental Ad Exposure. *The Journal of Consumer Research, 26*(1), 16–36. doi:10.1086/209548

Sheth, J. N., Newman, B. I., & Gross, B. L. (1991). *Consumption Values and Market Choices-Theory and Applications.* Cincinnati, OH: South-Western Publishing Co.

Shu, S., Strombeck, S., & Hsieh, C. (2013). *Consumer Ethnocentrism, Self-Image Congruence and Local Brand Preference : A Cross-National Examination.* doi:10.6126/APMR.2013.18.1.03

Simoes, A. J. G., & Hidalgo, C. A. (2011). The economic complexity observatory: An analytical tool for understanding the dynamics of economic development. *Workshops at the 25th AAAI Conference on Artificial Intelligence.*

Singh, J. P., Irani, S., Rana, N. P., Dwivedi, Y. K., Saumya, S., & Kumar Roy, P. (2017). Predicting the "helpfulness" of online consumer reviews. *Journal of Business Research, 70*, 346–355. doi:10.1016/j.jbusres.2016.08.008

Skillicorn, N. (2016). *What is innovation? 15 experts share their innovation definition.* Retrieved from https://www.ideatovalue.com/inno/nickskillicorn/2016/03/innovation-15-experts-share-innovation-definition

Skoric, M. M., Teo, L. L. C., & Neo, R. L. (2009). Children and Video Games: Addiction, Engagement, and Scholastic Achievement. *Cyberpsychology & Behavior, 12*(5), 567–572. doi:10.1089/cpb.2009.0079 PMID:19624263

Small and Medium Enterprises Corporation. (2017). *Definisi Baharu PKS.* Dicapai daripada http://www.smecorp.gov.my/images/pdf/GarisPanduan_Definisi_Baharu_PKS_updated.pdf

SME Annual Report. (2018). *Small and Medium Enterprise Annual Report 2018.* Available online from http://www.smecorp.gov.my/index.php/en/laporan-tahunan/3342-laporan-tahunan-pks-2017-18

Smith, T., Coyle, J. R., Lightfoot, E., & Scott, A. (2007). Reconsidering Models of Influence: The Relationship between Consumer Social Networks and Word-of-Mouth Effectiveness. *Journal of Advertising Research*, *47*(4), 387–397. doi:10.2501/S0021849907070407

Soetikno, I. (1996). *Analysis Wacana*. Jakarta: Gramedia Pustaka Utama.

Solomon, M. R. (1983). The role of products as social stimuli: A symbolic interactionism perspective. *The Journal of Consumer Research*, *10*(3), 319–329. doi:10.1086/208971

Sommer, R. (2017). Michael Kors - A Fashionable Trend. *Seeking Alpha*. Retrieved from https://seekingalpha.com/article/4133212-michael-kors-fashionable-trend

Song, X. M., & Montoya-Weiss, M. M. (1998). Critical Development Activities for Really New versus Incremental Products. *Journal of Product Innovation Management*, *15*(2), 124–135. doi:10.1111/1540-5885.1520124

Sparks, B. A., Perkins, H. E., & Buckley, R. (2013). Online travel reviews as persuasive communication: The effects of content type, source, and certification logos on consumer behavior. *Tourism Management*, *39*, 1–9. doi:10.1016/j.tourman.2013.03.007

Spence, M. (1973). Job Market Signaling. *The Quarterly Journal of Economics*, *87*(3), 355–374. doi:10.2307/1882010

Sreen, N., Purbey, S., & Sadarangani, P. (2018). Impact of culture, behavior and gender on green purchase intention. *Journal of Retailing and Consumer Services*, *41*, 177–189. doi:10.1016/j.jretconser.2017.12.002

Srikant, M. (2013). Materialism in consumer behavior and marketing: A review. *Management & Marketing*, *8*(2), 329.

Srinivasan, S. S., Anderson, R., & Ponnavolu, K. (2002). *Customer loyalty in e-commerce : an exploration of its antecedents and consequences*. Academic Press.

Srisutto, S. (2010). *Country Branding, Consumption Values, and Purchase Decision Confidence: A Case Study of Tourists to Thailand* (PhD thesis). Lincoln University.

Steenkamp, E. M. (2002). How perceived brand globalness creates brand value. *Journal of International Business Studies*, *34*(1), 53–65. doi:10.1057/palgrave.jibs.8400002

Steenkamp, J.-B. (2014). How global brands create firm value: The 4V model. *International Marketing Review*, *31*(1), 5–29. doi:10.1108/IMR-10-2013-0233

Steffes, E. M., & Burgee, L. E. (2009). Social ties and online word of mouth. *Internet Research*, *19*(1), 42–59. doi:10.1108/10662240910927812

Steiner, C. (1995). A Philosophy for Innovation: The Role of Unconventional Individuals in Innovation Success. *Journal of Product Innovation Management*, *12*(5), 431–440. doi:10.1111/1540-5885.1250431

Stern, P. C. (1999). A Value-Belief-Norm Theory of Support for Social Movements: The Case of Environmentalism. *Research in Human Ecology.*, *6*(2), 81–97.

Stevens, C. S. (2011). Touching the audience: Music and television advertising in Japan. *Japanese Studies*, *31*(1), 37–51. doi:10.1080/10371397.2011.560260

Stevenson, N. (2009). Talking to Bowie fans: Masculinity, ambivalence and cultural citizenship. *European Journal of Cultural Studies*, *12*(1), 79–98. doi:10.1177/1367549408098706

Suki, N. M. (2016). *Handbook of Research on Leveraging Consumer Psychology for Effective Customer Engagement*. https://www.igi-global.com/book/handbook-research-leveraging-consumer-psychology/149284

Suki, N. M., & Suki, N. M. (2015). Consumers' environmental behavior towards staying at a green hotel: Moderation of green hotel knowledge. *Management of Environmental Quality*, *26*(1), 103–117. doi:10.1108/MEQ-02-2014-0023

Suki, N. M., & Suki, N. M. (2015). Consumption values and consumer environmental concern regarding green products. *International Journal of Sustainable Development and World Ecology*, *22*(3), 269–278. doi:10.1080/13504509.2015.1013074

Suki, N. M., & Suki, N. M. (2019). *Correlations between awareness of green marketing, corporate social responsibility, product image, corporate reputation, and consumer purchase intention. In Corporate Social Responsibility: Concepts, Methodologies, Tools, and Applications* (pp. 143–154). IGI Global. doi:10.4018/978-1-5225-6192-7.ch008

Sultan, N. (2010). Cloud computing for education: A new dawn? *International Journal of Information Management*, *30*(2), 109–116. doi:10.1016/j.ijinfomgt.2009.09.004

Sun, Y., Zhao, Y., Jia, S. Q., & Zheng, D. Y. (2015). *Understanding the Antecedents of Mobile Game Addiction: The Roles of Perceived Visibility, Perceived Enjoyment and Flow*. Retrieved October 13, 2018, from https://pdfs.semanticscholar.org/419c/b97897f014d2d932afbf8c35b0b1e45fe424.pdf

Sundaram, D. S., Kaushik, M., & Webster, C. (1998). Word-of-mouth communications: A motivational analysis. *Advances in Consumer Research. Association for Consumer Research (U. S.).*

Sun, G., Wang, W., Cheng, Z., Li, J., & Chen, J. (2017). The intermediate linkage between materialism and luxury consumption: Evidence from the emerging market of China. *Social Indicators Research*, *132*(1), 475–487. doi:10.100711205-016-1273-x

Sun, N., Rau, P. P. L., & Ma, L. (2014). Understanding lurkers in online communities: A literature review. *Computers in Human Behavior*, *38*, 110–117. doi:10.1016/j.chb.2014.05.022

Suprayitno, E., Aslam, M., & Harun, A. (2017). Zakat and SDGs: Impact zakat on human development in the five states of Malaysia. *International Journal of Zakat*, *2*(1), 61–69.

Sussman, S. W., & Siegal, W. S. (2003). Informational influence in organizations: An integrated approach to knowledge adoption. *Information Systems Research*, *14*(1), 47–65. doi:10.1287/isre.14.1.47.14767

Sustainable Development Goals. (2019). Available online from https://sustainabledevelopment.un.org/sdgs

Swinyard, W. R., & Smith, S. M. (2003). Why people (dont) shop online: A lifestyle study of the internet consumer. *Psychology and Marketing*, *20*(7), 567–597. doi:10.1002/mar.10087

Sze, J., Ho, Y., Ong, D., Teik, L., Ing, W. P., Tay, G., … Peng, N. C. (2000). *Global Versus Local Brand : Perceived Quality And Status-Seeking Motivation In The Automobile Industry*. Academic Press.

Tabachnick, B. G., & Fidell, L. S. (2007). Using Multivariate Statistics (5th ed.). doi:10.1037/022267

Tafsir, M., Shaari, R., Muchtar, H., & Firmansya, F. (2018). The Effects of Product Quality and Interpersonal Communication on Customer Loyalty. *International Journal on Advanced Science, Education, and Religion*, *1*(1), 1–8. doi:10.33648/ijoaser.v1i1.1

Tajfel, H., & Turner, J.C. (1979). An integrative theory of intergroup conflict. *The Social Psychology of Intergroup Relations*, *33*(47), 74.

Tajfel, H. (1988). *Social Identity and Intergroup Behavior*. Cambridge, University Press.

Tajfel, H., & Turner, J. C. (1986). The Social Identity Theory of Intergroup Behavior. In S. G. Worchel & W. G. Austin (Eds.), *Psychology of Intergroup Relation* (pp. 7–24). Chicago: Nelson-Hall Publishers.

Taken Smith, K. (2012). Longitudinal study of digital marketing strategies targeting Millennials. *Journal of Consumer Marketing*, *29*(2), 86–92. doi:10.1108/07363761211206339

Tan, S. J. (1999). Strategies for reducing consumers' risk aversion in internet shopping. *Journal of Consumer Marketing, 16*(2), 163.

Tang, L. (2017). Mine your customers or mine your business: The moderating role of culture in online word-of-mouth reviews. *Journal of International Marketing*, *25*(2), 88–110. doi:10.1509/jim.16.0030

Tang, M. C. (2016). The effect of online word of mouth on fantasy readers' preference stability: The moderating role of involvement and knowledge. *Library & Information Science Research*, *38*(4), 292–300. doi:10.1016/j.lisr.2016.11.003

Tan, K. S., & Phang, S. Y. (2005). *From Efficiency-Driven to Innovation-Driven Economic Growth: Perspectives from Singapore*. The World Bank. doi:10.1596/1813-9450-3569

Tan, Y.-H., & Thoen, W. (2001). Toward a generic model of trust for electronic commerce. *International Journal of Electronic Commerce*, *5*(2), 61–74.

Taufique, K. M. R., & Vaithianathan, S. (2018). A fresh look at understanding Green consumer behavior among young urban Indian consumers through the lens of Theory of Planned Behavior. *Journal of Cleaner Production*, *183*, 46–55. doi:10.1016/j.jclepro.2018.02.097

Tavormina, M. G. M., & Tavormina, R. (2017). Playıng Wıth Vıdeo Games: Goıng To A New Addıctıon? *Psychiatria Danubina*, *29*(3), 422–426. PMID:28953802

Tee, P. K., Gharleghi, B., & Chan, B. Y. F. (2013). Malaysian young consumer preferences in choosing international fashion brand. *Journal of Human and Social Science Research*, *1*(1), 31–38.

Teichmann, K., Stokburger-sauer, N. E., Plank, A., & Strobl, A. (2015). Motivational drivers of content contribution to company- versus consumer-hosted online communities. doi:10.1002/mar

Tencent. (2017). China's Digital Transformation: An Analysis from a Socio-economic Perspective. *5th IMF Statistical Forum.*

Terranova, T. (2000). Free labor. In *Digital Labor* (pp. 41–65). Routledge.

Thakor, M. V., & Lavack, A. M. (2003). Effect of perceived brand origin associations on consumer perceptions of quality. *Journal of Product and Brand Management*, *12*(6), 394–407. doi:10.1108/10610420310498821

Thoumrungroje, A. (2014). The influence of social media intensity and EWOM on conspicuous consumption. *Procedia: Social and Behavioral Sciences*, *148*, 7–15. doi:10.1016/j.sbspro.2014.07.009

Tidd, J., & Bessant, J. (2014). *Strategic innovation management*. New York: John Wiley & Sons.

Timm, S. N., & Deal, B. M. (2016). Effective or ephemeral? The role of energy information dashboards in changing occupant energy behaviors. *Energy Research & Social Science*, *19*, 11–20. doi:10.1016/j.erss.2016.04.020

Tirunillai, S., & Tellis, G. J. (2012). Does chatter really matter? Dynamics of user-generated content and stock performance. *Marketing Science*, *31*(2), 198–215. doi:10.1287/mksc.1110.0682

Tizazu, Y. (2014). A linguistic analysis of errors in learners' compositions: The case of arba minch university students. *International Journal of English Language and Linguistics*, *2*(2), 69–101.

Tonis, R. (2015). SMEs role in achieving sustainable development. Journal of Economic Development. *Environment and People*, *4*(1), 41–50. doi:10.26458/jedep.v4i1.102

Trabucchi, D., Buganza, T., Dell'Era, C., & Pellizzoni, E. (2018). Exploring the inbound and outbound strategies enabled by user generated big data: Evidence from leading smartphone applications. *Creativity and Innovation Management, 27*(1), 42–55. doi:10.1111/caim.12241

Tregear, A., Kuznesof, S., & Moxey, A. (1998). Policy initiatives for regional foods: Some insights from consumer research. *Food Policy, 23*(5), 383–394. doi:10.1016/S0306-9192(98)00044-X

Trigg, A. B. (2001). Veblen, Bourdieu, and conspicuous consumption. *Journal of Economic Issues, 35*(1), 99–115. doi:10.1080/00213624.2001.11506342

Troise, C., & Ferrara, E. (2016). App economy: impact and effects of the phenomenon. *MC - Diritto ed economia dei mezzi di comunicazione, 2*, 7-28.

Troise. (2019a). Entrepreneurship and Equity Crowdfunding: Does It Matter? *International Journal of Business and Management, 14*(10), 72-86.

Troise. (2019b). Marketing Strategies in Equity Crowdfunding: a Comparative Study of Italian Platforms. *International Journal of Marketing Studies, 11*(4), 16-29.

Troise, C., Candelo, E., Matricano, D., & Sorrentino, M. (2018b). The role of Entrepreneurial Quality in Equity Crowdfunding success: An explorative analysis of Italian platforms. *ICSB Conference.*

Troise, C., Candelo, E., & Sorrentino, M. (2018a). Equity Crowdfunding: Investigating the Role of Entrepreneurial Quality in Affecting the Success of the Campaigns. *Sinergie Conference*, 315-319.

Troise, C., Matricano, D., & Sorrentino, M. (2019). Open innovation platforms: exploring the importance of knowledge in supporting online initiatives. *Ifkad Conference*, 1646-1658.

Tsai, K.-H., Chou, C., & Kuo, J.-H. (2008). The curvilinear relationships between responsive and proactive market orientations and new product performance: A contingent link. *Industrial Marketing Management, 37*(8), 884–894. doi:10.1016/j.indmarman.2007.03.005

Tu, J. C., Shih, M. C., Hsu, C. Y., & Lin, J. H. (2014). Developing Blue Ocean Strategy Of Sustainable Product Design And Development For Business Opportunities Of BOP Groups In Taiwan. *Mathematical Problems in Engineering, 2014*, 2014. doi:10.1155/2014/297524

Tyler, K. (2008). Generation Gaps. *HRMagazine, 53*, 69–73.

Underwood, R. L. (2003). the Communicative Power of Product Packaging: Creating Brand IdentityVia Lived and Mediated Experience. *Journal of Marketing Theory and Practice, 11*(1), 62–76. doi:10.1080/10696679.2003.11501933

United Nation System Task Team. (2015). *Post 2015 Development Agenda.* Science Technology and Innovation for Sustainable Development in The Global Partnership For Development Beyond 2015. Retrieved on 9 Dec 2019 from https://www.un.org/en/development/desa/policy/untaskteam_undf/thinkpieces/28_thinkpiece_science.pdf

United Nations Development Programme (UNDP). (2019). *Sustainable Developments Goals.* Available online from https://www.undp.org/content/undp/en/home/sustainable-development-goals.html

van Noort, G., & Willemsen, L. M. (2012). Online damage control: The effects of proactive versus reactive webcare interventions in consumer-generated and brand-generated platforms. *Journal of Interactive Marketing, 26*(3), 131–140. doi:10.1016/j.intmar.2011.07.001

Veblen, T. (1899). *The Theory of the Leisure Class: An Economic Study in the Evolution of Institutions.* Macmillan & Co.

Verstraten, R. (2015). *The Effect of Advertising Credibility: Could it Change Consumers' Attitude and Purchase Intentions?* (Unpublished dissertation). Erasmus University Rotterdam.

Vision Mobile. (2015). *European App Economy 2015: creating jobs e driving economic growth in Europe*. Author.

Vismara, S. (2016). Equity retention and social network theory in equity crowdfunding. *Small Business Economics, 46*(4), 579–590. doi:10.100711187-016-9710-4

Vogel, E. A., Rose, J. P., Roberts, L. R., & Eckles, K. (2014). Social comparison, social media, and self-esteem. *Psychology of Popular Media Culture, 3*(4), 206–222. doi:10.1037/ppm0000047

Vollmer, C., Randler, C., Horzum, M. B., & Ayas, T. (2014, January-March). Computer Game Addiction in Adolescents and Its Relationship to Chronotype and Personality. *SAGE Open, 4*(1), 1–9. doi:10.1177/2158244013518054

Voola, R., & O'Cass, A. (2010). Implementing competitive strategies: The role of responsive and proactive market orientations. *European Journal of Marketing, 44*(1/2), 245–266. doi:10.1108/03090561011008691

Wagner, S. A. (2002). *Understanding green consumer behavior: A qualitative cognitive approach*. Routledge. doi:10.4324/9780203444030

Wan, C. S., & Chiou, W. B. (2006). Why Are Adolescents Addicted to Online Gaming? An Interview Study in Taiwan. *Cyberpsychology & Behavior, 9*(6), 762–766. doi:10.1089/cpb.2006.9.762 PMID:17201603

Wang, C. W., Chan, C. I. W., Mak, K. K., Ho, S. Y., Wong, P. W. C., & Ho, R. T. H. (2014). Prevalence and Correlates of Video and Internet Gaming Addiction among Hong Kong Adolescents: A Pilot Study. *TheScientificWorldJournal, 2014*, 1–9. doi:10.1155/2014/874648 PMID:25032242

Wang, F., Liu, X., & Fang, E. (2015). User Reviews Variance, Critic Reviews Variance, and Product Sales: An Exploration of Customer Breadth and Depth Effects. *Journal of Retailing, 91*(3), 372–389. doi:10.1016/j.jretai.2015.04.007

Wang, H. Y., Liao, C., & Yang, L. H. (2013). What Affects Mobile Application Use? The Roles of Consumption Values. *International Journal of Marketing Studies, 5*(2), 11–22. doi:10.5539/ijms.v5n2p11

Wang, K., Nickerson, J., & Sakamoto, Y. (2018). Crowdsourced idea generation: The effect of exposure to an original idea. *Creativity and Innovation Management, 27*(2), 196–208. doi:10.1111/caim.12264

Wang, X., Yu, C., & Wei, Y. (2012). Social media peer communication and impacts on purchase intentions: A consumer socialization framework. *Journal of Interactive Marketing, 26*(4), 198–208. doi:10.1016/j.intmar.2011.11.004

Wang, Y., & Fesenmaier, D. R. (2004). Towards understanding members' general participation in and active contribution to an online travel community. *Tourism Management, 25*(6), 709–722. doi:10.1016/j.tourman.2003.09.011

Wan-Ismail, W. N. A., Zakaria, N., & Abdul-Talib, A. N. (2016). Craving vs. Compulsion for Luxury Goods?: Trends and Patterns of Conspicuous Consumption Behavior in Asian Culture. In *Neuroeconomics and the Decision-Making Process* (pp. 287–297). IGI Global. doi:10.4018/978-1-4666-9989-2.ch015

Wansink, B., & van Ittersum, K. (2003). Bottoms Up! The Influence of Elongation on Pouring and Consumption Volume. *The Journal of Consumer Research, 30*(3), 455–463. doi:10.1086/378621

Wei, Z., Zhao, J., & Zhang, C. (2014). Organizational ambidexterity, market orientation, and firm performance. *Journal of Engineering and Technology Management, 33*, 134–153. doi:10.1016/j.jengtecman.2014.06.001

Wells, J. D., Valacich, J. S., & Hess, T. J. (2011). What signal are you sending? How website quality influences perceptions of product quality and purchase intentions. *Management Information Systems Quarterly, 35*(2), 373–396. doi:10.2307/23044048

Werner, R. R. (2017). How to Protect Against Common Cyberattacks and Insure Against Potential Losses. (cover story). *The CPA Journal, 87*(3), 16. Retrieved from http://search.ebscohost.com.proxy.cecybrary.com/login.aspx?direct=true&db=f5h&AN=121733191&site=ehost-live&scope=site

West, J., & Lakhani, K. (2008). Getting clear about communities in open innovation. *Industry and Innovation, 15*(2), 223–231. doi:10.1080/13662710802033734

Whelan, T., & Fink, C. (2016). The Comprehensive Business Guide for Sustainability. *Harvard Business Review*. Retrieved on 9 Dec 2019 from https://hbr. org/2016/10/the-comprehensive-businesscase-for-sustainability

White, K., Habib, R., & Hardisty, D. J. (2019). How to SHIFT Consumer Behaviors to be More Sustainable: A Literature Review and Guiding Framework. *Journal of Marketing, 83*(3), 22–49. doi:10.1177/0022242919825649

Whitty, M. T. (2015). *Mass-marketing fraud: A growing concern*. Academic Press.

Whitty, M. T. (2018). 419 – It's just a Game : Pathways to Cyber- Fraud Criminality emanating from West Africa. doi:10.5281/zenodo.1467848

Whitty, M. T. (2013). The Scammers Persuasive Techniques Model: Development of a Stage Model to Explain the Online Dating Romance Scam. *British Journal of Criminology*. doi:10.1093/bjc/azt009

Whitty, M. T. (2017). Do You Love Me? Psychological Characteristics of Romance Scam Victims. *Cyberpsychology, Behavior, and Social Networking*. doi:10.1089/cyber.2016.0729 PMID:28657792

Whitty, M. T., & Buchanan, T. (2012). The Online Romance Scam: A Serious Cybercrime. *Cyberpsychology, Behavior, and Social Networking, 15*(3), 181–183. doi:10.1089/cyber.2011.0352 PMID:22304401

Wilcox, K., & Stephen, A. T. (2012). Are close friends the enemy? Online social networks, self-esteem, and self-control. *The Journal of Consumer Research, 40*(1), 90–103. doi:10.1086/668794

Winit, W., Gregory, G., Cleveland, M., & Verlegh, P. (2014). Global vs local brands: How home country bias and price differences impact brand evaluations. *International Marketing Review, 31*(2), 102–128. doi:10.1108/IMR-01-2012-0001

Wirtenberg, J., Russell, W., & Lipsky, D. (2009). *The Sustainable Enterprise Field Book*. Greenleaf Publishing Limited.

Wong, N. Y. (1997). Suppose you own the world and no one knows? In M. Brucks & D. MacInnis (Eds.), *Advances in consumer research* (Vol. 4, pp. 197–201). Provo, UT: Association for Consumer Research.

Wood, R. T. A. (2008). Problems with the Concept of Video Game "Addiction": Some Case Study Examples. *International Journal of Mental Health and Addiction, 6*(2), 169–178. doi:10.100711469-007-9118-0

Woodruff, R. B. (1997). Customer value: The next source for competitive advantage. *Journal of the Academy of Marketing Science, 25*(2), 139–153. doi:10.1007/BF02894350

Woog, K. (2016). Proposed Gaming Addiction Behavioral Treatment Method. Addicta: The Turkish. *Journal of Addiction, 3*(2), 271–279.

Worsham, J., & Gatrell, J. (2005). Multiple Principals, Multiple Signals: A Signaling Approach to Principal-Agent Relations. *Policy Studies Journal: the Journal of the Policy Studies Organization, 33*(3), 363–376. doi:10.1111/j.1541-0072.2005.00120.x

Wortmann, F., & Flüchter, K. (2015). Internet of Things: Technology and Value Added. *Business & Information Systems Engineering, 57*(3), 221–224. doi:10.100712599-015-0383-3

Wright, L. T., Newman, A., & Dennis, C. (2006). Enhancing consumer empowerment. *European Journal of Marketing*, *40*(9–10), 925–935. doi:10.1108/03090560610680934

Wu, J.H., Wang, S.C., & Tsai, H.H. (2010). Falling in love with online games: The uses and gratifications perspective. *Computers in Human Behavior, 26*(6), 1862–1871.

Wu, J., & Rangaswamy, A. (2003). A fuzzy set model of search and consideration with an application to an online market. *Marketing Science*, *22*(3), 411–434. doi:10.1287/mksc.22.3.411.17738

Wu, P. F. (2013). In search of negativity bias: An empirical study of perceived helpfulness of online reviews. *Psychology and Marketing*, *30*(11), 971–984. doi:10.1002/mar.20660

Xu, B., & Ouenniche, J. (2011). A multidimensional framework for performance evaluation of forecasting models: Context-dependent DEA. *Applied Financial Economics*, *21*(24), 1873–1890. doi:10.1080/09603107.2011.597722

Yablonsky, S. (2018). A Multidimensional Framework for Digital Platform Innovation and Management: From Business to Technological Platforms. *Systems Research and Behavioral Science*, *35*(4), 485–501. doi:10.1002res.2544

Yang, J., Kim, W., Amblee, N., & Jeong, J. (2012). The heterogeneous effect of WOM on product sales: Why the effect of WOM valence is mixed? *European Journal of Marketing*, *46*(11), 1523–1538. doi:10.1108/03090561211259961

Yang, J., Ma, J., Zhang, Y., & Hong, J. H. (2018). With whom should you have dinner? A multidimensional framework for understanding political ties in China. *Business Horizons*, *61*(6), 891–898. doi:10.1016/j.bushor.2018.07.010

Yang, L. (2009). All for love: The Corn fandom, prosumers, and the Chinese way of creating a superstar. *International Journal of Cultural Studies*, *12*(5), 527–543. doi:10.1177/1367877909337863

Yang, L., Yang, S. H., & Plotnick, L. (2013). How the internet of things technology enhances emergency response operations. *Technological Forecasting and Social Change*, *80*(9), 1854–1867. doi:10.1016/j.techfore.2012.07.011

Yenicioglu, B., & Christodoulides, G. (2014). Branding in the age of digital connectivity. In *The Routledge companion to the future of marketing* (pp. 268–281). London: Sage.

Yigitcanlar, T., Kamruzzamanf, M., Buys, L., Ioppolo, G., Sabatini-Marques, J., Moreira da Costa, E., & Yun, J. H. J. (2018). Understanding 'smart cities': Intertwining development drivers with desired outcomes in a multidimensional framework. *Cities (London, England)*, *81*, 145–160. doi:10.1016/j.cities.2018.04.003

Yıldırım, S., & Candan, B. (2015). Segmentation of Green Product Buyers Based On Their Personal Values and Consumption Values. *Environmental Values*, *24*(5), 641–661. doi:10.3197/096327115X14384223590212

Yin, R. K. (1994). *Case study research: Design and methods* (2nd ed.). Sage.

Yoo, K. H., & Gretzel, U. (2008). What motivates consumers to write online travel reviews? *Information Technology & Tourism*, *10*(4), 283–295. doi:10.3727/109830508788403114

You, K. H., Lee, S. A., Lee, J. K., & Kang, H. (2013). Why read online news? The structural relationships among motivations, behaviors, and consumption in South Korea. *Information Communication and Society*, *16*(10), 1574–1595. doi:10.1080/1369118X.2012.724435

Young, K. (1996). Psychology Of Computer Use: XL. Addictive Use Of The Internet: A Case That Breaks The Stereotype. *Psychological Reports*, *79*(3 Pt 1), 899–902. doi:10.2466/pr0.1996.79.3.899 PMID:8969098

Young, K. (2004). Internet Addiction: A New Clinical Phenomenon and Its Consequences. *The American Behavioral Scientist*, *48*(4), 402–415. doi:10.1177/0002764204270278

Young, K. (2009). Understanding Online Gaming Addiction and Teatment Issues for Adolescents. *The American Journal of Family Therapy*, *37*(5), 355–372. doi:10.1080/01926180902942191

Yuriev, A., Dahmen, M., Paillé, P., Boiral, O., & Guillaumie, L. (2020). Pro-environmental behaviors through the lens of the theory of planned behavior: A scoping review. *Resources, Conservation and Recycling*, *155*, 104660. doi:10.1016/j.resconrec.2019.104660

Zainal, H., Othman, Z., & Mustaffa, F. (2019). The Implementation of Sustainable Development Goals Model Through Initiative of Zakat Management in Kedah. *International Journal of Zakat and Islamic Philanthropy*, *1*(1), 1–6.

Zakaria, N., Wan-Ismail, W. N. A., & Abdul-Talib, A. N. (2015). Superfluous or Moderation?: The Effect of Religious Value on Conspicuous Consumption Behavior for Luxury Products. In Emerging Research on Islamic Marketing and Tourism in the Global Economy (pp. 1-18). IGI Global.

Zakaria, N., & Abdul Talib, A. (2010). Applying Islamic market-oriented cultural model to sensitize strategies towards global. *Journal of Islamic Marketing*, *1*(1), 51–62. doi:10.1108/17590831011026222

Zakaria, N., & Talib, A. N. A. (2011). What did you say? A cross-cultural analysis of the distributive communicative behaviors of global virtual teams. In *2011 International Conference on Computational Aspects of Social Networks (CASoN)* (pp. 7-12). IEEE. 10.1109/CASON.2011.6085910

Zamani, S. N. M., Abdul-Talib, A. N., & Ashari, H. (2016). Strategic orientations and new product success: The mediating impact of innovation speed. International Information Institute (Tokyo). Information, 19(7B), 2785.

Zaoui, I., Ben Ammar Mamlouk, Z., & Trahand, J. (2008). Analyse du processus d'achat sur Internet: nouvelles influences, nouveaux comportements, nouveaux challenges. *Actes du congrès de l'AFM*.

Zhang, J. Q., Craciun, G., & Shin, D. (2010). When does electronic word-of-mouth matter? A study of consumer product reviews. *Journal of Business Research*, *63*(12), 1336–1341. doi:10.1016/j.jbusres.2009.12.011

Zhang, J., & Duan, Y. (2010). The impact of different types of market orientation on product innovation performance: Evidence from Chinese manufacturers. *Management Decision*, *48*(6), 849–867. doi:10.1108/00251741011053433

Zhang, L., & Hanks, L. (2018). Online reviews: The effect of cosmopolitanism, incidental similarity, and dispersion on consumer attitudes toward ethnic restaurants. *International Journal of Hospitality Management*, *68*, 115–123. doi:10.1016/j.ijhm.2017.10.008

Zhang, L., Ma, B., & Cartwright, D. K. (2013). The impact of online user reviews on cameras sales. *European Journal of Marketing*, *47*(7), 1115–1128. doi:10.1108/03090561311324237

Zhang, Q., Cheng, L., & Boutaba, R. J. (2010). Cloud computing: State-of-the-art and research challenges. *Journal of Internet Services and Applications*, *1*(1), 1–7. doi:10.100713174-010-0007-6

Zhang, W., & Watts, S. A. (2008). Capitalizing on content : Information adoption in two online communities. *Journal of the Association for Information Systems*, *9*(2), 73–94. doi:10.17705/1jais.00149

Zhao, X., Zhao, K., & Deng, J. (2018). Geography Still Matters: Examine the Role of Location in Online Markets for Foreign Branded Products. *Decision Sciences*, *50*(2), 285–310. doi:10.1111/deci.12337

Zhao, Y., Yang, S., Narayan, V., & Zhao, Y. (2013). Modeling consumer learning from online product reviews. *Marketing Science*, *32*(1), 153–169. doi:10.1287/mksc.1120.0755

Zhou, E. L. (2013). Displeasure, star-chasing and the transcultural networking fandom. *Participations*, *10*(2), 139–167.

Zhou, N., & Belk, R. W. (2004). Chinese consumer readings of global and local advertising appeals. *Journal of Advertising, 33*(3), 63–76. doi:10.1080/00913367.2004.10639169

Zhu, N. (2011). Household consumption and personal bankruptcy. *The Journal of Legal Studies, 40*(1), 1–37. doi:10.1086/649033

Zmud, R. W., Croes, H., Shaft, T., & Zheng, W. (2010). Systematic differences in firm's information technology signaling: Implications for research design. *Journal of the Association for Information Systems, 11*(3), 149–181. doi:10.17705/1jais.00223

Zolkepli, I. A., & Kamarulzaman, Y. (2011). Understanding social media adoption: The role of perceived media needs and technology characteristics. *World Journal of Social Sciences, 1*(1), 188–199.

Zorbaz, S. D., Ulas, O., & Kızıldag, S. (2015). Relation between Video Game Addiction and Interfamily Relationships on Primary School Students. *Educational Sciences: Theory and Practice, 15*(2), 489–497.

Zou, S., Taylor, C. R., & Osland, G. E. (1998). The EXPERF Scale: A cross-national generalized export performance measure. *Journal of International Marketing, 6*(3), 37–58. doi:10.1177/1069031X9800600307

About the Contributors

Norazah Mohd Suki is a Professor of Marketing and E-Commerce at Othman Yeop Abdullah Graduate School of Business (OYAGSB), Universiti Utara Malaysia. She is the recipient of Malaysia's Research Star Award 2018, Highly Commended Paper in the 2015 and the 2017 Emerald Literati Network Awards for Excellence, Winners of the IGI Global Seventh Annual Awards Excellence in Research Journal, etc. She's also the recipient of Anugerah Tokoh Penyelidik 2015 UMS (Social Sciences). Her research interests include marketing research, consumer behaviour, M-commerce, E-commerce, E-marketing, green marketing, Islamic marketing, and areas related to marketing. She has mentored several post-graduate students, published more than 300 papers in referred journals, book chapters, books, and conference papers detailing her research activities, on top of coordinating and participating in several research projects. She is also the editor of several SCOPUS indexed books. She has sound experiences as speaker to public and private universities, government bodies on courses related to Structural Equation Modelling (SEM), Statistical Package for Social Sciences (SPSS), research methodology, etc. She can be contacted at: azahsuki@yahoo.com.

Norbayah Mohd Suki is an Associate Professor at School of Creative Industry Management & Performing Arts (SCIMPA), Universiti Utara Malaysia, Kedah, Malaysia. Her research interests include Creative Multimedia, Mobile Learning, Animation, HCI, Educational Technology, M-commerce, E-commerce, User Experience and Behavior, etc. She has mentored several postgraduate students; published papers in peer-review ISI and SCOPUS indexed journals, books chapters and international conference proceedings.

* * *

Ili-Salsabila Abd-Razak is a PhD candidate in International Marketing at Universiti Utara Malaysia and country manage for Orissa International's operation in Malaysia.

Arbaiah Abdul Razak was originally trained as a biomedical scientist at Faculty of Medicine, Universiti Malaya and had working experience as Medical Technologist at clinical diagnostic laboratory. Pursued postgraduate study in information technology and then completed a Doctorate degree in innovation management at the University of Southern Queensland, Australia. Previously worked as a senior lecturer at UMK.

Siti Khalilah Basarud-Din is an assistant manager at International Research Center of Zakat Kedah Board, Malaysia.

Rizalniyani Binti Abdul Razak has been an accounting lecturer for almost 20 years and is currently attached at Faculty of Business and Finance, Universiti Tunku Abdul Rahman, Malaysia. She is currently a PhD student in Management at Bangor University, North Wales, United Kingdom. Her research interests include consumer behaviour, consumer psychology, social media studies and behavioural accounting. She has been awarded MSc. International Accounting from Universiti Utara Malaysia and B.A (Hons.) Accounting and Finance from Manchester Metropolitan University, United Kingdom.

Asmat-Nizam Abdul-Talib teaches international business and international marketing at the Universiti Utara Malaysia. He received his PhD in International Marketing from Aston Business School, Aston University, UK, his MBA in International Business from Cardiff University, UK, and a Bachelors Degree in Economics from Concordia University, Canada. At current, his academic research has received financial support or support in kind from various institutions. His research interests lie primarily in international marketing and strategic marketing, especially in export market intelligence, and the use of export market intelligence in the firm's export decision process.

Muhammad Farooq Akhtar is a student of PhD at Othman Yeop Abdullah Graduate School of Business (OYAGSB), Universiti Utara Malaysia (UUM), Malaysia. His research interests include consumer behavior, green marketing, and areas related to marketing. He has the experience to work as a research fellow on US-AID funded research project at the University of Agriculture, Faisalabad, Pakistan. He is lecturer marketing (study leave) at The University of Lahore, Pakistan where he has experience of teaching marketing subjects i.e. seminar in consumer behavior, seminar in marketing theory, marketing research, customer relationship marketing, global marketing, consumer behavior, and strategic marketing etc.

Hanene Babay born April 5, 1980 in Nabeul. She obtained her master's degree in marketing at the Faculty of Economics and Management of Sfax, her master's degree and then doctoral degree in marketing at the Faculty of Economics and Management of Tunis with the distinction of very honorable. She has been a university teacher since 2005. She has also been a trainer since 2010. In fact, she has held several training sessions for Tunisian companies. His areas of expertise revolve around marketing, negotiation and sales techniques, communication techniques and pedagogy. She has also participated in several international events and symposia.

Norrina Din is a senior lecturer at Faculty of Hotel and Tourism Management and also a former International Liaison Officer for Universiti Teknologi MARA, Cawangan Pulau Pinang. She actively involved in internationalization activities for universities in Japan, China, Thailand and Indonesia. She has received numerous awards for publications and received gold and silver medals for product innovation. She also experienced as a reviewer for Cornell Hospitality Quarterly Journal and served as Editorial board for several journals and conferences. She also involved in organizing the workshop and served as Co-Chairman for a conference. Her research interest is in food safety, food allergy, teaching, and learning as well as human/consumer behavior.

Eugenia Ida Edward is an English language teacher at the Center for the Promotion of Knowledge and Language Learning, Universiti Malaysia Sabah, Malaysia. She holds a B.ed in TESL from Universiti Institut Teknologi MARA, Malaysia. She has been involved in the English as a Second Language (ESL) field as a teacher for 9 years.

Nozha Erragcha is a senior lecturer at Higher Business School of Tunisia, Tunisia.

Khader Omar Lawa is a DBA candidate at Universiti Utara Malaysia.

Dzulfikar Mahtar is a DBA candidate at Universiti Utara Malaysia.

Nur Aliah Mansor has developed an abiding interest in inter-disciplinary media, marketing and cultural studies. She is completing her PhD in new media at Bangor University. Reflecting part of her PhD studies, she focuses on information control, celebrity culture and fan engagement with the management company, Johnny & Associates. This research provides a close-up analysis of how a discrete commercial agency like Johnny & Associates uses information to manipulate and control its target audiences and make money from the fans through affective media experiences. Her research addresses the tensions and contradictions of Johnny's fangirls, of the love and attachment towards the idols and fans'conflicted feelings towards Johnny & Associates. Her work, Johnny's Idol Persona Constructions and Female Fandom Consumption, has been published in Disassembling the Celebrity Figure: Credibility and the Incredible (2018).

Zam Zuriyati Binti Mohamad earned her Doctor of Philosophy (Accounting) from Universiti Pendidikan Sultan Idris. She is a Chartered Accountant from Malaysian Institute of Accountants. After 14 years of experience in corporate sector, in year 2011 she decided to change her career and become an academic. She is currently an Assistant Professor at Universiti Tunku Abdul Rahman, teaching Advanced Financial Accounting, Business Accounting, Financial Information for Management, Corporate Reporting Current Issues and serves as Chairperson for research centre of Centre for Accounting, Banking and Finance. Her recent publications include "Comprehensive Board Diversity and Quality of Corporate Social Responsibility Disclosure: Evidence from an Emerging Market (Journal of Business Ethics) and Artificial Intelligence, Smart Contract and Islamic Finance (Asian Social Science). Her current research interests include corporate governance, corporate social responsibility, corporate disclosure, digital technology, housing affordability and sustainable development goals.

Syuhaily Osman obtained her first degree in Bac. of Sc. (Human Development) from Universiti Putra Malaysia (UPM) in 1997, Master of Science (Consumer Science) from UPM in 2000 and Ph.D (Consumer Behavior) from the University of Malaya in 2008. She currently holds the position of Associate Professor at Department of Resource Management and Consumer Studies, Faculty of Human Ecology, UPM in the field of Consumer Behavior. She is currently the Head of Department, Chief Editor of the Malaysian Consumer Journal, EXCO of the Malaysian Family and Consumer Economics Association (MACFEA) and a member of the Advertising Committee of the Ministry of Domestic Trade and Consumer Affairs. She is also an associate researcher at the Center for Sustainable Use Studies (SCoRE), Universiti Putra Malaysia. She is active in the writing and publication of articles in the field of consumer behavior and among other articles published on Muslim consumer buying behavior, online buyer typology, halal consumer buying and purchase perceptions, sustainable consumption behavior and etc.

Raife Meltem Yetkin Özbük is an Assistant Professor at the Department of Marketing, Faculty of Applied Sciences, Akdeniz University, Antalya, Turkey. Her research interests are in the area of Electronic Marketing, Tourism Marketing, and Consumer Behavior.

Chelster Sherralyn Jeoffrey Pudin is an English language lecturer at the Center for the Promotion of Knowledge and Language Learning, Universiti Malaysia Sabah, Malaysia. She holds an MA in Applied Linguistics from Edith Cowan University, Western Australia. She has been involved in the English as a Second Language (ESL) field as a teacher and a lecturer for 10 years.

Azlan Shah is a DBA candidate at Universiti Utara Malaysia.

Izwan Shukor is a DBA candidate at Universiti Utara Malaysia.

Maple Tan is a DBA candidate at Universiti Utara Malaysia.

Ciro Troise is a Knowledge Transfer Manager (KTM) at the Technology Transfer Office of University of Campania "L. Vanvitelli" and Research Fellow at the Department of Management of University of Campania "L. Vanvitelli". Visiting Research Fellow and Ph.D. at the Queen Mary University of London. Visiting in China "Technology-transfer tour" by Netval. Formely Stageur at AGCM (Antitrust) and AGCOM. Author of several papers (among the main topics: digital platforms, crowdfunding, open innovation, app economy). Attended several international conferences (e.g. Euram, Ineka, Ifkad, Icsb and Sinergie) and presented several works. Chaired several session (e.g. Ifkad 2019).

Lee Kar Wai was born in Ipoh, Perak, Malaysia. Before started her undergraduate studies in Universiti Putra Malaysia, she attended pre-university classes in SMK Sam Tet. She obtained her first-class degree, Bachelor of Consumer Studies with Consumer Finance as her minor in 2016, and the bachelor degree was fully sponsored by PTPTN. In the same year, she continued her postgraduate studies for Master of Science in the field of Consumer Science at Universiti Putra Malaysia and graduated in 2019.

Raife Meltem Yetkin Özbük (PhD) is an Assistant Professor at the Department of Marketing, Faculty of Applied Sciences, Akdeniz University, Antalya, Turkey. Her research interests are in the area of Electronic Marketing, Tourism Marketing, and Consumer Behaviour.

Seda Yıldırım was born in 1983. She graduated from Kocaeli University, Department of Business Administration in 2006. She completed her postgraduate and doctoral education at the Department of Business Administration, Kocaeli University, Production Management and Marketing. She worked as a research assistant in Kocaeli University between 2010-2013 and worked as an assistant professor in Recep Tayyip Erdoğan University between 2013-2016. Since 2017, she has been working as an Associate Professor at Namık Kemal University in Turkey. Her current research interests include sustainable development, green marketing, sustainable consumption, Islamic economics, marketing culture, and values. She works as an editorial board member and reviewer in various journals. She also studies as a member of the organizing committee of various international congresses.

Mahjabin Yusuf is a lecturer in Marketing Department, MARA Professional College Seri Iskandar, Perak, Malaysia. She holds a MSc. in International Business from Universiti Utara Malaysia and has been teaching Marketing as well as Business Management courses for more than 13 years.

Hafizah Zainal is a Manager at International Research Center of Zakat Kedah Board, Malaysia.

Index

N

O

P

S

T

V

W

Z

Ensure Quality Research is Introduced to the Academic Community

Become an IGI Global Reviewer for Authored Book Projects

The overall success of an authored book project is dependent on quality and timely reviews.

In this competitive age of scholarly publishing, constructive and timely feedback significantly expedites the turnaround time of manuscripts from submission to acceptance, allowing the publication and discovery of forward-thinking research at a much more expeditious rate. Several IGI Global authored book projects are currently seeking highly-qualified experts in the field to fill vacancies on their respective editorial review boards:

Applications and Inquiries may be sent to:

development@igi-global.com

Applicants must have a doctorate (or an equivalent degree) as well as publishing and reviewing experience. Reviewers are asked to complete the open-ended evaluation questions with as much detail as possible in a timely, collegial, and constructive manner. All reviewers' tenures run for one-year terms on the editorial review boards and are expected to complete at least three reviews per term. Upon successful completion of this term, reviewers can be considered for an additional term.

If you have a colleague that may be interested in this opportunity, we encourage you to share this information with them.